KU-490-259

B.S.U.C. - LIBRARY
00325264

# CRUISING WITH ROBERT LOUIS STEVENSON

# CRUISING WITH ROBERT LOUIS STEVENSON

*Travel, Narrative, and the Colonial Body*

OLIVER S. BUCKTON

Ohio University Press
Athens

Ohio University Press, Athens, Ohio 45701
www.ohio.edu/oupress


Printed in the United States of America


Ohio University Press books are printed on acid-free paper ♾ ™

14 13 12 11 10 09 08 07    5 4 3 2 1

*Library of Congress Cataloging-in-Publication Data*

Buckton, Oliver S.
Cruising with Robert Louis Stevenson : travel, narrative, and the colonial body / Oliver S. Buckton.
p. cm.
Includes bibliographical references and index.
ISBN-13: 978-0-8214-1756-0 (acid-free paper)
ISBN-10: 0-8214-1756-8 (acid-free paper)
1. Stevenson, Robert Louis, 1850–1894—Criticism and interpretation. 2. Stevenson, Robert Louis, 1850–1894—Travel. 3. Travel in literature. 4. Colonies in literature. 5. Homosexuality in literature. 6. Men in literature. 7. South Pacific Ocean—In literature. 8. Oceania—In literature. I. Title.
PR5497.B83 2007
823'.8—dc22

2007013089

For Laurice

*viva viola*

# CONTENTS

# ACKNOWLEDGMENTS

In the course of working on this project, I have accumulated numerous debts that it is a pleasure to acknowledge here. First, I am fortunate to have been part of a vibrant international community of Stevenson scholars whose intellectual energy and friendship have made working on Stevenson a great pleasure and who provided much stimulating exchange and discussion as this project progressed. The three international conferences on Stevenson I attended and participated in at Stirling, Scotland (2000), Gargnano, Italy (2002), and Edinburgh, Scotland (2004), were pivotal in generating new interest in Stevenson among scholars and general readers alike and in bringing new theoretical approaches to bear on Stevenson's work and life. In particular, I would like to thank Richard Ambrosini, Stephen Arata, Jenni Calder, Ann Colley, Richard Dury, Linda Dryden, Roslyn Jolly, William B. Jones Jr., Katherine Linehan, Eric Massie, Barry Menikoff, Alan Sandison, and Rory Watson for their passionate commitment to and outstanding work on Robert Louis Stevenson.

Other colleagues have been generous in reading and offering feedback on earlier versions of individual chapters. I thank Joseph Bristow, Lee Edelman, Richard Dellamora, Catherine Gallagher, Dorothy Mermin, Brian Richardson, and Hayden White for their willingness to offer constructive criticism, which has greatly benefited my work.

No project such as this could reach fruition without the generous support of various research institutions. I am grateful to the Beinecke Rare Book and Manuscript Library for awarding me the Jackson Brothers Fellowship in 2002, which allowed me to launch the project with a month at Yale researching in the world's largest collection of Stevenson manuscripts. I am also grateful to the Beinecke Library for permission to reproduce Stevenson's self-portrait on the cover. I am grateful to the Huntington Library, San Marino, California, for awarding me the Ernestine Richter Avery Fellowship in 2003, which allowed me to spend a month at the library researching Stevenson's South Seas journal. I would like to express my grateful appreciation to the staffs of both these libraries, and also to the staffs of the National Library of Scotland in Edinburgh and the Mitchell Library in Sydney, New South Wales, for their enthusiastic assistance and timely responses to my request for access to Stevenson manuscripts and for photocopies of archival material.

My work on this book has been stimulated by lively discussions with colleagues and students in the Department of English at Florida Atlantic University. I am grateful to the Dorothy F. Schmidt College of Arts and Letters at Florida Atlantic University for granting me a sabbatical semester during which a substantial portion of the research for this book was completed.

Several chapters of this book have appeared previously. An earlier version of chapter 1 was published as "Reanimating Stevenson's Corpus," in *Nineteenth-Century Literature* 55, no. 1 (June 2000): 22–58, copyright © 2000 by the Regents of the University of California. An earlier version of chapter 3 was first published as "'Faithful to his Map': Profit and Desire in Robert Louis Stevenson's *Treasure Island*," in *Journal of Stevenson Studies* 1 (2004): 138–49. A version of chapter 5 was first published as "Cruising with Robert Louis Stevenson: The South Seas from Journal to Fiction," in *Robert Louis Stevenson: Writer of Boundaries*, edited by Richard Ambrosini and Richard Dury (Madison: University of Wisconsin Press, 2006), 199–212. I gratefully acknowledge the University of California Press, the *Journal of Stevenson Studies*, and the University of Wisconsin Press, respectively, for permission to reproduce these articles in the present book.

I offer thanks to David Sanders at Ohio University Press for his belief in and enthusiasm for this project. I am also grateful to John Morris and Sally Bennett for their scrupulous attention to and outstanding copyediting of the manuscript, and Jean Cunningham for overseeing the marketing of the book. I also express appreciation to the anonymous readers for the Press for offering helpful and constructive suggestions for improvement of the manuscript.

Finally, there are the debts that are harder to put into words. I thank my parents, Christine and David Buckton, for their love, their inspiring energy, and their ongoing interest in my work. I dedicate this book to my wife, Laurice Campbell Buckton, who fills every day of my life with music.

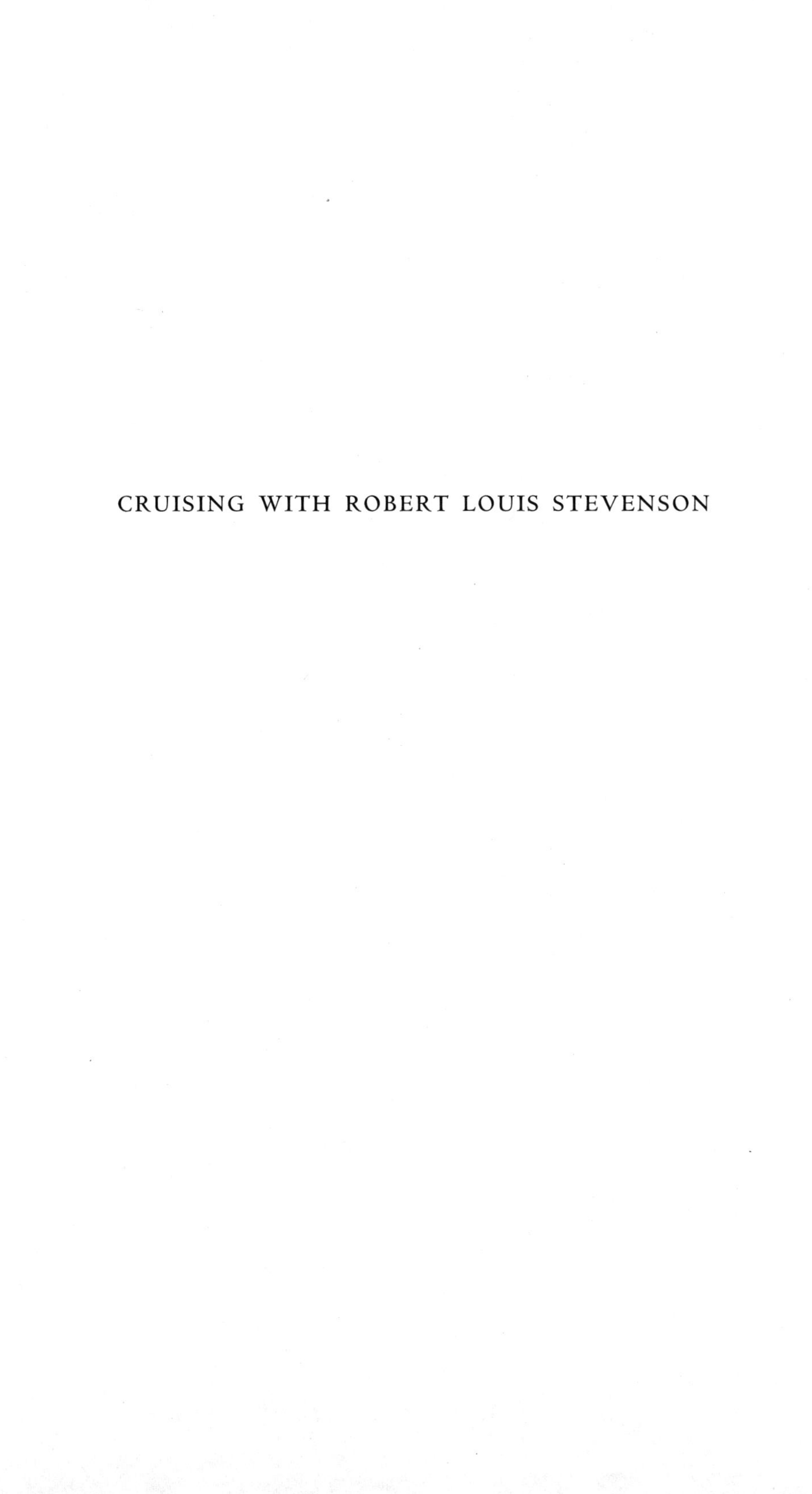

# CRUISING WITH ROBERT LOUIS STEVENSON

# Introduction

TOWARD THE END OF HIS LIFE, while living in the South Seas, Stevenson wrote an essay that did much to consolidate his reputation as, first and foremost, a writer of fiction. In "My First Book" (1894), published in the *Idler*, Stevenson overlooked his first six published volumes to pronounce *Treasure Island* (1883) his inaugural work, explaining that "when I am asked to talk of my first book, no question in the world but what is meant is my first novel." My investigation of Stevenson's travel writing was motivated in part by curiosity as to why, in 1894, there could have been "no question in the world" about Stevenson's fame being based on his work as a novelist, such that "the great public regards what else I have written with indifference, if not aversion."[1] In particular, I was struck by the fact that of Stevenson's first four books, two were works of travel writing while the third explored a specific location, that of his native Edinburgh. Why, I wondered, was Stevenson so willing to disown books that had garnered critical acclaim, as well as his collection of essays

(*Virginibus Puerisque*) that had identified him as one of the most accomplished stylists of English prose?[2] Further researches revealed that, at the time of writing "My First Book," Stevenson was still smarting under the hostile reception accorded his "South Sea Letters" and was doubtful of the success of his latest work, *The Ebb-Tide,* which was also based on his South Seas travels. The defensive note of the essay began to be comprehensible as a response to the lack of public interest in his travel writing in general and his South Seas material in particular.

Yet the appearance at the beginning of Stevenson's career of *An Inland Voyage*—his actual first book—and *Travels with a Donkey* reveals that the impetus to produce narratives based on his journeys was fundamental to his professional activity, and this original interest in travel would continue to direct his course in fiction and nonfiction. In addition to the group of Stevenson's texts usually categorized as travel writing—the two works mentioned, as well as *The Silverado Squatters, Across the Plains,* and *In the South Seas*—travel emerges as the energizing narrative dynamic of the majority of Stevenson's output. Hence, the neglect of his travel writing in "My First Book" is a screen to deflect attention from the actual vitality of travel in Stevenson's corpus of works. The themes that link the various literary styles and personae of Stevenson are the preoccupation with the pleasures and perils of travel and the pivotal influence of location on literary production.[3]

Moreover, Stevenson's approach to travel and his narrative use of travel motifs were transformed over time, as the circle of his wandering widened with his increasing independence from his parents and improved economic circumstances. An important shift occurs from Stevenson's youthful philosophy of "travel for travel's sake," which influenced the loose form of the first two travel books, and his later adaptation of the journey into a quest for profit that launched his commercially successful career as a novelist.[4] Later, while cruising in the South Seas, Stevenson was offered a lucrative contract to produce a series of letters describing his travels; however, the quest for profit was superseded by other ambitions, involving a desire for cultural knowledge of and insight into the peoples and societies of the South Seas, which Stevenson hoped would result in a definitive ethnographic study of the region's history and culture. The advantage of the approach I adopt in this book is that it is flexible enough to accommodate writing about travel pursued for various motives, including pleasure, profit, self-testing, exploration, new forms of knowledge, and the improvement of health. The concept that links these diverse approaches to travel is "cruising," a term that applies both to Stevenson's preferred leisurely mode of transport and to the narrative practices that derived from his travels.

## Stevenson's "Cruising"

Throughout this book, I use the term *cruising* to articulate Stevenson's practices of travel and travel writing in their various transformations and phases. This term, with its evocation of leisurely sea voyages, might seem to hark back to an earlier age of travel, prior to the technological changes that, in the nineteenth century, radically altered the access to and experience of mobility. Indeed, the actions of Stevenson's historical romances such as *Treasure Island* and *Kidnapped* are set before the age of steam, and these novels use the "cruise" to signify a sea voyage in a sailing vessel, whether pursued for profit or for some other purpose. Stevenson exhibited nostalgia for the preindustrial era of travel, and much of his early travel was carried out by "primitive" means (by canoe, by foot, on a donkey, by sailing ship).[5] Yet the term *cruising* is more inclusive than simply describing a mode of transport; it incorporates a variety of modes of travel and kinds of writing. While some of the uses of this term will be familiar to most readers, others may be more specialized or obscure.

In the first place, *cruising* signifies a process of travel characterized by leisurely movement and random progress, rather than a planned journey toward a specific destination. One of the definitions that the *Shorter OED* provides for *cruise* is "sail to and fro . . . for pleasure making for no particular place or calling at a series of places." To this definition the *OED* adds "walk or travel about making for no particular place or calling at a series of places; drive around at random." This notion of travel for pleasure rather than in pursuit of a destination informed Stevenson's ongoing emotional and intellectual investment in cruising. The idea of moving around at random is also important to the significance of cruising—the traveler may have no destination in mind when the journey begins, instead moving on impulse, following the promptings of whim or desire. Of course, even travel undertaken specifically for the sake of writing about it has a purpose, and Stevenson certainly sought to commodify and commercially exploit his travels in more popular works.[6] Yet he remained invested in the principle of pleasure in travel and resisted the constraint of a predetermined destination.

The second meaning of *cruising* is to designate Stevenson's narrative practice, which is based on his method of integrating the materials and experiences of travel into his writing. In the first place, Stevenson's texts were often composed in transit, written either in the midst of the journey or during intervals between travel.[7] From the outset, Stevenson's two early travel books, *An Inland Voyage* and *Travels with a Donkey,* were both based on journals that he kept while traveling by canoe and donkey, respectively. He began work on *The Amateur Emigrant,* the account of his epic journey from Scotland to California, shortly after completing the journey, while staying in Monterey in September 1879.[8] Later in his career, Stevenson again kept a journal of his cruises on the *Casco* and the *Equator* in the South Seas, recording his travels and adventures as they happened. This journal became the basis for both the South Seas letters and the book posthumously published as *In the South Seas* (see chapter 5). It also furnished materials for the account of colonial conflict in Samoa (published as *A Footnote to History*) and provided crucial sources for his fictional pieces. Hence, Stevenson's practices of writing while traveling and of incorporating materials gleaned from his voyages were not limited to his nonfiction. From early in his career, travel was also a stimulus to his practice of composing fiction. He wrote "Story of a Lie" while sailing on the SS *Devonia* from Greenock to New York, for example, and "Pavilion on the Links" was written after his arrival in Monterey.[9] Stevenson's first novel, *Treasure Island,* was strongly influenced by his early travel writings (see chapter 3). The narrative was begun in Scotland, yet Stevenson reached an impasse in his writing that could be overcome only by travel, as he wrote in "My First Book": "Arrived at my destination, down I sat one morning to the unfinished tale, and behold! It flowed from me like small talk" (282). For other Victorian writers, such as Dickens, travel was a disruption to the routine of writing. Even while away from England, Dickens preferred to remain for extended periods in one place so that "during another year of absence, I can at once work out the themes I have now in my mind, without interruption."[10] By contrast, Stevenson thrived on the relocations and changes of scene incurred by travel. Indeed, the work composed entirely in a single location is the exception rather than the rule in Stevenson's corpus. *Cruising,* then, aptly describes this narrative practice that has travel as an essential stimulus and features disruption and motion as part of the compositional process.[11]

Stevenson's narrative practice of cruising is also accompanied by a break with literary realism, as articulated in his debate about the form and purpose of the novel with Henry James.[12] James remained committed to the novel as a mode of realism par excellence, which sought to "compete with life."[13] For Stevenson, the novel had to be selective and impressionistic: "[F]or the welter of impressions, all forcible but all discreet, which life presents, it substitutes a certain artificial series of impressions . . . all aiming at the same effect." Whereas the travelogue shifted from focusing on the external world of the places visited to the impressions of the traveler, the novel, for Stevenson, reflected the subjective personality of its creator. The novel, Stevenson argued, succeeds "not by its resemblances to life, which are forced and material, . . . but by its immeasurable difference from life, which is designed and significant." Narrative art, for Stevenson, involved a dislocation from place, a self-conscious awareness of the artifice of all literary representation. Travel writing and fiction were not ultimately distinct for Stevenson, who argued, "The art of narrative, in fact, is the same, whether it is applied to the selection and illustration of a real series of events or of an imaginary series."[14] Stevenson's theory of narrative art thus challenges distinctions between forms in a way that anticipates later theorists such as Hayden White.

Cruising involves the deployment of travel as a basis for narrative structure, without being constrained by the conventions of realism or the expectation that the narrative should resemble life. Even though Stevenson utilized the materials of his own travels in his fiction and nonfiction, these narratives often rehearse or reflect the disruptions and provide other personal impressions of his voyages. Use of the term *cruising* registers that Stevenson's narrative practice—whether in *Treasure Island* and *Kidnapped* or in the "nonfictional" works such as *Travels with a Donkey* or *In the South Seas*—is based on the trajectories of journeys. However, the path of cruising is frequently disrupted by problems with narrative closure. Stevenson's travel writings tend to conclude abruptly, proving unable to resolve the various problems and contradictions raised by the encounters they narrate or to condense the significance of the journey following its termination.[15] Whereas travel narratives are often open-ended, closure is expected of the novel as a form: yet many of Stevenson's works of fiction also end suddenly or unsatisfactorily. Stevenson's correspondence provides evidence that the closure of a narrative was his greatest source of difficulty as a writer. In one famous instance, Stevenson avoided (or rather, deferred) the problem of the ending of *Kidnapped* by leaving his protagonist, David Balfour, in limbo outside the British Linen Company Bank in Edinburgh, until Stevenson felt inclined to write the sequel, *David Balfour,* seven years later (see chapter 4). Such problems with closure can be read symptomatically, as signs of the breakdown of the ideological conventions of realist narrative. If, as Fredric Jameson argues in *The Political Unconscious,* narrative analysis can fruitfully examine "those narrative frames or containment strategies which seek to endow their objects of representation with formal unity," then the fragility or incompleteness of Stevenson's narrative frames may allow useful ideological purchase on the shifting forms and functions of the novel. In particular, Jameson has argued that the ideological function of the novel is "to 'manage' historical and social, deeply political impulses, that is to say, to defuse them, to prepare substitute gratifications for them." In light of this, the strategy of containment will offer such gratifications in the form of ideological closure, highlighting the triumph of the individual against adversity, which Jameson terms "categories of the ethical and of the individual subject."[16] Stevenson's inconclusive, open-ended narratives expose the fragility of such containment strategies and foreshadow the emergence of new ideological machinations of prose in the twentieth century.

Even as Stevenson's narrative cruising deploys the journey as the hinge on which the plot turns, it shows how susceptible the journey is to disruption and abrupt termination. Such disordered journeys, of course, have narrative consequences: the generic form of Stevenson's texts is unstable, frequently mutating following an aborted voyage, as in *Kidnapped,* where the text shifts from the familial plot of inheritance to a historical adventure featuring Jacobites and the Appin murder.[17] *The Wrong Box* abruptly changes generic course following the train wreck, from a "tontine" plot and family drama to a black farce centered on an errant corpse, and *The Ebb-Tide,* which begins as a "beachcomber" narrative featuring a degenerate trio of adventurers, mutates into a scathing critique of colonial ideology and exploitation following the failure of the *Farallone*'s proposed journey to Peru and emergency stop at New Island. In these texts and others, cruising entails a narrative method that produces unstable texts of travel—texts that display a generic hybridity and formal flux.

Other meanings of *cruising* expand on the term's association with pleasurable travel. Particularly since the twentieth century, *cruising* has come to evoke a journey in search of sexual partners and erotic experience. Indeed, the *OED* defines one meaning of *cruise* as "walk or drive around looking for amusement, a sexual partner."[18] To a significant extent, Stevenson was attracted to the possibilities offered by travel for escape from the rigid gender and sexual codes of Victorian Britain. In particular, locations such as the south of France and the South Seas appealed to Stevenson as spaces of erotic renewal, a perception shared by other artists of the period, including the painter Paul Gauguin, whose first period of residence on Tahiti overlapped with Stevenson's on Samoa. As Lee Wallace writes, "the Pacific [is defined] as the safe distance at which feminine sexual difference can be known and rationally understood in order to reveal, if not remedy, the sterility, corruption, and hypocrisy of European social organization."[19] Such utopian views of Polynesian society were by no means uncommon, and they help to explain why, as Stevenson wrote, "It was suggested that I should try the South Seas," as though it were an established cure for moral and physical ills, and why he asserted that "no part of the world exerts the same attractive power upon the visitor," as though advertising its remedial and restorative properties.[20] The appeal of travel for Stevenson thus included the allure of erotic adventure, and one of the motives for Stevenson's travels was the search for sexual encounters and pleasures.[21] More specifically, *cruising* has emerged as a signifier within the discourse of homosexual desire to designate the pursuit of same-sex partners. The term could possibly have carried a specifically same-sex connotation in the late nineteenth century and may very well have formed part of the erotic vocabulary of cruising in Stevenson's texts, as when a cruise is offered as a seductive enticement by one man to another.[22] Moreover, the homoerotic sense of *cruising* opens the opportunity for a "queer" reading of Stevenson's texts that is surely overdue, despite the fact that specific texts in the Stevenson canon—most notably *Strange Case of Dr. Jekyll and Mr. Hyde*—have been scrutinized for traces of homoeroticism and homophobia.[23]

That there has as yet been no substantial review of Stevenson's work in the light of gender studies and queer theory is perhaps all the more remarkable given Stevenson's intimate personal and professional relationships with male writers who were known to be (or are now known to have been) homosexual, including John Addington Symonds, Henry James, and Edmund Gosse.[24] One can speculate as to how much Stevenson knew, or wanted to know, about the secret homosexual lives of his circle of male friends. Claire Harman states, in her biography of Stevenson, that "the list of sexually ambiguous and gay men who *did* find Stevenson almost mesmerisingly attractive is long, including Gosse, Andrew Lang and, later, Henry James. Added to this could be a subsidiary list of men who seemed to be responding to homosexual signals in Stevenson's work."[25] Significantly, Harman emphasizes Stevenson's attractiveness to gay men without asserting that he himself was attracted by homosexuality. That Stevenson was admired and desired by some of these men seems beyond question; that he sought or desired intimate or physical relationships with other men is less clear. Stevenson's marriage to Fanny, of course, is no evidence that he was not sexually attracted to men: Symonds and Oscar Wilde were also married, while actively pursuing male sexual partners. Certainly Symonds's response to *Jekyll and Hyde,* for example, indicated that he felt Stevenson had touched on aspects of Symonds's sexuality that he would preferred to have kept concealed: "[I]t has left such a deeply painful impression on my heart that I do not know how I am ever to turn to it again. The fact is that, viewed as an allegory, it touches one too closely. Most of us at some epoch of our lives have been upon the verge of developing a Mr Hyde."[26] Symonds's reference to "most of us" suggests a community of homosexual readers who are only too familiar with the need for a double life. In his reply, Stevenson sounded an apologetic note for having exposed what Symonds called "the abysmal deeps of personality": "Jekyll is a dreadful thing, I own; but the only thing I feel dreadful about is that damned old business of the war in the members. This time it came out; I hope it will stay in, in future."[27] The wish that the homoerotic implications of his texts would "stay in" has been amply fulfilled by most criticism of Stevenson's works.

Yet the focus of Stevenson's work on masculine intimacy and male camaraderie seems to invite readings that explore the homoerotic dynamics of these male relationships. To some extent, the masculine emphasis of Stevenson's narratives conforms to the perception of late-Victorian romance as "manly" literature that sought to displace the feminine domestic novel and degenerate foreign realism from the center stage of fiction. Along these lines, Nicholas Daly asserts, "From the beginning, romance is a gendered genre," pointing to the contemporary critical "assumption that the romance is a more healthily masculine form than the realist novel" and cites Andrew Lang, who "presented the romances of Haggard and Stevenson as an antidote to the feminizing—and thus morbid—effects of the virus of French realism." Furthermore, the belief that romance could contribute to the masculinizing of readers gained credence as "the romance was presented as restoring the manhood of British fiction, too long tied to the apron strings of the domestic novel."[28] Stevenson's declaration in "My First Book" that "women were excluded" (279) from *Treasure Island* might stand as a manifesto for much of his work in romance, though it has tended to cloud the extent to which women do appear in Stevenson's work, especially his later fiction. Henry James addressed the masculine "gallantry" of Stevenson's works, written "as if language were a pretty woman, and a person who proposes to handle it had of necessity to be something of a Don Juan." Yet this effort to portray Stevenson as a romantic heterosexual lover runs aground on James's recognition of the same-sex affiliation of Stevenson's writing: "[I]t is rather odd that at the same time a striking feature of that nature should be an absence of care for things feminine. His books are for the most part books without women, and it is not women who fall most in love with them. But Mr. Stevenson does not need, as we may say, a petticoat to inflame him."[29] James leaves the question of what did "inflame" Stevenson to the reader's imagination.

Of course, the case for "queer" readings of Stevenson's texts does not depend on biographical evidence of his homosexuality. One can explore the representation of same-sex relationships and currents of homoerotic affect in Stevenson's work without assuming, or seeking to prove, that he was actively homosexual in life. Given the legal and cultural hostility toward homosexuality in late-Victorian society, it is likely that such homoerotic representations are buried in narratives whose official or explicit focus lies elsewhere. As I argue in part 4 of this study, for example, the colonial context of Stevenson's Pacific writings is in some ways a screen for his exploration of intense, simultaneously antagonistic and erotically charged male bonds. Such bonds could be explored more fully away from the norms and conventions of Victorian England. Lee Wallace has argued that the heterosexual fixation of Western discourse about the South Seas has concealed a counterdiscourse in which the sexual allure of the Pacific foregrounds the fantasized accessibility of male bodies.[30] Indeed, the homosexual representations of Stevenson's texts are also coded in heterosexual or even nonhuman forms. The following chapters focus on material figures such as the animated corpse, in *The Wrong Box* and *The Suicide Club;* the abused she-ass Modestine, in *Travels with a Donkey;* and the eroticized body of the native woman Uma in "Beach of Falesá," all of which indicate the presence of "libidinal currents" (to use Joseph Allan Boone's term) that run through the text without surfacing in obvious ways.[31] In particular, the animated corpse—an inert body that is jolted into life by the force of desire and linguistic play—is a recurring feature of Stevenson's texts, serving to bring into circulation a desire that cannot be contained by the official narrative or plot (see chapter 1). Specifically, sodomitic desire between men is buried within narratives that focus on property, familial conflict, colonial conquest, and other major themes in the nineteenth-century novel.

Though often coded, the homoerotic dimensions of Stevenson's work are on other occasions strikingly evident. Many of Stevenson's narratives elicit a heavy investment in the vicissitudes of male-male relationships, dramatizing the bonds of friends, rivals, collaborators, brothers, and mortal enemies. Jekyll's confession that "I have really a very great interest in poor Hyde" and Utterson's speculation that Jekyll must, in his submission to Hyde, be paying the price for "the ghost of some old sin, the cancer of some concealed disgrace" are only the most well-known of Stevenson's insights into relationships between men that may have scandalous significance.[32] In tales as different as "Pavilion on the Links," "The Merry Men," "Markheim," *The Master of Ballantrae,* and "The Beach of Falesá," the male bond is represented as a source of antagonism and attraction, conflict and desire.[33] Of course, the plots of these narratives provide motives for this conflict—such as rivalry over a woman, property, or wealth—but such pretexts seem inadequate to account for the intensity of the passion. Rather, I argue, desire between men surfaces under the pressure of the kind of homophobic paranoia analyzed by Eve Kosofsky Sedgwick in *Between Men,* but fails to find an outlet in heterosexual intimacy and instead erupts in violence.[34]

Sedgwick's focus is nineteenth-century fiction, in which the pattern of triangulation that determines homosocial male bonds is linked to her emphasis on the variations on the gothic form of the novel. This use of the term *gothic* to apply to late-Victorian fiction has been challenged by Nicholas Daly, who argues that this usage of *gothic,* by linking late-Victorian romance too closely to earlier forms, has obscured its connections with modernist writing; Daly observes that "present-day critics have interpreted the romance as a revenant, as the ghost of eighteenth-century Gothic fiction, rather than as a new departure, labeling it as 'Victorian Gothic,' 'imperial Gothic,' or even 'urban Gothic.'"[35] Travel writing, as I argue, is a significant forum for challenging the narrative conventions of the Victorian novel, being a significantly more open-ended narrative form that lacks the formal architecture of plot and closural strategies on which the novel, whether gothic or realist, depends. Stevenson's earlier travel writing thus served as a precursor to the kinds of formal experimentation that he would later pursue in fiction, allowing the journey itself to provide the narrative momentum and structure.

Cruising may involve the idea of travel in search of a sexual partner, especially one of a different class, race, or nationality. But it may also involve traveling *with* a same-sex companion, as Stevenson does in his first narrated journey, *An Inland Voyage.* This text, which inaugurated Stevenson's career as a travel writer, introduces his practice of dedicating his books to close male friends, whom he addressed in a semiprivate language that constructs the journey as a shared experience only partially accessible to public knowledge. In dedicating his actual "first book" to his traveling partner, Walter Grindlay Simpson, Stevenson implies that a public scandal may attach to this textual linking of their names: "I could not in decency expose you to share the disgrace of another and more public shipwreck." Under the burden of his dependence on parental approval and the conventions of Victorian publishing, Stevenson cannot realize, or narrate, the dreamed-of romantic journey with another man but can only refer to their relationship "by new and alien names."[36]

The constraints on turning the pleasures of shared travel into narrative evaporated in the South Seas, where Stevenson cruised extensively and productively with various men, especially his stepson, Lloyd Osbourne, with whom he collaborated on several narratives of travel and adventure: *The Wrong Box, The*

*Wrecker*, and *The Ebb-Tide*. Their collaboration began (as I argue in chapter 3) with the map of Treasure Island, but it achieved its richest vein of production in the South Seas, where the more relaxed attitudes toward gender and sexual categories helped to foster their creative partnership.

Stevenson's interest in same-sex relations, as reflected in his life and his writing, became stronger during his time in the South Seas.[37] Such interest in the homosexual possibilities of the South Seas was not limited to Stevenson; Lee Wallace has argued that "the spectacle of male-male sexual relations" in Polynesia provided the groundwork for the emergence of homosexual roles in Europe: "Polynesian same-sex sexual activity makes, for the first time in history, reasonable or rational (rather than treasonous or offensive) the parallel possibility of similar relations among European men."[38] In the Gilberts—the realm of Tembinok', the cross-dressing king of Apemama—Stevenson's fascination with gender inversion and male sexuality reached its apotheosis.[39] In particular, the Gilbertian couple Nan Tok' and Nei Takauti provides an interesting example of a kind of gender inversion that fascinated Stevenson in the South Seas. In Stevenson's portrait of the "topsy-turvy couple" (*ISS*, 204), the wife, Nei Takauti, dominates her husband, being "a high chief-woman" (203), while Stevenson writes of Nan Tok' that "he was his wife's wife. They reversed the parts indeed, down to the least particular; it was the husband who showed himself the ministering angel in the hour of pain, while the wife displayed the apathy and heartlessness of the proverbial man" (203–4). Perhaps because Nan Tok', the husband, is so clearly the "decorative" partner—"Whatever pretty thing my wife might have given to Nei Takauti . . . appeared the next evening on the person of Nan Tok" (203)—Stevenson feels emboldened to admire the beauty of the husband, describing him as "young, extremely handsome, of the most approved good humour, and suffering in his precarious station from suppressed high spirits" (203).[40]

Travel in the South Seas brought Stevenson into contact with new races and locations that prompted the adaptation of his narrative methods to handle these materials. Indeed, the "seduction" and the "attractive power" (*ISS*, 5) of the South Seas and its inhabitants appear in a number of encounters with Polynesian natives. One particular episode stands out, as Stevenson recounts going out one moonlight night while in the Gilberts: "I walked in the bush, playing my pipe" (238). There he encounters "another wanderer of the night." Stevenson's admiration for the man's erotic appeal is emphatic: "[H]is body, his face, and his eyes, were all of an enchanting beauty. Every here and there in the Gilberts youths are to be found of this absurd perfection; I have seen five of us pass half an hour in admiration of a boy at Mariki; and Te Kop (my friend in the fine mat and garland) I had already several times remarked, and long ago set down as the loveliest animal in Apemama" (238). Though the description is reminiscent of Stevenson's praise of Java, his female Samoan servant (whom he similarly objectifies in his correspondence), Stevenson here defies Victorian sexual conventions by dwelling on the beauty of the male.

In so doing, Stevenson joined the company of authors who had either created scandal by representing the homoerotic fascination of beautiful young men (such as Oscar Wilde in *The Picture of Dorian Gray* [1891]) or had carefully concealed such admiration in unpublished texts, such as John Addington Symonds, who left unpublished at his death in 1893 an autobiography (the *Memoirs*) in which he disclosed his "secret" history as a homosexual.[41] Like Symonds, Stevenson depicts the man he admires as an "animal," yet insists that some reciprocity of human affection also occurred: "The philtre of admiration must be very strong, or these natives specially susceptible to its effects, for I have scarce ever admired a person in the islands but what he has sought my particular acquaintance" (*ISS*, 238). Stevenson discloses his habitual admiration of male beauty, which leads to further gestures of intimacy: Te Kop "apostrophised me as 'My name!' with an intonation exquisitely tender, laying his hand at the same time swiftly on my knee" (239).[42]

In this and other ways, Stevenson's travel writing participated in a movement that challenged orthodoxies of gender in the fin-de-siècle. Joseph Allan Boone has argued that in modernist texts, there is a pattern of representing female sexuality as it seeks to burst free from the bonds of patriarchal Victorian society. Referring to the "forbidden geography" and "subversive desire" of female sexuality, Boone argues that "it is the liberation of these constrained floods of libidinal and bodily desire . . . that forms the overt goal of the paradigmatic plot of female sexual awakening." Boone's argument that it is the woman's sexuality that is most insistently repressed by late-Victorian gender ideology is persuasive, so far as it goes. Yet Boone's focus on the plot of female sexual awakening leaves out the erotic facets of male-centered narratives such as Stevenson's, in which male desire—especially when oriented toward other men—may be no less disavowed or punished. Boone at times recognizes this transgressive force of male desire, using a geographic image to indicate its potential effects: "[E]ver since the Enlightenment's remapping of desire's streams as the flow of capital, protest against the colonization of the body and against the limitations mapped over its pleasures has increasingly become the province of male poets and novelists."[43] Stevenson's practice of cruising embraces a sustained project of "remapping" the body that resists and reverses the body's colonization by prohibition and erotic disavowal. As such, Stevenson's travel writing is in an oppositional relationship to the contemporary attempts to define, categorize, and "discipline" sexual identities in the late nineteenth century.

It is surely significant that Stevenson's attempt (in his essay "My First Book") to disavow the early travel writings with which he had begun his career was made while living in the South Seas, which he had come to recognize was his final abode. Stevenson understood that his nonfiction writings about the South Seas had generated little public interest but believed that he could redeem his reputation with a new work of fiction. Observing that Stevenson portrayed South Sea islanders not "in a state of careless happiness" but "as peoples in irreversible decline," Joan Pau Rubiés suggests that the public "expected Stevenson's book to be about romance and personal feelings, rather than a moralistic ethnography of native transformation." Rubiés deems this as "disturbing" the public's demand for "pure entertainment, in the form of identifiable passions, from the travel account."[44] Stevenson's disappointment with the reception of his South Seas writings prompts one to investigate the specific impact of the South Seas—the site of Stevenson's most extensive cruising—on the attitudes toward travel in his texts and of his writing on late-Victorian views of the South Seas in general. Lee Wallace argues that "Pacific sexuality, from its origins in colonial encounter to its current reprise in the sexual politics of postcoloniality, continues to be the very paradigm of a modern sexuality." Yet, Wallace argues, this paradigm has been misrepresented as exclusively heterosexual, representing Pacific sexuality as "a confirmation of an unspoken heterosexual warrant" that leads "desire to be understood as a unidirectional and unproblematic force that knits its male and female subjects into stable if inequitable relation." This blindness to the existence of same-sex relations in the Pacific results in "failure to recognize the disruptive force of Polynesian sexuality within European discourse." In the work of critics such as Edward Said, Wallace argues, "whose *Orientalism* insists on the centrality of sexual subjugation to the West's imperial project," such a "tendency to heterosexual metaphorization continues." The implications of Wallace's call for recognition of male-male sexual relations in the Pacific are far-reaching for this study of Stevenson's travel writing, for in the Pacific texts of Stevenson, the dynamic energies of cruising—which frequently invoke the sea-going images of freedom and pleasure—generally occur in the context of male desire.[45]

This is not to say that Stevenson enjoyed license to directly represent such homoerotic encounters in his fiction. Although Stevenson felt at liberty to include his engagement with native male beauty in the South Seas letters, in his fiction the encounter is transformed into a heterosexual liaison, as Wiltshire desires and bonds with a native woman, Uma. Wiltshire's marriage to Uma, even as it obeys the logic of compulsory heterosexuality, violates the conventions of imperial romance. As Nicholas Daly argues, "these novels do represent the colonial woman as exerting a peculiar fascination, but the exotic sexuality that the adventurers find . . . is never allowed to disturb the integrity of the male family." Yet such disturbance is precisely the effect of Uma, who functions less as a bond than as a source of conflict between members of the "male family": Wiltshire chooses Uma at Case's prompting but later learns that Case selected Uma for Wiltshire because she was tabooed. As Daly argues, in the imperial romance (such as H. Rider Haggard's *King Solomon's Mines*), when "there is the possibility of the male family being broken up by the attractions of such a woman, the text quickly shuts down this avenue of narrative development." Stevenson's narratives of cruising, however, fail or refuse to "shut down" the sexual intimacy of European colonizer and native woman. "The Beach of Falesá," for example, depicts a fantasized scenario of the desire for domestic settlement reconciled with the attraction of "exotic sexuality," breaking the rule that "there can be no 'going native.'"[46] In the South Seas, Stevenson's awareness of the deforming effects of Victorian gender ideology on men and women both would intensify. In a striking letter to Sidney Colvin, Stevenson writes that his Samoan maid, Java, exhibits physical beauty and liberty unattainable by the

European woman, and he describes her as "a miracle of *successful womanhood* in every line"(emphasis added). In a fashion reminiscent of Gauguin's exotic representation of Tahitian and Marquesan women in his paintings, Stevenson sets up the native female body as an icon of health and beauty, "a woman undeformed." In contrast, he finds the condition of women in the West repressive: "[T]he worst of civilisation is that you never see a woman. Hence my continual preference of the male, of which I used to grow ashamed."[47] Yet one can also detect in this response an anxiety about confronting the feminine sympathies and impulses in himself. As Colleen Lamos notes, "the much-noted and oft-decried virilization of women at the time had as its more disquieting corollary the effeminization of men which, after the trial of Oscar Wilde, implied the homosexualization of same-sex male affection and bonds."[48] For a male author to express sympathy for the feminine, then, was to open himself to charges of effeminacy and homosexuality.

Yet Stevenson's "preference of the male"—which he indicated was always evident in his fiction—also activates a cluster of anxieties about the permissibility of same-sex desire. On the one hand, Stevenson's experiences of cruising (specifically, the exposure to male beauty and physical freedom) enticed him with the prospect of new sexual freedom. On the other, such exposure threatened the dissolution of an identity founded on the exclusion or repression of such impulses. Lee Wallace argues, "Against the tide of European fantasies of the South Seas as heterosexual utopia . . . the body that stands as place-marker for erotic capacities both indulged and forsworn is indicatively male." Stevenson's South Seas narratives reveal this erotic fixation on the male body, illustrative of Wallace's claim that desire "among men proves particularly charged in Polynesian locations, where the desirability of the male body is foregrounded without shame."[49] This practice of eroticizing the male body informs Stevenson's critique of colonial power in the South Seas, while the view of the South Sea islands as a location in which male same-sex desire is accepted also appears in various of Stevenson's letters, in which he freely praises male beauty, defending his responses to it with the argument that "I am not ashamed of it now; it was good taste."[50]

Stevenson's ambivalent response to the erotic pleasures of cruising is symptomatic of his position at the end of the Victorian literary tradition and the beginning of the modernist era. Colleen Lamos has described the conflicted trajectory of homoerotic desire in modernism, arguing that the works of "male modernists were generated and inflected by homoerotic energies that they largely denied and by feminine identifications whose proximity to male self-constitution evoked both fantasies of escape from the strictures of masculinity and fears of same-sex desire." Lamos usefully addresses the productive rather than merely repressive role of same-sex desire in literary culture, while suggesting "fear" and "escape" as dual impulses of male subjectivity. The paradox of feminine identification, Lamos argues, is that it offers "the exciting possibility of freedom from restrictive masculine norms"; cruising reflects Stevenson's journey away from the patriarchal space of Victorian Scotland, toward encounters with the feminine in France and the United States, and ultimately toward the more feminized space of Polynesia. Yet this very embrace of freedom "also implied the potential of a feminizing sexual inversion. . . . The potential of a feminine interiority thus assumed a particular urgency for men at the time with the articulation of the concept of homosexuality by sexologists and the emergence of homosexuality as a social role, epitomized by Wilde."[51] Cruising thus complexly refracts both the fantasies and the anxieties of male sexual desire in the late nineteenth century.[52]

## The Colonial Body

The subtitle of this book addresses the significance of the "body" in Stevenson's travel writing: specifically, the "colonial body." While this term designates the bodies of colonized subjects encountered by Stevenson in the South Seas, it extends beyond that geographical place to include the colonial bodies of Scottish Highlanders, which formed a substantial subject of interest for Stevenson in his fiction and nonfiction. Moreover, the term also applies to Stevenson's body, both as a subject of a colonial power (England's colonization of Scotland) and as a man whose perpetual ill health made him subject to colonization by medical authority. In these several respects, the term invokes the body as a site of power and resistance, a space where the crossings of desire and mastery may be rendered visible; broadly, the body is part of "the system by which dominant groups in society constitute the field of truth by imposing specific knowledges, disciplines, and values upon dominated groups."[53] The colonial body then brings into play a range of somatic effects "within a society and culture deeply enmeshed in imperial domination." While for Said and other postcolonial critics the representation of the colonized body as "other" forms part of "a cultural discourse relegating and confining the non-European to a secondary racial, cultural, ontological status," this diminished status may also be accorded to those Europeans whose difference is a matter of economic class, nationality, or ill health.[54]

Helen Carr's argument that in the nineteenth century "much travel writing shows the complicity with imperialism" stands alongside her claim that the period also witnessed "the invention of distinct national identities" and "the establishment of firm racial hierarchies . . . and white supremacy." Stevenson's avoidance of the obvious landmarks of foreign travel and preference for less-populated areas such as the Cevennes and the South Seas reflects his desire to escape the "burgeoning droves of tourists" that repelled many travel writers of the time. Such writers feared that "modernity, in the shape of tourists if not colonialists, is about to sweep away the picturesque customs they have come to seek."[55]

Stevenson's oppositional stance may at times disguise complicity with such class and racial ideologies. The very concept of "adventure" from the 1880s is implicated in contexts of imperial ambition, what Carr calls "that vast expansion of territorial colonialism in the late nineteenth century." Stirring anxieties that he had "gone native," Stevenson's pleasure in his newly brown skin and his embarrassment at the remaining traces of his pale complexion connect to a discourse of robust health achieved through hardship that reaches back to his earlier travel writings. Stevenson's reference to "vile whiteness"[56] also indicates his critique of the white presence, as Stevenson (like others) "represents an important strand of anti-colonialism in the period, one which was conservative and anti-modern, and which associated imperialism with vulgar middle-class commerce."[57] There is an apparent contradiction in Stevenson's travel writing between, on the one hand, a discourse of oppression by bourgeois respectability and the impulse to escape to a "primitive" culture and, on the other, an ideology of national expansion with which his travels are complicit and which assumes a position of racial and cultural superiority. While cruising in the South

Seas, for example, Stevenson would frequently rejoice in his escape from stifling European clothing and other bodily restraint. In writing of the healthful, life-renewing impact of the South Seas cruise, he observes that "as for colour, hands, arms, feet, legs and face, I am browner than the berry; only my trunk and the aristocratic spot on which I sit, retains the vile whiteness of the north." Stevenson's dislike of modernity appears in his obvious delight that in the Pacific, "the nineteenth century only exists there in spots." He describes meeting whites who are "quite the lowest I have ever seen even in the slums of cities." The body as a sign of racial identity is unstable in Stevenson's travels, in that he often inverts the "white supremacy" of imperial discourse; indeed, he writes about "Beach of Falesá" (in a letter to Colvin), "that almost all that is ugly is in the whites."[58]

Yet despite the ugliness of colonial settings in texts by Stevenson and the public's disappointment in the lack of romance that they offered, Stevenson's travel writings nonetheless (like those by his contemporaries Rudyard Kipling and Joseph Conrad) "brought to a basically insular and provincial British audience the color, glamour, and romance of the British overseas enterprise." As Said has observed, British popular consciousness of empire was relatively slow to develop: "Not until well after mid-century did the empire become a principal subject of attention in writers like Haggard, Kipling, Doyle, Conrad as well as in emerging discourses in ethnography, colonial administration, theory and economy." The role that Said ascribes to literary culture is significant, for public fascination with this "enterprise" depended on an "othering" of the indigenous culture: "'[A]broad' was felt vaguely and ineptly to be out there, or exotic and strange, or in some way or other 'ours' to control, trade in 'freely,' or suppress when the natives were energized into overt military or political resistance."[59] This fixation on native resistance to imperial control is, of course, key to understanding Victorian attitudes toward the imperial project. Stevenson positioned himself in such a way as to jeopardize this purity, dwelling on the mixed aspects of his bodily appearance and racial heritage. At the same time, he did not always disguise his complicity with colonial violence: in proposing a "complete story of Polynesia," Stevenson specified that it would deal with the destruction of Polynesian culture by what he termed "our shabby civilization," using the first-person plural to associate himself with the very destructive forces he abhorred.[60] This idea of cultural and biological violence obviously locates the colonial subject as a victim of European invasion, a point Stevenson reiterates in *In the South Seas,* writing, "The Marquesan beholds with dismay the approaching extinction of his race. . . . [H]e lives and breathes under a shadow of mortality awful to support" (25). Stevenson's sympathy with the dismay of the Marquesan resonates with the dismay of the writer at the loss of authentic indigenous cultures for ethnographic study. Texts such as *The Ebb-Tide* exemplify how "[a]nimal imagery, used by earlier travelers to describe savage others, is now applied to the hapless . . . tourists" and colonizers.[61] Stevenson also raises the negative impact of European invaders with his supposition "that the coming of the whites, the change of habits, and the introduction of maladies and vices, fully explain the depopulation" (*ISS,* 31) of Polynesia. This perception of the devastating impact of European "civilization" in Polynesia circulates throughout Stevenson's South Seas fiction, arguably reaching its apotheosis in the opening sentence of *The Ebb-Tide,* in which Stevenson points to the destructive effects of "European races" (*SST,* 123).

The native body may serve a cultural function in Victorian society, as a focal point of European fantasy about what Vanessa Smith labels a Polynesian "post-lapsarian paradise." Yet Stevenson repeatedly undermines this fantasy by, for example, representing "the ravages of imported disease among Polynesian populations," which is responsible for, among other things, "a decline in local cultural production."[62] Moreover, even if the "other" is idealized or celebrated for its freedom from "the dead weight of European culture," there is an equally authoritative European discourse that presents the native as dangerous and degenerate "savage"; Said, for example, writes, "To be British meant to feel repugnance and injury—to say nothing of righteous vindication—given the terrible displays of cruelty by 'natives' who fulfilled the roles of savages cast for them."[63] By sympathizing with the native "other," Stevenson irrevocably invited the stigma that was frequently attached to those outside civilization. Sidney Colvin, perhaps Stevenson's closest friend in Britain, expressed the distaste shared by others at Stevenson's intimacy with Samoans in a letter of 21 March 1894: "Do these things interest you at all: or do any of our white affairs? I could remark in passing that for three letters or more you have not uttered a single word about anything but your beloved blacks—or chocolates—confound them; beloved no doubt to you; to us detested, as shutting out your thoughts . . . from the main currents of human affairs."[64] After Stevenson's death, Arthur Johnstone similarly wrote disapprovingly of Stevenson's "strong predilection for savagism" and "love for the natives, and his pity for their helplessness under the conditions in which he found them," which blinded him to "their precocious faults and unvarying instability." Johnstone further attacked Stevenson's "prejudice against civilized men," arguing that it "originated in caprice, just as his indiscriminate love for Polynesians likely sprang from another personal mood."[65]

The nature of Stevenson's travel had the effect of undermining clear-cut distinctions between nations, landscapes, and races. Stevenson's narrative device of finding parallels between the new location he visits and his native land tended to destabilize the hierarchy of "civilized" Britain (or Europe) and "savage" colonies. Moreover, Stevenson's body bore traces of immersion in Polynesian life that provided evidence of his having "gone native," anticipating Kipling's Kim, who "has grown up as a child of the Lahore bazaars" and lives as "a Sahib in native clothes."[66] As Ann Colley writes, "the Stevensons' vestimentary practices went against the dominant Western discourse and, worse, as far as their friends in Scotland and England were concerned, showed signs (were tangible proof) of the Stevensons' going native."[67] However, rather than interpreting Stevenson's body having "gone native" as signifying "contamination by absorption into native life and customs," one can view it as a mediating link between the binary opposites of colonial Self and Other. As such, Stevenson's position suggests a hybridity, an "'in-between' space that carries the burden and meaning of culture." Hybridity indicates "the creation of new transcultural forms within the contact zone produced by colonization" yet may also "reverse 'the structures of domination in the colonial situation.'"[68] Said, following Victor Turner, identifies a more positive role of "the liminal," noting that "societies . . . require a mediating character who can knit them together into community, turn them into something more than a collection of administrative or legal structures." This approach helps to cast light on the ideological nature of Stevenson's bodily and sartorial dissidence: Stevenson's predilection for "taking sea baths and living 'almost entirely in the open air as nearly without clothes as possible'" tended to confirm the belief that he had reverted to a savage state of nature. As Colley remarks, "This state of undress was a sign of the erasure of boundaries between what his friends perceived as the civilized and the uncivilized. Clothes were boundary markers and were supposed to protect one from being infected by whatever lurks beyond them. To be in a mode of undress was to violate those frontiers, to lose the covering /protection and status offered by European clothing, and to bring one too close to the unsettling otherness of an alien culture."[69] Stevenson's predilection for physical adversity, his desire "to come down off this feather-bed of civilization, and find the globe granite underfoot and strewn with cutting flints," was one of the powerful attractions that travel held for him, with the accompanying fantasy of living out of doors with his ideal "companion."[70] Such physical hardship was always a component of cruising, even in the tropics.

Western objections to the Stevensons' apparel were further founded on the erasure of gender divisions, "mixing up the gender of the clothing, so that like the Reverend Chalmers they have to persuade a male native in the Gulf of Papua to take off the woman's dress and put on a man's shirt."[71] One is here reminded of Stevenson's account of Tembinok', the king of Apemama, whose dress crossed a range of boundaries of race, gender, and class: as Stevenson remarked of his sartorially eclectic host, "Now he wears a woman's frock, now a naval uniform; now (and more usually) figures in a masquerade costume of his own design. . . . This masquerade becomes him admirably. In the woman's frock he looks ominous and weird beyond belief" (*ISS*, 211–12). The reference to the king's clothing as a masquerade recalls Judith Butler's argument about the performative aspects of gender, especially the claim that gender identities are secured by repeated bodily acts and practices, rather than grounded "naturally" in the biological body. Such bodily acts inevitably carry identifiers of race and class, as well as gender. This masquerade includes elements of the colonial powers ("naval uniform") and upper class ("jacket with shirt tails"), as well as cross-dressing ("woman's frock"). Tembinok' is fascinating to Stevenson in part because his appearance eludes classification, being powerfully hybrid in its references and performative in its design (see chapter 5). His eclectic bodily style seems connected to his refusal to be categorized as a "native," or made subject to colonial European rule. Stevenson, as a European traveler, expresses admiration for the king's resistance to white influence, writing that "The white man is everywhere else, building his houses, drinking his gin, getting in and out of trouble with the weak native governments. There is only one white on Apemama, and he on sufferance" (209). The incorporation of native and European styles is thus an empowering version of colonial mimicry, making Tembinok' feared and respected among whites as well as his own people.

By contrast, Stevenson's own bodily "performance" in the South Seas risks a loss of caste and status, as registered in European and American friends' objections to his violations of codes of gender, class, and race; in his unisex clothing that resembled too closely the garb of the "native"; and in his apparent lack of hygiene. Such bodily practices could be taken as evidence that Stevenson had "gone native"—as Colley observes, his friends, "from the very beginning of Stevenson's life in the islands, fretted over Stevenson's growing interest [in] and preoccupation with South Sea cultures and feared that he was involving himself too deeply in the life and study of the natives."[72] It seems more productive, however, to consider him as the kind of liminal figure sketched by anthropologist Victor Turner: such figures, argues Turner, "may be disguised as monsters, wear only a strip of clothing, or even go naked, to demonstrate that they have no status, property, insignia. . . . It is as if they are being reduced." Stevenson's seminaked, skeletal appearance exemplifies the kind of "reduction" outlined by Turner as a necessary precursor for the liminal figure's becoming "endowed with additional powers to enable [him] to cope with [his] new station in life."[73] Stevenson's "powers" did not depend on an official post under colonial rule—apart from a brief interest in the position of British consul on Samoa in 1892, he showed no desire for such a role—but rather lay in his communal function as a storyteller.[74] Designated as "Tusitala"—"Teller of Tales"—by the Samoans, Stevenson's cultural authority was based on gifts of narrative rather than an association with the British government, even as it earned him the material means to build the largest house on Samoa (Lloyd Osbourne wrote that "Stevenson made a very large income, and spent it all on Vailima").[75] Hence Stevenson's function as a writer was to gain him influence while creating new literary forms in the Pacific, a hybrid between native and European cultures that helped to tie the community together.[76] However, Europeans did not necessarily perceive his role in this positive light, preferring to dwell on signs of decline in his literary output. Oscar Wilde spoke for many when he wrote that

Stevenson had abandoned his true calling as a writer of romances: "In Gower Street, Stevenson could have written a new *Trois Mousquetaires.* In Samoa he wrote letters to *The Times* about Germans."[77] While Wilde obviously objected to what he saw as the literary decline in Stevenson's Samoan output, others found Stevenson's turn toward political critique disturbing for different reasons. Indeed, the German officials about whom he wrote were none too thrilled by his criticism of colonial practices: at one point, following the publication of *A Footnote to History,* the German commissioner on Samoa sought to have Stevenson deported.[78]

Stevenson's position placed him at odds with European colonial discourse of the period, which, as Said writes, was "supported and perhaps even impelled by impressive ideological formations that include notions that certain territories and people *require* and beseech domination, as well as forms of knowledge affiliated with domination." What Said terms "the vocabulary of classic nineteenth-century imperial culture . . . words and concepts like 'inferior' or 'subject races,' 'subordinate peoples,' 'dependency,' 'expansion,' and 'authority'" is either absent from Stevenson's writing or is used in a context that undermines its claims to authority.[79] For example, Stevenson's portrayal of the Polynesian body—its appearance, arts, and adornments—and his comparison of these with European practices were far from asserting the superiority of the latter. On the contrary, Stevenson often ascribed a higher value to the "primitive," voicing his objections to the proscription of native customs such as tattooing, of which he wrote, "Their art of tattooing stood by itself, the execution exquisite, the designs most beautiful and intricate; . . . I am sure it is far more becoming than the ignoble European practice of tight-lacing among women" (*ISS,* 71). Stevenson's attack on the deforming effects of female dress is unmistakable in this passage, as is his appeal against the ban on tattooing, one of the central Polynesian cultural practices: "And now it has been found needful to forbid the art" (71).

One of the frequent narrative strategies in Stevenson's travel writing is to foreground parallels between the culture, landscape, and language of locations he visits in his travels and those of his native Scotland; in *In the South Seas,* for example, he writes that "points of similarity between a South Sea people and some of my own folk at home ran much in my head in the islands," adding that "what I knew of the Cluny Macphersons, or the Appin Stewarts, enabled me to learn, and helped me to understand, about the Tevas of Tahiti" (*ISS*, 13). Stevenson's sense of, and desire for, kinship with the colonized subjects of the South Sea islands was crucial to his sympathetic portrayal of Polynesians in fiction and nonfiction, and that kinship was connected to his own history as a colonial subject. Though he sometimes referred to himself as an Englishman, Stevenson remained deeply identified with Scotland and trenchantly aware of the history of Scotland as a colonized land. In *David Balfour*, written while he resided on Samoa, Stevenson constructed a scathing critique of the British government's manipulation of Highland politics, and the monarchy's view of Scotland as "barbarous."[80] Though by birth a Lowlander, Stevenson had a strong interest in and attraction to Highland culture and history, as has been compellingly demonstrated by Barry Menikoff in *Narrating Scotland.* In Alan Breck, Stevenson represents the glamorous, exotic body of the Highland Jacobite who wears his cultural identity, literally, on his sleeve: "[A]s soon as [Breck] had taken off the greatcoat, he showed forth mighty fine for the round-house of a merchant brig: having a hat with feathers, a red waistcoat, breeches of black plush and a blue coat with silver buttons and handsome silver lace."[81]

As Breck's elaborately adorned physique demonstrates, the colonial body may also be an object of erotic interest, not least because the glamour of its appearance contrasts with the bourgeois norm. In the Polynesian context, the bodily adornment takes the form of "inscriptions of tattoo" (*ISS*, 72) that draw attention to the physical form of the native body. Lee Wallace observes, "Tattoo . . . visually enhances Marquesan flesh, accentuating the contours of the male form and further defining its perfectly developed musculature and torsion." Hence, "there is no defense against the peculiar erotic pull of tattoo, as it inevitably draws a sexualized look from its observer."[82] The colonial body thus is doubly constructed as "other" (that is, barbarous) and as an object of erotic desire. As an observer of bodily practices in foreign lands, Stevenson was drawn to the beauty of tattooed men in asserting that "nothing more handsomely sets off a handsome man; it may cost some pain in the beginning, but I doubt if it be near so painful in the long-run" (71), and then contrasting tattooing favorably with tight-lacing among European women, as cited above.

The notion of a "textual" body that is also sexualized sheds light on Stevenson's resistance to the inscription of an essential difference on the colonial body.

In the case of the Highlander, the wearing of tartan was read as the sign of an essential identity, one that was alien and hostile to the hegemonic English culture of the eighteenth century.[83] The kilt was also objected to, on the grounds of indecency, as it drew attention to parts of the body that should be concealed, as though inviting the prurient gaze of the observer: "The common Habit of the ordinary Highlands is far from being acceptable to the Eye; . . . This Dress is called the *Quelt,* and for the most part they wear the Petticoat so very short, that in a windy Day, going up a Hill, or stooping, the Indecency of it is plainly discovered."[84] If the indecency of the kilt lies in its ability to give one visual access to the body of the wearer—specifically, to his private parts—that the political objections to the garment were overlaid by this sexual significance is striking. If the dress is a visible sign of the assumed internal savagery that invites a disturbingly eroticized gaze, how much more so is the tattoo, which is actually written upon the Polynesian body, making it inescapably textual and "other." So deep was the European antipathy to the practice that Stevenson grouped it with cannibalism among the most despised Polynesian "arts and pleasures" (*ISS,* 71).

For Stevenson, like Melville before him, "tattoo stands as merely the final and most literal invasion of a white male subjectivity whose boundaries have already proven alarmingly permeable, dangerously susceptible to visual erasure and reinscription." One effect of such a blurring of boundaries is that it undermines any essentialist conception of colonial identity, challenging the binary of colonial "subjects" and "objects." Said provides an example of such challenging of essentialism: "If you know in advance that the African or Iranian or Chinese or Jewish or German experience is fundamentally integral, coherent, separate . . . you first of all posit as essential something which . . . is both historically created and the result of interpretation." In other words, Stevenson's texts, by asserting the parallels and resemblances between Polynesian and European practices, may have helped to challenge Orientalist perceptions of the Polynesian that were founded on the assumption of an essential difference.[85]

Throughout his travel writings, Stevenson emerges not as a detached observer but as one who becomes involved in the host culture and susceptible to its seductions. By displaying the extent to which his subjectivity is "invaded" and influenced by his surroundings on his travels, Stevenson reveals the "other" in himself, challenging what Timothy Mitchell argues is one of the critical effects of the "modern political order" of colonialism, that is, "the effect of seeming to exclude the other absolutely from the self, in a world divided absolutely into two. The establishing of this seemingly absolute difference is in fact an overcoming, or an overlooking, of difference."[86] Stevenson represents the female body without attempting what Joseph Allan Boone views as an important project of modernism, "the autoerotic recovery of the colonized female body."[87] Unlike Burt in the Highlands, Stevenson is far from being disturbed by any display of "indecency" in the exposed flesh of Java, his female Samoan servant. Instead, he celebrates and idealizes the freedom from restraint of the native female body as he subjects her body to his gaze to illustrate his theory of "successful womanhood" in the native: "An honest, almost ugly, bright good-natured face; the rest (to my sense) very exquisite; the inside of Java's knees, when she kilts her *lava-lava* high, is a thing I never saw equaled in a statue."[88]

Despite these objectifying tendencies and essentializing risks of Stevenson's discourse on the colonial body, I argue that he challenges the construction of the native body as inferior and "savage," both in his imitation of some of its aspects and in his deconstruction of the distinction between European and "other." Moreover, Stevenson's attention to the "masquerade"—to forms of native dress and behavior that resist essentializing, by incorporating elements from diverse races and classes—shows his desire to complicate the portrayal of the colonial body.[89] Similarly, rather than invoking the tropics as a region in which Europeans become diseased, Stevenson suggests that Europeans are responsible for the spread of infection. Stevenson's portrayal of the colonial body emphasizes its vulnerability to disease and extinction. Though he suggests that such frailty may be endemic to the race—as, for example, in writing, "The Polynesians are subject to a disease seemingly rather of the will than of the body" (*ISS*, 26)—Stevenson directly implicates European culture in the affliction by noting that "Where there have been fewest changes, important or unimportant, salutary or hurtful, there the race survives. Where there have been most . . . there it perishes" (33). In particular, Stevenson often uses disease to signify the subjection to colonial rule, as with the opening of *The Ebb-Tide*. Significantly, while almost all of Attwater's native servants have fallen prey to smallpox—"a dreadful sickness" (*SST,* 29)—Attwater remains immune, the picture of health in a deracinated community.

Disease was an apt metaphor by which Stevenson could represent subjection to power, being a state of oppression under which he had long suffered. One might say that Stevenson was himself colonized by disease, which brought him into the regime of medical knowledge (that is to say, power) embodied in figures such as Dr. Karl Ruedi at Davos, whom Stevenson expected "to have a worry at my human frame." Stevenson predicted, in writing to his parents about Ruedi, "He is going to attack me in every tender spot and make my life a burthen to me."[90] The vulnerability of the patient's body is analogous, in Stevenson's account, to that of the colonized subject, in whose "despondency there is an element of dread" (*ISS,* 27). Moreover, Stevenson's chronic illnesses made him subject to extended parental support and authority, determining many aspects of his life. Throughout his life, many of the key decisions about Stevenson's health and choice of location were made by others—his parents, his wife, his doctors—such that one can recognize in his situation the sensitivity to inert or passive bodies being compelled to conform to the will of others.

Stevenson's decision to delete the early works of travel writing from his curriculum vitae was undoubtedly connected to his belief that only the turn to fiction had allowed him to achieve commercial success as a writer. Abandoning the critique of bourgeois values apparent in *An Inland Voyage,* Stevenson jumped aboard the vessel of British imperial romance with his first novel. Significantly, Stevenson's attitudes toward colonial ideology hardened somewhat around the same time as the publication of *Treasure Island,* the turning point in this shift in attitudes being the crisis in the Sudan in the early 1880s, coinciding with the composition and publication of his first novel.[91] Yet even as Stevenson's support of Britain's imperial mission continued—not to dissipate until his arrival in the South Seas—he articulated a resistance in his writing to the colonial domination of Scotland by England. In October 1881, the same month in which *Treasure Island* began serialization in *Young Folks,* Stevenson published "Thrawn Janet" in *Cornhill Magazine;* this story launches an assault on England's cultural hegemony, not least in the material form of the Scots dialect in which it is written. By narrating the story in Scots, Stevenson erects a linguistic barrier against the English reader, who is thereby constructed as an "invader" of the

Scots cultural text. The English reader's alienation from the dialect reverses the relationship between literary and cultural "center" and colonial "outpost"; while reading the story, the English reader is compelled to accept the narrating authority of the Scots dialect, as well as the supernatural aspects of the story. The reader's surrogate in the story is the minister Soulis, whose skepticism about the supernatural meaning of Janet's appearance is founded on cultural ignorance. Barry Menikoff notes that "the devil is not the issue in this classic tale of witchcraft, but rather the minister's inability to perceive let alone acknowledge the fact of evil and its power in people's lives." Soulis struggles with the reality of "a core of evil in the world that can be denied only at one's peril," much as the reader grapples with the narrative's linguistic density.[92] As Stevenson wrote of the story, "I like [it] very much myself. . . . I do not think it is a wholesome part of me that broods on *the evil in the world and man;* but I do not think that I get harm from it; possibly my readers may, which is more serious."[93] Stevenson's concern about harming or alienating his readers led him to imbed his critiques of colonial corruption in narratives featuring the pleasures of cruising.

THE TRAJECTORY OF CRUISING in Stevenson's travel writing is a movement from Scotland and Europe outward to America and then to the South Seas, taking Stevenson to the farthest reaches of the globe. It is also a movement away from an exuberant bohemian pleasure in "travel for travel's sake" and toward a more pragmatic and critical engagement with colonial politics and cross-cultural encounters. This pragmatism was also grounded in Stevenson's increasing awareness of the literary marketplace and how he might flourish in it. Whereas Stevenson's early travel writings reflect his ebullience at escape from family and his contempt for bourgeois respectability, at times with little attention to his surroundings, the records of his cruises in the South Seas dwell on the fragility and ongoing corruption of Polynesian society as a result of the invasion of Europeans. While his early Scottish fiction such as "Thrawn Janet" portrays evil forces lurking in man and nature, eluding rational understanding, his South Sea tales identify evil explicitly with European colonial manipulation and greed. Their portrayals of disease and of brutal violence make tales such as "The Beach of Falesá" and *The Ebb-Tide* essential indices of anticolonial writing in the late-Victorian period, exposing the metropolitan center as the source of corruption in the quest for colonial plunder and domination. Of course, Stevenson's early romance, *Treasure Island,* is open to readings that identify a critique of colonial adventure in the narrative (see chapter 3). However, his later South Seas writings are far more trenchant in their use of evidence of the devastating impact of colonialism on indigenous peoples and cultures. Consequently, cruising as a practice of travel that seeks pleasure (that is, escape from Victorian prohibition) while acquiring "materials" from encounters with new places and peoples becomes imbued with Stevenson's darkening vision of colonial adventure and the violent energies of empire.

Seeking to reflect this trajectory of Stevenson's cruising, I have structured this book in four parts, each of which corresponds to a specific stage of Stevenson's travels and travel writing, unfolding Stevenson's changing relation to travel, location, and the literary marketplace. The text thus moves from the limited theme and figuration of the reanimated corpse (which both produces a change of narrative direction in the novel and represents the emergence of illicit forms of desire), to the role of the "beast" as a figure for the material body and its resistance to the transcendent impulses of travel, through Stevenson's transition from travel writer to author of "books for boys" and his leading role in the revival of "romance" and the creation of a new genre focusing on "incident" (within a "commodity-text" that exploits travel for commercial ends), and finally to the ways in which Stevenson's initial plan of writing a series of travel letters was converted to more ambitious projects, such as an ethnographic study of Polynesia and even his narrative account of the colonial and political struggles of Samoa. Following Stevenson's settlement in the South Seas, his disillusionment with the colonial enterprise grew, culminating in *The Ebb-Tide,* which presents Stevenson's most scathing portrait of European influence in the South Seas. In the figures of the trio of beachcombers, Stevenson exposes the degeneration of European culture in its contact with Polynesia, while his character Attwater embodies the corruption of the energies and pleasures of cruising, subsuming them under the drive for power and profit. With this text—one of critique and disillusionment—the initial promise of the islands has become contaminated by deeper knowledge of their diseased state and the unstoppable tide of European colonialism.[94]

*The Ebb-Tide* was published in September 1894, the month after "My First Book" appeared. That Stevenson's retrospective designation of his "first book" should coincide with the publication of his last provides a fitting sense of closure. As Wendy Katz points out, Stevenson's essay "recalls circumstances from well over a decade earlier."[95] Likewise, *The Ebb-Tide* rehearses the themes of adventure, cruising, and treasure hunting that had launched Stevenson's literary success a decade before. Yet the novel may be said to look ahead rather than back, providing a map for those literary adventurers such as Conrad, Kipling, and Graham Greene, who would continue the journey into the colonial darkness where Stevenson had left off.

# PART ONE

## Travel and the (Re)animated Body

# ONE

## Reanimating Stevenson's Corpus

THE 1994 CENTENARY of Robert Louis Stevenson's death was the impetus for a major reevaluation of his life and career. Indeed, given the recrudescence of scholarly and critical attention to Stevenson since 1994—including several new biographies, a number of critical studies, and the superb multivolume edition of his letters published by Yale University Press under the editorship of Ernest Mehew—one might justifiably speak of the reanimated corpus of a writer whose extraordinary popularity during his lifetime was followed by decades of critical neglect and dismissal.[1] Robert Kiely wrote, in his important 1964 study, of "the pedestal upon which Stevenson's contemporaries had set him being used as the ram to batter him with," and Stevenson's reputation has undergone several deaths and rebirths during the twentieth century.[2] Yet despite this renewed attention to his work, the significance of a vital source of narrative energy and interest in Stevenson's fiction has remained buried in obscurity: that of the reanimated corpse, a figure that surfaces in many of his fictions of adventure, including *Treasure Island* (1883), *The Master of Ballantrae* (1889), and *The Ebb-Tide* (1894), and plays a central role in Stevenson's comic masterpiece of 1889, *The Wrong Box*. This figure is of central importance not only to the impetus to travel and mobility in Stevenson's travel writing but also to the forms of narrative desire in Stevenson's late fiction. By attending to the narrative energies associated with the corpse, I argue, we are better able to grasp an important technique of romance fiction by which Stevenson and other writers, such as Oscar Wilde and Rider Haggard, sought to reanimate the corpse of Victorian realism through a revitalized use of gothic and sensational motifs.[3] Moreover, the reanimated corpse is, like cruising, a vital component of Stevenson's travel writing. In many of these works, travel is the stimulus needed to renew dying energies and restore the inert, moribund body to life.

Yet even as reanimation is crucial to the narrative energies of Stevenson's corpus, the desire brought into play by the reanimated corpse is, I argue, problematic: at once secret and homoerotic in nature, such desire emerges in a context of physical intimacy between men who seek to dissociate themselves from the contaminating effects of the corpse by burying it, by passing it on to another unsuspecting recipient, or by treating it as a joke. What one reviewer of *The Wrong Box* called "a kind of ghastly game at hide and seek with a dead man's body" becomes imbued with homoerotic import as the game enters into ever more promiscuous forms of exchange.[4] What is at stake in this game is the representation of the corpse as a reminder both of the materiality of the body and of its status as a site of illicit pleasure, specifically, "unspeakable" sexual practices between men. Such practices, which grew increasingly obtrusive in public discourse following the Labouchère Amendment of 1885 and the Cleveland Street scandal of 1889, were ripe for narrative treatment but only in cryptic or displaced form. Wayne Koestenbaum has argued that Stevenson was aware of the significance of this antihomosexual legislation and sought to give representation to illicit forms of masculine desire in *Strange Case of Dr. Jekyll and Mr. Hyde*, published a few months after the Labouchère Amendment was passed.[5] Reminding us that the original readers of the story would not have known of Jekyll and Hyde's shared identity, Koestenbaum argues that "the novel's opening pages suggest . . . a socially transgressive story about a Dr Jekyll and a Mr Hyde, two men from different social classes, who are involved in a shadowy, illicit relationship that is probably sexual, or at least involves the blackmail which was, by 1885, a sign for homosexuality."[6]

The shocking aspects of Stevenson's story, in this reading, derive significantly from its reanimation of desires that were at once repugnant and fascinating to Victorians, desires that the legislation of the period made increasingly visible and problematic. I argue that the "horror" generated by the presence of the corpse in Stevenson's text indicates the presence of erotic fantasies that are unmentionable and disturbing, which the corpse promotes by engendering dangerous intimacies and confusions of identity. Specifically, the contaminating effects of the corpse on the agents of narrative closure in Stevenson's fiction—including the narrators themselves—eventually require the deployment of various strategies of containment that seek to manage the disruptive effects of the corpse and close off the narrative desires it has produced.[7] This tendency of a disruptive narrative desire to elude strategies of containment is, I argue, emboldened by the reanimation of the corpse that suggests the impossibility of finally stifling the desire that it has brought into play. Hence, the reanimated corpse is symptomatic of a double bind of erotic disavowal by which, according to Joseph Bristow, "the more Western culture devise[s] methods for speaking about the unspeakability of sex, the more sex itself [becomes] a type of open secret, ushering into the public domain a scandal that ha[s] to be masked."[8]

The corpse is also significant in the transition from the dominant realist novel of the mid-Victorian age to the romance that has been read by Nicholas Daly as a precursor of modernist narrative. The erratic—and erotic—movements of the animated corpse bring into focus the radical emptiness—in realist terms, the "lifelessness"—of character within the adventure narrative typical of the late-Victorian romance. As Stevenson explains in his 1882 essay "A Gossip on Romance," the necessary focus of romance is on the extrinsic action—or "incident"—of the story at the expense of the intrinsic experience or traits of character. A key text in my discussion of reanimation is *The Wrong Box,* the composition of which marked a transition in Stevenson's location from Scotland to the South Seas. Not only does *The Wrong Box* typify Stevenson's practice of producing his works in multiple locations, but also its hybridity of form suggests the destabilizing of generic conventions that accompanies the reanimated corpse. The problems of the body are of a specific and peculiar kind in

*The Wrong Box,* involving the need to dispose of an unwanted corpse, while the characters are thoroughly absorbed in devising convoluted strategies for disposing of, transmitting, or concealing the taboo object. Although certainly not a realist novel, *The Wrong Box* cannot satisfactorily be characterized as a romance, as several of Stevenson's earlier narratives can. It is, in a word, unclassifiable: a hybrid work in which romance elements combine with comic misadventure to produce a narrative that refuses to conform to established generic conventions and cannot be contained within any narrative "box." As such, it is a symptom of late-Victorian narrative disorder, as well as of Stevenson's journey beyond the bounds of narrative convention. Stevenson's novel presents similar generic problems to James Hogg's 1824 gothic text, *Confessions of a Justified Sinner,* both works being "characterized by numerous false starts, false endings, and digressions."[9] Hogg's refusal to conform to generic expectations is designed to disorient the reader, "a plot to trap us in our own rigid expectations of the laws of genre," by refusing to provide satisfying closure to the narrative.[10] Hogg's and Stevenson's disruptions and derailings of plot undermine the narrative agenda of nineteenth-century realism, refusing to comply with the demand for lifelike characters and plausible plots. Moreover, the centrality of the corpse to the economies of desire in both *Justified Sinner* and *The Wrong Box* undermines the realist novel's emphasis on heterosexual desire, marriage, and class as the keys to subjectivity.

Although Stevenson has generally been aligned with "romance" in opposition to "realism"—in part because of his often-cited debate with Henry James—his position is best understood not as a refutation of realism, as such, but as a rejection of the system of generic classifications. Ultimately, Stevenson disputes both the entombment of narrative art into such theoretical "boxes" and the subsequent disavowal of romance as a secondary, inferior, or decadent aesthetic form: in "A Note on Realism," he writes, "This question of realism, let it be then clearly understood, regards not in the least degree the fundamental truth, but only the technical method, of a work of art." By focusing on style and method, Stevenson shifts the ground of the debate about realism from the ontological status of mimetic representation to the material techniques and readerly effects of narrative. Whereas the skilled artist is concerned primarily with "what to put in and what to leave out," the realist author—in an impossible quest to reproduce reality—risks burying his audience with words: "The immediate danger of the realist is to sacrifice the beauty and significance of the whole to local dexterity, or, in the insane pursuit of completion, to immolate his readers under facts."[11]

For Stevenson, therefore, the romance novel is energizing precisely in its refusal to be either inclusive or conclusive. As M. M. Bakhtin would later argue, the novel (or novelistic discourse) is less a genre in itself than a reanimating influence on other genres: "[T]he novel inserts into these other genres an indeterminacy, a certain semantic openendedness, a living contact with unfinished, still-evolving contemporary reality." As "the only developing genre," the novel "sparks the renovation of all other genres, it infects them with its spirit of process and inconclusiveness."[12] This Bakhtinian insight brings into focus Stevenson's embodiment of the subversive, anticanonical energies of the novel, embodying "whatever force is at work within a given literary system to reveal the limits, the artificial constraints of that system."[13]

Stevenson's errant and inconclusive narrative practice therefore raises a number of interesting and important questions concerning both the relationship between character and incident in late-Victorian narrative and the tension between subversive desire and strategies of containment that seek to produce closure. *Incident* is perhaps the key term in Stevenson's defense of romance; it entirely eclipses the significance of character, to the extent that (as he writes in "A Gossip on Romance") "the characters are no more than puppets. The bony fist of the showman visibly propels them; their springs are an open secret; their faces are of wood, their bellies filled with bran; and yet we thrillingly partake of their adventures."[14] In his designation of characters as "puppets," Stevenson suggests that they are merely the inert vehicles for narrative action, wholly dependent upon animation by author and reader.

*The Wrong Box*'s chief transgression of literary propriety—at least in the eyes of Victorian critics—was to expose this mortifying effect of literary realism, setting the nameless body adrift indefinitely until, carried off by an unsuspecting carter, the corpse further defers its own burial. In part, this critical uneasiness with the fiction is the manifestation of cultural taboos about death: as Christine Quigley observes, "fear of the dead may stem from the fear that their bodies are contagious."[15] The fear of contagion by the corpse—manifested in

*The Wrong Box* as the urgency with which each recipient of the body tries to get rid of it as soon as possible—is also linked to the novel's secret figuration of homoeroticism, a discourse of "unspeakable" desire that is hastily dissolved into comic scenarios of misunderstanding or exchange. I argue that the source of the jokes and wordplay in *The Wrong Box* may be located in anxieties about anality and sodomy and their metonymic displacement as burial in a secret site (the corpse as a "stiff," misdirected to the wrong orifice). I will discuss specific scenes of male intimacy in the text in which the corpse figures as an unspeakable secret that must be "buried." This suppression of anality is, according to Guy Hocquenghem, symptomatic of Western subjectivity: "[T]he anus is so well hidden that it forms the subsoil of the individual, his 'fundamental' core. . . . Your anus is so totally yours that you must not use it: keep it to yourself."[16] This paradox of secrecy—that which is most hidden is also most fundamental, both to text and to body—resurfaces time and again in Stevenson's fictions of reanimation. Like the "cloak of silence" (which, as Koestenbaum argues, "veils Jekyll's bachelor community"), the "unspeakability" of the corpse articulates a buried significance in Stevenson's narrative practices and so puts in reverse the intended effects of legislation of the period as noted by Koestenbaum: "[W]hen the Labouchère Amendment focused its eye on the homosexual, it articulated practices it had meant to silence." I will explore the function of such articulations in other texts by Stevenson, including those written collaboratively with his stepson, Lloyd Osbourne, a young man with whom Stevenson shared the "excitement" of "the metaphorically sexual conception of a 'romance.'"[17] Firstly, however, I will examine the theme of reanimation in one of Stevenson's least-discussed texts, yet one that has relevance to the entire corpus.

## Burying Desire in *The Wrong Box*

When published under the joint authorship of Robert Louis Stevenson and Lloyd Osbourne in June 1889, *The Wrong Box* was almost unanimously dismissed by critics as a kind of tasteless practical joke or as a mistaken attempt on Stevenson's part to boost the credibility of his amateurish collaborator. As Paul Maixner observes, this novel "provoked more adverse reviews than any book [Stevenson] would publish," and the hostility aroused by the work was initially attributable to uncertainty concerning the respective contributions of Stevenson and his collaborator: one critic, with discernible anxiety, wrote, "What Mr Osbourne's share in the story may be it is hard to determine."[18] In fact, as Stevenson's correspondence of the period reveals, there was a clear division of labor in the composition of the text. Lloyd had written the original draft, which Stevenson was so impressed with that he had "taken it in hand" and developed it. As Stevenson wrote to Henry James on October 6, 1887, "from the next room the bell of Lloyd's type-writer makes an agreeable music, as it patters off (at a rate which astonishes this experienced novelist) the early chapters of a humorous romance."[19] Asserting that "if it is not funny, I'm sure I don't know what is," Stevenson informed Charles Baxter that "*I have split* over writing it" and expressed no embarrassment in publishing the novel under their joint authorship. Stevenson's split subjectivity is a source of *jouissance* rather than anxiety. Indeed, he viewed the writing of it as an amusing pastime—what Michael Finsbury terms a "little judicious levity"[20]—promoting an escape from the laborious task of completing *The Master of Ballantrae*, of which he wrote, as though anticipating his own reanimation, "when that's done I shall breathe."[21] Hence, one can see the composition of this novel as itself an act of reanimation, in which the experienced author takes in hand the embryonic text of an enthusiastic amateur and injects it with life and comic vitality: Bernard Darwin writes that "Lloyd Osbourne was little more than a boy at the time and was Stevenson's stepson to whom he would be glad to give a helping hand." Darwin goes on to cite Lloyd's comment on the Frankenstein-like creative powers of his stepfather: "He [Stevenson] breathed into it, of course, his own incomparable power, humour and vivacity *and forced the thing to live* as it had never lived before."[22] At the same time, as Stevenson's letters reveal, his own creative energies were reanimated by this collaboration with the youthful novice.

Yet the critics of his time were unwilling to applaud either Stevenson's generosity to his protégé or the new lease on life that he gained from working on the "humorous romance." For example, Stevenson's fellow Scot Margaret Oliphant objected that he "had deluded us by the loan of his name into that undignified and unworthy exhibition," a comment that reflects the perhaps especially Victorian anxiety about the unique identity of the author and the value of the literary commodity-text as determined by the seal of the author's signature.[23] The (literally) decadent subject matter of the novel was offensive to Victorian sensibilities, as is evident from the angry assertion by the critic for the *Pall Mall Gazette* that Stevenson "ought to be ashamed of himself" for "the choice of so repellant a subject"; this critic added that "we must . . . enter our forcible protest against the funereal fun of a story which has as the pivot on which the whole plot turns the buffeting from pillar to post of a corpse." The indecency of making a corpse the protagonist of a prolonged narrative—even though the story moved fast enough "to prevent the olfactory nerve discovering the whereabouts of the concealed carcase"—was evidently enough to earn *The Wrong Box* the contempt of the critics, despite its similarity to "a weird story under the title of 'The Body Snatcher,'" which Stevenson had published in 1884.[24] The plot of *The Wrong Box* is no less byzantine than that of a sensation novel, and it shares with that popular genre of the 1860s a feature identified by Patrick Brantlinger as "the subordination of character to plot."[25] Consequently, the "box"—or plot—of this novel must be carefully measured in its various dimensions if we are to grasp its capacity to shock and appall, as well as entertain and amuse, the Victorian reader.[26]

Stevenson took Osbourne's initial idea of an unwieldy, economically motivated "box" involving the two elderly survivors of a "tontine fund"—an agreement by which a group of parents contribute to a fund on behalf of their children, with the last surviving member of the original group of children receiving the entire accumulated figure—and injected a grotesque game involving a misidentified corpse. The two surviving members of the original group are brothers, Joseph and Masterman Finsbury, who are jealously guarded by their youthful relatives—Joseph's nephews, Morris and John, and Masterman's son, Michael. Because of a prior episode in which they have been defrauded by their uncle Joseph of an inheritance, Morris and John consider themselves entitled to the proceeds of the tontine fund and anxiously protect Joseph so that he will outlive his rival: the narrative describes how, in Morris's view, "his uncle was rather gambling stock in which he had invested heavily; and he spared no pains in nursing the security" (*Wrong Box*, 7).

The course of this inheritance plot of sorts, however, is disrupted when a train transporting Joseph, Morris, and John Finsbury from Bournemouth to London is wrecked in a collision with another train.[27] In the ensuing carnage and confusion, Morris and John mistakenly identify the dead body of another passenger—dressed identically to Joseph, in "the uniform of Sir Faraday Bond" (*Wrong Box*, 16)—as the corpse of their uncle. This misidentification of the corpse is also promoted by the fact that in the train wreck "the face had suffered severely, and it was unrecognizable" (18). The two brothers temporarily bury the body until they can find some means of moving it to their London address, their chief concern being to prevent discovery of the death of their uncle, so as not to lose the tontine. They eventually pack the body into a water-butt and place it on a train to London, directing it to their address in Bloomsbury. On the journey, however, a prankster—coincidentally, a friend of Michael Finsbury's—switches the address label with another crate containing a statue, which is supposed "to lie at Waterloo till called for, and addressed to one 'William Dent Pitman'" (34). Meanwhile the real Joseph, who has survived the crash, has been wandering around the countryside and ends up on the same London-bound train as the packing cases. Pitman unwittingly receives the water-butt containing the corpse and is assisted by his lawyer—who happens to be Michael Finsbury—in disposing of it. They deposit the body in a Broadwood piano owned by a young man-about-town, Gideon Forsyth.

Meanwhile, Morris is appalled to discover that he has received a packing crate containing a statue of Hercules rather than the barrel containing the corpse of his uncle. The crate has been opened by Gideon Forsyth and Julia Hazeltine, a young woman who lives at Joseph's home. In a rage at the mistake, Morris attacks the statue with a hammer and destroys it. Gideon, having discovered the corpse concealed in his Broadwood piano, takes a houseboat under the false name of Jimson (supposedly a frustrated composer) and plans to drop the body into the canal, feigning the suicide of his alter ego. But the cart carrying the piano—inside which the corpse remains hidden—is stolen and is last seen driving away into the distance. As Gideon says of the cart driver, "the man has been ass enough to steal the cart and the dead body; what he hopes to do with it I neither know nor care" (122). The real Joseph Finsbury is finally restored to his relatives.

As this summary indicates, *The Wrong Box* is a story featuring error, mistaken identity, disrupted journeys, and aborted narrative designs. Though several calamities have already occurred as the narrative commences—in particular, the loss of Morris's and John's fortune in their uncle's declining leather business—the central disaster determining the plot occurs with the train wreck. Specifically, the wreck is an emblem of a recurring motif in Stevenson's travel narratives—the failure to reach one's intended destination, and the generation of new plots that results from this failure. Representing a relatively new technology of travel, the railway proves as vulnerable to breakdown as the recalcitrant ass in *Travels with a Donkey* or the shipwrecked brig *Covenant* in *Kidnapped.*

In a metafictional gesture, the narrator draws attention to the link between the work of fiction and the railway journey in the opening paragraph by lamenting the amount of labor, on the part of the author, necessary "to while away an hour for him [the reader] in a railway train" (3). The railway carriage is posited as the presumed locale in which the narrative is consumed: a point illustrative of the fact that "[t]he great Victorian railway expansion (or 'mania') took place in the late 1830s and early 1840s, creating a distinct new market for portable, entertaining books." In interpellating the reader as a railway traveler, the narrator invokes not only the transient, casual relationship between text and reader common to such consumers but also the tolerance they had for sensational or shocking subject matter: as John Sutherland remarks, "The railway boom created a new lease of life for the authors who were favourites with the travelling public, who tended to be broader in their tastes than circulating library subscribers."[28] Yet the story Stevenson has begun to construct around the tontine is effectively derailed with the train wreck, precipitating the characters into a wholly new and unexpected sequence of events defined by a series of aborted travels. This first violently interrupted journey inaugurates a series of failed or incomplete expeditions: just as the train fails to deliver Joseph's body—which is by this time a very valuable commodity—to its destination, so also will the corpse that results from the wreck never be properly delivered or, indeed, identified.

The motif of the random, aimless, or interrupted journey is an important feature not only of Stevenson's fiction but also of the travel writings with which he began his career. In the preface to his first published book, *An Inland Voyage* (1878), Stevenson warns the reader that "Caleb and Joshua brought back from Palestine a formidable bunch of grapes; alas! my book produces naught so nourishing," yet he then expresses the hope that "the eccentricity may please in frivolous circles."[29] This address to the frivolous reader identifies the journey as a quaintly unproductive, dilettante exercise. Framing the journey as a gentle rebellion against Victorian bourgeois work practices and efficiency, Stevenson describes his travels as "the most leisurely of progresses" (47), characterized by delay and disruption, "now waiting horses for days together on some inconsiderable junction" (47). Stevenson presents the journey itself as inconsiderable, a course determined by the whim and curiosity of the travelers rather than any rigid itinerary or grand tour. Yet the narrative takes on a serious purpose as the journey down the river becomes a metaphor for the vagaries of life and the deferral of inevitable death: "[W]e may look upon our little private war with death somewhat in this light. If a man knows he will sooner or later be robbed upon a journey, he will have a bottle of the best in every inn and look upon all his extravagances as so much gained upon the thieves. . . . So every bit of brisk living, and above all when it is healthful, is just so much gained upon the wholesale filcher, death" (52). Even as the journey highlights the novelty and excitement of travel—"I had never been in a canoe under sail in my life; and my first experiment out in the middle of this big river was not made without some trepitation" (7)—death returns to haunt the traveler/author, as even the shape of his canoe becomes a memento mori: "[T]here are people who call out to me that it is like a coffin" (58). Anticipating the ambivalent representation of travel—the blend of pleasure and anxiety it evokes—in his later works, *An Inland Voyage* depicts the journey as a futile struggle against death while nevertheless affirming its liberating force with the claim that "the most beautiful adventures are not those we go to seek" (107).

Whereas *An Inland Voyage* concludes with a scene of "travelers . . . telling their misadventure" (120), *The Wrong Box* ends with the jarring image of the corpse going astray on the stolen cart, symptomatic of the narrative as a risky journey on which things never go according to plan, characters fail to arrive at their proper destinations, and the narrative fails to reach a satisfactory conclusion. Though the final image of the errant corpse vividly signals the failure of closure, the damage has been done at an earlier juncture, with the rail crash. The railway, like the novel, came of age in a century of increasing speed, population growth, and travel; it was designed to accelerate the transportation of bodies from one location to another. Indeed, the novel and railway are alike in requiring an engine to generate motion. Peter Brooks, in his study of the dynamics of desire in narrative fiction, has compared the plot of the nineteenth-century novel to an engine or motor, which moves the reader forward in time and space. Representing the "fascination with engines and forces" characteristic of the period, the presence of machines in fiction indicates that "[l]ife in the text of the modern is a nearly thermodynamic process; plot is, most aptly, a steam engine."[30] In Stevenson's novel, the engine that moves the comic plot forward is, in fact, a steam engine: yet its progress suffers "a brutal stoppage" (*Wrong Box*, 17) in a collision with a more powerful locomotive, "the down express" (17), representing the dominant force of narrative realism, with which Stevenson's railway novel collides. In the resulting crash, the narrative is fragmented and the plot is transformed into utter chaos, requiring the utmost ingenuity to restore order. The corpse, then, emerges from the wreckage as an embodiment of the contingency and disorder produced by the derailing of realist narrative. This creates a new challenge for the author, who must generate narrative without the conventional strategies of containment. As the doctor says at the scene of accident (while "the vomit of steam . . . still spouted from the broken engines"), "there's terrible work before us" (18).

Of course, Stevenson has artfully engineered this wreckage of his plot to allow the emergence of a different kind of narrative desire, one that eschews the logic of narrative order for something more open-ended. What Brooks terms the "totalizing" movement of narrative desire, in which the "ultimate determinants of meaning lie at the end," is renounced for "a system of potentially unlimited energetic transformations and exchanges."[31] Paradoxically, the chief figure for this reanimation of the narrative from the wreckage of its own plot is the mutilated corpse: an object described, with a telling reference to the loss of lifelike characteristics, as "something that had once been human" (*Wrong Box*, 18). The mistaken identification of this corpse by Morris and John as the body of their uncle can occur only because—as has been made clear in a fascinating self-reflexive passage—the followers of Sir Faraday Bond are already so interchangeable that even at the moment of his first appearance, this character has already ceased to exist: "Many passengers put their heads to the window, and among the rest an old gentleman on whom I willingly dwell, for I am nearly done with him now. . . . His name is immaterial" (16). This refusal to name—to provide an identity for—a character who is so eminently dispensable rejects the sheer pleasure of creating and elaborating character that typifies a Dickens novel, for example, and shirks the obligation to furnish the precise details of character and location that are the hallmark of the realist narrative.

This gesture of negation is a far more final death than the one that follows in the train wreck. Indeed, the narrator makes clear that the transience and flux of modern society render individual subjects highly dispensable by noting that "if the whole of this wandering cohort were to disappear tomorrow, their absence would be wholly unremarked. How much more, if only one—say this one in the ventilating cloth—should vanish! . . . Perhaps the old gentleman thought something of the sort, for he looked melancholy enough as he pulled his bare, grey head back into the carriage, and the train smoked under the bridge, and forth, with ever quickening speed, across the mingled heaths and woods of the New Forest" (*Wrong Box*, 16–17). The only trace of interiority attributed to this anonymous figure is sadness at his obsolescence. Moreover, the rapidity and frequency of travel is assigned as a cause for the evacuation of identity. Yet another significant dynamic here is the narrative desire to destroy the "old gentleman," one of several substitutes in the novel for the father with whom Stevenson had a conflicted relationship. The desired death of the father—which in Stevenson's case had occurred two years earlier (in 1887), leaving the son financially independent—here anticipates the ending of the novel, leaving the narrative with no goal to pursue.[32] Yet this premature "death" leads to a crucial error—perhaps wish-fulfillment—as John and Morris hastily (mis)identify the deceased as their uncle and go on to engage in a series of new games and fictions, beginning with the brothers' decision to hide the body and their realization that "we must take assumed names" (21). Morris Finsbury, in fact, takes advantage of the wrecked plot to appropriate the authorial role in determining the fates of characters, saying of his uncle, "He's not dead, unless I choose." Morris decides that the fiction of his uncle's being alive has, unlike the life itself, no need for closure: "[T]here's no sort of limit to the game that I propose" (20).

The wrongness invoked by the novel's title, then, alludes in part to the destruction of the train that redirects the plot and the ensuing series of ill-chosen containers in which the corpse is deposited. Yet it also alludes to the novel's "repellant" subject matter, in which death and the deceased body are treated as prolonged jokes. Additionally, Margaret Oliphant's critique of Stevenson's text identifies another construction of wrongness, as when she refers to the novel as "a very wrong box indeed." Here an element apparently belonging to the plot—the confusion between packing cases or boxes that leads to the misdirection of the corpse—is appropriated for a critique of the "errors" of the narrative, especially its failure to conform to conventions of genre and authorial responsibility. What is wrong about *The Wrong Box*, from Oliphant's point of view, is that (a) Stevenson should never have written it but (b) having done so, he should never have published it, because (c) it deals with subject matter not suitable for fictional treatment and (d) does not belong to any particular "box" used to classify narrative fiction.

But Oliphant's comment also reveals a slippage—a pun—in the novel's title. If the "wrong box" refers at the level of plot to the confusion between the packing case and the water barrel, it also implicitly alludes to the failures of the "box"—whether the novel or the plot—to adequately contain the desires that it impermissibly represents. As an illicit object of desire, the corpse can be safely removed only by being buried in a coffin. None of the boxes in the novel, however, achieves the status of what D. A. Miller terms the "ultimate mortifying box" in which the corpse may finally, and with propriety, be laid to rest.[33] Consequently, the coffinless corpse is allowed—like Stevenson's body in the coffin-shaped canoe in *An Inland Voyage*—to wander aimlessly, functioning as a contaminated object of desire that eludes narrative containment. Far from being possessed in the novel, this "box" escapes its rightful owner and is passed from one unwilling host to another, so that by the novel's end, all characters are implicated in, and contaminated by, the transgressive desire of/for the errant body.

The body in motion is a focus of fascination and desire in Stevenson's travel writing. This desire inevitably surfaces in displaced form, for the body can be represented only in terms of its movements or its coverings, all of which imbue the body with a kind of unruly animation that the artifice of narrative plot manifestly fails to contain. In Stevenson's travel writing, the body is metonymically linked to the means of transportation, such that in *Travels with a Donkey*, the donkey both carries and substitutes for the narrator's body. In *The Wrong Box*, the body, following its discovery in a water barrel by Pitman and Michael

Finsbury, is described in terms that allude to its inhuman and inscrutable form: "In the midst of these [fragments of water barrel,] a certain dismal something, swathed in blankets, remained for an instant upright, and then toppled to one side and heavily collapsed before the fire. Even as the thing subsided, an eye-glass tingled to the floor and rolled toward the screaming Pitman" (*Wrong Box*, 64). This scene explicitly renders the corpse—as an object of dehumanized materiality and mortality—a source of disgust and horror. Yet this adverse reaction is productive of a screening discourse that displaces the response of sheer terror at the inanimate body into a sequence of ingenious jokes and puns tending to generate amusement at the appalling lifelessness of the object. One example of this is Gideon's return to his darkened apartment, whereupon he bumps into the Broadwood piano, which has been placed in the center of the room, or as the narrative playfully states, he "dashed himself against a heavy body; where . . . no heavy body should have been" (98–99). Attempting to play the piano, he is shocked to find that the keyboard will produce no sound: "He gave the Broadwood two great bangs with his clenched fist. All was still as the grave" (99). The inactive, silent bulk of the piano—its "heavy body"—metonymically represents the corpse it contains, while the powers of expression previously possessed by Gideon and his instrument are paralyzed by the corpse's mortifying presence.

Stevenson's ludic manipulation of novelistic discourse in *The Wrong Box* derives from the reliance of the plot on a presence that threatens to implode the artifice of novelistic character. The narrative mischievously generates a sequence of metonymic and euphemistic displacements for the corpse, which substitute for the inner life of character and endow the inanimate corpse with the illusion of substance and vitality. The self-reflexive mode of the characters' speech when in the vicinity of the corpse suggests the extent to which their discourse has ceased to be transparent and has become a problem of representation, best expressed by the words of one of the characters in this scene: "What language am I to find?" (65). A typical exchange occurs when Michael Finsbury and Pitman decide to "get him out of sight," by means of hiding the body in a closet, in the course of which the corpse is referred to evasively as "it," as "you know what" (66), as "that horror in my studio" (67), and once, bizarrely, as "Cleopatra" (67).

Following its concealment, the corpse's anonymity is preserved through reference to it as the "party in the closet" (65), at which point it becomes a dangerous yet unmentionable secret between the two men. Pitman's fear that his hitherto "eminently respectable" life, which he describes in textual terms as "entirely fit for publication," will be fatally scandalized by the presence of the corpse seems to play on authorial anxiety at the hostile reception in store for the novel, which was deemed as being entirely unfit for publication under Stevenson's imprimatur. Additionally, however, the scene invokes the specifically male sexual secret as a site of horror. From that scene onward, the morbid game of hide-and-seek played between characters in *The Wrong Box* involves, with its fixation on the materiality of the male body, a context of homoeroticism in which the proximity of the corpse becomes part of a transgressive scene of male intimacy. This leads to what might be termed the novel's primal scene, as Michael Finsbury suggests that he and Pitman bury the body: "[W]e should look devilish romantic shovelling out the sod by the moon's pale ray" (65). As Finsbury then states, the men have little alternative but to embrace the strategy of burial: "If you won't take the short cut and bury this in your back garden, we must find some one who will bury it in his" (66). "Sod" may be read as an abbreviated term for *sodomite,* such that "shovelling out the sod" (or, indeed, "bury[ing] . . . in your back garden") functions as a coded representation of sodomy.[34] This scenario is linked to the imminent threat of invasion by the police, whom Michael describes, to a terrified Pitman, as "digging up your back garden" (66). The sodomitic encryption of the secret burial suggests the threat that the corpse poses to the illusion of masculine character as possessing an inviolable inner life. This interiority, Leo Bersani has argued, is violated by the self-dissolving jouissance of anal pleasure. Bersani has carefully traced the discursive association between sodomy and the death of subjectivity, whereby the rectum becomes rhetorically configured as a grave for the masculine subject. Bersani's account is useful in this context because it examines the association between anal pleasure and the evacuation of subjectivity that is viewed, in Western culture, as the self-destructive abdication of masculine power and privilege.

At stake in Bersani's analysis is less the pleasures and problems of a specific sexual practice than the production of male sexual passivity as representing the abandonment of the Western masculine ideal of autonomy and selfhood. According to Bersani, the specter of anal penetration terrifies because it threatens the loss of a culturally privileged identity and represents a "death" that is figured by the disturbing receptivity of the rectum, an interpretation that helps to account for the astonishing persistence of homophobic prejudice. Though Bersani examines this "frenzied epic of displacements" in the context of AIDS discourse, his argument goes on to embrace the "suicidal" implications of male sexual passivity.[35] Pointing to "the heterosexual association of anal sex with a self-annihilation originally and primarily identified with the fantasmatic mystery of an insatiable, unstoppable female sexuality," Bersani celebrates the notion that "the rectum is the grave in which the masculine ideal . . . of proud subjectivity is buried" and encourages the assault on, or fragmentation of, "the sacrosanct value of selfhood" that sexual jouissance achieves.[36]

The notion of selfhood that Bersani invokes, only to discard, is one that the nineteenth-century realist novel establishes as the ideological basis for its fiction and reinforces through its strategies of containment. The attack on this hegemonic notion of the novelistic plot, specifically as one based on the individual life story, is carried out in *The Wrong Box* by the comic possibilities of the corpse. As an end to the contaminating influence of the corpse is sought through repeated attempts to control and box it in, the containment strategies of the novel—identified by Fredric Jameson as a repressive discourse that organizes "the rewriting of a narrative whose dynamics might otherwise elude categories of the ethical and of the individual subject"—are brought into play by means of the prospective burial of the body. As Jameson argues, such containment strategies work by managing impulses that represent the unthinkable, "to defuse them, to prepare substitute gratifications for them."[37] In the scene that I have cited from *The Wrong Box,* the grave is imagined as the final and proper container of the erotically charged corpse. Yet the intention of burial or "shovelling out the sod" is abandoned as a strategy of containment in favor of passing the corpse on to someone else, which only produces further chaos and failures of closure. The relation of this episode to the manipulation of narrative techniques is emphasized by the fact that the scene of burial is a doubly imaginary one—it is a prospect of disposing of the body as fantasized by a character in a novel yet never actually occurs, even in the plot of a fiction.

The homoeroticism of the scene, however, becomes a new narrative engine that drives the plot forward and keeps the body in circulation. Here, a strategy of closure by means of burial—initially attempted when the Finsbury brothers dig a shallow grave only to set the corpse on its course again—is deferred in favor of a new displacement, by which the corpse enters a new economy of desire. The dead body cannot remain lifeless: it must be reanimated by a series of competing intentions that take the form of the various containers—the boxes—in which the corpse is strategically deposited and transported. These boxes echo the coffin that Stevenson compared to his canoe and anticipate subsequent means of transport by which the body is at once contained and carried. They thus serve as both the metonymic displacements of the body, by means of which its disruptive influence is disseminated through the narrative, and the futile strategies of containment generated by the plot to contain the errant desires it has aroused. The Broadwood piano in which Michael and Pitman transfer the body to the unsuspecting Gideon's apartment is, perhaps, the most absurd of the "wrong boxes" in which the corpse is deposited. Indeed, the very wrongness of this box draws attention to the fact that the narrative produces no "right box" with which finally to govern and snuff out the errant energies of the corpse.

There is "no sort of limit to the game" in which the wandering body participates, no termination of the discursive transformations it might undergo. With no clear limit to the number of "wrong boxes" that might be invented, the narrative itself becomes a limitless "box," a space that cannot be measured, because it is without boundaries. Even when the corpse has outlived its function in the plot—when the body is eventually discovered not to be that of Joseph Finsbury and therefore loses its economic and narrative significance—it continues to dominate the discourse. Gideon's final "qualms of conscience" (*Wrong Box*, 152) concerning the unidentified dead body being carried away in a cart indicate the narrative's bypassing of the problematic question that it had posed earlier: "How does a gentleman dispose of a dead body, honestly come by?" (102). The situation is embarrassing, of course, because a gentleman ought not to be in the possession of a dead body in the first place: the code of bourgeois propriety is thoroughly violated by association with the corpse, and to desire (let alone to possess) such a corpse, as my discussion of the earlier scene argues, is to enter an unstable discourse of uncontrolled desire, sodomy, and secrecy. In a telling exchange between Gideon and Morris over the location of the corpse, a dangerous desire is at once foregrounded and disavowed by its very interrogation and repetition:

> "Where is the body? This is very strange," mused Gideon. "Do you want the body?"
>
> "Want it?" cried Morris. "My whole fortune depends upon it! I lost it. Where is it? Take me to it!"
>
> "O, you want it, do you? And the other man, Dickson—does he want it?" enquired Gideon. (142)

The vagueness of the "it" that is sought for by these men contributes to the destabilizing effects of the corpse on the structure of male relations in the novel. Though the corpse can never be decisively claimed or named—as it remains to the end an object in limbo, without a proper owner—this does not prevent it from becoming an object of disruptive desire in the narrative. The silence surrounding its decease is attributable to the scandalous associations that have accrued to the concept of possession and desiring the body, even—or especially—the desire to bury it: to "bury in the back garden" is to commit buggery, and the body must be kept in motion if only to defer the accomplishment of this unspeakable act indefinitely.

Consequently, the fate of the corpse—hence of the narrative—is left undecided, as its delivery to a new destination is never represented in the text or mastered by the plot. Concerning the ignominious fate of the corpse—"the man in the cart" (152)—these flagrantly fictional figures can, with an insouciance that betrays their relieved liberation from the corpse's scandalous presence, do "nothing but sympathize" (152) with its predicament. Though the body has not been buried, it has at least been (temporarily) banished. If, as D. A. Miller argues, the Dickensian character is "frequently coupled with boxes: bags, parcels, luggage," then the ending of *The Wrong Box* develops that coupling to a promiscuous extreme: the character has *become* a box, a parcel presumably to be packed off to the next unsuspecting host, perhaps to initiate another series of connected events, another plot.[38] The reviewers' protests against the "funereal fun" and "[c]hurchyard humours" of *The Wrong Box* register, among other things, a cultural uneasiness with a narrative in which the rhetorical and comic productivity of the corpse plays a central role.[39] Yet this disgust at the fictional corpse is also symptomatic of a deeper unease with the production of desire that cannot be contained by the familiar boxes of character and narrative closure, such as inheritance and marriage. Among the most disturbing features of

*The Wrong Box* is its power to suggest, without naming them, the presence of unspeakable desires that surface to disrupt the progress of the narrative toward ideological closure. Yet far from being the aberration that its critics claimed, *The Wrong Box* is in many ways definitive of the concerns and patterns of Stevenson's corpus. In the first place, the representation of the inert, recalcitrant body that is revived and energized by travel is a hallmark of the travel writings. In the second place, the reanimated corpse appears in many of Stevenson's works of fiction, including highly praised novels such as *Treasure Island, Kidnapped,* and *The Master of Ballantrae,* on which his literary reputation was chiefly based. This double function of the reanimated corpse—both driving narrative desire and disrupting its progress toward closure—emerges as a central element of Stevenson's narrative practice.

## Excavating the "Unburied"

From the time of his earliest successes as a writer, Stevenson displayed a keen interest in the reanimation of dead bodies. The story that most resembles *The Wrong Box*—in its macabre humor and its treatment of the corpse as a gruesome secret—is "The Suicide Club," first published in 1882 as part of the *New Arabian Nights.* The three sections of this story are loosely connected by the suicide club, an organization in London that offers a quick and easy death to men who are tired of life. In the "Story of the Physician and the Saratoga Trunk," Silas Q. Scuddamore, a young American in Paris, is unwittingly lured into a murder plot and returns from an assignation with a mysterious woman to find the corpse of a young man in his room. Like Pitman in *The Wrong Box,* Silas is persuaded by a stronger-willed, more worldly man, Dr. Noel, to conceal the unwanted corpse and accept the burden of desire it presents. The body becomes a homoerotic secret between the two men after Noel asks pointedly, "Do you think this piece of dead flesh on your pillow can alter in any degree the sympathy with which you have inspired me?"[40] Having noticed Silas's Saratoga trunk in the room, Noel suggests that "the object of such a box is to contain a human body" (42), and together they pack the corpse into the trunk: "Silas taking the heels and the Doctor supporting the shoulders—the body of the murdered man was carried from the bed, and, after some difficulty, doubled up and inserted whole into the empty box. With an effort on the part of both, the lid was forced down upon this unusual baggage" (42).

Silas's evident uneasiness at the unorthodox burial of the body suggests the guilt of the sinner and the fear of discovery: that the dead body is discovered in Silas's bed is significant, and the doctor's initial question, "[H]ow came this body in your room?" (40), seems to invite a confession of a sexual motive for its presence (the dead man had earlier been described as "a very handsome young fellow of small stature" [33]). Hence, the corpse becomes associated in the narrative with a stifled, unacknowledged sexuality, bringing into the open inclinations that Silas has not recognized. Silas becomes increasingly obsessed with the secret contents of his box, fearing that "a single false step . . . and the box might go over the bannisters and land its fatal contents, plainly discovered, on the pavement of the hall" (47). The same fear of discovery leads Silas to check the concealed corpse for signs of decay: "[A]s soon as he was alone the unfortunate New Englander nosed all the cracks and openings with the most passionate attention. But the weather was cool, and the trunk still managed to contain his shocking secret" (48). As in *The Wrong Box*—one reviewer of which was concerned that the "olfactory nerve" might be offended by the corpse—the container is metonymically substituted for the corpse it contains, the "cracks and openings" of the trunk substituting for the prohibited orifices of the body. In this early story, the corpse is incriminating not only because it implicates Silas in murder but also because it suggests the "unspeakable" vice of sodomy, elicited by what Silas terms "this object in my bed: not to be explained, not to be disposed of, not to be regarded without horror" (41). Silas's "shame and terror" (47) at the prospect of discovery reflect the fear of men whose sexual secrets had to be locked away.

The figure of the reanimated corpse makes several appearances in *Treasure Island*—the work that began Stevenson's career as a novelist, published in 1883, and inaugurated the practice of commodifying his travel experiences within a narrative designed to produce profit. Significantly, at this turning point in Stevenson's corpus of work, several of the more memorable scenes involve pirates who are presumed dead but come back to life. A crux in the narrative occurs when Jim Hawkins, having set the *Hispaniola* adrift, finds the apparently dead bodies of Israel Hands and the "red cap" O'Brien: "I observed, around both of them, splashes of dark blood upon the planks, and began to feel sure that they had killed each other in their drunken wrath." Hands's death proves to be illusory, as Jim writes that "in a calm moment, when the ship was still, Israel Hands turned partly round, and, with a low moan, writhed himself back to the position in which I had seen him first."[41] The horror of the ensuing scene, in which the reanimated Hands makes a villainous attempt on Jim's life before plunging to his own death, has as a prelude Hands's interrogation of Jim on the question of reanimation: "There was this here O'Brien, now—he's dead, ain't he? Well, now, I'm no scholar, and you're a lad as can read and figure; and, to put it straight, do you take it as a dead man is dead for good, or do he come alive again?" (152). There could hardly be anything less "straight" than this recurring figure of the corpse, the potential of the dead body to introduce the specter of pederasty. On being informed that the body may die but the spirit lives on, Hands succinctly replies, "[T]hat's unfort'nate—appears as if killing parties was a waste of time" (152). The life-and-death struggle between Hands and Jim unfolds in the grim company of O'Brien's corpse, which at one point is described as reanimated, "the dead red-cap with his arms still spread out, tumbling stiffly after us. . . . Blow and all, I was the first afoot again; for Hands had got involved with the dead body" (157). Threatening Hands with a pistol, Jim warns him, "Dead men don't bite, you know" (158); after Hands's thrown knife narrowly misses him, Jim shoots Hands dead. Yet even after he hits the water, Hands threatens to return to life: "He rose once to the surface in a lather of foam and blood, and then sank again for good. . . . Sometimes, by the quivering of the water, he appeared to move a little as if he were trying to rise. But he was dead enough, for all that, being both shot and drowned, and was food for fish in the very place where he had designed my slaughter" (159). Like Hands, Stevenson's text and its juvenile narrator have become "involved with the dead body," an intimacy that has subversive effects in a work nominally designed for an audience of boys.

Stevenson's most famous historical adventure narrative, *Kidnapped,* features a narrator and hero, David Balfour, who is reanimated by making two dramatic returns from presumed death. On first seeking the help of his uncle Ebenezer after his father's death, David is treacherously sent up a tower by his uncle to retrieve "the chest that's at the top."[42] While climbing the staircase, David turns a corner in the dark; his hand, "feeling forward as usual, . . . slipped upon an edge and found nothing but emptiness beyond it. The stair had been carried no higher: to set a stranger mounting it in the dark was to send him straight to his death" (39). Upon David's return to his uncle's house, Ebenezer "flung up his arms, and tumbled to the floor like a dead man" (40). He returns to consciousness apparently believing that David has returned from the dead: "'Are ye alive?' he sobbed. 'O, man, are ye alive?'" (41). Though David physically survives this episode, it effectively leads to the elimination of his identity as, following his kidnapping, David frequently has difficulty in proving who he is. On returning to Edinburgh at the end of the narrative, for example, he realizes that "I had no grounds to stand upon; and no clear proof of my rights, nor so much as of my own identity" (247). David has in fact returned from presumed death a second time: following his disappearance, as the lawyer explains, Captain Hoseason appeared "with the story of your drowning; whereupon all fell through" (251).

With his body restored to safety and again clothed in civilized fashion, the hero's reanimation is complete, as he finds "the beggarman a thing of the past, and David Balfour come to life again" (255). The restoration of his identity—his "coming back to life"—is the necessary precursor of the restoration of his property, which occurs after a final encounter with his conniving uncle. However, David's rebirth is again accompanied by the sudden loss of animation of his uncle, paralyzed by the return of the dead, "who stared upon us like a man turned to stone" (269). Finally, David's new life as a man of means is also compromised by a loss, as he remarks that "this good change in my case unmanned me more than any of the former evil ones" (272). In particular, the parting from Alan Breck—who acted as David's unofficial, surrogate father and tutored him in the skills of manhood and survival—produces a mourning for the lost self he had cultivated in physical intimacy with Alan, experienced as a feeling of remorse. Even as David comes back to life and gains his fortune, his return to Edinburgh establishes him, like Stevenson, as a guilty, fatherless son.

The narrative force of reanimation again emerges in a context of familial conflict in *The Master of Ballantrae* (1889), a work that, like *Kidnapped,* utilizes the Jacobite rebellion of 1745 as a historical setting. Whereas the corpse is an object of desire and competition between relatives in *The Wrong Box* and David's "death" is the result of fraternal hatred in *Kidnapped, The Master* features an animated corpse that returns to exacerbate an existing sibling rivalry. Though the laudatory critical reception enjoyed by *The Master* could hardly have contrasted more with the cries of derision and outrage that greeted *The Wrong Box* earlier the same year, the historical romance was also criticized for the confusion of narrative modes that resulted from the improper reanimation of a corpse. Indeed, *The Master* blends together narrative techniques from several of Stevenson's earlier works, including the pirate story (*Treasure Island*), the historical romance (*Kidnapped*), and the tale of reanimation (*The Wrong Box*).[43] This merging of narrative forms reflects Stevenson's penchant for textual experimentation, as well as his unsettled life during this period, with frequent journeying between the Adirondacks, California, and the South Seas. Writing Henry James of his concern that the later chapters "are not so soundly designed . . . they are fantastic, they shame, perhaps degrade, the beginning," Stevenson exposes the influence of location on the bizarre conclusion to the narrative in stating that "the devil and Saranac suggested this *dénouement.*"[44] But the hybridity of the novel also suggests Stevenson's resistance to being boxed in by narrative categories and generic conventions. Even as he struggled to construct a coffin for *The Master,* for example, Stevenson recognized that his hero could not be contained.

The venerable Mrs. Oliphant, who had dismissed Stevenson's collaboration with Osbourne on *The Wrong Box* as an "unworthy exhibition," wrote of *The Master* that the critic is "proportionately grateful and joyful now to find him [Stevenson] in his right mind, in a piece of work which would do credit to any name."[45] The implication that Stevenson had been "out of his mind"—that is, alienated from himself (in a manner at least implicitly comparable to the self-division of Henry Jekyll)—while writing *The Wrong Box* but was later restored to his "right mind" is attributable less to Oliphant's admiration of the aesthetic merits of the novel than to her relief that the proper role of the author as the unique creator of his work has been reestablished and the true (literary and economic) value of his commodity-text reaffirmed. The confusions and disturbances over identity, desire, and authorship generated by *The Wrong Box* and its errant corpse were, it seemed, reassuringly laid to rest by the appearance of *The Master.*

Yet even in the apparently positive verdict that "in *The Master of Ballantrae* [Stevenson] has produced something very like a classic," one may detect a lingering reservation about the literary value of Stevenson's art: a work that is very like a classic is still not quite a classic. The same critic singled out the very passages that had given Stevenson the most trouble as he completed the novel—the burial, resurrection, and ultimate death of the Master—for rebuke as "an inadmissible plunge into the supernatural."[46] Indeed, these were the chapters in which Stevenson abruptly shifted the location of the novel to the Adirondacks, where he and his family had spent the winter of 1887–88. Both in its concluding drama in the ice and in other key episodes, the novel brings into sharp focus the intensely homoerotic force of the proximity of bodies—of corpses—in its narrative of prolonged and violent fraternal conflict. The final disinterment of his corpse is the third of the Master's reanimations. The first occurs when James Durie returns to Durisdeer after being presumed killed fighting for the rebels in the Jacobite uprising of 1745. The second follows his apparent death in the duel between the brothers, a scene described by one critic as "one of the most powerful and touching in the annals of romance."[47] The duel takes place after Henry, jealous of his brother James's relationship with Alison, "struck the Master in the mouth," at which point Mackellar comments, "I had never seen the man so beautiful."[48] The ambiguity here—which man is he referring to?—registers the arousing and disorienting power of masculine beauty on a male spectator and continues with Mackellar's scattered account of the duel: "I cannot say I followed it, my untrained eye was never quick enough to seize details, but it appears he [James] caught his brother's blade with his left hand, a practice not permitted. Certainly Mr Henry only saved himself by leaping on one side; as certainly the Master, lungeing in the air, stumbled on his knee, and before he could move, the sword was through his body" (96).

Mackellar's uncertainty over exactly what happens suggests that he may be mistaken in his judgment that the Master has received a fatal wound—"the heart was quite still, it gave not a flutter" (96)—and thus prepares the reader for the return of the Master from the dead. At the same time, the reference to "a practice not permitted" evokes the prohibition of desire. Mackellar raises the possibility that the Master is possessed of some supernatural agency, as his disappearance from the scene of his death seems magical: "There was the blood-stain in the midst; and a little farther off Mr Henry's sword, the pommel of which was of silver, but of the body, not a trace" (104). Mackellar depends for the incident of his narrative on the Master's uncanny ability to return from the dead, yet these repeated resurrections threaten to disrupt the narrative's progress toward closure, by invoking the unstable dynamics of repetition and circularity.[49] Even as the narrative seeks to contain and terminate the Master, it also reveals its failure to proceed without the demonic hero's disruptive, vitalizing influence.[50] The vanishing corpse of the Master will reappear to cause further disruptions in both the Durisdeer family and the narrative to which he gives his name.

Exploring the violent ambivalence of this fraternal and filial conflict, Stevenson's narrative passes through a series of false conclusions marked by illusory terminations of the Master—his alleged death in the '45 rebellion, his apparent end in the duel—to reach its culmination in the "double funeral" (218–19), in which the brothers' corpses are reunited and laid to rest in a long-resisted intimacy. The desire to be rid of the Master and the disturbing energies he represents suggests a longing for purification, by dismissing the contaminated corpse and terminating the narrative. In relating his failure to destroy the Master, Henry Durie reenacts his violent encounter with his brother: "'He's not of this world' whispered my lord, 'neither him nor the black deil [devil] that serves him. I have struck my sword throughout his vitals,' he cried; 'I have felt the hilt dirl [ring] on his breastbone, and the hot blood spirt in my very face, time and again, time and again!' he repeated, with a gesture indescribable. 'But he was never dead for that,' said he and sighed aloud. 'Why should I think he was dead now? No, not till I see him rotting,' says he" (209).

In this passage, which strongly represents the duel as a gruesome enactment of sexual penetration and ejaculation, issuing in a reanimated corpse, we again confront the limits of Mackellar's narrative powers: Henry's gesture can only be represented as "indescribable." Henry's desire to bury his brother is apparent as he misremembers the outcome of the duel, claiming that Mackellar had "buried him with his own hands" (209–10). This mistake reveals a frustrated wish that he had, in fact, achieved this definitive separation from his brother's demonic body and, thus, the termination of the story it dominates. But the wish to bury the Master—which recalls the urge to "shovel out the sod" in *The Wrong Box*—is at the same time a return in displaced form of the desire to bury his weapon in the Master's body, to penetrate him. This wish is first realized in Mackellar's description "the sword was through his body" and is then obsessively repeated in Henry's discourse: "I have struck my sword throughout his vitals . . . time and again." As in *The Wrong Box,* the desire for burial takes on a prohibited, displaced association with the "indescribable" act—"a practice not permitted"—of sodomy.

The Master's end, moreover, brings to a climax the productive hybridity of literary genres and foregrounds the feature of the narrative perceived as inadmissible—the improper animation of a dead body. This transgression, however, is precisely what links *The Master* to the narrative practices that had offended critics of *The Wrong Box.*[51] The key episode—in which the Master, James Durie, after being buried alive in the Adirondacks by his Indian servant, Secundra Dass, is brought back to life—is recounted by the Durie family's retainer and the story's chief narrator, Mackellar:

> I thought I could myself perceive a change upon that icy countenance of the unburied. The next moment I beheld his eyelids flutter; the next they rose entirely, and the week-old corpse looked me for a moment in the face. So much display of life I can myself swear to. I have heard from others that he visibly strove to speak, that his teeth showed in his beard, and that his brow was contorted as with an agony of pain and effort. And this may have been; I know not, I was otherwise engaged. For at that first disclosure of the dead man's eyes my Lord Durisdeer fell to the ground, and when I raised him up he was a corpse. (218)

Paradoxically, the exhumation scene's most powerful effect is on Henry Durie, who dies of the shock of seeing his "dead" brother return to life. This is perhaps the most dramatic instance in Stevenson's fiction of the contaminating effect of the corpse on a living body. The younger brother falls, as it were, into the grave created for the elder—as he has previously stepped into his brother's position as Lord Durisdeer and intended husband of Alison—and they are subsequently buried side by side. Hence, one might say that the Master's reanimation, which seems to defer the end, actually produces an excess of closure—both brothers die at once, the noble life is erased along with the demonic one, and thus the end of *The Master* represents the death of the novel's official values, as embodied by Henry. Yet Mackellar's conclusion discloses a perhaps unconscious preference for the Master over his less animated brother: there is a note of regret in the servant's account of "the earth heaped for ever on his once so active limbs" (213). Moreover, the epitaph "with a copy of which I may fitly bring my narrative to a close" (218) contains an encomium of the "Master of the arts and graces" that dims the light of his brother's "[l]ife of unmerited distress." Hence, this double grave and its epitaph uncover the location of the novel's official values as being where, perhaps, they have always been buried: in Mackellar's unreliable and inconsistent plot.

The fantasy of "burying the Master" cannot be contained by the narrative but spills over into Stevenson's correspondence, in which he described his relief at finishing the work that he had feared would never reach its terminus: "I have at length finished *The Master;* it has been a sore cross to me; but now he is buried, his body's under hatches,—his soul, if there is any hell to go to, gone to Hell."[52] Dependent on the highly narratable potency of the Master's subversive speech, inventive plotting, and erotically charged body, Stevenson's narrative must nonetheless strive ineluctably toward the conclusive event of the Master's burial. Yet what the narrative ultimately, perhaps perversely, renounces is precisely this satisfying equation of burial with (narrative) closure. By inserting the highly gothic scene of exhumation, following which the Master returns to life, the narrative once more defers its closural strategy and reveals instead its investment in a circuit of repetition, powered by an inadmissible erotic fascination with the dead body. Hence, the grimly prophetic paradox uttered by Secundra—"He bury, he not dead" (216)—indicates the disruption of the narrative's desire for "burial" as the final resting-place, both of the Master's body and of the text it names.

## Stevenson's Ebb

In the year following the publication of *The Wrong Box* and *The Master,* Stevenson moved permanently to the island of Samoa in the South Seas, becoming deeply involved in Samoan politics and scathingly critical of the interference of colonial powers, including Britain and the United States, in the affairs of the Polynesian South Pacific. Stevenson's late fictions of the South Sea islands, especially "The Beach of Falesá" and *The Ebb-Tide,* reflect his initial optimism and ultimate disillusionment concerning the political stability and social progress of his chosen home.[53] The final work he published during his lifetime, *The Ebb-Tide,* transports the trope of reanimation to the South Seas to develop a critique of colonial power, amoral materialism, and religious fanaticism. Eschewing the humorous and macabre treatment of the corpse in *The Wrong Box* and "The Suicide Club," *The Ebb-Tide* is closer to *The Master* in its view of reanimation as a sinister, perhaps inhuman power of evil, adding a new dimension in the character of the English colonialist, Attwater, a religious fanatic who justifies his plundering of the Pacific island's wealth by appealing to God: "I was a man of the world before I was a Christian; I'm a man of the world still, and I made my mission pay."[54] Attwater is not a missionary in any conventional sense: indeed, he criticizes missionaries for being "too parsonish, too much of the old wife" (203) and describes his religion as "a savage thing" (204).

Through Attwater's discourse, the narrative links the reanimation of the dead to the resurrection of Christ in what becomes, from one perspective, a religious parable of redemption. The degenerate trio of beachcomber-adventurers—Herrick, Captain Davis, and Huish—first appear as human refuse stranded on the beach in Tahiti before being reanimated by the chance of a new "mission" when Davis is offered the captaincy of a ship, *The Farallone.* Despite the opening of a new prospect, however, this "forbidden ship" turns out to be a floating coffin, the previous captain and mate of which have died of smallpox: the imagined presence of a "disfigured corpse" (153) haunts the men as they pursue their illicit journey, and Herrick in particular is tormented by "the horror of that grave that we've escaped from" (160). The purpose of this doomed voyage, to steal the cargo of champagne and sell the ship, is abandoned when the cargo is discovered to be fraudulent, consisting mainly of water in champagne bottles. Arriving at Attwater's island in search of a new source of wealth, the men soon penetrate the secret beneath the facade of peace and civilization, the island proving to be not an escape from but an intensification of the link between colonialism and deadly disease. The ominous "silence of death" (188) and "sense of desertion" (190) on the island are soon explained by Attwater's announcement that the island has been infested with smallpox and "that is why the house is empty and the graveyard full" (194). In answer to Herrick's immediate question as to how they disposed of all the bodies, Attwater refers to the natives' corpses as "empty bottles" (194), which inevitably links them with the fraudulent cargo of champagne, epitomizing the European view of the native islander as a commodity to be exploited and then discarded when its "content"—its labor—is used up. Additionally, the reference returns us to the idea of a box or container as the metonymic figure for the body, whose disposal is a matter of convenience, as it removes the traces of an unwanted materiality.

Significantly, given Herrick's interest in death and burial, the crucial encounter between him and Attwater takes place in "the cemetery of the island," where "nothing but the number of the mounds, and their disquieting shape, indicated the presence of the dead" (204). Attwater, whom Ann Colley characterizes as "a hybrid of the worst elements delineating a destructive colonial presence," reanimates the spirits of the dead islanders, calling into being their living characters: "'Here was one I liked though,' and he set his foot upon a mound. 'He was a fine savage fellow; he had a dark soul; yes, I liked this one'" (205).[55] As Vanessa Smith observes, by this strategy "the populace of his island, decimated by disease, are resurrected as the subjects of story."[56] Curiously, the cemetery is where the relationship between the two Englishmen attains a new intimacy, as Attwater tells Herrick, "You are attractive, very attractive" (205). This leads Herrick to an erotic fascination with his host and a desire to save Attwater from the "two wolves"; he experiences "an immense temptation to go up, to touch him on the arm and breathe a word in his ear: 'Beware, they are going to murder you'" (207).

Perhaps the most intriguing symbol of reanimation in *The Ebb-Tide* is the diving suit, which is transformed by Attwater into a metaphor for "God's grace" and by Herrick into a symbol of human "self-conceit" (202). The practical function of the diving suits is to assist in Attwater's accumulation of pearls (the original title of the story was "The Pearl Fisher"), but he describes the effects of the suits in a striking scene of reanimation: "It . . . was a queer sight when they were at it, and these marine monsters . . . kept appearing and reappearing in the midst of the lagoon" (202).[57] This reappearance of the divers suggests the uncanny reanimation of the corpses that Attwater has "buried" in the lagoon, perhaps returning to rebuke the colonialist for their exploited lives and ignominious resting place. The connection between the resurfacing divers and reanimation of the dead is strengthened when Attwater links the diving suit to the resurrected Christ, "He who died for you, He who upholds you, He whom you daily crucify afresh" (203). Offering Herrick a parable for the suits, Attwater says, "I saw these machines come up dripping and go down again, and come up dripping and go down again . . . and I thought we all wanted a dress to go down into the world in, and come up scatheless" (202). The body inside the "diving suit" of faith has become a resurrected corpse, an animated machine, with its human quality drained by the mechanical analogy: the body as machine appears again when Attwater tries to convert Herrick, who is shocked "to find the whole machine thus glow with the reverberation of religious zeal" (203).

Stevenson's readers were no less appalled to find the "machine" of his anticolonial narrative fueled by religious zeal, especially embodied in such a debased incarnation. The novel was viewed by critics—and to some extent by Stevenson himself—as a kind of barely animated literary corpse, "bringing together parts that failed to cohere, producing waste material, rather than a useful new object."[58] As one critic wrote in the *Speaker*, "Of grace, virtue, beauty, we get no glimpse. All we have in exchange is a picture of the fag-ends of certain useless and degraded lives."[59] Signaling the final chapter of the collaboration between Stevenson and his stepson, *The Ebb-Tide* was taken by its critics as the symptom of exhaustion of the novel at the fin de siècle. Moreover, it was read as Stevenson's literary ebb and creative demise, serving in fact as the "fag-end" of his career. As one critic expressed it, "This is not the Stevenson we love."[60] When the time came to evaluate Stevenson's career after his death in 1894, the South Sea tales were quietly buried by neglect, "as if this body of work simply did not exist."[61]

Stevenson's animated corpses both vitalize and disrupt the narratives in which they appear, at once driving the engine of the plot and introducing a disorderly dynamic of circularity and bodily intimacy. Obtruding its obscene presence in narrative—refusing to be contained or boxed in—the corpse blatantly violates the cultural conventions of taste and secrecy in Stevenson's corpus, according to which "the dead are shielded from view to protect them and us from our natural curiosity."[62] Further undermining the unity of character and plot, these uncontained and contaminating bodies circulate freely through their narratives, blurring the lines between gothic romance, adventure, domestic tragedy, and macabre humor. The animation of the corpse in *The Wrong Box* is developed within a discourse of morbid humor and homoerotic desire, thus elaborating the corpse's comic treatment in "The Suicide Club." However, reanimation takes on much darker significance in the adventure romances and South Sea tales, in which evil—in its most extreme case, demonic possession—is associated with the reanimation of an abject, colonized body. Attwater's fatalism and powers of reanimation link him to the Master, while the three degenerate beachcombers, traveling under assumed names, join the anonymous railway victim of *The Wrong Box* as animated corpses whose restless journeying betrays a submission to narrative contingency, moral futility, and abdication of agency. Provocatively burying an unstable body of desire—a "romance"—at the heart of Stevenson's corpus, the corpse's mobile, unpredictable progress might finally be characterized as a narrative journey that ends up where it began.

# TWO

## The Beast in the Mountains

### Misusing the Ass in *Travels with a Donkey*

> I have heard it said, that drums are covered with asses' skin, what a picturesque irony is there in that! As if this long-suffering animal's hide had not been sufficiently belaboured during life . . . it must be stripped from his poor hinder quarters after death, stretched on a drum, and beaten night after night round the streets of every garrison town in Europe. . . . Generally a man is never more uselessly employed than when he is at this trick of bastinadoing asses' hide. We know what effect it has in life, and how your dull ass will not mend his pace with beating.
>
> —Stevenson, *An Inland Voyage* [1]

ONE OF THE most intriguing narrative features of Stevenson's *Travels with a Donkey in the Cevennes*—his second travel book—is that it devotes as much attention to the donkey, Modestine, as it does to the places in which Stevenson travels. As Clare Harman remarks, "In the published version of his journey through the Cevennes, it was Stevenson's relations with Modestine that became the subject, rather than the walking tour itself."[2] What might have been, in the hands of another writer, merely a conventional book of travels relating a journey through an attractive and historically significant region of France is animated by the intrusion of a memorable and sympathetic "character"—Stevenson's purchased she-ass, Modestine. Far from being treated impersonally as a convenient mode of transport—a means to an end, necessary to carry his belongings through the mountainous terrain that Stevenson is traversing—Modestine (whom Stevenson named) is given a share of the title and a personality that allows her to play a significant role in the narrative. The conjunction in the book's title is significant—*Travels* with *a Donkey*—as it suggests that the relationship between Stevenson and Modestine is that of traveling companions or partners, rather than owner and beast of burden.

Of course, Stevenson's emphasis on the donkey might appear to be merely a device or a ruse designed precisely to prevent the work from being treated as an ordinary book of travels and to avoid repeating the disappointing reception of his previous effort in the genre, *An Inland Voyage.*[3] Yet although Modestine's presence does distinguish the work from other travel writing, reducing her role to the status of a gimmick would be overly simplistic. Rather, the presence of Modestine serves as a constant reminder of the material body and the resistance it offers to travel and reaching the intended destinations. As a counterweight to Stevenson's enthusiasm for "travel for travel's sake" (163), the donkey—characterized as "the reluctant Modestine" (203)—represents what one might call the spirit of antitravel: inertia, resistance, and rebellion. She also presents a challenge to Stevenson's will, preferring to follow her own instinctive course rather than to obey his directions. As such, Modestine is the physical body, driven by instinct rather than conscious control, at once an obstacle to Stevenson's authority and a reminder of his errant, disobedient desire.[4]

Strikingly, Stevenson suggests in his dedication to the book that his journey through the French mountains is illustrative or exemplary of a general condition: "But we are all travelers in which John Bunyan calls the wilderness of this world—all, too, travelers with a donkey; and the best that we find in our travels is an honest friend" (122). In this dedication to Sidney Colvin—his friend and literary mentor—Stevenson idealistically defines friendship as the "end" of travel, the purpose of life's journey: "He is a fortunate voyager who finds many [honest friends]. We travel, indeed, to find them. They are the end and the reward of life" (122). While this encomium to friendship might be read as a conventional gesture for a dedication, we should not dismiss its significance for Stevenson's attitude toward travel, for the preface makes an implicit distinction between "travelers" and "travelers with a donkey." Even as he ascribes universality to the condition of traveling, Stevenson implies the difference that the donkey makes, in adding "all, *too,* travelers with a donkey." If, as he suggests, one's travels can be taken as a metaphor for life's journey, then what is the significance or role of this addition of the donkey to the proceedings?[5]

As the foregoing epigraph from *An Inland Voyage* makes clear, Stevenson viewed the ass as an image of pitiable suffering, a victim whose oppression and abuse makes possible the journeys of others. The traveler, in other words, needs a donkey less for its companionship than for its hard labor. Carrying the traveler's baggage, the donkey, by minimizing the physical hardship of the traveler, frees him or her to enjoy the journey's aesthetic and topographical pleasures. This pragmatic view of the donkey suggests a division between the donkey as suffering body and the traveler as enlightened intellect and sensory apparatus. As Stevenson narrates the journey in *Travels,* however, a different picture emerges, in which traveling with a donkey is itself an additional responsibility or burden for the traveler. Initially, of course, Stevenson purchases the donkey to reduce his burden: "It will readily be conceived that I could not carry this huge package on my own, merely human shoulders. It remained to choose a beast of burden" (135). Even in this paragraph, however, Stevenson indicates that the selection of such a beast is fraught with risk. Stevenson genders such beasts of burden, comparing the ass with a "horse . . . a fine lady among animals" but considers that with a horse "you are chained to your brute as to a fellow galley-slave" (135). The language reveals that the traveler and the beast are both "galley-slaves," neither of whom is able to attain or enjoy the freedom promised by travel. A less "exacting" animal is preferable, hence Stevenson chooses "something cheap and small and hardy, and of a stolid and peaceful temper . . . a donkey." His purchase of the donkey, "for the consideration of sixty-five francs and a glass of brandy" (135), establishes Modestine as a commodity to be bought and sold—a representation that persists until the end of the journey and the narrative. Stevenson shows that he has been warned about the refractory inclination of the ass: "To prove her good temper, one child after another was set upon her back to ride, and one after another went head over heels into the air; until a want of confidence began to reign in youthful bosoms, and the experiment was discontinued from a dearth of subjects" (135). Modestine's hostility toward children inscribes her as part of Stevenson's plan to escape from domestic confinement and anticipates her resemblance to another beast, the far more dangerous "Beast of Gevaudan" (150). The purchase, rather than solving Stevenson's travel problems, inaugurates a new series of crises, in which his pack repeatedly collapses: in another Bunyan allusion, Stevenson writes that "like Christian, it was from my pack I suffered" (137).

Stevenson's travels through the Cevennes, this opening to the narrative reveals, are partly a rehearsal for the next journey to another country: an epic voyage that will have as its destination a specific romantic object, Fanny Osbourne (though this object would be suppressed in the published narrative, *The Amateur Emigrant*). In practicing solitude and confronting a self-imposed adversity, Stevenson is preparing himself for the hardships and loneliness of his subsequent journey to America.[6] Yet there are doubts about the viability of his present journey, which he calls "my projected excursion southward through the Cevennes," let alone his forthcoming transatlantic odyssey. Stevenson writes, "A traveller of my sort was a thing hitherto unheard-of in that district. I was looked upon with contempt, like a man who should project a journey to the moon" (133). The public's contempt for a traveler would naturally be a concern for Stevenson as a travel writer, who might fear that his audience would find his book unappealing. In his dedication, Stevenson writes optimistically, "Every book is, in an intimate sense, *a circular letter* to the friends of him who writes it. . . . The public is but a generous patron who defrays the postage" (122; emphasis added). Yet Stevenson's expectation that the public will defray the postage obviously depends on the popular appeal of his work, its ability to reach beyond the "private" circle of his friends. Like the preface to *An Inland Voyage,* with its concern "that I might not only be the first to read these pages, but the last as well" (*Travels,* 3), the dedication to *Travels* reveals anxiety about his readership. If the letter is "circular," the journey must not be so, or the public may refuse to fulfill its part of the bargain and deny payment of the postage.

Given this anxiety about audience, the prominence given to the donkey is legible as the key to the text's general appeal. If, as Stevenson writes, "[w]e are all . . . travelers with a donkey" (122), then the animal is sure to secure his readers' interest. Yet Modestine is portrayed as a burden rather than a support for the traveler. Before the journey proper even begins, in fact, Modestine is a source of frustration and disappointment to her new owner. As he attempts to load the donkey, "ten minutes after, my hopes were in the dust" (137). In a second attempt, Stevenson "once more loaded her with my effects," which "were all corded together in a very elaborate system of knots"—an arrangement in which "even a very careless traveller should have seen disaster brewing" (137). The account is unusual for its humorous attention to the very aspects of travel that most Victorian travel narratives repress: the material preparations and problems that must be faced before the trip can be launched and which return to impede its progress. At the end of these preparations, Stevenson's body is suffering: "my shoulder was cut, so that it hurt sharply; my arm ached like toothache" (145). Subsequently, one of the functions of Modestine will be to occupy the role of the suffering body, as the symptoms of physical pain are displaced onto the donkey.[7] This focus on the material problems of travel—in this case, the recalcitrant body of the donkey and the inexperience of the driver—is one of Stevenson's most distinctive features as a travel writer. The narrator gains the advantage of amusement but risks self-ridicule, portraying himself as an incompetent traveler (a status suggested in the chapter title "The Green Donkey-Driver").[8] In the teeth of such failure, Stevenson "had to invent a new and better system" (143)—a revision of his method that also applies to the transition from *An Inland Voyage* to *Travels with a Donkey,* in which Stevenson seeks a better "system" for narrating his random journey in a way that will gain popular appeal.

Stevenson's search for literary and commercial success with *Travels* suggests a paradox regarding his use of the donkey. For on the practical level of the journey, the donkey—far from being of assistance to Stevenson the traveler, or releasing him from care—becomes an additional burden. Modestine's stubbornness and resistance to forward motion—"Modestine would be neither softened nor intimidated. She held doggedly to her pace" (140–41)—is punished by Stevenson's repeated acts of violence, as "nothing but a blow would move her" (141). Ostensibly, these acts are designed to propel Modestine toward their destination, yet they also suggest a sadistic pleasure in her suffering that risks alienating the reader. Stevenson criticizes the donkey's previous owner, who "had a name in the village for brutally misusing the ass" (136) and states his intention to be more compassionate: "God forbid, thought I, that I should brutalise this innocent creature" (138). Yet the narrative contains a catalog of Stevenson's violent acts against Modestine, as he uses a switch to beat her: "I promise you, the stick was not idle; I think every decent step that Modestine took must have cost me at least two emphatic blows" (143).[10] Far from being a good and faithful servant, Modestine has a will of her own that places her in constant conflict with her driver. Failing in her function as a beast of burden, she becomes part of "this infamous burden" (142) that Stevenson carries on his journey.

At the level of literary signification, Modestine is an essential figure having two key representational functions. First, she embodies the burden of physical being and the oppressions of servitude from which Stevenson seeks liberation. Second, she symbolizes the femininity that Stevenson elsewhere excludes or marginalizes in his writing. Through her given name ("Modestine, as I instantly baptized her" [135]), the references to her sexuality, and most of all her human qualities, the femininity of Modestine is constantly in the foreground. Her femininity proves problematic to Stevenson, as he pursues travel as a form of solitude and seclusion, including escape from female influence. Stevenson's violence toward the donkey is frequently tempered by a sense of her humanity and comes into conflict with his proclaimed code of chivalry toward a lady. He writes that Modestine had a "resemblance to a lady of my acquaintance who formerly loaded me with kindness, and this actually increased my horror of my cruelty" (141). Critics have found biographical relevance in this passage—and in Stevenson's portrayal of Modestine more generally—citing the context of Stevenson's nascent romance with Fanny Vandegrift Osbourne, whom Stevenson had met in France in 1877. There is some evidence for this in Stevenson's correspondence, as he wrote of the book to his cousin Bob Stevenson that "lots of it is mere protestations to F., most of which I think you will understand."[10] Richard Holmes, who wrote his own travelogue about following Stevenson's footsteps in the Cevennes, found himself "puzzling over these words. Were they just the famous Stevensonian whimsy? Or was he thinking of some particular woman?"[11] Holmes quickly reaches the conclusion that this particular woman was Fanny Osbourne, to whom he devotes a chapter of his account of Stevenson's journey. Holmes points out that the Cevennes journey began in the same month that Fanny returned to California, and one can detect numerous traces of her influence in Stevenson's ambivalence toward his solitary state.

Yet one should hesitate before ascribing this reference automatically to his recent lover and future wife. In the first place, the phrase "*formerly* loaded me with kindness" suggests someone whose affection for Stevenson was in the past rather than the present or (hoped-for) future. Moreover, the passage is immediately followed by one in which Stevenson encounters a rival for Modestine's affections, "another donkey" that "chanced to be a gentleman" (*Travels,* 141). Stevenson's anger at being challenged by this intruder—whom he eventually beats away—might on first glance suggest animosity toward his cousin Bob Stevenson, whom Fanny Osbourne at first preferred to him. Yet it was Bob who eventually persuaded Fanny to accept the attentions of Louis, as Fanny, "aided by Bob's tactful maneuverings, was able to transfer her interest to Stennis frere with no visible dints to her pride." This was in 1876, and Claire Harman believes that "Bob and Louis were obviously in cahoots" in securing Fanny's affections for the latter. In this light, Bob would seem less a rival than an advocate for Stevenson's romance.[12]

More plausibly, the "triangle" of Stevenson and the two donkeys represents his relationship with Sidney Colvin and another Fanny—Frances Sitwell—which had reached a frustrating impasse. Falling in love with Frances Sitwell, a woman several years his elder whom he had met in Suffolk in the summer of 1873, Stevenson was dismayed to learn that he had a rival suitor in Sidney Colvin. Colvin became a close friend and mentor and helped to advance Stevenson's career. Yet he nonetheless appeared on the scene at Cockfield as "a serious rival for Mrs Sitwell's attentions," and some of this resentment lingers in *Travels.*[13] Colvin and Sitwell became a couple, eventually marrying. Modestine is therefore being punished for the perceived sexual betrayal of the "lady" she resembles.

Ironically, given Stevenson's adopted persona as an ardent lover separated from his mate, he becomes a patriarchal repressor of Modestine's sexuality, which introduces another distraction to his intended travel: "He and Modestine met nickering for joy, and I had to separate the pair and beat down their young romance with a renewed and feverish bastinado" (*Travels,* 141). Stevenson seems to enjoy disrupting this "young romance," unconsciously anticipating his father Thomas Stevenson's role in objecting to the union with Fanny. Indeed, the scene reinforces the idea that Modestine's femininity is part of the burden she places on Stevenson and strengthens her function as a material obstacle to Stevenson's travel. As Holmes states, Stevenson "eventually discovered that Modestine was on heat for almost their entire journey. This disturbed him; for as I gradually came to suspect, problems of friendship, romance, and sexuality were much on his mind throughout this lonely autumn tour."[14] Yet the problems disturbing Stevenson's mind are associated in the narrative with the problems of Modestine's body—specifically, what M. M. Bakhtin would call the "lower bodily stratum"—as exemplified by the fact that during the trip

"Modestine was on heat and bleeding" and tended "to be mounted by any stray male."[15] Stevenson writes of the thwarted romance that "the incident saddened me, as did everything that spoke of my donkey's sex" (*Travels,* 141). Modestine's sex is painful to Stevenson not only because it implicitly reprimands him for his ungallant behavior toward her but also because it highlights his own loneliness and isolation. Stevenson longs for a specific female companion, and Modestine is a poor substitute for the woman he desires. As is revealed in the chapter entitled "A Night among the Pines," Stevenson's role as a romantic, solitary traveler is under constant pressure from his need for sexual and emotional companionship: "And yet even while I was exulting in my solitude I became aware of a strange lack. I wished a companion to lie near me in the starlight, silent and not moving, but ever within touch. For there is a fellowship more quiet even than solitude, and which, rightly understood, is solitude made perfect. And to live out of doors with the woman a man loves is of all lives the most complete and free" (188). Stevenson is in fact living outdoors with a female, but she is not the woman he loves. The sentiment is prophetic, however, of Stevenson's "outdoor" future with Fanny, specifically, their honeymoon in California, which Stevenson would record in *The Silverado Squatters* (1883). Indeed, the passage is one of the most confessional in *Travels,* in that Stevenson admits to the suffering that his separation from Fanny is causing him and identifies Modestine as an inadequate substitute. His physical proximity to Modestine mimics his desired intimacy with Fanny, no more so than when Stevenson is separated from his donkey at night, about which he comments that "the first thing was to return to Modestine. I am pretty sure I was twenty minutes groping for my lady in the dark; and if it had not been for the unkindly services of the bog, into which I once more stumbled, I might have still been groping for her at the dawn" (157). The mock-chivalrous reference to "my lady" is undercut by the sexual connotations of "groping," suggesting Stevenson's frustrated physical desire.

Travel, in this early text, is an activity linked with solitude and exclusion from erotic intimacy, as is highlighted in a scene at the "*auberge* of Bouchet St Nicholas" (146), in which Stevenson is required to share a room with "a young man and his wife and child" (147). His embarrassment at finding them "in the act of mounting" suggests that he has discovered the couple in flagrante delicto: an unwitting act of voyeurism that Stevenson's dubious assertion "I kept my eyes to myself" (147) does little to mitigate. Indeed, the narrative reveals the detail of his observation, noting that the woman "had beautiful arms, and seemed no whit abashed by my appearance" (147); the woman's exhibitionism thus complements his voyeuristic impulse. He previously commented on the "kind breeding" (146) that the traveler encounters at the inn, a phrase evocative of the reproductive impulses on display in his "sleeping-room" (147). Though he refers to this inn as "among the least pretentious I have ever visited" (146), it stands out by providing "something better" (147) than the routine accommodation, namely, a vicarious access to others' union. Stevenson's comment that "I little knew what he was offering" (147) implies gratitude for the unasked-for spectacle. Stevenson attributes his embarrassment at witnessing the sexual intimacy of this couple to his solitary and celibate status: "A pair keep each other in countenance; it is the single gentleman who has to blush" (147).[16] Yet Stevenson is part of a couple or pair, bound together with his donkey in the very title of the book. The word *mounting* also conveys his position atop Modestine, whom he dominates by the use of the goad given to him by the landlord. Stevenson exclaims, "Blessed be the man who invented goads!" (148), and he celebrates the instrument as a symbol of power over his donkey in declaring that "this plain wand, with an eighth of an inch of pin, was indeed a scepter when he put it in my hands" (148). While the term *wand* suggests the appurtenance of a magician and *scepter* evokes the sovereignty of the driver, the phallic force and significance of the object are what emerge in Stevenson's account of its use: "Thenceforward Modestine was my slave. A prick, and she passed the most inviting stable-door. A prick, and she broke forth into a gallant little trotlet that devoured the miles" (148–49). Stevenson's fragile chivalry—he had protested that "it goes against my conscience to lay my hand rudely on a female" (138)—is rapidly abandoned in his elation at possessing the power of the "prick," with which he torments Modestine into submission. This goad is a substitute for the hand that Stevenson forbids himself from using as a weapon. Indeed, far from being troubled by his dominance, he seems to enjoy torturing her: "[W]hat although now and then a drop of blood should appear on Modestine's mouse-coloured wedge-like rump? . . . The perverse little devil, since she would not be taken with kindness, must even go with pricking" (149). The blood—mimicking her menstrual bleeding—confirms her "low" status and "perverse" sexuality.

Stevenson has thus become a man known "for brutally misusing the ass" (136), to which critics of the book objected. The sodomitic implications of this violation are displayed by the emphasis on Modestine's "rump" or "stern-works" (139) as the focus of Stevenson's attentions, while his remark "I dropped . . . into the rear" (138) again invokes an unspeakable abuse of the donkey. Stevenson's "secret shame" (138) at his misuse of the "beast" is belied by the public nature of his utterance, his assurance that this sodomitic discourse can be nullified by humor, serving as "a piece of comedy" (139). This "comic incredulous air" (139) pervades the account of Modestine, yet it jars in juxtaposition with the violence of the treatment he metes out to her.

Stevenson's ongoing conflict with the donkey is not the only source of violence in the narrative. In the midst of his struggles with Modestine—on whose body, as I have argued, he takes out his own hostility toward the feminine—Stevenson introduces another character, "the ever-memorable BEAST, the Napoleon Bonaparte of wolves" (150), into the picture. As the capitals suggest, Stevenson attributes great importance to this wolf, the "Beast of Gevaudan," whose "favourite victims were women, young girls, and little children," such that "their bodies were often found drained of blood and sometimes partially devoured" (327n). The vampiric effects of this beast suggest the wolf as a precursor of Bram Stoker's Dracula—the most famous vampire in late-Victorian romance—who also preys on women and children. Under the threat of this beast, Stevenson—like the team of men in Stoker's novel—can claim "fragments of an older idea of masculine heroism" through his willingness to risk an encounter with the "monster."[17] Yet this beast, rather than being a recipient of Stevenson's violent impulses, enacts them on his behalf. For despite the horrific details of its attacks, Stevenson seems to admire its extraordinary powers of destruction: "What a career was his! He lived ten months at free quarters in Gevaudan and Vivarais: he ate women and children and 'shepherdesses celebrated for their beauty'" (150). Stevenson's use of the term *career* inevitably suggests parallels with his own nascent career as an author, while the trace of envy derives from the beast's freedom to act out its hostility toward women and children with impunity. I have referred to Dracula, but the beast also anticipates Mr. Hyde, whose savage violence is likewise directed at the most vulnerable citizens on the streets of London.

Travel, for Stevenson, is both an escape from his parental family and a deferral of commitment to a new family, composed of Fanny Osbourne and her children. Stevenson's resistance to being domestically tied to women and children and to being a child of his own parents is projected into the wolf's "career" of spectacular violence, emphasizing its public significance. Stevenson is simultaneously acting out hostility toward another beast; "goading Modestine down the steep descent" (10); like the "beast of Gevaudan," Stevenson shows no mercy—indeed takes a sadistic pleasure—in drawing blood from his female victim.[18]

I have argued that Modestine does not necessarily represent one woman in particular (as Holmes has argued) but suggests a more general incarnation of femininity by which Stevenson is deeply troubled. Certainly the charge of misogyny may be leveled at Stevenson in those passages in which he details the abuse of the donkey while also emphasizing her femininity. His ambivalence toward the feminine is revealed in a duality of desire in the narrative. On the one hand, Stevenson is in flight from the feminine, stung by Fanny's perceived rejection and abandonment of him with her return to California. On the other, however, he seeks to prolong his escape from the parental home and the stigmas of physical and financial dependency that attach to it. He is also cautious about committing himself to a woman who is already married (to Sam Osbourne) and brings the additional burden of children. Even as he travels away from his domestic "center" in Scotland, Stevenson is constantly reminded of the very things that he seeks to escape: the inns in which he stays are typically family homes, in which "in the kitchen cooking and eating go forward side by side, and the family sleep at night" (146). The solitary traveler finds himself welcomed as though part of a family: "As soon as you cross the doors you cease to be a stranger," and the hosts are "friendly and considerate" (146). The tension between these domestic scenes and Stevenson's preference for a "secret" camp away from the domestic space appears throughout the narrative (134). Indeed, Stevenson's professed rejection of "the feather bed of civilization" (163) is incongruous, given his residence at such cozy inns. Equally, however, his solitude is a persistent reminder of the "strange lack" (188) from which he suffers. The word "strange" both anticipates one of his most famous stories *(Strange Case of Dr. Jekyll and Mr. Hyde)* and calls to mind the goal of his journey, which he refers to as "my strange destination, the Trappist monastery of Our Lady of the Snows" (166). Stevenson's "lack" and his "destination" are both "strange" in that they indicate a willful division of self and suppression of desire. One of the connotations of *strange* is "estrange": to alienate or separate from. Like Jekyll and Hyde, Stevenson is both bound together with and estranged from the being closest to him, one who is "knit to him closer than a wife" and "lay caged in his flesh, where he heard it mutter and felt it struggle to be born."[19] In Jekyll's account, Hyde is both a "wife" and an unborn child. Moreover, one inevitably notices that "Hyde" is homophonous with "hide"—Jekyll's alter ego is a skin that he must wear and shed. Similarly, Modestine's hide allows Stevenson to hide his animosity toward Fanny, displacing it onto the suffering body of the donkey.

The destination of a monastery—this is the first reference in the narrative to a specific goal of the journey—might indicate that Stevenson seeks a religious confirmation of his solitary status and celibacy. His entrance to the monastery, an exclusively masculine space, would also complete his separation from women, reminding us that Stevenson is at this point estranged from Fanny, the woman he loves. Yet crucially the monastery is named after the Virgin Mary: an image of female purity, even sanctity, that sharply contrasts with both the physical longing for "the woman a man loves" and the heightened corporeality of Modestine. This opposition is rendered in narrative terms as a journey, as Stevenson approaches the monastery: "A spidery cross on every hill-top marked the neighbourhood of a religious house; and a quarter of a mile beyond . . . a white statue of the Virgin at the corner of a young plantation directed the traveler to Our Lady of the Snows. Here, then, I struck leftward, and pursued my way, driving my secular donkey before me" (*Travels,* 166). The designation "of the snows" enforces the radical purity and frigidity of the virgin, while the white statue also indicates a stainless ideal of femininity.[20] Hence, I would argue that Stevenson's movement is less a flight from or rejection of the feminine than a flight from one version of femininity (sexual, physical, secular) toward another (pure, virginal, spiritual): by entering the monastery, Stevenson joins a world in which the "secular donkey" can have no place.[21]

Stevenson's narrative continues to emphasize the female sex of the donkey, reminding us of the sexual dynamics of the journey. Yet I would argue that the donkey represents the problem of the body more generally, with specific reference to Stevenson's frail physiognomy and failing health. To read any Stevenson biography, or indeed his correspondence, is to witness at several removes an unremitting series of physical breakdowns and episodes of severe illness. In this particular case, on his journey through the Cevennes, Stevenson "was in a state of collapse and wanted only to be alone," writing to Baxter, "I am so ill and so tired that I can scarce finish these words."[22] Under the threat of his physical collapse, Stevenson's donkey comes to function as much more than a useful supplement to his travel equipment, despite his dismissive statement that "she was only an appurtenance of my mattress, or self-acting bedstead on four castors" (135). Modestine is, rather, a suffering animal that reiterates the narrator's physical frailty and dependence. Above and beyond the donkey's representation of the "other" (the feminine), therefore, the donkey also figures as Stevenson's suffering body and its resistance to the will or control of its owner. In this respect, Modestine's effect on Stevenson resembles Hyde's bringing a vitality and robustness to Jekyll that he otherwise lacks. Like Jekyll, Stevenson feels "younger, lighter, happier in body" and experiences "an unknown but not an innocent freedom of the soul" in his travels with the donkey. Yet also, like Jekyll "aware that I had lost in stature," Stevenson feels the diminishing effects of his dependence on Modestine.[23]

Stevenson frequently referred to his body as something apart from himself, objectifying it in light of its tendency toward mechanical failure. Perhaps the most famous of these self-objectifying references to his body occurs in a letter to Sidney Colvin in May 1892, in which he alludes to himself in the past as "the pallid brute that lived in Skerryvore like a weevil in a biscuit."[24] Yet an earlier reference is more germane to the text at hand: in November 1884, Stevenson writes to W. E. Henley complaining of "fever and chills, with really very considerable suffering" and describes his difficulty in writing: "I am not sure that my incapacity to work is wholly due to illness; I believe the morphine I have been taking for my bray, may have a hand in it. It moderates the bray; but I think sews up the donkey."[25] Stevenson's play on words here is in the jocular register that he used to correspond with Henley and other friends, yet his reference to himself—specifically, to his failing corpus—as "the donkey" illustrates the function that this animal plays in his earlier narrative. This usage sheds further light on Stevenson's dedication to Colvin, that "we are all . . .

travelers with a donkey" (*Travels,* 122). The donkey as appendage represents the body, the burden of physical activity and suffering that afflicts everyone who travels in "the wilderness of this world" (122). Stevenson's donkey, however, is not a robust animal: rather, she is a "diminutive she-ass" whose physical frailty mirrors (or mimics) Stevenson's. In confessing to Colvin that his narrative—like his journey—has "an uncouth beginning" (122), Stevenson draws attention to those early episodes in which the donkey plays the most conspicuous part. Yet in alluding to "the end and the reward of life" (122), the dedicatory text also suggests the part about which Stevenson is most embarrassed and self-conscious, the "ass" or what he alludes to in a later text as "the backward parts and 'abject rear.'"[26] Strikingly, Stevenson's account of his physical and economic vulnerability in his letter to Henley dwells upon this nether region: "I hope it [his illness] will not last long; for the bum-baily is panting at my rump, and when I turn a scared eye across my shoulder, I behold his talons quivering above my frock-coat tails."[27] Stevenson's archaic usage of *bum-baily* (that is, *bum-bailiff,* one employed in the arrests of the insolvent) draws attention to the threat to his rear end posed by this official, "so called as approaching from behind" (*Shorter OED*). Whereas it is Modestine's "rump" (*Travels,* 149) or "stern-works" (139) that are victimized in *Travels,* it is Stevenson who is threatened a posteriori, the "talons quivering" representing all too vividly the imminent brutalizing of his ass. Stevenson's letter suggests another instance of "a revenge upon the donkey's persecutors" (*Travels,* 43) as his severe cough, metaphorized as a "bray," afflicts him by making him donkeylike. In writing "I am now at the cough stage and torn simply to ribbons," Stevenson reiterated the analogy in a November 1884 letter to Baxter: "We are all vilely unwell. I put in the dark watches, imitating a donkey with some success but little pleasure." For Stevenson, the donkey serves as a shorthand for his afflicted body, otherwise represented in a compendium of terms, as "a miserable, snuffling, shivering, fever-stricken, night-mare ridden, knee-jottering, hoast-hoast-hoasting shadow and remains of man."[28] As an image for the "remains of man," the donkey serves less as an aid to travel than as a reminder of its futility. The journey that gives "little pleasure" to the traveler is characterized as a "misadventure" (161) in which the body suffers, while "the destination I had hunted so long" is dismissed as "little worthy of all this searching" (160–61).

Having apparently attained mastery over Modestine by means of the goad, Stevenson is free to focus his attention—and that of his narrative—on the course of his journey. Though he still portrays himself as "a man encumbered with a donkey" (152)—that is, Modestine remains a material impediment to smooth progress—Stevenson has gained control over his means of transport, and the material problems of the journey temporarily recede into the background. Stevenson uses the opportunity of travel in the Upper Gevaudans to articulate two important themes that will recur in his later travel writings. The first is a comparison between the landscape and culture through which he travels and those of his native land. In this case, the comparison is unfavorable to both, as he observes that "my road lay through one of the most beggarly countries in the world. It was like the worst of the Scottish Highlands, only worse; cold, naked, and ignoble" (163). Though he would later—especially in the South Seas—look back nostalgically on the Highlands and seek parallels to its geography and history in Polynesian settings, he is here too close both temporally and spatially to romanticize his origins.

Second, Stevenson articulates, at this early stage of his career, a philosophy of travel that will play an influential role in his career as a travel writer: questioning whether this region is worth visiting, he explains, "For my part, I travel not to go anywhere, but to go. I travel for travel's sake. The great affair is to move; to feel the needs and hitches of our life more nearly; to come down off this feather-bed of civilization, and find the globe granite underfoot and strewn with cutting flints" (*Travels,* 163). I have already alluded to the apparent contradiction between this pose of renunciation and Stevenson's residence at cozy and domesticated inns. However, the renunciation of a destination as the purpose of the journey is a key part of the random, eclectic, and spontaneous approach to travel that I refer to throughout this book as "cruising." The chief modification of the term *cruising* as I apply it to Stevenson's later works is that it comes increasingly to invoke pleasure and escape from conventions of narrative form. Whereas such travel is linked, in this instance, to a critique of the bourgeois comforts of civilization, with its featherbed, cruising increasingly comes to signify the enjoyment of the body in its encounters with alien landscapes and climates. It also evokes the freedom to experiment with narrative forms and develop hybrid texts that exploit numerous genres.

Though cruising—a method of travel as a pleasurable process and random voyage rather than a means to an end—reaches its apotheosis in the South Seas writings, the sentiment is already present in *An Inland Voyage,* where Stevenson expresses his distaste for the regular work habits of bourgeois society, a bohemianism that deeply informs cruising: "I am sure I would rather be a bargee than occupy any position under Heaven that required attendance at an office. There are few callings, I should say, where a man gives up less of his liberty in return for regular meals" (12). In *Travels with a Donkey,* it is the material comfort rather than the monotony of "civilization" that Stevenson rejects, embracing travel as a form of self-imposed physical adversity. Travel becomes, at least temporarily, an expression of Stevenson's bohemianism.

When Stevenson refers to his "strange destination" in *Travels,* perhaps the strangest thing about it is that he has made no mention of it before. The destination is "strange" because Stevenson has by this time renounced religious orthodoxy, as he ironically remarks: "I pursued my way, driving my secular donkey before me, and creaking in my secular boots and gaiters, toward the asylum of silence" (166).[29] The monastery is "a scene of some attraction for the human heart" (166), yet Stevenson is out of place there on several counts. In addition to being "secular," he does not fit the monks' expectations of national identity or occupation: when Stevenson declares himself a Scotsman, his host announces that he "had never seen a Scotsman before" and "looked me all over . . . as a boy might look upon a lion or an alligator" (167). Appearing to the monks as a kind of beast, Stevenson is at pains to prove both his humanity and his class status, insisting, "I was not a pedlar, but a literary man" (167)—a change of profession that he hopes will procure him an upgrade of accommodations. When Stevenson was mistaken for a pedlar in *An Inland Voyage,* he lacked any defined identity to oppose this misapprehension. In *Travels,* by contrast, he is anxious to be recognized as "a literary man" and—refusing the monk's suggested alternative, "a geographer" (167)—asks to be introduced to the community as "an author" (168).

Significantly, Stevenson parts company with Modestine at the entrance to the monastery, which "was the first door . . . which she had not shown an indecent haste to enter" (168). This reference suggests that it would indeed be indecent for a female animal even to attempt access to the exclusively male space of the monastery, to which Stevenson aspires. Stevenson draws attention to "the exclusion of women" (173) from the sanctuary, a phrase that anticipates his account in "My First Book" (1894) of writing *Treasure Island:* "It was to be a story for boys; no need of psychology or fine writing; and I had a boy at hand to be a touchstone. Women were excluded."[30] Stevenson's career as an author of romances would be founded on the exclusion of women, even though it began with the composition of *Treasure Island,* in a domestic setting featuring Fanny Stevenson and Lloyd Osbourne: the cottage at Braemar. Like the monastery, the romance would be constructed as an all-male space that it would be indecent for women to enter. Stevenson's anxiety about "petticoats," which he would later claim to have overcome, finds expression in his eagerness to join the all-male community.

On this journey that occurs on the back of a separation from Fanny, I have argued that Stevenson is anxious to escape reminders of femininity—which are also reminders of his own incomplete identity without the woman he loves. Yet the sex of his donkey prevents him from forgetting his dependence on the female influence, hence it saddens him. At the monastery, Stevenson seems attracted to the monks' lifestyle, including the "vow of silence" (*Travels with a Donkey,* 173), yet this setting leads Stevenson back to a previous experience of "lay phalansteries" (173): the artists' colony at Grez, outside Paris, where he met Fanny in 1876. This community had provided Stevenson with convivial mixed company and the opportunity to meet his future wife, and yet in *Travels* he dwells on the disadvantage of female company for a monastic and an artistic community, observing that "in the neighbourhood of women it is but a touch-and-go association that can be formed among defenceless men; the stronger electricity is sure to triumph; the dreams of boyhood, the schemes of youth, are abandoned after an interview of ten minutes, and the arts and sciences, and professional male jollity, deserted at once for two sweet eyes and a caressing accent" (174). The autobiographical relevance of this passage is unmistakable, as Stevenson contemplates abandoning his ambitious "schemes of youth" for the pursuit of a woman across the Atlantic: a journey he would make soon after the Cevennes trip, in the same year (1879) in which *Travels with a Donkey* was published. Stevenson's ambivalence about this change of course provoked by "two sweet eyes and a caressing accent" is hardly disguised by the ironic tone. Yet the passage uses autobiography to offer insight into Stevenson's approach to travel writing and fiction. In his subsequent journey—from Scotland to California—Stevenson would again enact flight from parental authority and domestic comfort, but in this case the journey (recorded in *The Amateur Emigrant*) is made specifically to pursue a woman rather than to escape feminine influence.[31] In *Travels*, by contrast, Stevenson's dependence on the feminine is inscribed in the very title of his book: "with a donkey," indicating the compromise of solitude necessary for Stevenson to make his journey. Excluding women from his company, as he would from his first novel, Stevenson enters the monastery alone, jettisoning the reminder of his material corpus to be received in a spiritual enclave. The monastery offers a possibility to Stevenson of living and working in an all-male environment, and perhaps of the homoerotic frissons of attractive male company: the monks are "sweet-tempered, with . . . a holy cheerfulness in air and conversation" (173). Stevenson admires their "strong manly singing" (175), while the "romance of the surroundings" and company provoke emotional turmoil: "I made my escape into the court with somewhat whirling fancies" (175).

Stevenson would establish some aspects of this intimate male community in his literary circle, based around the Savile Club, to which he had been elected in 1874.[32] Moreover, Stevenson looks ahead to the male camaraderie portrayed in his fictional work: not just *Treasure Island* but also *Jekyll and Hyde*, with its all-male "club" of professionals. Yet in the absence of domestic bonds or women, Dr. Jekyll and his cohorts can scarcely be said to exhibit "professional male jollity." Rather, the group is rife with anxiety, melancholy, disorder, and suppressed rivalry, while their vows of silence—"I am ashamed of my long tongue. Let us make a bargain never to refer to this again," as Enfield tells Utterson—are designed not to advance the "arts and sciences" but to conceal the monstrous symptom of Hyde, who has emerged from the "back door" of respectable Victorian society.[33] In the midst of the all-male professional enclave, the novella discloses an anal fixation that is also evident, as I have argued, in *Travels*. Whereas in the novella, Hyde's association with the "back door" encodes anality, that concept is embedded in *Travels* by the use of *ass* as a variant term for *donkey* (the label she is ascribed in the title); Modestine is first introduced as "a diminutive she-ass" that "passed into my service" (135). The previous owner's reputation "for brutally misusing the ass" (136) is a practice Stevenson ostensibly renounces, but in practice he is no less brutal than his predecessor toward the donkey's "stern-works." The name "Modestine"—with its suggestion of "modesty"—dictates that the "ass" should be concealed, protected from violation. Yet the ass in fact exposes Stevenson's vulnerability and increases his liability to unwanted interference. In a memorable scene, Stevenson seeks a campsite for the night and "goaded and kicked the reluctant Modestine" up a hill. However, the company of the donkey renders his position precarious: "There was only room for myself upon the plateau, and I had to go nearly as high again before I found so much as standing room for the ass" (203). Stevenson's ass both is and is not a part of him—anticipating how Jekyll at once acknowledges and disavows the anal Hyde as part of his identity, admitting on looking at Hyde's reflection that "[t]his, too, was myself" while subsequently removing such traces of union: "He, I say—I cannot say I."[34] The donkey represents a dilemma, as Stevenson cannot complete his day's travels until he has found "room for the ass," yet this "position was unpleasantly exposed" (203). Fearing nocturnal invasion, Stevenson writes, "I was passionately afraid of discovery, and the visit of jocular persons in the night" (203). Stevenson's sense of insecurity verges toward paranoia, as he detects "the movement of something swift and indistinct between the chestnuts" (204) and is later awakened by "such a noise as a person would make scratching loudly with a finger-nail" (205). The hallucinatory quality of this experience is suggested by the remark that "nothing was to be seen, nothing more was to be heard" (205). Though Stevenson provides an explanation—"I learned next day that the chestnut gardens are infested by rats" (205)—he admits that "the puzzle, for the moment, was insoluble" and that he remained "in wondering uncertainty about my neighbours" (205). The rat, of course, is another creature associated with anality and waste because of its frequent residence in sewers. Yet Stevenson's dread of intrusion is not wholly caused by the distaste for the rodent (Modestine, we recall, was "the colour of a mouse" [135]); it also derives from fear of the "peasantry" who are "abroad" and who are "terrible" to Stevenson. Stevenson's class anxiety is palpable in the implicit equation between the rats with which the area is infested and the peasants whose intrusion terrifies him. When he is finally caught and interrogated, Stevenson detects hostility in the "unfriendly tones" (205) with which the man asks him questions, reiterated in "his unfriendly voice" (206).

Yet Stevenson's identification with "a criminal" suggests a guilt for which he must make atonement by giving alms to a beggar (206). The chief humiliation Stevenson suffers is that the peasant talks to him as though "merely to an inferior" (206), assuming a position of superiority to the foreign traveler. This class confusion ironically recalls Stevenson and his companion being mistaken for "pedlars" in *An Inland Voyage,* although Stevenson's being in a position to "pay for my night's lodgings" (206) restores his superior status.

For much of the narrative of his journey, Stevenson seems eager to embrace the opportunity to meet new people and fellow travelers, writing that strangers "in nine cases out of ten, show themselves friendly and considerate. As soon as you cross the doors you cease to be a stranger" (146), even at Our Lady of the Snows, where he "found no difficulty as to [his] reception" (169). Yet recurring traces of misanthropy in Stevenson's narrative remind us that he is traveling to escape rather than to encounter people. Stevenson's admiration for the Beast of Gevaudan reveals not only his animosity toward women and children but also his hostile impulses toward the local people generally. Encountering two girls, he calls them "a pair of impudent sly sluts" (153) who mock him, and he recalls with evident relish that the "Beast of Gevaudan ate about a hundred children of this district; I began to think of him with sympathy" (154). Similarly, Hyde first attracts public attention by "an act of cruelty to a child." Stevenson's identification with a beast recalls his denomination of Modestine as "a beast of burden" (135) whose role is to carry his pack and receive his abuse. It also, however, anticipates the dualism of Dr. Jekyll and Mr. Hyde: the former using the latter to direct his sadistic impulses toward women, children, and other vulnerable beings. Jekyll writes that his "pleasures . . . began to turn towards the monstrous" and involved "drinking pleasure with bestial avidity from any degree of torture to another."[35]

The description of Hyde as "bestial" reminds us that, in this post-Darwinian culture, the "lower elements in my soul" inevitably involved symptoms of animality. Significantly, not only does Hyde exhibit signs of "deformity and decay," but he also starts to sprout "a swart growth of hair," revealing the animalistic traits of his double.[36] Yet in *Travels,* Stevenson creates a duality out of the beast itself, one side of which (Modestine) passively accepts punishment while refusing to obey Stevenson's commands, while the other side (the Beast of Gevaudan) acts out Stevenson's violent impulses with Hyde-like savagery. If this beast can represent Stevenson's violent impulses, then he is no less ready than Jekyll to project this side of himself onto external beings. In one scene he asks for guidance from a local man, who queries him about his destination. Stevenson insists, "I was not going to indulge his bestial curiosity" (156), and he requests that the man help him find a guide. When the man refuses to cross the door, Stevenson comments, "I saw unaffected terror struggling on his face with unaffected shame. . . . Here was the Beast of Gevaudan and no mistake" (156–57)—alluding to the terror of the beast among the local population but also suggesting that Stevenson himself is the beast, since the man is terrified of him. Indeed, as Stevenson is excluded by the "family party" who "retire within their fortifications," he acerbically remarks, "Let me say it in the plural: the Beasts of Gevaudan" (157), identifying his unhelpful hosts as a family of beasts, while leaving open the possibility that Stevenson himself is one of the "beasts."

Stevenson's loss of bearings suggests the downside of a random itinerary: his sense of direction is fragile, and he seeks help in vain from an old man who "turned a deaf ear," while another "did not care a stalk of parsley if I wandered all night upon the hills!" (153). In his desperation, Stevenson seeks assistance from his donkey: "Soon the road that I was following split, after the fashion of the country, into three or four in a piece of rocky meadow" (154). Like Jekyll, Stevenson "had come to the fatal cross roads," and his choice of direction would determine his fate. In Jekyll's case, the outcome depends on whether he emerges as "an angel" or "a fiend" from the "thick cloak . . . of Hyde."[37] Stevenson's dilemma is no less acute, as he is absorbed in "a black night . . . never in a blacker" (154), at which juncture Stevenson strangely relies on the judgment of his donkey: "Since Modestine had shown such a fancy for beaten roads, I tried her instinct in this predicament" (154). Stevenson, having previously described himself as "a man encumbered with a donkey" (152), finds no succor from his beast, for "the instinct of an ass is what might be expected from the name; in half a minute she was clambering round and round among some boulders, as lost a donkey as you would wish to see" (155).

The image of Modestine going "round and round" conjures up the circularity of Stevenson's journey: despite his intended destination, the actual experience of travel is like going round in circles. Jekyll also uses the metaphor of a thwarted journey, relating "that truth, by whose partial discovery I have been doomed to such a dreadful shipwreck." Indeed, the journey is a powerful image throughout this passage, as Jekyll admits that "the state of my knowledge does not pass beyond that point" while "[o]thers will follow, others will outstrip me on the same lines." Likewise, he describes how he "advanced infallibly . . . in one direction only."[38] Having plotted a rigid course, Jekyll is incapable of either diversion or retreat and so is doomed to be shipwrecked.

Yet Stevenson, whose route is far less fixed, becomes equally lost; indeed it becomes clear that Modestine's aimless circularity is a projection of his own state of confusion and misery. Modestine becomes a vehicle for Stevenson to express his own physical distress and suffering under the rigors of travel, as he writes, "I tied Modestine, a haggard, drenched, desponding donkey" (157) while making no direct allusion to his own state. Similarly, Stevenson writes that Modestine was "growing angry, pawed and stamped upon the road" (159), adding tellingly that "I was recalled for a brief while to consciousness" (159)—as though Modestine's actions and Stevenson's consciousness were connected. His reference to the "instinct of an ass" evokes the stubbornness and stupidity that he elsewhere attributes to her. Yet this instinct of the animal proves remarkably similar to Stevenson's: Modestine is no more or less adept at finding her way in the dark than is her master.

Just as her emotional state is a version of Stevenson's distress, so are Modestine's physical sufferings a projection of his own: "[W]e had shared some misadventures, and my heart was still as cold as a potato towards my beast of burden," he remarks, describing "her two forelegs [as] no better than raw beef on the inside, and blood was running from under her tail" (162). Modestine embodies the suffering corpus, allowing Stevenson to occupy the role of the romantic traveler "in a pleasant frame of mind with all men" (160). It is the beast who has given "proof of dead stupidity" (162), allowing Stevenson to enter the spiritual realm of the monastery without the reminder of his material body.

The narrative's primary focus—indeed, dependence—on Modestine as a figure of suffering physicality and material resistance to travel is nowhere more apparent than at the termination of *Travels with a Donkey*. Problems of closure are endemic to the narrative mode I characterize as "cruising"—for the random motion, unplanned direction, and pleasure sought in cruising as "travel for travel's sake" all militate against a structured plot and a definitive conclusion. By flaunting the contingent, impulsive, and hedonistic dimensions to travel, cruising forgoes the detailed itinerary and careful mapping of the more organized journey. At what point, therefore, does a narrative that exemplifies cruising—such as *Travels with a Donkey*—attain closure, or reach its destination? Stevenson partially resolves this problem by substituting a temporal for a spatial or geographic plot. The journey—originally recorded in a daily journal—extends through time, and it has a beginning and an end that are determined only by hindsight: the penultimate chapter is titled "The Last Day," indicating that the end point of Stevenson's journey and his narrative both are determined only by this temporal statement, much as a book is concluded by the words "The End."

The final chapter contains further allusions to the distant object of Fanny Osbourne, allusions that seem coy and evasive, as Stevenson writes, "I moved in an atmosphere of pleasure. . . . But perhaps it was not the place alone that so disposed my spirit. Perhaps some one was thinking of me in another country; or perhaps some thought of my own had come and gone unnoticed, and yet done me good" (227). In the absence of any confession to the reader of the identity of the someone in question, Stevenson's allusion seems to be a private reference that excludes the reader (reflecting the basis of the narrative in a journal). Yet what matters is that the object of Stevenson's "journey" is elsewhere, a remote figure about whose desires and intentions he can only speculate (the doubt implied by the repeated "perhaps" seems genuine). Like Our Lady of the Snows, this woman is an idealized figure, possessing a mystical power to do him good despite her physical absence. Yet in his account of a Catholic couple who condemn another Catholic for converting to Protestantism, Stevenson agrees that it is "a great flight of confidence for a man to change his creed and go out of his family for heaven's sake" (227). Here the use of the term *flight* recalls travel's appeal as a form of escape, while the allusion to the traveler's need to "go out of his family" suggests an outcome of isolation or perhaps exile.

By contrast to the unnamed woman in another country, Modestine is physically present yet undesired by the narrator: he is willing to part with her despite her "sort of affection" for him (229). One is reminded of Stevenson's previous parting from Modestine at the monastery, in which "Modestine was led away by a layman to the stables, and I and my pack were received into Our Lady of the Snows" (169). Stevenson's reception into this space of feminine purity is conditional on his parting from the material, secular donkey who "seemed to have a disaffection for monasteries" (168). In search of an ideal—whether of male brotherhood or female purity—Stevenson hastily renounces his attachment to the "diminutive she-ass."[39]

Throughout the journey, Modestine has been associated with the body and has served as a reminder of animality. I have suggested parallels between Modestine and an apparently more sinister beast, Mr. Hyde, whose animality is frequently asserted in Stevenson's text. One of the many reminders of Hyde's animality—along with the reference to his "apelike tricks" (72) and "ape-like fury" (25)—is the echo of hide, or animal skin, in his name. Stevenson, in writing about the practice of making drums from asses' skin (see epigraph), writes that "a man is never more uselessly employed than when he is at this trick of bastinadoing asses' hide" (*Travels*, 43). Like Hyde, Modestine—whose ass Stevenson has no hesitation in giving a hiding—embodies with stubborn insistence the demands of the corpus and the travails of the flesh. While Stevenson is not, like Jekyll, transformed into his bodily alter ego, he is anxious lest his bond with Modestine become permanent, an unshakeable part of his "infamous burden" (142). We recall that Jekyll is afraid that he and Hyde might exchange identities: "I began to spy a danger that, if this were much prolonged, the balance of my nature might be permanently overthrown, the power of voluntary change be forfeited, and the character of Edward Hyde become irrevocably mine."[40] Stevenson's dismay when his pack is overthrown, as "the whole hypothec turned round and groveled in the dust below the donkey's belly" (141), mirrors anxiety that their roles will be reversed, that he too will be "below the donkey's belly." Indeed, just as Modestine shoulders Stevenson's burden—in the form of the "monstrous deck-cargo, all poised above the donkey's shoulders" (137)—so too must Stevenson carry Modestine, "must make a sacrifice to the gods of shipwreck" (142), and he fears that he will collapse under the strain.

Yet perhaps this parallel between Stevenson and Jekyll, Modestine and Hyde, is too neat; moreover, it leaves Stevenson in the comfortable position of respectable middle-class identity, with Modestine as his abject "other." At times, Stevenson's pleasure in inflicting suffering represents the dark impulses of Hyde, such as his attack on Carew: "With a transport of glee, I mauled the unresisting body, tasting delight from every blow."[41] Indeed, the confessional tone of the narrative in *Travels* is reminiscent of Jekyll's shame at "losing hold of my original and better self, and becoming slowly incorporated with my second and worse."[42] Stevenson's guilt at his brutalizing of Modestine is plain for all to see: "I am ashamed to say [that I] struck the poor sinner twice across the face. It was pitiful to see her lift up her head with shut eyes, as if waiting for another blow. I came very near crying" (143). Yet shortly afterwards, Stevenson gets "an arm free to thrash Modestine, and cruelly I chastised her" (143). Modestine, like the young girl Hyde tramples and elderly Carew whom he murders, appears to be the innocent victim of "a being inherently malign and villainous."[43]

The final chapter of the narrative is, fittingly, that in which Stevenson parts company with his donkey. This is the proper end of the travels, both as a physical journey and as a narrative project. Stevenson has prepared the reader for this separation by recounting a passionate love story between Castanet and Mariette that demonstrates how "even in a public tragedy, love will have its way" (229). The story concludes with "an exchange of prisoners" (229) that is an apt metaphor for the release of Modestine, who has been the traveler's slave. Writing that Modestine "had a sort of affection for me, which I was soon to betray" (229), Stevenson portrays himself as an inconstant lover, the converse of the passionate devotion of Castanet to his lady. The sense of bondage and coercion invoked by use of the term *prisoners* is apt in another way: Stevenson's master-slave relation with Modestine demonstrates a sadomasochistic dynamic in which Stevenson's pleasure in inflicting pain is matched by Modestine's apparent affability in the face of brutality.

The title of the chapter, "Farewell, Modestine!" might suggest fondness for or even sadness at his separation from the donkey, his traveling companion, which brings the journey to a close. Yet the tone of the chapter conveys eagerness and relief at the prospect of separation: "I determined to sell my lady friend and be off by the diligence that afternoon" (230). Having obtained what he wants from Modestine—both a beast of burden for his pack and an appealing character for his narrative—Stevenson ungratefully abandons her for a speedier mode of transport, the diligence—surely an ironic comment on Modestine's lack of speed and purpose. Indeed, so keen is he to disappear that he seems to be turning the tables on Fanny, who abandoned him with equal abruptness earlier that year. His callousness in selling a female friend seems calculated, while he proclaims that "the pecuniary gain is not obvious, but I had bought freedom into the bargain" (230). Whose freedom, one wonders, has Stevenson purchased? While Modestine is manifestly the "slave" (148) who has been liberated from a tyrannical "driver," the context suggests that it is Stevenson's own freedom that he believes has been acquired. Having traveled for several weeks with a donkey, he is now free to journey without this encumbrance. Modestine thus appears to be the "sacrifice to the gods of shipwreck" necessary for Stevenson's romance—in both senses—to prosper and for his narrative to conclude.

Yet this curt dismissal is not the final note: while being driven away in the carriage, Stevenson "became aware of my bereavement. I had lost Modestine" (230). Stevenson rhapsodizes on Modestine as though the two were estranged lovers, stating that "although sometimes I was hurt and distant in manner, I still kept my patience; and as for her, poor soul! She had come to regard me as a god. She loved to eat out of my hand. She was patient, elegant in form, the colour of an ideal mouse, and inimitably small. Her faults were those of her race and sex; her virtues were her own" (231). This ambivalent passage both parodies and mocks the convention of love poetry and articulates a sense of loss that cannot be dismissed as purely parodic, especially as it concludes the narrative. Recalling how "Father Adam wept when he sold her to me," Stevenson admits that he did the same and "did not hesitate to yield to my emotion" (231). Throughout the narrative, Modestine's failure to greatly accelerate Stevenson's motion is balanced by her stimulating effect on his emotions. As a practical aid to travel she is useless, a fact that threatens the very possibility of a travel narrative: "Of all conceivable journeys, this promised to be the most tedious" (138), Stevenson observes, and evoking a Sisyphean image of the futility of travel, he describes them as "a pair of figures ever infinitesimally moving, foot by foot, a yard to the minute, and, like things enchanted in a nightmare, approaching no nearer to the goal" (139). This nightmare of stasis tests Stevenson's commitment to "travel for travel's sake" (163): for even while a specific destination may be unnecessary, a sense of progress is required for the narrative to assert the claims of "travel." In the absence of clear advancement toward a goal, Stevenson's narrative instead dwells in the affective register of desire and lack. Missing his "lady friend," anonymously signified as "the woman a man loves" (188), he desires her company and imagines scenes of romantic intimacy. The presence of Modestine, by contrast, is portrayed as irksome and troubling, a reminder both of the absence of the loved one and of a range of physical symptoms that Stevenson would prefer to disavow. Indeed, Modestine presents what for the writer is the most disabling predicament, the failure of language, as "no words can render an idea of my difficulties" (142).

Only when Modestine is absent can she in turn be idealized in an encomium that reads like an epitaph. Stevenson tautly registers this change of perspective: "Up to that moment I had thought I hated her; but now she was gone, 'And, Oh, / The difference to me!'" (231). Significantly, Stevenson quotes from one of Wordsworth's "Lucy" poems—"She dwelt among th' untrodden ways"—in which the speaker commemorates a deceased woman he loves. Wordsworth's italicizing of *lived* in the final stanza emphasizes that his ideal woman is no more among the living:

> She *lived* unknown. And few could know
> When Lucy ceased to be.
> But she is in her grave, and oh!
> The difference to me!

With neither an explanation of how Lucy died, nor the history of the speaker's attachment to her, the lyric presents an enigmatic tragedy of loss defined by the absence of the subject. Stevenson's version might seem a parody, not least because his "lady," Modestine, possesses none of the mystery or delicacy of Lucy, while the history of their relationship has been disclosed in too much detail. However, just as it is Lucy's death that leads to her being idealized by the speaker, so too is it the separation from Modestine that reduces Stevenson to tears. No longer chided as the "infamous burden," Modestine by her absence deprives Stevenson indefinitely of the pleasures of traveling light.

# PART TWO

# Mapping the Historical Romance

# THREE

## "Faithful to his map"

### Profit, Desire, and the Ends of Travel in *Treasure Island*

> Yet most cultural historians, and certainly all literary scholars, have failed to remark the *geographical* notation, the theoretical mapping and charting of territory that underlies Western fiction, historical writing, and philosophical discourse of the time. There is first the authority of the European observer—traveller, merchant, scholar, historian, novelist. Then there is the hierarchy of spaces by which the metropolitan center and, gradually, the metropolitan economy are seen as dependent upon an overseas system of territorial control, economic exploitation, and a socio-cultural vision; without these stability and prosperity at home—"home" being a word with extremely potent resonances—would not be possible.
>
> —Said, *Culture and Imperialism*[1]

As WE HAVE SEEN, *Travels with a Donkey* concludes with Stevenson selling the donkey Modestine, receiving "an offer of twenty-five francs" and informing the reader that "after a desperate engagement, I sold her, saddle and all for five-and-thirty." In this way, Stevenson draws attention to the fact that the mode of transport, despite his affection for her, remains a commodity. At the same time, he reminds us that the journey and the text are also commodities. As in his dedication, where he assigned the public to the role of "generous patron, who defrays the postage," Stevenson is intensely conscious of the commercial possibilities of his travels. Yet he admits at the end of *Travels with a Donkey* that "the pecuniary gain is not obvious," a phrase that refers to the lack of profit he obtained from his travel writings.[2] In the early 1880s, with a wife and family to support, Stevenson was eagerly searching for a more lucrative form of literary labor. Indeed, as I argue in this chapter, the conception, composition, and publication of *Treasure Island* arose from a desire to realize the profitable potential of travel in the marketplace. In this way, Stevenson tapped into a new audience for fiction that emerged in the late nineteenth century. If, as Nicholas Daly argues, *Treasure Island* "did much to create the popular perception of a new direction in fiction," Stevenson had "many rivals for the attention of the popular reading public" and had to distinguish his work from that of his peers.[3] Moreover, Stevenson depended for this favorable reception on changes in the publishing of fiction during the period, as both "H. Rider Haggard and Robert Louis Stevenson were to the vanguard in the shift to first-time single-volume publication." The works of Stevenson, Haggard, and others, Daly notes, "were aimed at an expanded middle-class readership, possessed of a certain amount of leisure and money." This "literary equivalent of the burgeoning consumer culture" was necessary, in Stevenson's case, for the transition from dilettante, bohemian travel writer to professional novelist.[4] If at the end of *Travels* the mode of transport is a commodity, in the case of *Treasure Island* the narrative itself is commodified from the outset. Daly's point that "the treasure hunt and the team of men relate to the new imperialism and the rise of professionalism" is significant, especially if one includes authorship within this expansion of professionalism. Daly believes that "changes in the material culture of Britain in the late nineteenth and early twentieth centuries . . . caused people—intellectuals and popular readers alike—to conceive it in terms of consumption rather than production."[5] Such a change helps to account for Stevenson's increased focus on the reader, his realization that a work of fiction, to be successful, must address a specific audience. In the case of *Treasure Island,* the prominence accorded to the map is not its documentary function as a record of travel but its commodity-status as logo of the treasure hunt. As Stevenson's accounts of the composition of the novel attest, the map is the most significant part of the fiction.

## Stevenson's First Commodity-Text

Although *Treasure Island* was published relatively early in Stevenson's career, my discussion of the novel begins with a text that was produced close to the end of his life. In August 1894, four months before his death, Robert Louis Stevenson published an article entitled "My First Book" as part of a series that appeared in the journal the *Idler.* If the title of this journal harked back to Stevenson's early literary experience as a bohemian adventurer-author, traveling with no clear destination, the essay went far to demonstrate how much time had elapsed since its author had ceased to be an "idler." The essay charts Stevenson's course from a struggling, impecunious writer of travel books, literary essays, and short stories to a productive, successful, professional man of letters. Indeed, by 1894 a famous author, Stevenson was in a position to advise young writers on the best route to success.

Yet in recalling his early career, Stevenson significantly distorted his curriculum vitae—not by adding but by deleting texts he had published. The "first book" of the essay's title is, of course, *Treasure Island,* his first novel. As Wendy R. Katz points out, this essay offers "RLS's reconstruction of events surrounding the text," in which the "crucial elements of map, island, sailing ship and pirate are all part of RLS's retrospective account of his first book."[6] Yet Katz does not contest Stevenson's designation of *Treasure Island* as his "first book," despite the fact that the essay discreetly erases six previously published works from his corpus of publications. In fact, Stevenson's first book was *An Inland Voyage,* published in 1878, a narrative of his journey in a canoe along the canals and waterways of France and Belgium. This was immediately followed by a study of the topography and history of his native city, *Edinburgh: Picturesque Notes.* In the following year, 1879, Stevenson consolidated his reputation as a travel writer, publishing *Travels with a Donkey in the Cevennes.* The obvious question for any reader interested in Stevenson's early work is why he would bury several books that were praised at the time for their "light and graceful touch."[7] Stevenson refers to this act of omission in the 1894 essay by reminding the reader, "I am not a novelist alone. But I am well aware that my paymaster, the Great Public, regards what else I have written with indifference, if not aversion. If it call upon me at all, it calls on me in the familiar and indelible character; and when I am asked to talk of my first book, *no question in the world* but what is meant is my first novel."[8] One explanation for the complete erasure of his literary origins as a travel writer in "My First Book" can be found, I think, in Stevenson's description of the public as his "paymaster," placing him in the role of obedient servant—indeed, the hired hand—who has come to recognize the economic necessity of giving the public what it wants. Yet Stevenson's confidence that there is "no question" about the public's preference for his fiction seems at odds with his increasing interest in writing nonfiction while living in Samoa. Moreover, the composition of Stevenson's first novel depended fundamentally—for its locations and narrative secrets—on the travels and contexts of his earlier career.

Ironically, Stevenson had turned to travel writing at the beginning of his career specifically to free himself from financial dependence upon his father. As Paul Maixner notes, "Accounts of travel were then in vogue and judged against other examples these volumes were clearly superior, though they did not rank high in Stevenson's own opinion, having been written according to him chiefly because they could be turned out easily and might be profitable."[9] In actuality, they earned little for him, although the reviews were generally favorable. Hence, the travel narratives were eventually dismissed as wasteful digressions and were consigned by Stevenson to "the succession of defeats [that] lasted unbroken till I was thirty-one" ("My First Book," 277).[10]

What is apparent in this late essay is that Stevenson's definition of success was largely a commercial one; likewise, his use of the term *defeats* applies specifically to works that were unprofitable. Throughout "My First Book," in fact, Stevenson's recollections of his early literary labors are inextricably intertwined with the profit motive: his initial pleasure in writing *Treasure Island*—which Stevenson describes as the "funds of entertainment" ("My First Book," 279) derived from creating characters such as John Silver—becomes inseparable from the monetary funds he hoped to realize with a successful venture of writing fiction for boys. The turning point in the conception of his first novel, Stevenson makes clear, was the drawing of the imaginary map in collaboration with his stepson, Lloyd Osbourne: "I made the map of an island; it was elaborately and (I thought) beautifully coloured; the shape of it took my fancy beyond expression" (279). It was only after the map had been drawn that "the future characters of the book began to appear there visibly among imaginary woods" (279).[11] The map served as a stimulus for the creation of the novel and thus lies at the origin of *Treasure Island.* Stevenson concludes his essay with advice to the young writer about achieving literary success: "[It] is my contention—my superstition, if you like—that he who is faithful to his map, and consults it, and draws from it his inspiration, daily and hourly, gains positive support, and not mere negative immunity from accident. The tale has a root there: it grows in that soil; it has a spine of its own behind the words" (283).

Here the contingency of Stevenson's account of writing *Treasure Island* is displaced by the portrayal of an essential relation between image and text, in which the former is the prerequisite of the latter. In suggesting that young writers imitate his fidelity to the map, Stevenson grafts his own recollection into a theory of composition that deploys an organic metaphor ("the tale has its root there"). The profitable results of this fidelity to the map are demonstrated in a particularly telling passage in which Stevenson admits that he realized, in the midst of writing *Treasure Island,* that he had for the first time produced a valuable literary commodity, a work that others desired to take possession of. A visitor, Dr. Alexander Japp, played the role of deus ex machina; he served temporarily as Stevenson's literary agent and arranged for the story's publication in *Young Folks Magazine,* thereby launching Stevenson in what he would call "this boy's book business."[12] Japp's role in piloting Stevenson toward a new audience—introducing his work to a nascent, lucrative class of readers—is crucial in the author's accession to profit and the creation of his first commodity-text. At the same time, there is a suggestion of theft in the recollection that Japp "carried away the manuscript in his portmanteau" ("My First Book," 197), an image strangely mirroring that of Jim absconding with Billy Bones's map, pilfered from the pirate's portmanteau. The implication that Stevenson's organic connection to his text was severed by its publication is part of his recognition of the story as a commodity-text.[13]

The commodity-text, according to N. N. Feltes, should not be confused with the simple category of "best seller," which "simply indicates value accrued through distribution and exchange, rather than through the production process." Nor can the notion of writing to a formula, for a prefabricated audience, accommodate the concept of the commodity-text, for "whereas a formula novel takes its value from something reduced and mechanical, and prior to its production, a commodity-text takes its value from the labor power ("imagination") expended in the very process of interpellation."[14] The key to the commodity-text is that it is produced within the capitalist mode of production, is aimed at mass distribution, and seeks to create a surplus value from which both publisher and author will claim a share of the profit. Rather than appealing to a preexisting audience, the commodity-text produces its own readership, and this work of creating desire in the reader is the "labor" that the text performs.

Feltes argues that the actual format of the work is less significant than this (capitalist) mode of production and extraction of surplus value: "[W]hether the commodity-text is to take the particular form of a series of books, a magazine serial, or a part-issue novel, series production, by allowing the bourgeois audience's ideological engagement to be sensed and expanded, [it] allows as well the extraction of ever greater surplus value from the very production (or "creative") process itself." Though the transition from petty commodity to a capitalist mode of production had occurred long before *Treasure Island*—Feltes claims that Dickens's *Pickwick Papers* (1836–37) was the first commodity-text—the mode of production shifted significantly with the rapid expansion of magazine fiction in the 1880s and 1890s, an expansion from which Stevenson benefited. These magazines were instrumental in invoking new markets of readers, for the "class" journal "did not address social groupings as it found them, always/already given (a class, for instance) but rather reconstituted their members into a specialized clientele . . . an audience with 'a market character' consuming a new kind of 'branded goods.'"[15] Significant among such "class journals" were the magazines designed for young readers, including James Henderson's *Young Folks* (founded 1871), in which Stevenson published three of his novels, as well as the *Boy's Own* and *Girl's Own* magazines (which appeared in 1879 and 1880, respectively).

Stevenson's retention of his copyright to *Treasure Island* allowed for the introduction of a final key component of this commodity-text: the map, which was not published in the serial version, was lost in transit when sent to Cassell (who published the novel in volume form) and therefore had to be reconstituted from the text. The map, I argue, was both an indicator of the commodity status of *Treasure Island*—it became, in effect, the logo for the book—and a material residue of Stevenson's travel writings: unprofitable journeys from which he had nevertheless learned the value and marketability of travel, adventure, and the quest for profit. As Daly observes, "the treasure hunt in particular, most memorably in Stevenson's *Treasure Island* (1883) and Haggard's *King Solomon's Mines* (1885), placed the map at the heart of the imperial imaginary." Key to this "imaginary" is the idea of the "untold riches that are to be had from the body of the colonial territory." Moreover, the text is itself a source of riches, as "an expanding consumer culture demands narratives to explain the new relations of subjects and objects."[16] This demand for explanatory narrative would be supplied by the proponents of romance, such as Stevenson and Haggard.

Embittered by the lack of commercial success for his travel writings, particularly for *Travels with a Donkey,* Stevenson would conceive *Treasure Island* from the outset as an assay on the literary marketplace from which he would struggle to extract his share of the bounty. If the early travel writings were in part "a fantasy of escape from commodified literature" embracing an antimodern primitivism,[17] in *Treasure Island* Stevenson deploys the treasure hunt as a deliberate anachronism, making profit out of depicting "ships, roadside inns, robbers, old sailors, and commercial travelers before the era of steam" ("My First Book," 280). A key to Stevenson's realization of the profit from his travels is the use of such historical referents to attract the audience of "boy" readers: a group that actually comprised not only juvenile readers but also adult readers who were willing, indeed eager, to be addressed as boys. This readership included several of the "full-grown, experienced [men] of letters" ("My First Book," 281) who would adopt Stevenson's cause and provide invaluable support for his literary career: important literary allies such as W. E. Henley, Henry James, Andrew Lang, and Edmund Gosse, who recognized in Stevenson's work a new voice of romance. As Henry James wrote in 1888, "everything he has written is a direct apology for boyhood. . . . [W]hat makes him so [rare] is the singular maturity of the expression that he has given to young sentiments." For James and his fellow admirers, Stevenson's gift was to invite sophisticated adults to participate in a boy's game: "[T]he execution is so serious that the idea (the idea of a boy's romantic adventures) becomes a matter of universal relations."[18] By reading *Treasure Island* and enjoying the fantasy inscribed in the map, James and his peers would join a homosocial community of readers through the guise of romance.

The image of Japp leaving Braemar with the manuscript of *Treasure Island* in his portmanteau is evocative of someone going on a journey, a point that should prompt us to recognize that Stevenson's preparation for the successful voyage into fiction undoubtedly came during his travel-writing years. Indeed, many of the techniques of description, narrative voice, characterization, and economy (in the literary sense) for which Stevenson became famous in his novels were recycled from his early travel books. For example, the development of

Modestine, with whom Stevenson shared an intimate love-hate relationship, as a character in *Travels with a Donkey* prepared the ground for subsequent traveling companions in a relationship likewise marked by ambivalence, such as Jim Hawkins and Long John Silver, David Balfour and Alan Breck, and even the debauched trio of Herrick, Davis, and Huish, who alternately support and berate each other in *The Ebb-Tide.*

Equally, however, Stevenson's travel writings demonstrate a keen concern with the economics of travel and questions of profit and loss, and they reveal at times an ardent desire for treasure: if this nascent capitalist impulse seems incongruous with the narratives' rejection of respectable bourgeois life and productive labor, it does anticipate the flagrant profit motive of *Treasure Island.* Stevenson's first successful venture into the novelist's art would reconfigure and repackage his preoccupation with travel as a random process, by sending his characters on a carefully planned itinerary that leads to an intended and profitable destination. Yet in *Treasure Island* there remain traces, sometimes buried, of the questioning of the profit motive, the critique of capitalist enterprise.

The shifting convergence of commerce, profit, and national identity within Stevenson's early works thus emerges as a distinct variation on being "faithful to his map." But his faithfulness to his own map may be questioned in light of the dramatic transformation of his literary career that occurred with his first novel. Rather than merely providing a "reading" of *Treasure Island,* this journey through the travel writings will, I hope, suggest a new location or set of coordinates for the novel on the map of Stevenson's career.

## A Wayward Voyage

Stevenson's first book, *An Inland Voyage,* published in April 1878, traces the canoe journey made by the author and his traveling companion, Sir Walter Grindlay Simpson, in 1876 along the rivers and canals of France and Belgium. Stevenson's and Simpson's canoes were named *Arethusa* and *Cigarette,* respectively, and by metonymic displacement, Stevenson and his companion are rechristened after their vessels: Stevenson dedicates the book to "My dear 'Cigarette'"—designating Simpson—and refers to himself as "Arethusa." The identities of the travelers are thus merged with the journey, becoming combined in a double identity with their mode of transport, their vessels. However, the dedication of the text anticipates the severing of this identity, with the eventual selling of their canoes, which "[n]ow . . . fly the tricoleur and are known by new and alien names." *An Inland Voyage*, therefore, constructs a world in which travel is everything, yet its opening pages already gesture toward the eventual dissolution of this world.[19]

In this work, the journey is narrated less as a purposeful voyage following a strict itinerary toward a specific destination and more as a rambling, disconnected series of escapades featuring male camaraderie, frequent mishaps and misadventure, and strange (sometimes disturbing) encounters with the native populace. Renouncing the tourist mentality and ignoring the official sites usually flocked to by foreign visitors, Stevenson anticipates the sentiment that he would express in *The Silverado Squatters:*

> Sight-seeing is the art of disappointment.
>
> > There's nothing under heaven so blue
> > That's fairly worth the travelling to.
>
> But, fortunately, Heaven rewards us with many agreeable prospects and adventures by the way.[20]

As its title indicates, the book does not narrate a sea-voyage, although the sea would subsequently become the chief location for Stevenson's travels. Instead, the journey is a paradox, being inland yet on water. As the topography of Stevenson's travels is always significant, one should note also that the title suggests a movement inland, away from the coastal zone that, in Scotland, his family had marked with its lighthouses.[21] In his first volume, Stevenson thus launched his literary career with a voyage that turned away from his family's profession, toward his own future as a writer "inland." The coast represents a kind of boundary between land and sea, which the Stevensons had made safer through their works of engineering, while also less romantic as a setting for fiction. Yet Stevenson's first recorded voyage moves away from this boundary, toward a "very smiling tract of country" into which he hopes to welcome his audience: "I am not yet able to dissemble the warmth of my sentiments towards a reader; and if I meet him on the threshold, it is to invite him in with country cordiality" (*Inland Voyage*, 3).

This valuation of travel for the process of movement—rather than the result or destination—is characteristic of *An Inland Voyage*, in which an aesthetics of wandering is opposed to the more purpose-driven travels of the tourist. In this early text, Stevenson emphasizes the "mystery [of] how things ever get to their destination" (12) and celebrates travel as the art of escape from bourgeois civilization or, as he metaphorically describes it, "the bear's hug of custom gradually squeezing the life out of a man's soul" (17). The aesthetics of travel is portrayed as a form of nonattachment, and Stevenson writes eloquently about the pleasures of detached observation—"I think the spectacle of a whole life in which you have no part paralyses personal desire. You are content to become a mere spectator" (21). Yet at several points in the text, Stevenson and Simpson become objects of the gaze, making a spectacle of themselves. For example, Stevenson readily accepts his identification by the local people as an outsider, a "pedlar" (36), which suggests the bohemian, antibourgeois impetus of Stevenson's travel, while also introducing the possibility that he might have something to sell. The commodity that he will have to sell, it turns out, is the book of his travels.

Yet as the narrative makes abundantly clear, the journey, in a practical and economic sense, amounts to nothing. It is carelessly planned and poorly executed. A revealing scene, in this respect, occurs when the two travelers are approached during a torrential rainfall by an old man, who, Stevenson writes, "Questioned me about our journey. In the fullness of my heart I laid bare our plans before him. He said it was the silliest enterprise that ever he heard of. Why, did I not know, he asked me, that it was nothing but locks, locks, locks, the whole way?" (41). Apparently trusting that he would receive a positive response, Stevenson instead encounters his severest critic, and the dismissal of the value of the journey anticipates the mixed reception of the travel narrative itself. If, as some reviewers suggested, the purpose of producing a book was too obviously the motive for the journey, then to condemn the journey was to damn the narrative that reproduces it. Moreover, the old man's gloomy repetition of "locks" invokes the obstacles that would impede Stevenson's progress as a traveler and as a writer, serving as a fitting emblem for Stevenson's struggling literary career. The man's concluding advice, "Get into a train, my little young man, and go you away home to your parents" (41)—both infantilizes Stevenson (for whom travel and travel writing are, ironically, attempts to escape parental control and gain independence from their economic support) and deflates his romantic idealism—trains are much more practical, though less romantic, than canoes. In this encounter, the romantic traveler confronts the voice of hard, unsympathetic realism in the form of a figure "whom I take to have been the devil" (41).[22]

Yet despite these obstacles, the voyage is determinedly presented by Stevenson as an excuse for relaxation, idleness, pleasure, and insouciant delay. He writes, "It was to be the most leisurely of progresses, now on a swift river at the tail of a steamboat, now waiting horses for days together on some inconsiderable junction" (*Inland Voyage*, 47). The journey for Stevenson is an escape, in the first instance, from the Victorian shibboleth of respectability, which he terms "a very good thing in its way, but it does not rise superior to all considerations" (23).[23] The appeal of the journey as narrated in *An Inland Voyage* is that it offers a holiday from the real, material pressures of life in late-Victorian society. An important part of the pleasure of this escape is provided by the map, which Stevenson and his companion study at length: "[W]e neither of us read anything in the world, and employed the very little while we were awake between bed and dinner in poring upon maps. I have always been fond of maps, and can voyage in an atlas with the greatest enjoyment" (89). Stevenson's rhapsody on the pleasure of maps anticipates the sentiments of "My First Book," in which he writes, "I am told there are people who do not care for maps, and find it hard to believe. The names, the shapes of the woodlands, the courses of the roads and rivers, the prehistoric footsteps of man still distinctly traceable up hill and down dale. . . . [H]ere is an inexhaustible fund of interest for any man with eyes to see" ("My First Book," 279). In accounts such as these, the map is less an accompaniment or illustration for a text, than a text itself, which offers the reader a "fund of interest." Significantly, the delighted perusal of the map in *An Inland Voyage* provides a substitute for an unsatisfactory work of fiction, "the current novel," of which "I never could bear more than three instalments; and even the second was a disappointment" (*Inland Voyage*, 89). One might say that at this stage of his career, the map was the material basis for

Stevenson's preference for travel writing over fiction; when he turned to fiction, he would again incorporate the map to ensure that his novel was not a disappointment. His paradoxical remark "the less I saw of the novel, the better I liked it" (89) anticipates his preference for concise, streamlined narratives, jettisoning the triple-decker beloved by Victorians.

Yet this preoccupation with maps is by no means evidence of a well-planned journey. Rather, the map gives an opportunity for childlike fantasy and play, as "we thumbed our charts on those evenings, with the blankest unconcern. We cared not a fraction for this place or that. We started at the sheet as children listen to their rattle" (*Inland Voyage*, 89). Hence, as the random, carefree voyage ends, Stevenson concludes with philosophic wisdom that "the most beautiful adventures are not those we go to seek" (107). In both its random structure and its carefree approach to travel, *An Inland Voyage* is thus a refutation of the profit motive, a denial of the logic of late-Victorian capitalism, which judges a man's life and activity by how much he produces, accumulates, or consumes. Yet the escape is a temporary one, for "to the civilised man there must come, sooner, or later, a desire for civilization" (106), and so traveling is recognized by Stevenson as a temporary distraction from (or deferral of) the reality, the urge "to get to work" (106). In Stevenson's case, getting to work meant writing up the narrative, passing the bodily experiences through the fictional techniques of the imagination. Although the reward of his labours was not as profitable as Stevenson had hoped, the travel book laid the foundation stone (3) on which Stevenson the architect-author would construct his edifice of fiction.[24]

The reviews of *An Inland Voyage* pointed not to the excitement or appeal of the journey but to many of the attractive features of Stevenson's style, which is perhaps best summed up in the last word of Sidney Colvin's review: "Charm." George Meredith, one of the acclaimed late-Victorian stylists, affirmed that Stevenson's "writing is of the rare kind which is naturally simple yet picked and choice. It is literature." Yet in the reviews there were repeated references to a certain aimless quality to the narrative and objections to the bohemian persona presented by Stevenson. A reviewer for the *Saturday Review* wrote that "his drift becomes sometimes so ambiguous that possibly we may be misled as to his meaning. . . . He lets his mind follow its wayward impulses as he lets his canoe glide downwards with the eddies of the streams." Colvin's review used the same term to criticize the narrator's errant behavior, describing the author's pose as "wayward and socially rebellious, with a rebelliousness much tempered by humour," while an Indian reviewer from the *Allahabad Pioneer* objected to the "affectation founded on the faddling hedonism" and the reviewer from the *Examiner* detected a "Bohemianism . . . too determined and ostentatious."[25] Stevenson's response was to refine his style and prune the excesses of bohemian philosophy from his next travel narrative, *Travels with a Donkey,* in an effort to eliminate what Meredith termed "Osric's vein" in the narrative.

While *Travels with a Donkey in the Cevennes* offers in some respects a continuation of the bohemian vacation from the pressures of respectable, commercialized existence, Stevenson balances the freedom of the unstructured journey with a new focus to his narrative and a clearer sense of a "plotted" journey. In general, Stevenson expresses less resentment and criticism about the norms of bourgeois society and its oppressive effects on the imagination. His companion is no longer an aristocratic male colleague but a beast of burden with whom Stevenson establishes a close if ambivalent relationship. Whereas *An Inland Voyage* features male camaraderie between "Cigarette" and "Arethusa," the strong female presence in *Travels* is far from being treated on terms of equality (see chapter 2).

A new anxiety about his commercial status creeps into *Travels with a Donkey:* in the earlier narrative, Stevenson had accepted with good humor and even pleasure the local people's mistaking of him and his companion for "pedlars"—indeed, this contributes to the process of his "becoming a more and more romantic figure" (27). One chapter is entitled "We Are Pedlars," while the succeeding one continues the theme with "The Travelling Merchant," and there is a ready willingness to accept the nomination, as when one landlady asks, "These gentlemen are pedlars?" (31), after which the narrator observes, "We began to think we might be pedlars, after all" (31). Stevenson then humorously switches his old identity for the new one, accepting the commercial role even though it involves a decline in social status: "You see what it is to be a gentleman—I beg your pardon, what it is to be a pedlar" (32), and he adds, "On the whole, I was not much hurt at being taken for a pedlar" (36).

By contrast, in *Travels with a Donkey,* Stevenson shows considerable irritation at being mistaken for a traveling merchant in this way. On one occasion, an elderly traveler calls him back; Stevenson writes, "The old gentleman had forgot to ask the pedlar what he sold, and wished to remedy this neglect. I told him sternly, 'Nothing.' 'Nothing?' cried he. I repeated 'Nothing,' and made off. It's odd to think of, but perhaps I thus became as inexplicable to the old man as he had been to me" (222). On the one hand, Stevenson evidently resents the insulting assumption that he has something to sell and wishes to reaffirm his class status as a gentleman-traveler. On the other, one might detect a note of sadness at being outside the realm of the commercial marketplace—"I thus became . . . inexplicable." Reflecting Stevenson's growing awareness, circa 1879, of the need to sell his writing to make a living, as well as his shame at being unable to support himself financially, the text relates that he is passed by "an empty carriage" and hailed by a carriage driver who "like the rest of the world, was sure I was a pedlar; but, unlike others, he was sure of what I had to sell" (228). This certainty of having something to sell is one that Stevenson would like to share.

Although, as Emma Letley states of *Travels,* "It reached a wider audience than had *An Inland Voyage,* and on the whole the critical reception was more favourable," the book was far from being a commercial success.[26] As Stevenson wrote with manifest disappointment about *Travels* to his cousin Bob, "My book is through the press. It has good passages, I can say no more. . . . Whether the damned public—But that's all one; I've got thirty quid for it, and should have had fifty."[27] The discrepancy between the dedicatory reference to the "generous patron" and the private reference to the "damned public" is jarring, to say the least. Presumably, the first was written in hopeful expectation of profit from his literary adventures, the latter penned in disillusionment at this hope being thwarted.

Stevenson's father—whom he hoped to impress with the success of his writings—was among the first and severest critics of *Travels with a Donkey:* though praising its "strong core of facts" (probably not the praise Stevenson most wished to hear), Thomas Stevenson objected to "three or four irreverent uses of the name of God which offend me and must offend many others" and chastised his son's "absurdity in not letting me see your proof sheets"—a comment that anticipated the censoring (and censorious) role that he would play in altering or withholding later works, especially *The Amateur Emigrant.*[28] Grant Allen, writing in the *Fortnightly Review,* objected both to Stevenson's harsh treatment of his donkey and to the aloof, hedonistic tone that Allen detected in its pages: "He and his donkey move in philosophic indifferentism up and down the Cevennes, and the remainder of the moral or material universe, with no other determination than to enjoy life themselves, each after his kind, and help others by telling the story of their enjoyment."[29]

Crucially, then, Stevenson's real-life travels—the trips he made in France and Belgium, by canoe and donkey—were viewed in hindsight as random, unprofitable, and wasteful journeys, involving a pose of adventure. It is not difficult to understand why Stevenson ultimately elected to erase the published accounts of these journeys from the record. Lacking "exciting incidents," the travel narratives failed to acquire the mass readership required for the commodity-text and its attendant profit. By contrast, the imaginary journey in *Treasure Island,* rooted in a map and narrated by Stevenson's fictional protagonist Jim Hawkins, is at once materialistic, commercial, and packed with "striking incident . . . to satisfy the nameless longings of the reader."[30] This new dependence on the map—valued no longer as a childish plaything but as an essential guide to success—points to a dramatic contrast between the unstructured journeys of the travel narratives and the disciplined, profit-driven venture of Jim Hawkins, Dr. Livesey, and Squire Trelawney, and of course the pirates, in *Treasure Island.* Crucial to this transition from dilettante writer to professional author, the map gives direction both to Stevenson's fiction and to Jim's journey, leading both to a carefully concealed treasure: a new audience of "boys." The map is an example of what Daly terms "the object which becomes a commodity simply because it becomes desirable for consumers, and is thereby drawn into economic exchange." Ironically, this economic value could be realized only as a result of the nexus of an imaginary journey and a small group of influential men, including several Scotsmen: his father, Thomas Stevenson; Alexander Japp; James Henderson, the owner of *Young Folks;* and Andrew Lang, whose early review of *Treasure Island* would be instrumental in bringing about the romance revival, which, as Daly argues, created "a publishing boom that looked forward to the mass-publishing trends of the twentieth century."[31] Hence, the bond of imagined boyhood, cemented by the commercial logo of the map, would be a determining factor in the commodification of Stevenson's art.

## Cruising to Treasure Island

Stevenson's fictional voyage to the land of boyhood, chaperoned by his stepson, Lloyd Osbourne, is indeed the journey that led him to literary treasure. Yet boyhood is an authorial ruse by which grown men are encouraged to participate in what Stevenson dubbed "a story for boys." One of the most significant effects of the late-Victorian romance pioneered by Stevenson in *Treasure Island* is this emergence of a readership that allows adult men to return imaginatively to boyhood. In this vein, H. Rider Haggard, who wrote *King Solomon's Mines* (1885) in a spirit of emulation of *Treasure Island,* dedicated his novel, using the persona of Allan Quatermain, "To all the big and little boys who read it."[32]

Identifying Osbourne as the original auditor of *Treasure Island,* Stevenson writes of an unexpected addition to this select circle: "I had counted on one boy, I found I had two in my audience. My father caught fire at once with all the romance and childishness of his original nature" ("My First Book," 280). The image of his father's enthusiasm contrasts sharply with Thomas's earlier, and subsequent, acts of criticism and censorship. In "A Gossip on Romance"—contemporary with *Treasure Island*—Stevenson argues that "reading . . . should be absorbing and voluptuous; we should gloat over a book, be rapt clean out of ourselves."[33] This theory of enraptured reading is vividly illustrated by Thomas Stevenson's impassioned response to his son's first novel: "[I]n *Treasure Island* he recognized something kindred to his own imagination; it was his kind of picturesque; and he not only heard with delight the daily chapter, but set himself actively to collaborate" (280). Thus, from its very inception, the power of *Treasure Island* to address adult males—even the stern patriarch, Thomas Stevenson—as boys willing to collaborate, by appealing to the childishness of their nature, was crucial to its success.

The pivotal role of the logo-map—inducing grown men to become adventurous boys eager to abandon their responsible duties and go in quest of buried treasure and imperial plunder—appears in the story through the excited reactions of the characters in the presence of the map. The map emerges as an object of desire with Jim and his mother's search of Billy Bones's possessions; in a kind of violation of Bones's corpse, Jim "tore open his shirt at the neck, and there, sure enough, hanging to a bit of tarry string, which I cut with his own gully, we found the key."[34] Having opened the chest, the pair find "a bundle tied up in oilcloth, and looking like papers, and a canvas bag, that gave forth, at a touch, the jingle of gold" (32). The proximity of the bundle to gold is significant, being the only indication that it has economic value. As Jim's mother counts out the sum owed to her by the dead pirate, Jim's attention is focused on the bundle, and he states, "'I'll take this to square the count' . . . picking up the oilskin packet" (33).

Jim's boyish fascination with the material form of this bundle is soon imitated by Squire Trelawney and Dr. Livesey, adult men who will accompany him on the quest for treasure. Faced with the oilskin packet, "the doctor looked it all over, as if his fingers were itching to open it" (41). Jim states of the map that though it was to him "incomprehensible, it filled the squire and Dr Livesey with delight. 'Livesey' said the squire, 'you will give up this wretched practice at once. Tomorrow I start for Bristol'" (44). Though Stevenson identifies *Treasure Island* as "a story for boys," the boy in the story is at first excluded from the pleasures of the map—he finds it incomprehensible—which addresses an audience of grown men. Their juvenile fantasy of adventure leads to prophesies of immeasurable wealth: "We'll have favourable winds, a quick passage, and not the least difficulty in finding the spot, and money to eat—to roll in—to play duck and drake with ever after" (44). One might say that the map—as the narrative secret at the heart of Stevenson's ideal romance—has the power to transform men into boys.

The map is an object that gives material form to a distant location in the novel. In "A Gossip on Romance," Stevenson writes that "some places speak distinctly," "certain coasts are set apart for shipwreck," it being the writer's task "to invent appropriate games for them . . . to fit them with the proper story."[35] The map is itself a kind of place, a representation of an island that has yet to be visited, and Stevenson's task is similarly to find the proper story to fit the map. As he states in "My First Book," "I had written it [*Treasure Island*] up to the map. The map was the chief part of my plot" (282). Created by Stevenson and Osbourne as an imaginary location, the task of the novel is to make it seem real, and the map is crucial in achieving this effect of authenticity. Appearing in the frontispiece of *Treasure Island,* the map is no longer a "coloured drawing" (279) produced from a "shilling box of water-colours" (278) but is instead a vividly detailed graphic image that draws on the resources of the capitalist mode of production. As such, the map contains the commodity status of the text it prefaces. Indeed, as Stevenson reveals in "My First Book," the map that the reader consumes in 1883 is not the same one originally drawn by the author. Stevenson relates how he too was forced to settle for a substitute when the original was lost: "I heard nothing of the map. I wrote and asked; was told it had never been received, and sat aghast" (282). This loss compelled Stevenson "with a pair of compasses [to] painfully design a map to suit the data. I did it, and the map was drawn again in my father's office. . . . But somehow it was never *Treasure Island* to me" (283). In contrast to the map that inspired the text and its narrative of journey—the creation that was a source of pleasure—the new map was painfully designed, a laborious process that had to mimic the journey already inscribed in the text. In preparation for its assimilation into the commodity-text published by Cassell, Stevenson's map had to be copied in a form that would make it a logo-map, infinitely reproducible as the frontispiece of *Treasure Island.*[36] The loss of authenticity accompanying this process is registered in Stevenson's remark that his father "elaborately *forged* the signature of Captain Flint and the sailing directions of Billy Bones" (283; original emphasis). It is this "forgery" that eventually constructs the community of readers of *Treasure Island.*

The potent fantasy appeal of the map to its community of readers is vividly captured by W. E. Henley's vignette of one Professor Beesley, discovered by his family while secreted in his study, "his history books thrown by . . . his Herbert Spencer all forgotten, sunk to the throat in 'Treasure Island.' He had a magnifier at his eye, and through that magnifier he was (historian-like) a-studying the map of Captain Flint." The reference to the studious Beesley absorbed in the perusal of the map suggests the power of the story to make fiction as compelling as fact—Henley states that Beesley might have been studying the map of Hadrian's campaign—but it also discloses the key to the romance's success in the secret cartographical pleasure of the text as disclosed in this Victorian "study."[37] The compelling object of the map links author (Stevenson), narrator (Jim), and reader (Beesley), all of whom are deeply absorbed by its secret pleasures.

Martin Green has commented on the importance of the map to "changing the conventions of adventure" in observing that "the story began with the drawing of the map and . . . it was told to his stepson, with his father's collaboration. It is palpably the fantasy of men-being-boys."[38] While Green explores the ideological force of this fantasy for the growth of empire, he does not emphasize its commercial profitability in the literary marketplace. Nicholas Daly has analyzed the rise of romance within a late-capitalist context of mass literature and brilliantly surveys "the role of the new fiction in modernizing the literary market." Pointing to analogies between subgenres such as mummy fiction and "the alienated conditions of production under capitalism," Daly's analysis helps to situate Stevenson and his peers at the vanguard of literary and cultural change in the fin de siècle. Yet Daly does not address the key role of a juvenile audience in shaping this new literary market, even though he notes that literary culture "was effectively becoming a 'niche market'" such that "writers had to suit their work to the carefully targeted readership of a particular periodical, and to trim the length of their text to suit that periodical's format." Interestingly, none of the journals that Daly mentions was targeted at a juvenile audience, even though such journals were among the most important publishing venues for the romance revival.[39] For example, the *Boy's Own Paper,* founded in 1879, published stories by G. A. Henty, R. M. Ballantyne, Arthur Conan Doyle, and W. H. G. Kingston.[40] *Treasure Island* was the first of three adventure novels that Stevenson published in *Young Folks,* followed by *The Black Arrow* and *Kidnapped.*

Jacqueline Rose has explored the immense profitability of children's literature, focusing on the lucrative history of *Peter Pan,* authored by Stevenson's friend and fellow Scot J. M. Barrie. Rose writes of the late-Victorian "expansiveness in the field of children's books" and points out that "books, no less than theatre, were part of a visual display in which children offered up some of the richest potential for the trade. The late nineteenth-century child was 'grist to the mill' of the miscellaneous bookseller." Rose points to the history of the Victorian book trade, noting that "in 1896, *The Bookman* added a special section of children's books to its Christmas Supplement . . . which, together with popular magazines and fairy tales, were the most commercially viable products of the market." Rose points out that "the association of children and trade is, however, a dangerous one," raising the threat of exploitation and even prostitution. The preoccupation of *Treasure Island* with money is disturbing in the context of the child reader, for, as Rose argues, "money is something impure.

It circulates and passes from hand to hand (children are warned that coins are *dirty*)."[41]

*Treasure Island* is, one hardly needs to point out, centrally concerned with the pursuit of money. The purpose of the map in *Treasure Island*—as it would be in Haggard's *King Solomon's Mines*—is to lead the author, the central characters, and the reader to the buried treasure at the heart of the story. Henley indeed stated boldly at the opening of his review of *Treasure Island*, "Buried treasure is one of the very foundations of romance." What has been neglected is how far Stevenson actively pursued the profit of an audience of boys even while manipulating his texts to appeal to men also. If Stevenson had missed commercial success with his previous works of travel writing, this was because he had not only underestimated the extent to which "grown men . . . have the sentiment of treasure-hunting" but also overlooked the reader's desire for a map—a carefully tailored (indeed, commodified) secret—to arouse and direct that readerly pleasure. Moreover, the map would provide a logo for its community of readers.[42] Having previously guided his reader through random sentimental journeys—and he recognized that "the child is somewhat deaf to the sentimental"—Stevenson had profited little from his excursions because he excluded the crucial motivation of profit, the romance of treasure, which for the boyish reader—or "The Hesitating Purchaser," as he titled the prefatory verse to *Treasure Island* (7)—was an essential lure if money was to change hands, the purchase to be made.[43]

The practical issue facing Stevenson was how to transform the map from a childish plaything into an object demanding serious scrutiny by professional male readers. This interest is partly acquired once the map is identified with profit—the squire and Dr. Livesey are, of course, excited less by the map's aesthetic qualities than by its practical use as a guide to wealth: "money to eat." In this respect, the most important part of the map's script is "in the same red ink, and in a small, neat hand, very different from the captain's tottery characters, these words—'Bulk of treasure here'" (*Treasure Island*, 43–44). The map, moreover, is a key object in the expansion of empire, providing a grid of knowledge and power that allows the colonizing peoples to claim possession of the colonized. As Bill Ashcroft writes, "maps and mapping are dominant practices of colonial and post-colonial cultures. Colonization itself is often consequent on a voyage of 'discovery,' a bringing into being of 'undiscovered' lands. The process of discovery is reinforced by the construction of maps, whose existence is a means of textualizing the spatial reality of the other, naming or, in almost all cases, renaming spaces in a symbolic and literal act of mastery and control."[44]

In a crucial passage from *Treasure Island,* Jim's narrative indicates how his imaginative immersion in the map prepares him for the exploits of colonization and expropriation: "I brooded by the hour together over the map, all the details of which I well remember. Sitting by the fire in the housekeeper's room, I approached that island in my fancy, from every possible direction; I explored every acre of its surface; I climbed a thousand times to that tall hill they call the Spy-glass, and from the top enjoyed the most wonderful and changing prospects" (47). The map is the source of access to the island and thus participates in what Green terms "the energizing myth of English imperialism."[45] Yet as a fantasy object, it mediates between the reader and the actual location, inviting an imaginative participation in an adventure that precedes "our actual adventures" (47). Jim's complete absorption by the map anticipates Stevenson's similar surrender to the pleasures of the map in "My First Book" as he recalls that "the shape of it took my fancy beyond expression; it contained harbours that pleased me like sonnets; and with the unconsciousness of the predestined, I ticketed my performance *Treasure Island*" (279). Even as Stevenson emphasizes the poetic faculty of his fancy, his allusion to the production as a performance for which one might require a ticket draws attention to the commercial potential of his new project, a profit value that is predestined. The subsequent phrase "fund of interest" reveals the economic advantages of the map, both for his characters and for the author (similarly, it recalls the "funds of entertainment" that Stevenson expected from John Silver).

The efficacy of the map as a tool for bridging the gap between child and adult readers and adventurers and establishing the commodity-text derives in part from its role in imperialist and nationalist projects. In *The Silverado Squatters,* Stevenson comments on the role of the map in producing the idea of national identity: "Scotland is indefinable; it has no unity except on the map. . . . Yet let us meet in some far country, and, whether we hail from the braes of Manor or the braes of Mar, some ready-made affection joins us on the instant."[46] As

Benedict Anderson writes, however, the map became of even greater importance as the European powers began to emerge as imperial nations: Anderson examines "three institutions of power which, although invented before the mid nineteenth century, changed their form and function as the colonized zones entered the age of mechanical reproduction. These three institutions were the census, the map, and the museum." Mapping was the means of "'filling in' the boxes [which] was to be accomplished by explorers, surveyors, and military forces."[47]

Pointing out that the map became a crucial instrument both in the construction of imperial identity and "for the anticolonial nationalisms being born," Anderson argues that the possibility of mass reproduction is what gave the map its charisma. Immediately recognizable as a logo, the map could even dispense with much of its informational content in that "all explanatory glosses could be summarily removed: lines of longitude and latitude, place names, signs for rivers, seas, and mountains, neighbours. Pure sign, no longer compass to the world. In this shape, the map entered an infinitely reproducible series, available for transfer to posters, official seals, letterheads, magazine and textbook covers, tablecloths, and hotel walls. Instantly recognizable, everywhere visible, the logo-map penetrated deep into the popular imagination."[48]

However, this transformation of the map into a logo (which occurs through reproduction) also brings a sense of loss. The original map discovered by Jim had all the lines and place-names "and every particular that would be needed to bring a ship to a safe anchorage upon its shores" (43). Replete with information, this map is later replaced by another, which lacks its detail: as it is handed to Silver, Jim states, "I knew he was doomed to disappointment. This was not the map we found in Billy Bones's chest, but an accurate copy, complete in all things . . . with the single exception of the red crosses and the written notes" (*Treasure Island,* 74). The missing information is, of course, precisely what is required to locate the treasure. The very act of reproduction necessary to make the logo-map entails a loss of "aura" that leads to disappointment. Stevenson, as we have seen, was also disappointed with the map that had to be produced as a substitute for the original ("My First Book," 283).

Hence, what distinguishes his new effort is its strictly limited appeal to a specialized audience or class of readers, a choice that in turn dictates the style of the work. Stevenson had previously been working on a collection of "crawlers" *(New Arabian Nights)* with his wife, Fanny; his new story, as he recalls in "My First Book," "was to be a story for boys; no need of psychology or fine writing. . . . Women were excluded" ("My First Book," 193, 195). This abrupt dismissal of women from the scene of the fiction is apparently a declaration of Stevenson's new fictional manifesto, and it foreshadows the extent to which women are excluded from (or at least marginalized in) most of his fictional ventures.[49] In this case, the woman—at least, the invading mother—is seen as a threat to the romance of the boyish collaboration with Lloyd and so must be excluded from it. This collaboration—which Stevenson would continue far beyond his "joint volume" with Fanny or W. E. Henley—thus provided both a return to childhood and an escape from domesticity and marriage, fulfilling the function of what Wayne Koestenbaum terms the "bachelor literature" of the late nineteenth century, which "enacted flight from wedlock and from the narrative conventions of bourgeois realism."[50]

Stevenson inevitably foregrounds the gender-specific appeal of the work for his imaginary society of readers. Such an imagined community of map-obsessed men was precisely the audience created by Stevenson's commodity-text, inspiring both admiration and emulation in fellow writers such as Henley, Haggard, Lang, and Kipling. Marking the location of an imaginary boundary separating the domestic domain of women—as wives, mothers, readers—from the external spaces of male empire and adventure, the map of this romance inevitably takes on a specifically masculine (indeed, homoerotic) significance.[51] Yet membership in this community required a willingness to—as Stevenson did with Lloyd—"unbend a little" ("My First Book," 279), that is, surrender to the childish pleasures of imaginary treasure hunting. In their reviews of *Treasure Island,* Stevenson's friends W. E. Henley and Andrew Lang both commented on the novel's likely appeal to men as well as to boys. Henley indeed wrote, "Primarily it is a book for boys. . . . But it is a book for boys which will be delightful to all grown men who have the sentiment of treasure-hunting and are touched with the true spirit of the Spanish Main." After asking, "[W]ill 'Treasure Island' be as popular with boys as it is sure to be with men who retain something of the boy?" Lang had no hesitation answering in the affirmative.[52]

Yet not all adult male readers were willing to "unbend," to participate in the shared fiction of boyish adventure. The possibility of resistance to joining this community founded on boyhood, romantic adventure, and profit was revealed the following year, 1884, in Henry James's influential essay "The Art of Fiction." In response, Stevenson wrote "A Humble Remonstrance," an essay in which he not only advocates the claims of romance against realism but also defines treasure hunting as an appropriate subject for romance and identifies the lucrative potential of juvenile fantasy. In doing so, Stevenson would define the limits of his community of readers, according to their ability to enter such fantasy.

Though James praises "the delightful story of *Treasure Island*" because "it appears to me to have succeeded wonderfully in what it attempts," he also indicates a refusal to fully enter its fictional world, pointing out that "I have been a child, but I have never been on a quest for a buried treasure."[53] In his famous rejoinder in "A Humble Remonstrance," Stevenson describes James's statement as a "wilful paradox; for if he has never been on a quest for buried treasure, it can be demonstrated that he has never been a child." Without disputing that "neither Mr James nor the author of the work in question has ever, in the fleshly sense, gone questing after gold," Stevenson identifies the fantasy of such a quest as the defining fact of childhood, a literary map from which James is thenceforth barred: "There never was a child (unless Master James) but has hunted gold, and been a pirate, and a military commander, and a bandit in the mountains." James's lack of a childhood disqualifies him, in Stevenson's account, from the community of men committed to romance, those who, he relates, "have ardently desired and fondly imagined the details of such a life in youthful daydreams." Stevenson's admission—in 1884, only a year after *Treasure Island* has been published in volume form—that he has calculatedly exploited these daydreams of boys and childlike men for profit discloses the commercial ambitions of his commodity-text: "[T]he author, counting upon that, and well aware (cunning and low-minded man!) that this class of interest, having been frequently treated, finds a readily accessible and beaten road to the sympathies of the reader, addressed himself throughout to the building up and circumstantiation of this boyish dream."[54]

Stevenson's ironic reference to himself as "cunning and low-minded" indicates that he has left behind his high-minded and unpopular renunciation of

Victorian capitalism and bourgeois labor in *An Inland Voyage.* But it also reveals the growth of confidence in his ability to secure his share of the market of readers by exploiting the "boyish dream" of adventure. In the preface to *An Inland Voyage,* Stevenson writes, "It occurred to me that I might not only be the first to read these pages, but the last as well; that I might have pioneered this very smiling tract of country all in vain, and find not a soul to follow in my steps." Depicting the book as a journey through a "tract of country," Stevenson fears that his literary "map" will find no followers (or readers) and so, "in a sort of panic terror . . . I rushed into this Preface, which is no more than an advertisement for readers."[55] The resort to advertisement reflects Stevenson's anxiety to commodify his work, that is, to gain commercial rewards for it. In 1884, Stevenson was assured that the "sympathies of the reader" would be translated into profits: no longer the "generous patron," the reader had become the "hesitating purchaser," whose economic investment in the narrative would have to be secured by its artful manipulation of fantasy.[56]

By recycling his ultimately rejected travel writings, Stevenson wrote a book that was not only "a composite of earlier books in that tradition" but also, I would argue, a significant innovation, dovetailing the classic adventure tale with the mass-market appeal of the commodity-text.[57] In his address "To the Hesitating Purchaser," Stevenson presents the outline of his novel expressly as an advertisement to attract a consumer. Stevenson wonders

> If sailor tales to sailor tunes,
> Storm and adventure, heat and cold,
> If schooners, islands, and maroons
> And Buccaneers and buried Gold,
> And all the old romance, retold
> Exactly in the ancient way,
> Can please, as me they pleased of old,
> The wiser youngsters of to-day. (7)

By flattering his reader and publicizing his wares to a juvenile public, Stevenson seeks to secure his share of a readership that had many alternatives from which to choose.[58]

Yet under the guise of this address to "youngsters," *Treasure Island* is a text that does the cultural work of producing desire in its adult male readers, a desire that the text rerouted from potentially subversive masculine desire toward the "innocent" object of adventure and buried treasure. Stevenson—who wrote in "A Note on Realism" that the romancer "must . . . suppress much and omit more"—produces romance as an art of sublimation, in which desire is buried with the treasure and subsequently excavated by its adult male readers posing as boys, or its boy readers posing as pirate-adventurers.[59] For the "secret" of *Treasure Island* is, after all, that there is no secret: its commitment to profit seeking is blatant throughout, its divestment from the "moral purity" ethos of childhood all but absolute. The treasure, though referred to as "hidden" and "buried" (42), is declared at the outset of the narrative as having already been found (11). Hence, as the pirates discover when their search party stumbles upon "a great excavation, not very recent" (197), the promise of discovering the treasure has always been illusory, as the gold has moved into a kind of symbolic circulation demanded by the novel as commodity-text: "[T]he cache had been found and rifled: the seven hundred thousand pounds were gone" (197).[60] The map, which has been sought and killed for as a valuable commodity with a direct link to the treasure, retains traces of its status as a useless artifact, one of a schoolboy's "coloured drawings" ("My First Book," 279).

Stevenson's artful combination of mapping, boyhood fantasy, and buried treasure is thus a skillfully commodified package, a lure designed to convert the "hesitating purchaser" into an active consumer. As he wrote to Henley on August 24, 1881, "I am now on another lay for the moment, purely owing to Sam [Lloyd Osbourne] this one; but I believe there's more coin in it than in any amount of crawlers. . . . If this don't fetch the kids, why, they have gone rotten since my day."[61] What would "fetch the kids" is that the narrator is one of them: as Green observes, "what is strikingly new about it [*Treasure Island*] in a generic way is that a boy plays the leading part and tells the story."[62] Stevenson's conviction that there is "more coin" in *Treasure Island* than the "crawlers"—referring to his collaboration with Fanny on *New Arabian Nights*—reflects the greater commercial potential of collaborating with his stepson. His indebtedness to Lloyd, the original "boy" reader, was evidently profit driven; in the following month (September 1881), Stevenson wrote to Henley with enthusiasm,

"I'll make this boy's book business pay; but I have to make a beginning. When I'm done with—*Young Folks,* I'll try Routledge or some one."[63]

In "A Humble Remonstrance," Stevenson describes "himself [as] more or less grown up," a fact that led him to "admit character, within certain limits, into his design."[64] The construction of this persona, "the boyish man," author of boys' books for men, appears to have been a carefully calculated move to exploit a growing market in fiction and bring to an end the "succession of defeats" of Stevenson's early travel writings, much as Stevenson's public image, increasingly associated with his adventure stories, demonstrated "the compulsion . . . to live out something of an adventure himself."[65] There is indeed a vast amount of "coin" in the story—such as the "jingling of gold" in Billy Bones's canvas bag, which serves to reveal "coins of all countries and sizes—doubloons, and louis-d'ors, and guineas, and pieces of eight, and I know not what besides, all shaken together at random" (32). Far more spectacularly, of course, there is the "coin" hoarded by Flint and discovered in Ben Gunn's cave, which is "like Billy Bones's hoard for the diversity of coinage, but so much larger and so much more varied that I think I never had more pleasure than in sorting them. English, French, Spanish, Portuguese, Georges, and Louises, doubloons and double guineas and moidores and sequins, the pictures of all the kings of Europe for the last hundred years . . . nearly every variety of money in the world must, I think, have found a place in that collection" (204). This passage registers the treasure as a map of the pirates' travels and adventures throughout the world, plundering all ships and nations with equal avarice. The treasure is thus marked not only as the profit of travel—which will become the reward of the journey for the members of the *Hispaniola* expedition—but also as the profit of collaborative project. Jim reveals this point to the reader: "All of us had an ample share of the treasure, and used it wisely or foolishly, according to our natures" (208).[66]

However, the boyhood romance ends not with a dream but with a nightmare, as the desired destination promised by the map becomes the last place on earth one wishes to return to. Disillusionment with the outcome of the journey is a feature that carries over from Stevenson's travel narratives and their emphasis on disappointment, as is evidenced by Jim's confession, "Oxen and wain-ropes would not bring me back again to that accursed island; and the worst dreams that ever I have are when I hear the surf booming about its coasts, or start upright in bed, with the sharp voice of Captain Flint still ringing in my ears: 'Pieces of eight! Pieces of eight!'" (208). The acquisition of profit, which has been the sole purpose of travel, makes further travel unnecessary and, in Jim's case, abhorrent. But what if—as Jim tells the reader on the opening page of his narrative, as an explanation for withholding the precise location of the island—"there is still treasure not yet lifted" (11)? A reviewer in the *Academy* gave Stevenson credit for daring "to depict an island the sole attraction of which lies in its hidden treasure," and this attraction surely retains some of its potency at the very end of the narrative: "The bar silver and the arms still lie, for all that I know, where Flint buried them; and certainly they shall lie there for me" (208).[67] Jim disavows any desire to return in search of this treasure, but note the ambivalence of his words: "certainly they shall lie there for me" means both "I will leave them lying there" and "they lie there awaiting me (or awaiting my return)." Despite the ship captain's statement, "I don't think you and me'll go to sea again" (202), the possibility of another quest for treasure has not been convincingly ruled out by Jim's narrative. Though Stevenson does not leave the door open for a sequel—as he flagrantly would at the end of *Kidnapped*—he certainly conceives of further installments in the "boy's book business."

Thus, the economic lesson of *Treasure Island* is that there is no more compelling reason for travel than the search for treasure—just as there is no more powerful motive for writing romance than commercial success. If each of the *Hispaniola*'s crew gains an "ample share of the treasure," then the same can be said of Stevenson. Although he wrote to Henley in September 1881 of his disappointment that the publication of *Treasure Island* in *Young Folks* did not realize the sum he had hoped—"The 100 pounds fell through, or dwindled at least into somewhere about 30 pounds"—Stevenson, eighteen months later, was triumphantly celebrating the sale of *Treasure Island* to Cassell in language worthy of John Silver himself: "There has been offered for *Treasure Island*—how much, do you suppose? . . . A hundred pounds, all alive oh! A hundred jingling, tingling, golden, minted quid. Is not this wonderful?" Stevenson's revealing postscript to this letter to his parents—"It has been, for me, a Treasure Island verily"—alerts us to the double valence of the novel's title, as the novel proved but the first of Stevenson's many literary islands to yield him profit.[68] Moreover, other benefits accrued from the story, as Henley observed in a letter to Stevenson: "The thing is that 'Treasure Island' has sent your name sky high and tripled the value of your work; . . . [it] will make more commissions for you than I know how to handle." Indeed, Stevenson's stock, as Henley pointed out, had risen: his initials, RLS—initially mistaken for "Real Leslie Stephen" when they appeared beneath his contributions in *The Cornhill*—had become uniquely his, the "logo" of a going concern, a valuable commodity with a suddenly inflated value.[69] No longer a drifting, recusant, impecunious "pedlar" but rather a well-paid pied piper of literature, Stevenson reveled in his newfound power to "fetch the kids," which he would realize in subsequent publications in *Young Folks.* Stevenson's plans to exact the reward from the public—which he called "the beast whom we feed" (299)—helped him to reject the condescending suggestion of some reviewers that he abandon the quest for buried treasure.[70] Publicly judging that Stevenson's treasure-hunting fiction was stronger "than even [his] humorous and sentimental journeying," Lang discreetly endorsed Stevenson's transition from travel writer to successful author for boys yet urged, "After this romance for boys he must give us a novel for men and women."[71] Even a proponent of romance, such as Lang, who helped to create "an expanded middle-class readership" for his friend, thus fell back into the hierarchy of the novel as a more mature form than the romance.[72] Similarly, the reviewer for the *Graphic,* who found "passages in this romance surpassing in power anything that Mr Stevenson has yet done," concluded by stating, "Yet we want no more boys' books from Mr Stevenson."[73] Nevertheless, Stevenson reaped the rewards of his conviction that "even when a map is not all the plot, as it was in *Treasure Island,* it will be found to be a mine of suggestion" ("My First Book," 284). Still lured by the prospect of the map, Stevenson's subsequent journeys into fiction, such as *The Black Arrow* (1883/1888), *Kidnapped* (1886), and *David Balfour* (1893) articulated this dismissal of the critics' short-sighted advice. Stevenson's ensuing successes in romance indicated not a refusal to grow up or a desire to escape but a clear-sighted vision that, according to his chart, there was indeed profit still to be lifted from *Treasure Island.*

# FOUR

## "Mr. Betwixt-and-Between"

### History, Travel, and Narrative Indeterminacy in *Kidnapped*

FOLLOWING THE SUCCESS of *Treasure Island,* published in volume form in 1883, Stevenson relished the prospect of writing another "story for boys," this time set in the aftermath of the Jacobite uprising of 1745. In March 1885, he wrote to W. E. Henley, giving details of his current project: "I have a great story on hand; boy's story: a crackler: very picturesque I think. As at present advised, it would be called somewhat thus: '(*Kidnapped:* continuing) memoirs of the adventures of *David Shaw;* how he was kidnapped and cast away.'" Stevenson continued, "I have proposed to Henderson to print from the sheets and to let the book appear when it is about half way through. . . . [T]he book as you may smell for yourself is to be (say) half as long again as *Treasure Island.* What would Cassell be up to?"[1] The references to James Henderson, editor of *Young Folks* (which had published *Treasure Island* in serial form in 1881–82) and Cassell (which had published the novel in volume form), indicate Stevenson's desire to repeat the successful publication formula of his previous commodity-text. Indeed, his claim that the new work would be "half as long again" indicates hopes for even greater success.

An important continuity with *Treasure Island,* as signaled by the serial publication in *Young Folks,* is that *Kidnapped* was designed for a juvenile audience. According to Barry Menikoff, "the conviction that *Kidnapped* is a children's book derives from two major sources: its initial publication in *Young Folks* and Stevenson's own dedication-preface to the first edition, identifying the purpose of the novel: 'to steal some young gentleman's attention from his Ovid, carry him awhile into the Highlands and the last century, and pack him to bed with some engaging images to mingle with his dreams.'"[2] Yet Stevenson's emphasis on the continuity between the two novels tends to mask an important difference. Whereas *Treasure Island* was engendered by a colored drawing of a map and used materials from earlier romances, *Kidnapped* was based on an actual historical incident. Menikoff observes, "This is not to make the absurd statement that Stevenson invented nothing in *Kidnapped.* . . . But what he imagined was set within a frame of historical reality so meticulously charted that it was almost impossible to separate the invention from the history."[3] Hence, Stevenson's sources were not works of fiction but documentary materials, offering "an authentic eyewitness account of life in the Highlands at a particular historical moment." David's journey through the Highlands is not, like Jim's voyage on the *Hispaniola,* a quest for treasure; rather, it is an opportunity to examine stark differences between English and Highland culture, "to reveal and capture life in the Highlands through the refracting lens of his young and open-eyed narrator."[4]

Although Stevenson struggled with the completion of both novels, his difficulties arose from different narrative problems. Late in his life, Stevenson recalled the difficulty of finishing his first novel: "Fifteen days I stuck to it, and turned out fifteen chapters; and then, in the early paragraphs of the sixteenth, ignominiously lost hold. . . . [T]here was not one word more of *Treasure Island* in my bosom." In this case, a journey made by Stevenson to Davos helped to end his writer's block: "Arrived at my destination, down I sat one morning to the unfinished tale, and behold! it flowed from me like small talk; and in a second tide of delighted industry, and again at the rate of a chapter a day, I finished *Treasure Island.*"[5] Fittingly, for a novel in which travel provides the basis for the plot, it was a journey that allowed its completion. Moreover, the efficient mode of production, "a chapter a day," emphasizes *Treasure Island* as Stevenson's first commodity-text, produced according to the specifications of a literary market.

As this example suggests, difficulties with closure were endemic to Stevenson's literary career.[6] Yet only once did Stevenson resort to the extreme step of abandoning a narrative in midplot, leaving the story incomplete and postponing its closure to a sequel, to be written at an unspecified time in the future. Though it is usually read as a self-contained work, *Kidnapped* (1886) is in fact only the first installment of a two-part text eventually published (posthumously) as *The Adventures of David Balfour* (1895). The second part, which appeared in 1893, had a double life of its own: published serially as *David Balfour* in *Atalanta* magazine, the novel retained this title in the U.S. volume published by Scribner's. The British publisher, Cassell, however, was concerned that a novel with this title would be confused with *Kidnapped* and therefore secured Stevenson's permission to change the title to *Catriona.* Bibliographically divided into two novels, the "adventures" of David Balfour are riven by the indeterminacy of their narrator-protagonist, with all the confusion of naming and identity that this entails.[7] This chapter examines the vacillating journey of David Balfour in *Kidnapped,* which concludes with his arrival at the doors of the British Linen Company Bank in Edinburgh. Though in one sense David's journey has concluded—David has secured his inheritance by the end of *Kidnapped*—Stevenson later wrote of "my David having been left to kick his heels for more than a luster [five years] in the British Linen Company's office," recognizing that his protagonist was left in limbo.[8] Throughout Stevenson's novel, indeed, David Balfour is characterized by an indeterminacy that requires the introduction of another protagonist, Alan Breck, in order to advance the historical plot.

## Kidnapping the Novel

Anticipating the eventual confusion surrounding its textual identity, the composition of *Kidnapped* began with Stevenson expressing doubts about his ability to finish it. Stevenson wrote to his father in March 1885 about his "new boys' story (which is a very good story by the way, and which you will like, if ever I can write it, which seems almost too much to hope for. I have no name for it but only a title page . . . 'Memoirs of the Adventures of David Balfour.'"[9]

Stevenson here hints at the difficulties of composition that would return to haunt him, while his admission of the text's lack of a name indicates his difficulty in defining the identity, and the central focus, of his narrative. Reflecting his tendency to think of his works in two sections, Stevenson wrote later in the month, "I am at David again, and have just murdered James Stewart semi-historically. I am now fairly in part two: the Highland part. I don't think it will be so interesting to read, but it is curious and picturesque."[10] According to Menikoff, the "Highland part" is what signals the real originality of *Kidnapped,* as Stevenson "selected the historical novel for his design, but he gave it a deliberate twist. He chose to reproduce and conceal history, to invent a fiction that would paradoxically reveal and veil historical truth."[11] The interweaving of fiction and historical truth adds another layer to a text that features the conjunction of opposites.

This splitting of his novel into two parts anticipates problems that Stevenson would have with the form of the work as a whole (specifically, with concluding his novel). He wrote to W. E. Henley in February, "*David* sticks in the mud," while to Thomas Dixon Galpin he wrote in May that "the trouble I am having over the last chapters of *Kidnapped* is incredible. I have written one chapter seven times, and it is no great shakes now it is done."[12] These obstacles to concluding the novel proved insurmountable, and Stevenson wrote to James Henderson—editor of the periodical *Young Folks,* which had agreed to serialize the novel—advising him that the fate of the story hung in the balance: "I warn you my health is not to be trusted; I may break down again, and the cup and the lip be once again divorced. Please consider this in your own interests and do as you please. Perhaps some qualified announcement, owning the uncertainty of this vile author's health would serve your end." In May 1886, he wrote to his father with a proposed solution: "The David problem has today been decided. I am to leave the door open for a sequel if the public take to it; and this will save me from butchering a lot of good material to no purpose."[13] Significantly, David Balfour is left in limbo outside the doors of the British Linen Company Bank—on the threshold (literally) of recovering his birthright, the inheritance of the House of Shaws.

Stevenson abruptly terminates the novel with an editorial postscript that reiterates the role of the public in ensuring the continuation of the novel: "Just there, with his hand upon his fortune, the present editor inclines for the time to say farewell to David. How Alan escaped, and what was done about the murder, with a variety of other delectable particulars, may be some day set forth. That is a thing, however, that hinges on the public fancy."[14] This postscript recalls Stevenson's address to "The Hesitating Purchaser" in *Treasure Island,* as both texts are designed to create consumers for Stevenson's narrative. But whereas the address appears at the beginning of *Treasure Island,* it marks the end of *Kidnapped,* speaking to a future audience that has already invested time and money in the narrative of David's adventures.

The use of an editor who merely "inclines . . . to say farewell to David" (277) glosses over both Stevenson's deep investment in the novel and its hero, and the problems of closure that resulted from his enthusiasm (as he later wrote, "I love my Davy"). In fact, the abandoning of David was a result of necessity rather than inclination. Revealing his dependence on public approval for his novel to continue, Stevenson in effect kidnaps his own narrative, holding it for ransom until the public accepts his demands for commercial success. With this strategy, the problem of concluding the novel has not been resolved, however, only deferred to a later time. The alternative is an act of textual violence that he refers to as "butchering" his own narrative, an unthinkable recourse to literary self-destruction.[15]

As the kidnapper of his own novel, Stevenson surely plays on words by naming the cabin boy on board the *Covenant* "Ransome." Given that David is first lured away from the House of Shaws by a message delivered by Ransome, then subsequently "kidnapped" and taken away from his familiar surroundings, it might seem that the boy is the "ransom" that must be paid to secure his release. Ransome's role as a surrogate for David is apparent when the cabin boy appears at the House of Shaws with "a letter from old Heasy-oasy to Mr Belflower" (44)—a direct repetition of David's earlier arrival with a "letter of introduction" (23) to his uncle Ebenezer. Ransome's appearance as "a half-grown boy in sea-clothes" (43) parodies David's pretense at adulthood, with both boys acting in a way that they "considered manly" (44). Furthermore, Ransome's physical injury, "a great, raw, red wound that made my blood run cold" (47), establishes him as a victim of violence, much as David is, having narrowly escaped an attempt on his life by his uncle. Most tellingly, following Shaun's deadly attack on Ransome, the two boys change places: as Hoseason informs David, "we want ye to serve in the round-house. You and Ransome are to change berths" (66). If David takes Ransome's place, this is only because Ransome has already taken his: the cabin boy has died so that David may live.

Yet this exchange of roles also serves the ideological purpose of displacing the intensifying class conflicts of Victorian Britain into an earlier, romanticized mode of opposition. Fredric Jameson has argued in *The Political Unconscious* that the ideological function of the nineteenth-century novel as a "strategy of containment" is to provide imaginary resolutions to actual social and historical conflicts that are incapable of such closure. The strategy of containment "allows what can be thought to seem internally coherent in its own terms, while repressing the unthinkable . . . which lies beyond its boundaries." One can recognize in *Kidnapped* a confrontation between David's "bourgeois individualism" (with his sheltered childhood and concern with the acquisition of property) and the working-class origins of Ransome, who "had followed the sea since he was nine, but could not say how old he was" (46).[16] Though David insists to Ransome "you are no slave, to be so handled!" (47), in reality Ransome is a slave, at the mercy of his brutal "owners." Yet rather than achieve a reconciliation of the ideological differences between bourgeois "subject" (David) and working-class "object," the narration offers an effacement or suppression of them, killing off Ransome and letting David take his place. This anticipates the strategy by which ideological differences between David and Alan are managed by displacing them into differences of individual temperament. Their famous quarrel—which does dramatize a profound difference in values—is resolved through Alan's pity for David's helplessness ("I cannae draw upon ye, David. It's fair murder" [221]), and Alan's disappearance from the novel—like David's indeterminacy—prevents the union necessary for narrative closure. This would be an example of what Jameson terms "ethical thought," which "projects as permanent features of human 'experience,' and thus as a kind of 'wisdom' about personal life and interpersonal relations, what are in reality the historical and institutional specifics of a determinate type of group solidarity or class cohesion."[17]

The textual indeterminacy of *Kidnapped* is thus related to its premature attempt at closure but is also an effect of its negotiation between Scott-like historical romance and popular boys' fiction, which was Stevenson's most marketable commodity. Of course, this generic indeterminacy is a feature of much writing in the romance mode and would also affect Stevenson's successors. As Fredric Jameson argues at the beginning of his influential reading of *Lord Jim,* for example, Joseph Conrad's place is "still unstable, undecidable, and his work unclassifiable . . . floating uncertainly somewhere in between Proust and Robert Louis Stevenson." Ironically, given this opposition that Jameson suggests between "high" modernism (Proust) and "popular" literature (Stevenson), Conrad was deeply influenced by Stevenson, both in his use of the sea as a setting—"the privileged place of the strategy of containment in Conrad," according to Jameson—and in his use of the first-person narrator of romance.[18] This influence is evident in the opening chapter of *Lord Jim,* in which Jim's imaginative formation takes place through his immersion in "light literature": "He saw himself saving people from sinking ships, cutting away masts in a hurricane, swimming through a surf with a line; or as a lonely castaway, barefooted and half naked, walking on uncovered reefs in search of shellfish to stave off starvation. He confronted savages on tropical shores, quelled mutinies on the high seas, and in a small boat upon the ocean kept up the hearts of despairing men—always an example of devotion to duty, and as unflinching as a hero in a book."[19]

The reference to the "lonely castaway . . . walking on uncovered reefs in search of shellfish to stave off starvation" clearly alludes to the situation of David Balfour, stranded on the isle of Earraid in *Kidnapped,* while other influences from Stevenson might be cited, especially *The Ebb-Tide* and *The Wrecker.* Jim's failure to act in a moment of crisis on board the *Patna* similarly suggests David Balfour's hesitancy rather than the more headstrong conduct of Jim Hawkins from *Treasure Island.* Yet Conrad's assignment of the Stevensonian "romance" (on which he drew) to the category of "light literature" reveals his ambivalence about the tale of adventure. Seeking the status of "serious" literature, Conrad is uneasy about the similarities of his work to "romance." Nicholas Daly has written of Fredric Jameson's account of Conrad, "In arguing for the kinship of modernism and mass culture Jameson is at pains not to collapse the two. Crucial to his argument is the idea that they handle their 'raw materials' in quite different ways, modernism providing certain stylistic compensations for the loss of the ability to map the historical totality, while mass culture operates in an essentially narrative register, harmonizing perceived contradictions."[20] Part of my argument here, however, is that although *Kidnapped* is recognizably a romance, it does not harmonize contradictions but manifests them in the ambivalence of the protagonist and the duality he creates with Alan Breck.

Equally significant as a sign of Stevenson's influence is Conrad's use of the first-person narrator in his fiction, conjuring up the material setting of Marlow's "yarn."[21] This return "to the older fiction of the storyteller and the storytelling situation," according to Jameson, reflects "impatience with the objective yet ever intensifying alienation of the printed book." Hence, the use of first person "marks the vain attempt to conjure back the older unity of the literary institution, to return to that older concrete social situation of which narrative transmission was but a part."[22] Stevensonian romance, equally, evokes the fantasy of direct personal communication within a concrete historical setting, as when *Treasure Island* begins with Jim's direct address, citing both the date and the place—which situate Jim as a historical subject within a paternal lineage. This formula is almost exactly replicated at the opening of *Kidnapped:* "I will begin the story of my adventures with a certain morning early in the month of June, the year of grace 1751, when I took the key for the last time out of the door of my father's house" (11). The greater specificity of David's date indicates the crucial role of historical action in his narrative, yet both examples evoke a concrete "storytelling situation." Moreover, much of Stevenson's narrative apparatus—the use of "editors" and other figures who mediate between text and reader; the distant historical setting; and the first-person narrator—derives from Sir Walter Scott and represents Stevenson's professional investment in the historical novel as representing "the older unity of the literary institution." As Menikoff argues, "with *Kidnapped* and *David Balfour* Stevenson was in the world of his great forebear, Sir Walter Scott—the world of Scottish history—and he was obliged, if not constrained, to commit himself to serious questions about the origins of the text in historical reality."[23] Yet Scott was writing in the infancy of the industrial revolution, which, as Eric Hobsbawm writes, eventually "established the limitless capacity of the productive system pioneered by capitalism for economic growth and global penetration."[24] Stevenson's texts, by contrast, were produced in the late-Victorian era of high capitalism, a society featuring "a new concentration of metropolitan power, a new imperialism, the spread of consumerism."[25]

Stevenson's use of the first-person narrator in *Kidnapped* seeks to overcome or resist the alienation of storytelling within what Jameson terms "the corrosive effects of market relations."[26] Stevenson grounds this first-person storytelling, moreover, in the travel narrative, as David's account of his adventures is directly based on his journey, drawing extensively on Stevenson's travels through the Highlands. As Barry Menikoff reveals, Stevenson originally planned a historical study of the Highlands, and he traveled and researched extensively in preparation for the volume; Menikoff asserts, "If Stevenson failed to use his notebook for a conventional Highland history, he made very good use of it for a fictional counterpart."[27] The novel's subtitle, "Being the Adventures of David Balfour," is supplemented by the title of the opening chapter, "I set off upon my journey," which inaugurates the central role of travel in the novel. The foundation of David's narrative in travel is further revealed in the map that appears in the front of the book, titled "Sketch of the Cruise of the Brig Covenant and the probable course of David Balfour's wanderings" (1). The phrase "probable course" suggests uncertainty, warning the reader that the route plotted on the map might not match the actual travels. Yet the map is a guide not only to David's travels but also to the narrative itself—on this map the reader can plot the course of David's narrative, to determine the geographical points where his adventures occur, discovering where they begin and end. In this sense, the map guarantees a closure to the narrative that Stevenson is bound to reflect in his text. Although Stevenson never claims of *Kidnapped,* as he did of *Treasure Island,* that "I had written it up to the map," the prominence of the map suggests that it will dictate the course of the adventures.[28] Indeed, the map is significant in that it gives away the events of the story—we know by looking at the map that David survives the shipwreck, escapes Earraid, and makes it back to Edinburgh.

Yet this only confirms visually what we already knew logically—David, as first-person narrator, must have survived to tell his tale. In this respect, the map and the first-person narrator serve parallel functions: both reveal that the storyteller has survived, that the end is already present in the beginning, that David has come full circle and is now in a position to narrate his adventures.

What the map cannot disclose, however, is the sudden abortion of David's narrative at the end of *Kidnapped.* Indicating a complete journey—if we combine the map of the *Covenant*'s voyage with that of David's wanderings—that begins and ends in Edinburgh, the map is misleading; in fact, David's adventures are only half complete at the end of the novel. The travel narrative that promises a specific end or destination is fraught with risk, for, as Stevenson wrote in *Travels with a Donkey,* the purpose of the journey is "not to go anywhere, but to go."[29] Incomplete in itself, the narrative of David's travels in *Kidnapped* will require a supplement or sequel, the dual title of which—*Catriona* and *David Balfour*—further suggests the text's indeterminacy, to which another map, "Map of Edinburgh and its Neighbourhood," will be appended.[30]

To compensate for the formal rupture at the heart of David Balfour's adventures and to help diminish the narrative trauma of the hiatus of seven years between the two novels, Stevenson offers the narrative persona provided by David Balfour as a means of establishing continuity between the texts. This strategy of containment attempts a seamless transition between two radically dissimilar texts: a Scott-like historical romance and a narrative of contemporary colonial intrigue and political corruption (*David Balfour*).[31] The efficacy of this strategy is compromised, however, by the indeterminacy of David Balfour—an indeterminacy at the heart of the problems of closure that haunt both *Kidnapped* and the novel identified as its sequel.[32]

Yet why does *Kidnapped* grind to a halt in the first place, requiring the ruse of leaving the door open for a sequel? I submit that this failure of narrative closure derives from problems inherent in the role of the central narrator and protagonist, David Balfour. These are problems not of psychology but of narrative function. Stevenson had written in "A Gossip on Romance" (1882) that "a certain interest can be communicated by the art of narrative" but that the appeal of romance depends for its effect on compelling incident, "not upon what a man shall choose to do, but on how he manages to do it; not on the passionate slips and hesitations of the conscience, but on the problems of the body and of the practical intelligence, in clean, open-air adventure."[33] Although these narrative features apply to *Kidnapped,* they do not accurately describe David Balfour. A brief comparison with Jim Hawkins in *Treasure Island* is helpful to illustrate these problems. Jim, though somewhat younger than

David, is an active, assertive figure who knows his own interests. He proclaims from the outset that he is writing his narrative to fulfill a demand: "Squire Trelawney, Dr Livesey and the rest of these gentlemen having asked me to write down the whole particulars about Treasure Island." Hence, his narrative is part of the commercial transaction that includes the treasure (some of which is "not yet lifted"—an allusion, perhaps, to the profits to be earned from publication). Despite his proclaimed abhorrence for "that accursed island," Jim never hesitates in his pursuit of the treasure: he is the one who takes the oilskin packet containing the map and presents it to the squire and doctor, thereby initiating the quest. He shows extraordinary resourcefulness in steering the *Hispaniola* on his own when the doctor and squire are on the island and in killing the pirate Israel Hands. Jim, who acts rather than thinks, is the ideal protagonist of a romance.[34]

David Balfour, by contrast, is compelled into action by demands from others—for example, he travels to the House of Shaws at the prompting of Minister Campbell, to whom he admits ignorance of his own intentions in saying that "if I knew where I was going or what was likely to become of me, I would tell you candidly" (11). Subsequently, David is easily prompted by his uncle to climb the lethal unfinished staircase, with "nothing but emptiness beyond it" (39). David's statement that "I was already half blinded, when I stepped into the tower" (37) applies to his moral no less than ocular sense, and only following his brush with death does he become enlightened, as "a blinding flash . . . showed me my uncle plainly" (39). Having been kidnapped by Captain Hoseason, he is effectively helpless until the arrival of Alan Breck Stewart, the Highland Jacobite who is picked up from the sea and does battle with the crew of the *Covenant.*

Alan Breck emerges as the key figure in the novel's historical plot, diverting the narrative away from its concern with inheritance and family and toward a complex engagement with Scotland's Jacobite history. This shift in generic conventions is reflected in the journey itself, as David's kidnapping is displaced by a travelogue of the Highlands. Alan is a key figure, also, for the novel's attempts at closure, as well as in the supplementary narrative of *David Balfour.* One of the most frequent plot devices for such closure in the nineteenth-century novel is the marriage—which may be used either to consolidate the class unity of the middle classes or to bring members of opposing groups or classes into romantic union, thereby suggesting (fictively) that the actual conflicts between these groups have been, or will be, resolved. One thinks, for example, of the marriage between Sybil and Charles Egremont in Benjamin Disraeli's *Sybil, or the Two Nations* (1845), which seeks to provide an imaginary resolution to the split between the "two nations," or the marriage of Margaret Hale and John Thornton in Elizabeth Gaskell's *North and South* (1855), which represents a union of the industrial middle class and the Southern "genteel" class. Generically, such a resolution by marriage seems improbable in a "book for boys," such as *Kidnapped*. Yet the novel does contain a relationship in which the political contradictions of the Scottish eighteenth century are contained by a union of "opposites"—that of David Balfour and Alan Breck.[35]

As a "loyal subject of King George," David has pledged allegiance to the Hanoverian government, for whom the Jacobite rebel is a dangerous incendiary, as Alan himself recognizes with his introduction: "[T]o be quite plain with ye, I am one of those honest gentlemen that were in trouble about the years forty-five and six; and (to be still quite plain with ye) if I got into the hands of any of the red-coated gentry, it's like it would go hard with me" (75). Yet David's personal attraction to, and practical dependence on, Alan Breck will override their ideological differences. The occasion of the quarrel between them is the exception that proves the rule, for it transforms a deep political contradiction into a squabble over money and gambling, provoked by David's exhaustion, that seems close to a lover's argument. In fact, David and Alan display many of the traits of lovers: they are physically intimate during their flight through the heather, they are emotionally attached to and affectionate toward each other, and they occasionally argue. The tension between them that prompts such arguments suggests an erotic attraction in conflict with cultural and ideological difference. It is certainly the most important relationship in the novel, and when they part at the end of *Kidnapped*, David is bereft without his companion: "I felt so lost and lonesome that I could have found it in my heart to sit down by the dyke, and cry and weep like any baby" (276).

Indeed, it is Alan's abandonment of David that leaves the protagonist and novel both bereft and in a state of incompletion: David is incapable of decisive action without Alan's assistance and example of resolute conduct. Yet if Alan's presence is required for the narrative to conclude, what is the specific role that he might play? Evidently, Alan is the figure who disrupts the original plot of *Kidnapped,* leading David into a new adventure concerning the Appin murder and propelling him on a new journey through the Highlands. Furthermore, he helps to secure David's access to the property of the House of Shaws, a key event in David's attainment of adult status. Yet a final resolution to the plot, following the conventions of the Victorian novel, would be a marriage—a confirmation of the union of opposing forces represented by David and Alan. Such a marriage between men is unthinkable in the nineteenth-century novel, bringing forward the spectre of homosexuality—or "gross indecency," the official name given to sexual acts between men in the Labouchère Amendment, passed in 1885, the year before *Kidnapped* was published.[36] As Nicholas Daly argues, whereas "the domestic novel revolves around the family and the heterosexual love plot, the adventure romance constructs an all-male 'family' or team, and replaces the heterosexual romance with strong affective (though also hierarchical) ties between men."[37] Yet the possibility of attaining closure is compromised by this abandonment of marriage as a strategy of containment. One of the principal tasks of *David Balfour,* the sequel, will be finding a female substitute for Alan, a woman who would represent his qualities of the active Highlander.

Interestingly, one woman does play a pivotal role in *Kidnapped:* namely, the innkeeper who provides David and Alan with sustenance and helps them obtain a boat to cross the river. Alan proves adept at manipulating female sympathy for the advance of their interests: "I don't want the lass to fall in love with ye, I want her to be sorry for ye, David; to which end, there is no manner of need that she should take you for a beauty" (238). Yet this result is produced by engaging the woman's interest in their male bond: "It was small wonder if the maid were taken with the picture we presented, of a poor, sick, overwrought lad and his most tender comrade" (240). *Comrade* was of course the term Whitman used in *Leaves of Grass* to indicate the "adhesiveness" between men, an affect that included sexual attraction. Stevenson wrote, in 1878, of Whitman's philosophy of love, quoting several lines from "Leaves of Grass":

> But next in order of truths to a person's sublime conviction of himself, comes the attraction of one person for another, and all that we mean by the word love:

> The dear love of man for his comrade—the attraction of friend
>   for friend,
> Of the well-married husband and wife, of children and parents,
> Of city for city and land for land.[38]

Significantly, Whitman lists the "love of man for his comrade" first among intimate relationships. Focusing on Whitman's figure of the "ideal man," Stevenson comments that "Whitman's ideal man must not only be strong, free, and self-reliant in himself, but his freedom must be bounded and his strength perfected by the most intimate, eager, and long-suffering love for others." Stevenson points out the same-sex dimension to this love, noting that "Whitman insists not only on love between sex and sex" but also "between friends of the same sex" and "in the field of the less intense political sympathies."[39] Significantly, the relationship between David and Alan in *Kidnapped* would illustrate both the love between men and the crossing of a political divide demanded by Whitman. Yet even while endorsing the high value that Whitman places on friendship, Stevenson registers an uneasiness at Whitman's invitation to "practise a most quixotic code of morals," concerned that "morality has been ceremoniously extruded from the door." Stevenson carefully circumnavigates Whitman's discourse on "the most delicate of subjects," love between men, which is "looked upon as ridiculous or shameful." Evidently, the sensitive issue of love between men results in Stevenson's tentative language. On the one hand he calls for complete openness, stating that "it would be a good thing if a window were opened on these close privacies of life," yet on the other he asserts that Whitman "loses our sympathy . . . by attracting too much of our attention."[40] Stevenson's desire to bring Whitman out into the open recalls Utterson urging Dr. Jekyll to leave his study—"You stay too much indoors. . . . You should be out, whipping up the circulation." Yet Jekyll's reply might speak for Whitman's decision to remain closeted: "I should like to very much; but no, no, no, it is quite impossible; I dare not."[41]

Yet the preference for relationships between men that Stevenson identified in Whitman's work was also a commented-upon feature of Stevenson's corpus during his time. In an essay on Stevenson in 1888—two years after *Kidnapped*—Henry James remarks that "it is rather odd that . . . a striking feature of that nature should be an absence of care for things feminine. His books are for the most part books without women, and it is not women who fall most in love with them. But Mr Stevenson does not need, as we may say, a petticoat to inflame him." If a petticoat does not inflame Stevenson, the reader might wonder, what is it that does so? An answer is quickly forthcoming: seeking to provide an "explanation of his [Stevenson's] perversities," James argues that "everything he has written is a direct apology for boyhood." James goes on to comment on "the idea of a boy's romantic adventures" in *Kidnapped* as being "more divine, for instance, than the passion usually regarded as the supremely tender one. The idea of making believe appeals to him much more than the idea of making love." Hinting frequently at the presence of a queer desire circulating in Stevenson's work, James makes clear that "the romance of boyhood" contains love of men, specifically, David's love for Alan. Invoking "the love of brave words as well as brave deeds," James seeks to explain these as "simply Mr Stevenson's essential love of style," yet immediately attributes them to the specific figure of Alan Breck, "a wonderful picture of the union of courage and swagger; the little Jacobite adventurer, a figure worthy of Scott at his best, and representing the highest point that Mr Stevenson's talent has reached." Stevenson's talent, James makes clear, is for portraying wonderful and courageous men, not depicting heterosexual intimacy.[42]

Although James remarks defensively that "it is not odd, but extremely usual, to marry," he insists on Stevenson's tendency "to regard women as so many superfluous girls in a boy's game. They are almost wholly absent from his pages. . . . Why should a person marry when he might be swinging a cutlass or looking for a buried treasure? Why should he waste at the nuptial altar precious hours in which he might be polishing periods?" Perhaps the most striking aspect of James's inquiry is the shift from incident to style, from character to author, suggesting that both Alan and Stevenson seek alternatives to marriage in the pleasures of the sword and the pen, respectively. With classic insouciance, James both alludes frequently to Stevenson's desire, "his personal situation," and reproaches himself for doing so, fearing that "I have already been indiscreet." In focusing on Stevenson's "talent for reproducing the feeling of queer situations and contacts," James seeks to identify a difference in Stevenson and seems to be intent on discovering the author's secret: "I have been wondering whether there is something more than this that our author's pages would tell us about him."[43]

Stevenson himself recognized the obstacles to representing passion between men, indicating to his friend Sidney Colvin the difficulty of translating the relationship between Alan and David into publicly acceptable discourse: "I am a realist and a prosaist, and a most fanatical lover of plain physical sensations plainly and expressly rendered; hence my perils. To do love in the same spirit as I did (for instance) D. Balfour's fatigue in the heather; my dear sir, there were grossness ready made!"[44] To narrate David's feelings for Alan "plainly" would result in "grossness," and these twin impossibilities—either a marriage between David and Alan, or David's continuing to function as a historical agent in Alan's absence—leave the novel in its irresolute state.

David's physical passivity is compounded by his political indeterminacy. Referring to Stevenson as "the historian of Alan Breck," James remarks that "his appreciation of the active side of life . . . proceeds in a considerable measure from an intimate acquaintance with the passive." This opposition of active/passive is aptly represented by the friendship of David and Alan. Yet James also diminishes the ideological differences between the characters, emphasizing instead Stevenson's brilliance in depicting character (David is an "unfortunate though circumspect youth" who gives "beautiful . . . expression" to the "Scottish character"). Praising the quarrel between the two in chapter 24 as "a real stroke of genius," James adds that "we feel [it] to be inevitable, though it is about nothing, or almost nothing, and which springs from exasperated nerves and the simple shock of temperaments."[45]

Yet the quarrel actually emerges from David's reluctant exposure to the culture of the Jacobites in Cluny's Cave. David's puritan objections to Alan's gambling continue even after the lost money is returned by Cluny: "Wheedling my money from me while I lay half-conscious, was scarce better than theft" (213). In conveying his sense that he has been violated by Alan's invasion of his resources, David represents his antagonism as the mirror image of his desire, "these two violent and sinful feelings" (212). The quarrel reaches its greatest intensity when the political differences between them resurface, as Alan "began to whistle a Jacobite air" (220) and David provocatively asserts that "you shall henceforth speak civilly of my King and my good friends the Campbells" (220).

By dismissing the profound political and cultural divide between David and Alan, Lowlander and Jacobite, as "nothing," Henry James in effects severs

Stevenson's artistic achievement from the political and historical framework of the novel, reducing the Jacobite rebellion to "the charm of the most romantic episode in the world."[46] Yet Stevenson's text insists on the deep political and cultural divide between the two protagonists. Indeed, at their first meeting, David observes that Alan's identity as an outlawed Jacobite is proclaimed by his appearance and discourse both: "[H]e laid a pair of fine, silver-mounted pistols on the table, and I saw that he was belted with a great sword. His manners, besides, were elegant and he pledged the captain handsomely" (73). David glosses Alan's question "[A]re ye of the honest party?" as "meaning, was he a Jacobite? For each side, in these sort of civil broils, takes the name of honesty for its own" (74). Hence, David is an astute observer of political divisions. Alan answers David's question, "And so you're a Jacobite?" directly: "Ay" (78). Yet on being asked by Alan in turn whether he is a Whig, David evades the issue: "Betwixt and Between," he replies, a vacillation that Alan seizes upon immediately, dubbing him "Mr Betwixt-and-Between" (78). This exchange demonstrates David's inability (or refusal) to choose sides in the central political and historical conflict of the period, the Jacobite uprising against the Hanoverian government of George II. Although he claims to be "as good a Whig as Mr Campbell could make me" (78), David will waver when it proves convenient.

David's political indeterminacy is dramatized in the paradoxical situation of a Lowland loyalist traveling through the Highlands with an outlawed Jacobite, determined to "avoid whigs, Campbells and the 'red-soldiers'" (139) and consorting with the allies of the exiled King James and Prince Charlie. David again proclaims his independence to Colin Campbell, "The Red Fox," precisely by disclaiming any local allegiance: "I am neither of his people nor yours, but an honest subject of King George, owing no man and fearing no man" (148). One might argue that his indeterminacy is precisely what allows David to function as a narrator, by distancing him from investment in either side of the struggle. Indeed, only by strategically suppressing his loyalty to King George (as when Cluny MacPherson and Alan toast "The Restoration" [204]) can David narrate the encounter with a proclaimed traitor and enemy of the king.

David's narrative is increasingly dominated by the compelling figure of Alan, and his course is redirected by their joint involvement in the Appin murder. Yet the crises in which Alan is involved—the shipwreck, Appin murder, and flight through the heather—also impede the conclusion of David's narrative, which can produce no resolution between competing ideologies. As James remarks, "the history stops without ending, as it were," yet he defends the author who "has often to lay down his pen for reasons that have nothing to do with the failure of inspiration."[47] James neglects the extent to which the "romantic" Jacobite plot (beginning with Alan's rescue and the shipwreck of the *Covenant*) is indeed a digression from the plot of inheritance with which the novel begins—a distraction of such force that the narrative can neither contain it nor conclude with David's inheritance, the logical termination of the original.

This leads to the larger point, that David's adventures in *Kidnapped* derive from aborted journeys, travels that fail to reach their destination. Comparing the poet to "a traveller on the hunt for his book of travels," Stevenson argues in "Walt Whitman" that "there is a sense, of course, in which all true books are books of travels."[48] Stevenson here anticipates the central and productive role of travel in his works of fiction. Yet the journey in *Kidnapped* exists in an uneasy relation to the novel's plot, tending to disturb and divert its course toward closure. At each key juncture of the novel, David's journeys and his plans are disrupted, leading to a new chain of events and a different series of adventures. Indeed, the point made by Stephen Arata about a later novel, *The Wrecker,* can also be applied to *Kidnapped:* "[W]e are continually invited to imagine other forms the story might take, as well as other stories the novel's materials might give rise to," involving figures that "function like switching points on a rail line, prodding us momentarily to consider the possibility that the novel as a whole might get shunted on to that track and move off in an entirely new direction."[49] In *Kidnapped,* such narrative redirecting occurs so often that the reader is, like David atop the ruined tower, compelled to grope in the dark for a secure point on which to rest, while faced with the prospect of "nothing but emptiness beyond it" (*Kidnapped,* 39).

The most dramatic instances of narrative redirection must begin with David's original intention to make his fortune by claiming kinship with Ebenezer, which is disrupted by his uncle's attempt on his life. David's temporary ascendancy over his uncle is then short-circuited by the kidnapping on

Hoseason's ship, including plans to convey him to slavery in the Carolinas. This narrative direction is in turn undone by another twist, the arrival of Alan Breck on board the *Covenant,* the plot against his life, and the siege of the roundhouse. David's alliance with Alan is then interrupted by the shipwreck of the *Covenant,* which leaves David stranded upon the isle of Earraid. No sooner is David back on the mainland than he is plunged into the political plot of Jacobite conspiracy and the Appin murder.

None of these incidents can claim the status of being central to the narrative; all are, rather, aspects of a journey that attains a fictive unity only through the figure of David himself. Just as "Scotland . . . has no unity except upon the map," so too does David's identity lack any unity except in the narrative, in which he may represent the "Scottish character."[50] Of all these episodes, David's captivity on Earraid is the one that can, I believe, be read as symptomatic of the novel as a whole. It is, in a narrative sense, a deferral of David's progress, a kind of textual limbo rather than a stage of his adventures. As such, it anticipates the ending of the novel, where David is left stranded outside the Edinburgh bank. For the most striking aspect of the Earraid episode is that nothing happens. Despite Stevenson's insistence on "the demand for fit and striking incident" in a romance, one of the most famous chapters of *Kidnapped* contains almost no action.[51] David's description of his stay on "The Islet" as "the most unhappy part of my adventures" (116) surely registers this indeterminate state, as does his experience of the isle as "barren," "desert and desolate" (115), involving "horrid solitude" (120), with "nothing living on it but game birds" (119)—all descriptions emphasizing absence and negation. This absence of signs of habitation—"neither house nor man" (116)—that would seem enticing when Stevenson cruises through the South Seas is here a "still so horrible thought to me" (118), echoing Jim's recollection of Treasure Island as "that accursed island; and the worst dreams that ever I have are when I hear the surf booming about its coasts."[52]

Yet whereas Jim's horror of the island is reserved for the end of his narrative, David's experience on the isle occurs in the middle, reflective of his narrative dilemma. In the first place, his arrival is the result of a random event—the wreck of the ship on the "Torran rocks" (110). David makes clear that his own incompetence and ignorance are what cause these "adventures" to happen at all. The fact that he "had no skill of swimming" (115) leads him to take refuge on the islet, and his ignorance of survival in the wild leads him to eat periwinkles, which make him sick. His ignorance of tidal patterns makes him believe "that I was cast upon a little barren isle and cut off from every side by the salt seas" (117), and his ignorance of Gaelic, in which language the fishermen attempt to enlighten him about his environment, prevents him from sooner overcoming his "pitiful illusion" (125). David's blindness is self-inflicted, for he observes that "if I had but sat down to think, instead of raging at my fate, [I] must have soon guessed the secret and got free" (125). The episode therefore shows the double bind of travel: the traveler may become diverted from his course or, worse, become stuck and unable to free himself, at which point the narrative must cease. As a hiatus in the narrative, the episode might be included as an example of Stevenson's "literary trick—that of dodging off in a new direction—upon those who might have fancied they knew all about him."[53]

Moreover, the stay on Earraid gives new meaning to the name bestowed on the narrator by Alan, as the tidal islet is "betwixt and between" land and sea, neither one nor the other—though he says of the island that "it was dry land" (115), David's progress is soon "stopped by a creek or inlet of the sea which seemed to run pretty deep into the land" (117). This invasion of the land by the sea makes the islet an apt image for David, whose personality is likewise surrounded and encroached upon by characters and landscape. In particular, the island represents David's dependence on Alan Breck for his identity. By (re)naming David, Alan takes on the role of surrogate father, a role that is later developed by his training of David in the skills of fighting and survival. Because David's story begins following the death of his father and mother, the search for parental substitutes is one of the key concerns of the narrative. David's identity is defined by his name, as Campbell reminds him: "[T]he name of that family, Davie boy, is the name you bear; Balfours of Shaws: an ancient, honest, reputable house, peradventure in these latter days decayed" (12). His hopes having been disappointed in his uncle, David turns to Alan, who renames him. Yet, curiously, this naming does not confer an identity on the "son" but rather highlights the lack of one and, indeed, prevents the formation of one. Proud that he, as a Stewart, bears a "King's name" (55), Alan in effect holds David hostage for a king's ransom by rejecting David's lowland, "whiggish" surname in favor of one that represents, even emblazons, his indeterminacy: "Mr. Betwixt-and-Between." Such a name, as Alan says, is "naething," making its bearer a cipher, a blank. Consequently, David's claim to identity that he makes as narrator, by telling "the story of my adventures" (11), is undone by his reliance on a supplementary figure. David can only function, it appears, in Alan's presence. It is significant, therefore, that the suspension of *Kidnapped* occurs immediately following the separation of David and Alan as they approach Edinburgh. David's reaction to the loss of his partner is reminiscent of an abandoned child. One might say that David sheds tears not only for the loss of a friend but also for the collapse of his narrative and the impossibility of its conclusion. The penultimate sentence of the novel confirms David's dependence: "[A]ll the time what I was thinking of was Alan . . . and all the time . . . there was a cold gnawing in my inside like a remorse for something wrong" (277).[54]

The title of the novel indicates this loss of control and agency, a journey made in captivity rather as an exercise in free will. Yet it is striking that the title *Kidnapped*—if taken to refer to David's captivity on the *Covenant*—accurately represents less than half of the novel: David gains his freedom from the ship in the thirteenth of thirty chapters, after which the journey through the Highlands with Alan and their involvement with the Appin murder dominates the novel. Henry James, in his essay on Stevenson, refers to *Kidnapped* as a novel "whose inadequate title I may deplore in passing."[55] I have already offered one interpretation of the title, namely, that Stevenson "kidnaps" his novel and demands a ransom from the public before continuing the narrative Let me here suggest another: that the narrative, and indeed David as narrator, are "kidnapped" by Alan, the Jacobite who usurps the protagonist's role, determines David's journey, and in his Highland speech contributes the most vital part of the discourse.[56] Appropriately enough, the "editor" places Alan's name first in proposing a sequel: "The editor has a great kindness *for both Alan and David*" (277; emphasis added). Henry James also devotes far more attention and praise to Alan than to David in his article of 1888. This order reflects the readers' preference for Alan's company, a pleasure that Stevenson planned to thwart in composing his sequel. In responding, on April 1, 1893, to Colvin's criticism of *David Balfour* ("You seem to hint that *Davie* is not finished in the writing, which cuts me"), Stevenson emphasized the merits of his protagonist: "[T]here has been no such drawing of Scots character since Scott; and even he never drew a full length like Davie, with his shrewdness and simplicity, and stockishness and charm. Yet you'll see, the public won't want it; they want more Alan. Well, they can't get it."[57]

In contrast to the propitiatory tone of the "editor," who concludes *Kidnapped* with promises of more "delectable particulars" (277) of Alan's adventures, Stevenson here stymies the public's desire, insisting that they accept "Davie" as a substitute for Alan. Stevenson resolutely concludes *Kidnapped* with images of completed travel, with David observing that "the beggar in the ballad had come home" (272); he goes on, "So far as I was concerned myself, I had come to port" (273). As "a man of means" (272), David is entitled to expect a new lease on life, and he "lay till dawn . . . planning the future" (272). Yet even as his fortune seems to promise full masculinity, rendering Alan's aid unnecessary, David admits that "this good change in my case unmanned me more than any of the former evil ones" (272). Indeed, despite Stevenson's intention to restore David to narrative sovereignty—of which his preference for the title *David Balfour* is symptomatic—the protagonist's dependence and indeterminacy and the narrative symptoms of division would continue to plague Stevenson in the sequel.

# PART THREE

## Travel and Ethnography in the South Seas

# FIVE

## "A quarry of materials"
### The Fictional History of Stevenson's South Seas Cruises

> There has been a good deal of disappointment among the few who have read the approaching South Sea letters. The fact seems to me that it is very nice to live in Samoa, but not healthy to write there. Within a three-mile radius of Charing Cross is the literary atmosphere, I suspect.
>
> —Edmund Gosse[1]

> I think *David Balfour* a nice little book, and very artistic, and just the thing to occupy the leisure of a busy man; but for the top flower of a man's life it seems to me inadequate. . . . I ought to have been able to build lighthouses and write *David Balfours* too.
>
> —Stevenson[2]

ROBERT LOUIS STEVENSON'S decision to leave Europe and settle in the South Seas was greeted by cries of dismay by his British friends and advisors, such as Sidney Colvin and Edmund Gosse. Others, however, were more enthusiastic, such as the American entrepreneur Samuel McClure, who, on learning of Stevenson's plans to travel in the South Seas, immediately commissioned him to write a series of "fifty letters, (2–3,000 words each) from the Pacific on subjects of his own choice, for which he would receive a fee of £20 per letter in England and a further $200 each in the USA."[3]

Despite this strong financial incentive for literary labor, Stevenson's belief that his literary output was inadequate reached a crescendo during his cruises in the South Seas (from 1888) and residence on Samoa (from 1890), far from the Protestant work ethic of his native Scotland and what his friend Edmund Gosse termed the "literary atmosphere" of London.[4] A significant source of Stevenson's malaise was his inability to produce the magnum opus on the history, society, traditions, and culture of the South Seas that he had envisaged almost from the beginning of his cruise. Stevenson described his purpose in a letter to Marcel Schwob on August 19, 1890: "I am about waist-deep in my big book on the South Seas: *the* big book on the South Seas it ought to be, and shall."[5] Stevenson conceived of this book as an ethnographic "prose-epic" that would undo generations of misrepresentation of Polynesia and portray "the unjust (yet I can see the inevitable) extinction of the Polynesian Islanders by our shabby civilization."[6] To some extent, the lack of a settled home—even after he purchased the land on Samoa, it was some time before the estate at Vailima was completed—hampered the execution of Stevenson's ambitious South Seas project, even though the cruises had provided the materials. The spontaneous and random propulsions of cruising—Stevenson's preferred mode of travel—were not propitious for the laborious production of a major volume of historical, cultural, and anthropological analysis. Rather, cruising was conducive to the writing of more informal texts, such as journals, letters, and "yarns," which would be published in installments. Hence, daunted by the scale and complexity of undertaking a big book, Stevenson would ultimately abandon this project and find other outlets for his South Sea materials: letters and yarns designed as marketable commodities that would both exploit his existing materials and yield profit from further excursions in the South Seas.

In a letter to Sidney Colvin written in April 1890 while on board the *Janet Nicoll,* Stevenson made clear that he needed not simply the South Seas climate but also the stimulation of cruising: "[T]his life is the only one that suits me; so long as I cruise in the South Seas, I shall be well and happy— . . . I mean that, so soon as I cease from cruising, the nerves are strained, the decline commences."[7] The antithesis of strain and labor, *cruising* was a code word for Stevenson's state of well-being, both physical and emotional. Yet Stevenson also resisted (and resented) the external demands on him to write his letters for publication, as well as the expectation that they would deliver the insights of the "romantic" writer. Cruising, for Stevenson, meant traveling *without* a specific destination or external compulsion—travel pursued for sensual pleasure and rewarded by enticing encounters with new people and scenes.[8] Cruising also entailed a new practice of writing for Stevenson, resulting from his resistance to the public's expectations and pressures to commodify his experiences of the South Seas for consumption by distant readers. Hence Stevenson continued to conceive of his nonfiction pieces as chapters of an imagined book rather than occasional letters designed to purvey the flavor of the South Seas to the casual reader.

This ambitious literary project was undermined to some extent by the lucrative commercial arrangement that Stevenson had made with Sam McClure: as early as March 1888, Stevenson had signed a contract with McClure to write a series of fifty letters from the South Seas, letters that would be syndicated in newspapers in Britain, the United States, Australia, and New Zealand. McClure wrote to Stevenson (in May 1888) that he hoped to be able to get Stevenson $300 per letter, a sum that Stevenson expected would defray the considerable expense of chartering the yacht *Casco* and crew: as he wrote to Bob Stevenson in February 1889, "I ought to get all I have laid out and a profit."[9] McClure wrote to Stevenson about the proposed South Seas letters from Kensington on March 9, 1889, with undisguised optimism:

> My dear Mr Stevenson:—
>
> How glad we all were to get your dear letter, & in your own hand-writing too, & from a definite address within the influence of the post office!!! And first business:— Everything has been done in strict accord with your wishes. *The New York Sun* simply purchases the serial use of the letters, exclusively for North America for $200 per letter of 2,000 to 3,000 words & they agree to take the letters up to 50—so if you write 50 letters 100,000 to 150,000 you get $10,000. I am arranging here for the letters in an English syndicate in accordance with your wishes.[10]

As it turned out, the *New York Sun* cancelled the serialization well before the fifty letters agreed upon had been completed, and Stevenson therefore never received the $10,000 offered by McClure. Moreover, despite McClure's conciliatory approach, Frank McLynn points out that there were numerous problems with the serial format in which Stevenson had agreed to produce his Pacific travel writing: "The conflict between his serious intentions and the colourful traveller's tales eventually led to the cancellation of the series of letters commissioned by McClure after thirty-four of them had appeared in print." McLynn also asserts that the financial results of the letters were ultimately disappointing: "The disappointment over the *In the South Seas* letters had been egregious. He had made just £1000, about a third of the money McClure promised him, after the cancellation of the series."[11] To these financial setbacks must be added Stevenson's disappointment at the negative critical reactions from home.

The early response to these letters from British readers was particularly discouraging, as Stevenson had counted on the exotic allure of the South Seas or his ability to communicate "some sense of its seduction" (5) to win him a new audience. Instead, the critics who had always doubted the wisdom of Stevenson's cruise—and even more so his decision to settle permanently on Samoa—became more vocal in their opposition. Colvin, rarely inclined to boost Stevenson's confidence, reported that *Black and White* had decided to cancel its publication of the letters because they were "too monotonous," a report that clearly reveals the thwarted expectation that Stevenson's letters would be as entertaining as his fiction.[12] By contrast, Gosse's criticism, cited above, ironically calls into question Stevenson's central conviction that cruising in the South Seas had restored his health (as he began his first letter by stating). In describing Samoa as "not healthy," however, Gosse evidently referred not to physical disease but to a moral or intellectual malady, the chief symptom of which is inferior literature.

## "Part by part in pieces"

As published in the *New York Sun* between February 1 and December 13, 1891, the South Seas letters appeared under the subtitle "Letters from a Leisurely Traveller," evoking a context of ease and suggesting that the act of cruising was casual and pleasurable rather than pursued for profit or with literary labor as its pretext.[13] Such an ambience of dilettante leisure was likely to alienate those Victorians who lived by the Protestant work ethic.[14] The first seven parts of the series were not individually titled, making this emphasis on the leisurely traveler rather than on specific locations even more pronounced. The series also included the material on the "Kona Coast" of Hawaii, which was later omitted from the 1896 Edinburgh edition, edited by Colvin, and (in the *New York Sun*) the account of "Pearl Island: Penrhyn," which was likewise cut out in 1896.

Yet Gosse and the other early critics of the South Seas material were not commenting on the serial publication of the letters; rather, they were responding to an unusual (indeed unique) publication, the 1890 copyright edition that included only the Marquesas material. Henry James, for example, was explicit in attributing his comments to the copyright edition, writing to Stevenson in January 1891 (before the letters had begun to appear serially) that he had read "the first chapters of your prose volume (kindly vouchsafed me in the little copyright-catching red volume" while complaining, "I missed the visible in them."[15]

Gosse clearly assumed that Stevenson did not begin to write the South Seas letters until his third cruise, on the *Janet Nicoll,* and that he did not find it possible to write while moving from island to island. Hence, Gosse believed that the 1890 copyright edition, which he termed the "rarest" of Stevenson's volumes, was the first incarnation of the South Seas materials. However, Gosse's claim is clearly contradicted by the extensive journal (now in the collection of the Huntington Library) that Stevenson kept during his cruises.[16] This journal has dated entries extending throughout the first two cruises (on the *Casco* and the *Equator*) and in effect presents the first draft of the work that eventually became *In the South Seas.*[17]

Stevenson made evident his own distinction between the South Seas letters and the proposed book in a letter to Samuel McClure written on board the SS *Janet Nicoll* on July 19, 1890. In this letter, we can detect the seeds of the future misunderstandings and recriminations between Stevenson and his commercial agent:

> My dear McClure,
>
> This is to announce to your anxious heart that the letters are at last under weigh. A considerable budget of them will go to London where it will be set up and whence it will reach you in proof. I take this plan first because it is necessary for me to have proof of the whole immediately which it might not be convenient for you to give me, and second because I can have this set copyrighted in England. Now I must explain to you that what you are to receive is not so much a certain number of letters, *as a certain number of chapters in my book.*[18]

Stevenson went on to advise McClure how to proceed with publication of the letters and expressed his wish that the texts should not be tampered with or censored in any way. It is striking to note that, even before the fiasco over the censorship of "The Beach of Falesá," Stevenson was aware that some suppression of his South Seas material might have been impending:

> I wish you in short to use your special knowledge freely with regard to the refusal or acceptance of individual letters. . . . But if you choose to print any of these letters, you understand that they are to be printed as you receive them without suppression and without typographical embellishments. . . . In the matter of suppressions I willingly make one exception. If the papers object to running over (which I do not suppose they will) where you shall have put two letters into one, I conceive some suppression may be necessary, and I willingly leave you to make it, should there be not time to communicate with me and receive my answer from Samoa.[19]

Finally, in this letter Stevenson conveyed his commitment to fulfilling his end of the bargain, assuring McClure that "I have very little doubt that before the end of the year, or at the latest before Easter '91, you shall have received the two and fifty letters. I hope that this will meet your views and those of your constituents."[20] Stevenson's reference to "constituents" indicates his awareness of McClure's readership as a commercial audience for his South Seas writing and of the demands they might make on his productivity.

Stevenson's frustration at the splitting up of his South Seas manuscript into "letters" required by serial publication—especially as the conflict emerged between the serial form and the book project—is evident in a letter he wrote to Henry James in December 1890: "[W]hat a strain is a long book! The time it took me to design this volume, before I could dream of putting pen to paper was excessive. And then think of writing a book of travels on the spot; when I am continually extending my information, revising my opinions, and seeing the most finely finished portions of my work come part by part in pieces."[21] Stevenson's language is telling, alluding to the impending fragmentation of his textual body "part by part" during the process of serial publication and expressing the fear that the magnum opus would be dismembered for what he privately referred to as the "grisly letters."[22] As Robert Irwin Hillier observes, Stevenson "felt that the complex savagery and grandeur he was experiencing could inspire an epic masterpiece, which he would call *In the South Seas* and which would encompass history, ethnology, geology, and folklore, rather than the mere collection of observations and anecdotes on exotica McClure had hired him to write."[23]

The key to Stevenson's conception of his literary labor in the South Seas, however, is to be found in his response to Colvin's criticism of the letters: in his defense, Stevenson asserted, "These letters were never meant and are not now meant to be other than *a quarry of materials* from which the book may be drawn."[24] While cruising in the South Sea islands, Stevenson would creatively "quarry" materials for the purposes of constructing literary narratives (as his family's firm of engineers had quarried materials for the construction of lighthouses). Clearly, Stevenson's desire to write a "big book" on the South Seas was spurred by the amount and variety of material that he had accumulated in his journal. Writing to Colvin in June 1889, Stevenson expressed his confidence that his book project was taking shape: "By the time I am done with this cruise I shall have the material for a very singular book of travels: masses of strange stories and characters, cannibals, pirates, ancient legends, old Polynesian poetry, never was so generous a farrago."[25] The fruit of Stevenson's cruises, however—the narrative built using the "quarry of materials"—was not the "South Sea book" (which remained unwritten, at least according to his original conception) but South Sea tales such as "The Beach of Falesá" and *The Ebb-Tide.* Stevenson recycled episodes, encounters, and characters that had been initially recorded in the South Seas journal and then published in the South Seas letters—or in some cases had not been published at all—for use in the "fictional" narratives that he at times termed dismissively as his "South Sea yarns."

## From Journal to Yarn

Stevenson's recycling of documentary material, acquired during his cruises, into yarns is ironic in that the wide generic discrepancy between his romance fiction—works such as *Treasure Island* and *Kidnapped*—and his nonfiction prose is what had alienated the early readers of the South Seas letters. McClure, for example, expressed his dissatisfaction with the letters by invoking Stevenson's duality: "There were two men in Stevenson—the romantic adventurer of the eighteenth century and the Scotch covenanter of the nineteenth century. Contrary to our expectation, it was the moralist and not the romancer which his observations in the South Seas awoke in him, and the public found the moralist less interesting than the romancer."[26] Thus, the expectations generated by the popular appeal of his romances led to disappointment when the letters paid more attention to the varieties of Polynesian languages, the art of tattooing, and the causes of disease than to Stevenson's adventures. Clearly, much of the disturbance surrounding the first appearance of the letters in the pages of *Black and White* and the *New York Sun* derived from Stevenson's international reputation for fiction—which was, of course, the very reason he had been commissioned to write the letters in the first place. As Stevenson would later write in "My First Book," "the great public regards what else I have written with indifference, if not aversion ."[27]

Such public aversion was evident in the reaction to the South Seas letters; but there were also misleading signs in the journals that the pieces were meant to be read as fiction. For example, there was no indication in the *Black and White* serial that this was a correspondence from Stevenson. While the *New York Sun* described these pages as "letters from a leisurely traveler," this could be plausibly constructed as a guise for fiction, as *The Master of Ballantrae* had begun with such a narrative frame. Significantly, the illustrations in *Black and White* were lavish and detailed, masterly engravings designed to illuminate key episodes of the text and using the same style of illustration as for the pieces of fiction it published. Moreover, the letters were juxtaposed with works of fiction by authors such as Arthur Conan Doyle, Rudyard Kipling, and H. Rider Haggard, all proponents of the romance school pioneered by Stevenson.[28] Readers would have been further confused when the March 28, 1891, volume of *Black and White* contained an installment of "The Bottle Imp" (a South Sea tale also by Stevenson) instead of the latest section of *The South Seas.* Was this part of the serialization? Was it an independent work of fiction? Or was the whole series of "letters" an elaborate work of fiction by the master of romance? These would have been legitimate questions for the reader of 1891.

The crucial point is that a combination of the "horizon of expectations" governing the reception of Stevenson's work and the serial format of the letters meant that they were received as an interweaving of fact and fiction, history and romance. In this light, Stevenson's attempts to distinguish sharply between his "South Seas book" and the "yarns" were perhaps disingenuous, or at least perplexing. In his correspondence, he emphasizes the fantastic, romantic aspects of the South Seas, writing to his cousin Bob that "the cruise has been a wonderful success. I never knew the world was so amusing. On the last voyage we had grown so used to sea life that no one wearied. . . . All the time, our visits to the islands have been more like dreams than realities: the people, the life, the beachcombers, the old stories and songs I have picked up, so interesting; . . . The women are handsomest in Tahiti; the men in the Marquesas."[29]

Stevenson's literary practice contributed to this effect, as he quarried the record of his cruises for the letters (or chapters) and the yarns, often recycling episodes, characters, and materials published in the former for use in the latter. Such recycling is never innocent, nor is it a matter simply of efficiency. For example, in the yarns, Stevenson replaces the seemingly neutral observer of the journal with an eccentric first-person narrator (in the case of "The Beach of Falesá") or a third-person narrator whose point of view shifts between several characters (as in *The Ebb-Tide*). In each case, the fictional narrator draws attention to his own biases of race, nation, and gender, displacing any notion of objectivity. Hence, Stevenson's revision of his material allowed him to develop a subtle critique of the European presence in the South Seas.

Stevenson's practice of quarrying literary materials can be compared in some ways to the engineering of his forefathers (as mentioned above). Martin Green has argued that Stevenson in effect applied the engineering techniques developed by his family to literature: "He had difficulty in reconciling his parents to his vocation to be a writer, but in fact he turned their engineering work to fictional images."[30] Certainly, Stevenson's emphasis on construction, as well as his repeated analogies between works of fiction and engines or machines (such as the watch image in "My First Book") would support such a theory. In "Memoirs of an Islet," Stevenson suggests that the possibility of "recycling" materials—in this case, his memories of being on Earraid—is inexhaustible: "[T]he memories are a fairy gift which cannot be worn out in using. After a dozen services in various tales, the little sunbright pictures of the past still shine in the mind's eye with not a lineament defaced, not a tint impaired."[31] The quarry takes on added engineering significance in this essay, in the context of Stevenson's youthful training as an engineer on the islet of Earraid, off the coast of Mull, in August 1870, when he oversaw the construction of Dhu Heartach lighthouse.[32]

Undoubtedly, Stevenson saw connections between his training as an engineer and his apprenticeship as a writer, as evidenced by his previously cited lament to Will Low (used as the chapter epigraph): "I ought to have been able to build lighthouses and write *David Balfours* too." Stevenson felt that his literary career ought to have been a supplement to his engineering career, rather than a substitute for it. Yet I want to suggest that Stevenson reinvented such techniques of "construction"—using materials from a "quarry"—so that they became a form of bricolage, a borrowing of methods and materials to produce something new. As Vanessa Smith has argued in her account of Pacific writing, "authorship in the atolls is bricolage rather than revelation. . . . To make literature, rather than natural history, in the atolls Stevenson adopts a genre that invests absence with significance: that of the fantastic. The details that the naturalist uncovers provide the uncanny elements of horror story . . . a narrative of terror can be uncovered below the surface of the atoll."[33] One can certainly identify elements of the fantastic in *The Ebb-Tide,* especially the uncanny desertion of the island and the sinister quality to the figurehead, which I discuss later. Moreover, the surface beauty of New Island masks a tale of terror. Stevenson thus adopts the more scientific accounts of previous travelers and naturalists in the South Seas, such as James Cook and Charles Darwin, making explicit the hidden menace that their accounts only implied.

As Smith argues, the theory of bricolage in the Pacific derives from the work of French anthropologist Claude Lévi-Strauss, whose contrast between engineer and bricoleur in *The Savage Mind* is illuminating of Stevenson's literary practice:

> In *The Savage Mind,* Lévi-Strauss adopted the notion of *bricolage* as a model for describing "savage" creative processes. He contrasted the activities of the *bricoleur* with those of the engineer, who, he claimed,

> epitomized the conceptual mode of Western thought: "The 'bricoleur' is adept at performing a large number of diverse tasks; but unlike the engineer, he does not subordinate each of them to the availability of raw materials and tools conceived and procured for the purpose of the project. His universe of instruments is closed and the rules of his game are always to make do with 'whatever is at hand,' that is to say with a set of tools and materials which is always finite and is also heterogeneous."[34]

The heterogeneity of materials and methods is one of the most important features of Stevenson's South Seas fiction. Indeed, Stevenson's use of recycled documentary materials and techniques reshaped his approach to fiction and brought a new, peculiarly modern complexity and intertextuality to his yarns.

The South Seas were, above all, a place of seduction for Stevenson. His desire to seek out and seduce the reader anticipates in some ways the critical practice of Roland Barthes, who also deploys the metaphor of cruising to articulate the tension between distance and desire at work in textual production: "Does writing in pleasure guarantee—guarantee me, the writer—my reader's pleasure? Not at all. I must seek out this reader (must 'cruise' him) without knowing where he is. A site of bliss is then created. It is not the reader's 'person' that is necessary to me, it is this site."[35] Stevenson's ideal, imaginary island—and islands are key locations in many of his writings, both fictional and nonfictional—would become his site of bliss and serve as the setting for his most powerful late works of fiction. Yet Stevenson was not content to rest with the "pleasure" of the South Seas. Discovering that many of the region's problems, such as disease, depopulation, and war, had resulted from European colonialism, Stevenson would probe beneath the surface of island beauty in his fiction to examine a more sinister reality.

Nonetheless, the first South Seas letter (originally published on February 1, 1891) begins by inviting the reader to participate vicariously in an idyllic, indeed erotic, first encounter with island beauty: "The first experience can never be repeated. The first love, the first sunrise, the first South Sea island are memories apart and touched a virginity of sense" (*ISS*, 6). This passage, while conveying the "thrill of landfall heightened by the strangeness of the shores," also implies that the European's paradise has already been lost—that the "virginity of sense" is no longer susceptible to such intense impressions. Stevenson's account also offers a warning that to succumb to the seductive power of such beauty is to lose one's freedom of action, and he suggests that the island's beauty has "deceived the eye" (6).

This mixture of the seductive and the sinister in the letter is adapted for the opening of "The Beach of Falesá," where the island is first described in an idealized (indeed, eroticized) language that echoes Stevenson's account of an "island landfall" in *The South Seas.* Wiltshire's narration opens with a potent evocation of the island's dreamy allure: "I saw that island first when it was neither night nor morning. The land breeze blew in our faces, and smelt strong of wild lime and vanilla. . . . Here was a fresh experience: even the tongue would be quite strange to me; and the look of these woods and mountains and the rare smell of them renewed my blood."[36] Of course, Wiltshire's blood is also renewed by the sight of Uma, the beautiful native woman whose sexual attractiveness leads him into his illicit, short-term marriage, which became the most controversial aspect of the story. As has been ably documented by Barry Menikoff, Stevenson's narrative underwent severe editorial dismemberment; among other changes, Wiltshire's notorious "contract" did not appear at all in the *Illustrated London News'* serialization of the story. Yet the contract had already appeared in the South Seas letters, being based on an event that Stevenson records in "The Gilberts" section of *The South Seas:* "All these women were legitimately married. It is true that the certificate of one, when she proudly showed it, proved to run thus, that she was 'married for one night' and her gracious partner was at liberty to 'send her to hell' the next morning" (*ISS,* 200).

Other episodes in "The Beach of Falesá" also derived from Stevenson's cruises, as when the missionary Tarleton describes a horrifying incident in which the trader Underhill, one of Wiltshire's predecessors, is buried alive at Case's instigation: "At last a grave was dug, and the living body buried at the far end of the village" (*SST,* 40). The incident, like others in the South Sea tales, was inspired by actual stories told to Stevenson and Fanny—in this case, one that Fanny recorded in her journal, published in 1914 as *Cruise of the "Janet Nichol."*[37]

The decisive narrative for assessing the influence of cruising the South Seas on Stevenson's fictional art, however, is the final story published during his lifetime, *The Ebb-Tide.* As Robert Irwin Hillier remarks, the complex literary treatment of the South Seas reached its apogee in this yarn, rather than in the proposed South Seas book: "*The Ebb-Tide,* which Stevenson and Osbourne first planned almost as a sequel to *The Wrecker* appeared as a serial in *McClure's Magazine* in the United States and *To-Day* in England at the end of 1893 and came out as a book in the spring of 1894. However, the South Seas book which Stevenson had once hoped would be his masterpiece turned out to be the unrevised 'Letters' written for McClure published in book form, minus the Hawaii 'Letters,' two years after his death."[38]

Other critics have detected, in this narrative, the end of the line for Stevenson as a novelist. Vanessa Smith argues, "For *The Ebb-Tide*'s trio . . . a general failure of enterprise is signaled by the exhaustion of narrative possibility that marks their aleatory or shallow creative endeavours." A significant critical debate has developed around the character of Attwater, the English colonist of New Island, representative as he is of a hybrid of aristocrat, evangelical missionary, and colonial trader. Several models or sources have been suggested for Attwater. Smith argues that in Attwater, "the missionary's authority and influence defeat the projects of the superseded beachcomber" and that "Stevenson represents in the figure of Attwater the dominance of evangelical discourse: a discourse which, in the later nineteenth-century Pacific, prospered through association with colonial policy."[39] Frank McLynn goes further, describing Attwater as a "terrifying figure . . . [a] monster who conflates the 'business' of profiteering with fundamentalist Christianity in the typical manner of the Victorians." Yet McLynn suggests a more specific, autobiographical source for the tyrant of New Island: "At a deeper level Attwater is a barely disguised portrait of Thomas Stevenson and represents in hyperbolic form all that Louis most feared and despised in his father."[40] Of course, there are other instances of Stevenson's depicting his troubled relationship with his father in fiction. Yet this intriguing link between Attwater and Victorian evangelism in general, and Thomas Stevenson in particular, has led critics to overlook an equally important—and arguably more far-reaching—source for Attwater's character in the characters Stevenson encounters during his South Seas cruises. Stevenson's narrative in *The Ebb-Tide* leads us from idyllic "first encounter" to the grim figure of Attwater. In similar manner, the narrative of *In the South Seas* leads us from the first island to the native tyrant, Tembinok', the most compelling figure of the book.

In *The Ebb-Tide,* the aptly named New Island is described from Herrick's idealizing point of view aboard the *Farallone* at the opening of the second part ("The Quartette"), in terms that echo the opening of "The Beach of Falesá": "[T]he isle—the undiscovered, the scarce-believed in—now lay before them and close aboard; and Herrick thought that never in his dreams had he beheld anything more strange and delicate. The beach was excellently white, the continuous barrier of trees inimitably green; the land perhaps ten feet high, the trees thirty more. . . . [S]o slender it seemed amidst the outrageous breakers, so frail and pretty, he would scarce have wondered to see it sink and disappear without a sound" (*SST,* 188). This pointing to the fragility of the island is tantamount to a warning: the atoll is not what it seems.

The narrator remarks the uncanny impression of abandonment conveyed by the island, despite the trio's initial surprise at seeing "the roofs of men . . . a substantial country farm with its attendant hamlet; a long line of sheds and store-houses; apart, upon the one side, a deep-verandae'd dwelling-house" (189). For despite these signs of life, "there breathed from it a sense of desertion that was almost poignant, no human figure was to be observed going to and fro about the houses, and there was no sound of human industry or enjoyment" (190). This image of desertion echoes Stevenson's account of visiting one of the Eight Islands, which he called "The Free Island":

> Here and there along the foreshore stood a lone pandamus, and once a trinity of disheveled palms. In all the first part of that journey, I recall but three houses and a single church. Plenty of houses, kine, and sullen-looking hills were there; but not a human countenance. "Where are the people?" I asked.—"Pau Kanaka make—Done; people dead," replied Apaka, with the singular childish giggle which the traveler soon learns to be a mark of Polynesian sensibility . . . the remark, such as it was, became the burthen of our ride.—"no people? No houses?" I would cry, at the turn of every bay; and back would come the antiphone: "Pau Kanake make."[41]

Similarly, when Stevenson describes a visit to Fakarava atoll in the Paumotus, the uncanny absence of life on these islands anticipates *The Ebb-Tide:* a story that features the problem of depopulation—a result of disease, premature death, and migration—that Stevenson addresses in many parts of *In the South Seas.* Of course, in the chapter from *In the South Seas* cited above, Stevenson learns of the deaths from a surviving islander. By contrast, the depredation of humanity in *The Ebb-Tide* is disclosed not by a native but by a colonialist—and the object that serves as his surrogate.

The narrator of *The Ebb-Tide* does not, like Wiltshire, transfer the seductive appeal of the island onto a native woman. Instead, he draws attention to a prominent discarded object that, despite its femininity, serves as an emblem of the white man's colonization of the islands: "[O]n the top of the beach and hard by the flagstaff, a woman of exorbitant stature and as white as snow was to be seen beckoning with uplifted arm. The second glance identified her as a piece of naval sculpture, the figure-head of a ship" (*SST,* 190). The most striking aspect of this figurehead—its extreme whiteness—is soon identified not as a sign of purity but as a symptom of disease: "its leprous whiteness reigned alone in that hamlet" (190), a phrase that recalls the opening sentence of the novel: "Throughout the island world of the Pacific, scattered men of many European races and from almost every grade of society carry activity and disseminate disease" (123).

In Stevenson's narrative, disease is represented not simply as a consequence of European colonialism but as a metaphor for it. Stevenson wrote widely about the effects of leprosy on Polynesian society and even stayed for a while at a leper colony in the region. Yet his sympathy for lepers did not prevent him from using the disease as sign for European corruption. This "leprous" figurehead—which plays a key symbolic role in the story—is another object quarried from Stevenson's record of his cruise, in this case a visit made to the "pearl island" of Penrhyn (significantly, the original title of the story was "The Pearl Fisher"). The local sailors on Penrhyn possessed such a figurehead, Lloyd Osbourne's photographs of which are included in Fanny's book *Cruise of the "Janet Nichol."* Stevenson and Fanny visited Penrhyn on May 9 and 10, 1890, and Stevenson described the visit in a section of his narrative called "A Pearl Island: Penrhyn" that appeared in the *New York Sun* (May 24, 1891) but not in *Black and White* and was not published in the 1896 edition of *The South Seas.* The following extract is from Stevenson's typescript:

> All that was here and that could be called wealth came from the sea: pearl shell and wreck wood <were> everywhere. On one side of the trader's house, they were weighing shell; on the other was a yard of stacked timber that had never grown upon that island; between on the verandah, the figure head of the lost ship stood sentinel: a very white and haughty lady, roman nosed and dressed in the costume of the directory, contumeliously, with head thrown back, she gazed on the house and the crowding natives. There was a piano in the sitting room; but the poor instrument had suffered in the shipwreck, and when the notes were struck, replied at random. Yet another waif from that disaster was a lad of my own land and city; and I thought it strange to stand by the figure head, in the tropic sun, beset by a throng of Penrhyn Islanders, and be talking of the Glasgow road, the Haymarket station, and the huge distillery.[42]

What proves most striking to Stevenson is the proud, almost aristocratic demeanor of the figure. The queenlike pose of superiority prepares the reader for *The Ebb-Tide,* as it "reigned alone in that hamlet." Fanny's description of the figurehead in her journal is written in terms that echo those of Stevenson: "From the first, I had been puzzled by a strange figure on the trader's veranda. When we were nearer I discovered it to be the figurehead of a wrecked ship, a very haughty lady in a magnificent costume. She held her head proudly in the air and had a fine, hooked nose." Fanny goes on to describe the troubling influence of the figurehead on the natives of Penrhyn: "When the figurehead came ashore people were terribly alarmed by the appearance of the 'white lady.' The children are still frightened into submission by threats of being handed over to her."[43] Given its regal bearing and "magnificent costume," the figurehead could represent Queen Victoria, the distant monarch who might be expected to remind Stevenson of his native roots, "the Glasgow Road, the Haymarket Station." If so, then Victoria is as ambivalent a figure here as she is in Kipling's poem "The Widow at Windsor" or his short story "The Man Who Would Be King," in which the monarch becomes a shallow artifice or pretext for colonial expansion. Although the nautical meaning of "figurehead"—"an ornamental carving, usually a bust or full-length figure, placed over the cutwater of a ship"—dates from the mid-eighteenth century, the *Shorter OED* identifies a secondary meaning that emerged in the late nineteenth century: "[A] nominal leader, president, etc, who has little or no authority or influence." This was of course the period in which two powerful prime ministers—Benjamin Disraeli and William Gladstone (who was in office when *The Ebb-Tide* was published in 1894, as he had been when *Treasure Island* appeared in 1883)—dominated the British political scene and largely eclipsed the political authority of the monarchy. Moreover, the power of the queen over her distant possessions—despite having been declared "Empress of India" in 1877—was doubtful at best. Hence, at the end of the nineteenth century, the queen was increasingly becoming a figurehead who officially "reigned alone" but whose actual power was compromised by her dependence on her prime ministers.

This insight into the limited influence of Queen Victoria—especially in distant lands, even those over which she nominally reigned—is also shown in an episode from "The Beach of Falesá." Uma, trying to convince her "husband," Wiltshire, of the need to cultivate an alliance with the local chief, Maea, asks him, "Victoreea, he big chief?" to which Wiltshire replies in the affirmative and adds that "I believed the old lady [Queen Victoria] was rather partial to me" (*SST*, 48). However, his confidence in being under the protection of a distant monarch is dismissed by Uma, who warns him, "Victoreea he big chief, like you too much. No can help you here in Falesá; no can do—too far off. Maea he small chief—stop here. Suppose he like you—make you all right" (48). Uma advocates the superior practical importance of local allegiances over some notional relationship to a distant center of empire or a remote monarch, a position that is validated when Maea defies the taboo on Wiltshire, comes to his store, and buys "like a gentleman" (58). As this phrase suggests, Maea's munificence leads Wiltshire to reveal his racial prejudice, stating, "I tell you I shook hands with that Kanaka like as if he was the best white man in Europe" (57). In a significant phrase, Wiltshire refers to Uma's speech as "a specimen about Queen Victoria and the devil" (60)—suggesting a parallel between the monarch and Case, who is known as "Tiapolo."

In Stevenson and Osbourne's story, the figurehead becomes a poignant symbol of the devastation wreaked by colonial control and manipulation by Europeans in the South Seas.[44] Yet despite its authoritative (even intimidating) appearance, the statue is impotent and passive, remaining on a beach as a helpless witness to—and eventual victim of—the greed and cruelty of the four men. The figurehead is specifically linked—in its large stature, its whiteness, and its menace—to the English colonialist Attwater, who is described as "a huge fellow, six foot four in height, and of a build proportionally strong" (191) and is invariably associated with white clothing. First appearing in his "white clothes, the full dress of the tropics" (191), Attwater is later described as being "dressed in white drill" (192) and is identified on the shore by "his white clothes shining in the chequered dusk" (196). In addition to these physical parallels between object and man, the story may suggest a kind of image-worship of the figurehead by Attwater (for whom religion is "a savage thing"), as Davis describes his enviable situation in having "all your gods about you, and in as snug a berth as this" (195).

Frank McLynn argues that the white figurehead is "a symbol of hope . . . whose whiteness turns out on closer inspection to be 'leprous'" and asserts—erroneously, I believe—that the story depicts the corruption of innocence in the South Seas.[45] I cannot agree that the figurehead ever symbolizes either hope or innocence in the novel. First, its "leprous" quality does not appear only "on closer inspection" but is observed on first sighting from the *Farallone,* while the trio is still at sea. Hence the figure is associated from the outset with corruption and betrayal, appearing to welcome visitors to the tropical atoll ("beckoning with uplifted arm") while its leprous appearance warns new arrivals of the actual diseased state of the island. In an unpublished chapter of *The South Seas* called "Leprosy on Penrhyn," Stevenson describes in more detail the ravages of the disease in Polynesia: "The facts are not clear: we are told, on the one hand, that some indigenous form of the disease was known in Samoa within the memory of man; we are assured, on the other, that there is not even a name for it in any island language. There is no doubt, at least, about the savage rapidity with which it spreads when introduced. And there is none that, when a leper is first seen, the islanders approach him without disaffection and are never backward to supply him with a wife."[46] The lack of fear with which the trio approach both the figurehead and Attwater mirrors this courage of the natives in the face of a deadly disease, while the phrase "supply him with a wife" recalls "The Beach of Falesá," in which Case does just this for Wiltshire, thereby "infecting" him with a tapu (i.e., taboo).

The figurehead thus serves as a constant reminder that disease has already devastated the island population. Indeed, the statue is one of the only "survivors" of what Attwater describes as "a dreadful sickness" (*SST*, 193), admitting that the population has been decimated by smallpox.

The symbolism of the figurehead becomes more sinister as the trio remain longer on the island. Where it had initially seemed to be beckoning, Herrick later perceives it in a posture of assault, "her formidable arm apparently hurling something, whether shell or missile, in the direction of the anchored schooner" (*SST*, 200). The figurehead thus has been transmuted from a token of the conquest of the island by the white man (as "a blind conductress of a ship among the waves" [200]) to an emblem of native defense against colonization. As such, it may suggest "the ruins of an empire," which, Attwater admits, "would leave me frigid" (201–2). The narrative elaborates on this symbolism of native resistance, as the figurehead comes to appear as a martial figure, "her helmeted head tossed back," or "a defiant deity from the island, coming forth to its threshold with a rush as of one about to fly" (200). The idea of the figurehead as inspiring reverence, absorbed into native religious practices (I have already suggested that she is one of Attwater's "gods") is continued as Herrick "found it in his heart to regret that she was not a goddess, nor yet he a pagan, that he might have bowed down before her" (200). Yet the figurehead also inspires in Herrick "singular feelings of curiosity and romance, and suffered his mind to travel to and fro in her life-history" (200). Identifying her with the romance of cruising—indeed, of adventure—Herrick wonders, "[W]as even this the end of so many adventures . . . or were more behind?" (200). In fact, although the travels of the figurehead are over, its greatest trial is yet to come.

In the climactic scene of the story, Attwater shoots at the figurehead as part of a "cruel game," in which the bullet apparently meant for Davis finds its mark in the wooden statue, with which the captain becomes curiously conflated, as the statue suffers a wound on his behalf: the shot causes "a spasmodic movement of the victim, and immediately above the middle of his forehead, a black hole marred the whiteness of the figurehead" (248). Two more shots are fired, and after the "third shot . . . he was bleeding from one ear. . . . The cruel game of which he was the puppet was now clear to Davis; three times he had drunk of death, and he must look to drink of it seven times more before he was despatched" (248). Eventually, however, Attwater spares Davis, instructing him, "Go, and sin no more, sinful father" (248), as a result of which Davis becomes a religious zealot, serving as "Attwater's spoiled darling and pet penitent" (252). Yet the violence of the scene suggests Attwater's savage nature through his use of force to manipulate those weaker than him. The whiteness of the figurehead and its disease and wounds suggest that the white man will suffer from the ravages of colonialism.

McLynn offers an interpretation of the scene that attempts to weave together Stevenson's life in the Pacific with his fictions in claiming, "The abandonment of the hope implicit in 'The Beach of Falesá' is symbolized by Attwater's destruction of the figurehead; in terms of RLS's life it is possible to read this as the destruction of the utopian dreams he took to Samoa, the end of innocence, the impossibility of believing in 'noble savages' or the possibility of a better world."[47] Leaving aside the question of whether there is "hope implicit in 'The Beach of Falesá,'" McLynn's argument that the figurehead originally suggests innocence in *The Ebb-Tide* is scarcely credible. By the time they arrive on the island, the trio are thoroughly corrupted and guilty, having stolen a ship (whose previous captain died of smallpox) and its cargo. Hence they immediately suspect a plot, or perhaps their paranoia makes them aware of the reality of colonial manipulation on the island: "[T]here came to them, in these pregnant seconds, a sense of being watched and played with, and of a blow impending, that was hardly bearable" (*SST,* 190–91). Moreover, the figure itself is, as we have seen, identified from the start as an image of corruption.

As the narrative makes clear, Attwater's "cruel game" began long before the trio's arrival on New Island. His treatment of the newcomers is merely an extension of his ruthless tyranny over the natives in his quest for pearls. However, the ritual of shooting at the figurehead in place of Davis does expose the ideological complexity of Stevenson's fictional reworking of material from his South Seas journal. Indeed, the episode illuminates a neglected source for the character of Attwater in one of the most impressive and memorable figures whom Stevenson encountered on his travels in the South Seas: King Tembinok', "The King of Apemama" in the Gilbert Islands. Neil Rennie, in his introduction to the 1996 edition, has pointed out the novelistic quality of this section of *In the South Seas,* terming it "an entertaining narrative [with] a powerful character around whom all the material naturally revolves."[48] Indeed, more text is dedicated to Tembinok' than to any other individual in the journal and letters—Stevenson introduces him as the "one great personage in the Gilberts," who is "solely conspicuous, the hero of song, the butt of gossip" (*ISS*, 209).[49]

The status of Tembinok' derives from the independence of his domain. As Vanessa Smith observes, Apemama was an exception to the rule of white dominion in Polynesia, "a territory not yet penetrated by the European" in which "Europeans resided only as employees of the high chiefs, and for specified periods; trade and importation were strictly controlled, and foreign innovations were either prohibited or made the prerogative of the ruler."[50] Yet the king's "literary territory" does not end with the South Seas letters (only the *New York Sun* ran the pieces on the Gilberts, as *Black and White* concluded its serialization with the letters on Hawaii). Rather, his influence reappears in the surprising form of the Cambridge-educated colonialist of New Island, Attwater.

The parallels between Attwater and Tembinok' are numerous in Stevenson's text. In the first place, Tembinok' rules his island with a Winchester rifle and tyrannizes his subjects—for example, following the Stevensons' arrival on Apemama, Tembinok' orders his men to build them a temporary residence, named Equator Town, after their schooner. On being told by Stevenson that the men had not completed the building, Tembinok' "rose, called for a Winchester, stepped without the royal palisade, and fired two shots in the air. A shot in the air is the first Apemama warning; it has the force of a proclamation in more loquacious countries" (*ISS*, 219). Moreover, his method of punishing a disobedient subject directly parallels Attwater's "cruel game" of torture with a rifle: "As soon as he was well within range, the travestied monarch fired the six shots over his head, at his feet, and on either hand of him: the second Apemama warning, startling in itself, fatal in significance, for the next time his majesty will aim to hit. I am told the king is a crack shot; that when he aims to kill the grave may be got ready; and when he aims to miss, misses by so near a margin that the culprit tastes six times the bitterness of death" (230).

Clearly, the king's expertise with a rifle resembles Attwater's. Indeed, Stevenson frequently associates marksmanship and possession of the famed repeating rifle with tyranny, as when Wiltshire, in his final showdown with Case in "The Beach of Falesá," exclaims that "the brute had a Winchester, and before

I could as much as see him his second shot knocked me over like a ninepin" (*SST,* 66). Attwater is rarely seen unarmed and defends his property with "the muzzle of a pointed rifle" (230). When Attwater arrives by boat to greet the *Farallone,* "on the thwart beside him there leaned a Winchester rifle" (192). In a striking intertextual moment in *The Ebb-Tide,* Attwater alludes admiringly to his counterpart on Apemama, telling Herrick of "an old king one knew in the western islands, who used to empty a Winchester all round a man, and stir his hair or nick a rag out of his clothes with every ball except the last; and that went plump between the eyes. It was pretty practice" (209). Attwater's appreciation of the king's marksmanship is another count against him morally but reflects their kinship as ruthless rulers.

Stevenson portrays Tembinok' not only as a despotic native king but also as an avid trader and collector whose desperate acquisitiveness mirrors the Englishman's avarice: he is "greedy of things new and foreign" and "possessed by the seven devils of the collector" (*ISS,* 213). This is similar to Attwater, who resides on the island solely to collect pearls and shell. There are also parallels between Tembinok' and Stevenson, who eagerly collected relics of the South Seas on his travels. In one episode recorded in the South Seas journal, Stevenson attempts to bribe Temtak, a priest in the Gilberts, to sell him a handcrafted box that is used in rites for healing the sick: "My appetite had been whetted by Temtak's boxes; and Captain Reid having obtained the King's leave to buy one if he could, he and I went down to the big medicine tree in the afternoon. We pushed into the square enclosure lifted the mat and began to examine the boxes. They were very neatly made of Pandanus wood, with an effect of pillaring along the sides . . . and standing on four legs."[51]

Stevenson goes on to recount the reluctance of the native priest to bargain away the sacred objects of his profession: "Temtak refused to sell, he was pressed and insisted in his refusal. It was explained we only wanted one: no matter: two were necessary for the healing of the sick. A pound was named: in vain; two pounds followed with the like result. . . . At length the Captain named the incredible figure of five pounds: At which sound, the maniaps were emptied. . . . The sum, I could clearly perceive, transcended, or at least fulfilled, the highest dreams of island avarice."[52] Stevenson's method of bargaining when faced with resistance to his acquisitiveness strongly resembles that of Tembinok' on being told that "the article is not for sale": "His autocratic nature rears at the affront of opposition. He accepts it for a challenge; sets his teeth like a hunter going at a fence; and with no mark of emotion, scarce even of interest, stolidly piles up the price" (*ISS*, 213). Stevenson's use of the term *interest* suggests the commercial practices of the West in the context of the accumulation of wealth by a native king.

Attwater's materialism, however, is still more sinister, not least because it is masked by a missionary purpose. Davis, the mercenary sailor, is the one who correctly divines Attwater's true motives for being on the island in observing that "for ten years he's been doing a great business. It's pearl and shell, of course; there couldn't be nothing else in such a place, and no doubt the shell goes off regularly by this *Trinity Hall*, and the money for it straight into the bank. . . . Yes, sir; the pearls!" (*SST*, 197). What Herrick calls his "ten years' collection" (198) of pearls has been acquired through the ruthless sacrifice of countless native lives. Moreover, Attwater's Christianity, far from moderating his profiteering, is in fact its ideological engine: as he explains to Herrick, "I have had a business, and a colony, and a mission of my own. I was a man of the world before I was a Christian; I'm a man of the world still, and I made my mission pay" (204). Beneath the veneer of Christian gentleman and Cambridge graduate, Stevenson suggests, Attwater has "gone native," acting out his primitive and acquisitive impulses and setting free his aggression from moral restraint. With his claim to Herrick that "I was making a new people here" (204), Attwater clearly demonstrates his godlike ambition but also his thorough absorption into island culture. The "island dinner" he prepares for his guests is a sign of his complete immersion in native customs, consisting as it does of "turtle-soup and steak, fish, fowls, a sucking pig, a cocoanut salad, and sprouting cocoanut roasted for desert . . . not even the condiments were European" (212). Indeed, Attwater is compared with native islanders from his first appearance, where the narrator observes, "A complexion, naturally dark, had been tanned in the island to a hue hardly distinguishable from that of a Tahitian" (192). In the denouement, while aiming his rifle at Davis, "Attwater smiled like a red Indian" (248), a description that further strengthens his association with native peoples.

With these parallel portraits of Attwater and Tembinok', Stevenson suggests that the boundary between white man and savage is largely imaginary.

Despite Attwater's missionary zeal, in worshipping idols such as the figurehead he may be only "half Christian" (202), suggesting a hybrid between Western and Polynesian influences. Further corporeal and sartorial parallels emerge between the king of Apemama and the English trader, both of whom embody a hybridity of cultures. Both are larger-than-life figures: Attwater is described as over six feet tall and strongly built (191), while Tembinok' is remarkable for "his weighty body" and, although corpulent, being "lusty rather than fat" (*ISS*, 211). In a passage later deleted from the South Seas journal, Stevenson describes how Tembinok' greets the new arrivals in person:

> The ship was no sooner at anchor, than a boat came out with Timpanok's [*sic*] ladder: and presently after, his majesty appears upon the scene himself and comes on board. . . . This visit to a ship is the end and the reward of the King's lips. A big man, heavy with a somewhat elephantine gait, a bold, strong eye, a singular {hooked} beaked profile, and a considerable mane of straight black hair: always elegantly dressed <perhaps> in green velveteen, <perhaps in pajamas of> cardinal red silk: {his manners plain but agreeable}. He has a way of sharply considering a stranger. It was not till the second day of acquaintance that he expressed the result in these flattering terms: "I look you eye; you good man; you no lie."[53]

That Tembinok' has a hooked or beaked nose, resembling the figurehead seen by the Stevensons on Penrhyn, is striking. Like her, he "reigns alone," as "he alone remains, the last tyrant, the last erect vestige of a dead society" (*ISS*, 209). Tembinok' greets the *Equator* personally, appearing as though out of nowhere: "The village adjoins on the south, a cluster of high-roofed maniaps. And village and palace seemed deserted. We were scarce yet moored, however, before distant and busy figures appeared upon the beach, a boat was launched, and a crew pulled out to us bringing the king's ladder" (210–11). Similarly, Attwater appears from a scene of desolation (*SST*, 190) to welcome the crew of the *Farallone:* "A boat put suddenly and briskly out, and a voice hailed. . . . The boat was manned with a couple of brown oarsmen in scanty kilts of blue. The speaker, who was steering, wore white clothes, the full dress of the tropics; a wide hat shaded his face; but it could be seen that he was of stalwart size, and his voice sounded like a gentleman's" (191). There is an important ambiguity in this first appearance of Attwater, especially respecting his race. He is in the company of "brown oarsmen," and his whiteness is signified by his clothing rather than his skin, as his face is shaded. A gentleman in voice, Attwater in his appearance is also immaculate, "dressed in white twill, exquisitely made; his scarf and tie were of tender-coloured silks" (192). Tembinok' is likewise distinguished by his elegant attire, dressed either in a "naval uniform" or "trousers and a singular jacket with shirt tails, the cut and fit wonderful for island workmanship, the material always handsome, sometimes green velvet, sometimes cardinal red silk" (*ISS*, 211–12).

Despite their dapper appearance, both rulers are brutal oppressors of their peoples. Stevenson describes Tembinok' as "the only master, the only male, the sole dispenser of honours" and shares horrifying rumors of his savagery: "I hear of him shooting at a wife for some levity on board a schooner. Another, on some more serious offence, he slew outright; he exposed her body in an open box, and (to make the warning more memorable) suffered it to putrefy before the palace gate" (*ISS*, 224). In the manuscript journal, Stevenson writes at greater length about the draconian disciplinary measures employed by Tembinok' on Apemama: "The laws are strict and strictly but very justly enforced. No native must drink except with the King's leave, none go naked, none be abroad without a lantern between the hours of 9 and 4. Punishment is by fine; enforced by mortgage on crops, convict labour, and imprisonment on the insular prison. This last is considered highly dishonourable; and the convict sometimes escapes from his disgrace by suicide."[54] Stevenson's comment that the laws of Tembinok' are "very justly enforced" reveals a sympathy for the king that emerges elsewhere in his narrative and may also be detected in Herrick's ambivalent response to Attwater.

Despite this brutality exhibited by Tembinok' toward his people, as Stevenson relates, "they made rather a hero of the man" (*ISS* 224). Indeed, Vanessa Smith has argued that Stevenson was far from being a neutral observer of the autocracy of Tembinok': "Tem Binoka [*sic*]mimics, but also effectively embodies, an imperialist presence. He supervises the building of Equator city [*sic*], a special compound in which the Stevensons are to reside, in colonial costume. . . .

His host's grand gesture enables Stevenson to play out a further fantasy of primacy: the founding of the city. . . . The primacy he experiences in Abemama [*sic*] is merely an experiment in imperialism, of which, by desiring to play first author, he has become the subject."[55] This sympathy between Stevenson and Tembinok' has also been observed by other critics: Robert Irwin Hillier, for example, has pointed to Stevenson's tendency to idealize, or even idolize, the powerful king in stating that "in Abemama [*sic*] . . . [King] Tembinok' grew fond of his guests, and Stevenson, who was not immune from the appeal of the cult of the hero, admired the tyrant's rule rather than being appalled at the whimsical cruelty which accompanied it."[56]

Yet despite Stevenson's admiration for Tembinok', when reinvented as an English colonialist, the island tyrant becomes a viable and visible target of scathing criticism from Stevenson. One might argue that the reanimation of Tembinok' as Attwater gives Stevenson license to attack the callousness of the despot without pandering to racial stereotypes. Though Herrick admits to being "attracted and repelled" (*SST*, 197) by Attwater, the narrative illustrates the host's callous indifference to native suffering as he changes abruptly from discussing the decimation of the islanders by smallpox to confirming a dinner invitation. Attwater narrates his version of punishment when his system of "justice had been made a fool of" in terms that recall the discipline of Tembinok'. Attwater tells his guests a story of how one native, called "Sullens," is falsely accused of breaking the rules and is accordingly punished. Attwater relates that he found Sullens "hanging in a cocoa-palm—I'm not botanist enough to tell you how—but it's the way, in nine cases out of ten, these natives commit suicide" (218), a description echoing the practice that Stevenson recorded in his journal. Sullens's suicide is followed by Attwater's sending the native he names "Obsequiousness" up a tree to retrieve the mutilated corpse and then shooting him dead so "they came to ground together" (219). Attwater's summary punishment of the native is a more extreme version of the way Tembinok' treats those who dare to disobey him. Yet Herrick's impassioned outburst against Attwater's atrocity—"It was a murder . . . a cold-hearted, bloody-minded murder! You monstrous being!" (219)—is notably lacking in Stevenson's account of Tembinok'.

Indeed, one episode from the journal suggests that Stevenson exploited the rough justice meted out by Tembinok': he writes,

> His cook, a big handsome mulatto looking fellow, was to come to us and learn; he was imprudent, unutterably lazy; I ran with him one day thrusting him before me by the shoulders through a delighted village, and he declared that I had been the death of him. It was serious to complain to Timpanok [*sic*] of a man; but my own cook was being killed with overwork, and my first duty was to him. I put it carefully to the sovereign that he was too old and too lazy. "I think he savy too much" observed the musing Timpanok. And the next I knew was that the cook cut me on the road; and the new man (steward, he was called who came to take his place) informed Foo [Ah Fu, Stevenson's cook] in the kitchen that his majesty had fired all around the cook and frightened him to death.[57]

As with the building of Equator Town, Stevenson finds it easy to approve of the despotism of Tembinok' when this suits his own interests. Notwithstanding Smith's assessment, Stevenson does not always seem to be aware of the extent of his complicity with Tembinok'.

## Colonial Cruising

If, as I have argued, Stevenson based the character of Attwater on his knowledge of Tembinok', the critical question that we must ask is, why did Stevenson not directly represent the ruler of New Island as a native king, rather than as an English colonialist, in his fiction? It might seem puzzling that Stevenson did not make explicit his dependence on this intriguing original for *The Ebb-Tide.* There are several possible explanations for this disguised transmutation of the Gilbertian tyrant of Apemama into his Cambridge-educated counterpart.

The first explanation is that Stevenson lacked confidence in his ability to portray native characters in fiction. It is plausible, certainly, that Stevenson felt more confident in critically portraying an upper-class English colonialist who incorporated certain characteristics of the native king than he would depicting the native king directly. Yet one can refute this theory with evidence from Stevenson's previous writings, especially "The Beach of Falesá," in which he had successfully portrayed Uma, a native woman—developing in the process his own literary version of Polynesian speech. "The Beach of Falesá" demonstrates the possibility of combining British and Polynesian characters in the same story. Moreover, the characters in "The Bottle Imp" are Hawaiians who speak Stevenson's version of Polynesian English.[58]

A second possibility is that Stevenson wished to conceal how extensively he was drawing on "documentary" material for his South Seas stories. Renowned as an exemplar of romance—with its emphasis on the fertile creative imagination, the ability to defy realism and create highly romantic characters and situations—Stevenson might have resisted his fiction's dependence on "fact." In an interesting allusion to this tension, Stevenson states that the praise Tembinok' gives him, "You no lie," represents "a doubtful compliment to a writer of romance" (*ISS,* 218). The reception of the letters, criticized as unromantic and monotonous, would not have encouraged Stevenson to make the link between letter and yarn explicit. Thus, the unreal quality present at Attwater's island and in the man—in the apparition of the white-clad colonialist from a presumably deserted island—derives from the concealed history of the Gilbert Islands. Had Stevenson made obvious his reliance on a native "original," this effect might have been tarnished.

A third theory is that it was, in fact, Stevenson's design to call into question the distinction between native tyrant and English autocrat. One of the central justifications for colonialism in the South Seas—as elsewhere in the "undeveloped" world—was that the natives were inferior, savage, and thus in need of being converted and civilized. Whether through missionary influence or trade, therefore, colonialism could be claimed as a natural assertion of the white man's superior civilization. In addition, Stevenson's portrayal of Attwater allows a "commentary upon the false promise, implicit in missionary discourse, that metropolitan techniques can transform natives into white men."[59] Stevenson's story rather demonstrates the reverse dynamic, depicting Attwater as an Englishman with a veneer of civilization, beneath which he is the most savage individual in the story, shooting at his enemies and sacrificing the natives to his lust for riches. One could speculate about the influence of atavism on this portrait of a white man "gone native." But the dislocation between Tembinok' and Attwater allows Stevenson to disrupt the rigid hierarchy of white man and savage and thus dispute the ideological basis for colonialism.

A more historical explanation would be that the substitution of Attwater for Tembinok' (if *substitution* is the right word) as "king" of the island reflects the historical transition of the Gilbert Islands from native self-government to British control. In his editorial note to the 1896 Edinburgh edition of *The South Seas*—also published independently by Scribner's the same year—Sidney Colvin writes that the Gilberts "at the time of [Stevenson's] visit was under independent native government, but has since been annexed by Great Britain" and that the account of Tembinok' therefore "derives additional interest from describing a state of manners and government which has now passed away."[60] As Attwater makes clear, his island has not yet even been mapped: he tells Herrick, "If it gets upon the chart, the skippers will make nice work of it" (*SST*, 202). This invisibility of New Island suggests the instability of many of the islands in the South Seas, which were named, renamed, conquered, and ruled over by distant colonial powers. Stevenson first visited the Gilberts in 1889, whereas *The Ebb-Tide* was not published until 1894. As the Gilberts were annexed by Britain in 1892, before the publication of his novel, Stevenson may have decided to represent this loss of independence or identity by turning the native king into an English colonial ruler, one whose only interest in the island is mercenary.

Yet the most convincing reason for the transformation is that Stevenson saw his South Sea tales as quite different in purpose and status from his documentary writing about the region. To include a portrayal of a native king in one of his stories would have blurred the boundary between genres in a way that Stevenson would have wished to avoid. In his desire to be "a serious chronicler of the Pacific," Stevenson made a sharp distinction between his "South Sea Book"—to which he dedicated his best literary labor—and the yarns that he was producing for popular consumption.[61] Writing to Colvin in September 1889 (in a letter dated August 22), Stevenson set out his plans for his "South Sea Yarns," commenting on the "strange ways of life, I think, they set forth: things that I can scarce touch upon, or even not at all, in my travel book." Of *The Wrecker*, for example, Stevenson wrote to Colvin, "[O]f course it don't set up to be a book—only a long tough yarn with some pictures of the manners of today in the greater world."[62]

Stevenson's cherished distinction between yarn and book broke down, however, during the serial publication of the "letters" when his insights into South

Seas culture and society were juxtaposed with fictional works by authors such as Doyle, Kipling, Haggard, and himself. Stevenson came to recognize that the South Seas journal and letters could be quarried for more than a nonfictional work on the South Seas. These materials could also serve to revive Stevenson's interest in romance, providing settings and characters for a new style of fiction. Stevenson's realization that his life in the South Seas demanded a new relationship with the reader is reflected in his assessment that "I must learn to address readers from the uttermost parts of the sea" (*ISS*, 5), but he lamented to Colvin that in the South Seas letters "I have told too much" and "had not sufficient confidence in the reader, and have overfed him."[63] Desiring to "cruise" in Roland Barthes's sense of seducing the reader, Stevenson's insight was that he must dismember his corpus and publish his literary remains in more appealing portions if he was to satisfy the voracious appetite of the "fireside travellers" (5) who constituted his audience.

# SIX

## "Buridan's donkey"

### The (Para)texts of Samoan Colonial History in *David Balfour* and *A Footnote to History*

ONE OF THE PARADOXES of Stevenson's literary activity on Samoa is that he wrote a number of texts dwelling on the history and culture of his native country and city. As he wrote to J. M. Barrie, "It is a singular thing that I should live here in the South Seas under conditions so new and so striking, and yet my imagination so continually inhabit the cold old huddle of gray hills from which we come. I have just finished *David Balfour*."[1] The segue to his completed novel is revealing, for it implies that writing *David Balfour* allowed Stevenson to travel imaginatively to his old home and to reestablish the connection that he had lost. The novel's status as a sequel to *Kidnapped,* moreover, contributes to the impression that time has stood still, that the world is the same in 1893 as it was in 1886.

Perhaps influenced by Stevenson's accounts, critics have tended to view his late Scottish writings as expressing nostalgia for Scotland and to insist on treating them as a distinct category from his South Seas writings. Ann Colley, for example, observes that Stevenson "continued to write extensively, often romantically and lovingly about Scotland, and to revisit its highlands and lowlands through his work on *Catriona (David Balfour), The Master of Ballantrae,* and *Weir of Hermiston.* But Stevenson also launched upon what has now come to be known as his South Seas or Pacific fiction. In these texts he took as his subject the white man's presence in the Pacific and depicted, as forthrightly as he was able, the encounters between colonials and islanders."[2] The assumption behind this analysis is that Stevenson's Scottish writings and Pacific texts are attempting quite distinct purposes. In this chapter I argue that Stevenson used his Scottish fiction—specifically, *David Balfour*—not as an outlet for nostalgia but to develop a critique of the colonial conditions on Samoa. As such, *David Balfour* belongs in the company of *A Footnote to History,* the nonfiction text in which he developed his most scathing dissection of the impact of European colonialism on his adopted country.

In August 1892, in the midst of fervid literary and political activity on Samoa, Stevenson had recourse to the figure of the donkey to articulate a narrative dilemma, as he had once used it in an earlier work, *Travels with a Donkey* (1879), to express ambivalence about travel and his relations to the feminine (see chapter 2): in writing Sidney Colvin that "I have come to a collapse this morning on D[avid].B[alfour].," Stevenson explained that he "wrote a chapter one way, half re-copied it in another, and now stand halting between the two like Buridan's donkey. These sorts of cruces are to me the most insoluble, and I should not wonder if D.B. stuck there for a week or two."[3] His invocation of the problem ascribed to the medieval French philosopher, concerning an ass unable to choose between a bundle of hay and a pail of water, suggests a poignant image of authorial indecision: the ass, of course, dies of hunger and thirst, unable to resolve its dilemma. In making reference to the difficulty that he experienced in writing the novel intended as a sequel to *Kidnapped*—eventually published in 1893 under the titles of *David Balfour* (U.S.) and *Catriona* (U.K.)—Stevenson addresses a problem of indeterminacy that hampered completion of the original novel (which had been published in 1886) as well as its successor.[4]

At the end of *Kidnapped,* Stevenson indicates that the story is incomplete and that its continuation rests in the hands of its readers: "The editor has a great kindness for both Alan and David, and would gladly spend much of his life in their society; but in this he may find himself to stand alone."[5] *David Balfour,* with its subtitle of "Further Adventures," appears to fulfill Stevenson's pledge to continue the narrative, yet the circumstances of its composition are so different as to make the term *sequel* problematic.

The division and incompletion that haunt the composition of *David Balfour* derived, of course, from the long delay after the publication of *Kidnapped,* a deferral that threatened the success of the sequel. During this long hiatus, Stevenson's life had been transformed. The success of *Strange Case of Dr. Jekyll and Mr. Hyde* had brought him worldwide fame and an increased income. The death of his father in 1887 had been a severe emotional blow but had left him financially independent for the first time in his life and also freed him to travel far from Britain—something he had not done since his epic pursuit of Fanny Vandegrift Osborne (the woman who became his wife) to California in 1879. In 1887, Stevenson had traveled with his family to the United States and, after a nine-month stay, began a cruise to the South Sea islands. There, on the island of Samoa, the Stevensons eventually settled in 1890, buying a property and building a large house that became his residence until his death in 1894. Hence, whereas *Kidnapped* was written in the mundane surroundings of Bournemouth, *David Balfour* was composed in the tropical luxuriance of Vailima, Stevenson's estate on Samoa. Colley states that "Stevenson periodically broke away from the glorified narratives of boys' adventure stories and the pervasive imperial myth of Robinson Crusoe, to write ballads based upon Samoan legends and to compose tales, fables, and short novels that drew upon his immediate experiences as a colonial."[6] Yet I argue that *David Balfour* is itself a turning away from the "boys' adventure story" and reflects Stevenson's engagement with the complex political realities of Samoa.

## Dedicating *David Balfour*

Stevenson's long absence from Britain—and the even longer absence of David Balfour from the pages of his work—dictated that he reestablish his links with (indeed, his authorship of) the earlier novel. In the dedication of *David Balfour,* Stevenson warns Charles Baxter that "it is the fate of sequels to disappoint those who have waited for them" (*K*, 211), a phrase that effectively does the work of establishing the novel as sequel even while it suggests that the book will not live up to expectations. Indeed, the dedication helps to establish continuity with the earlier novel, which Stevenson had likewise dedicated to Baxter. The dedication is an example of what Jerome McGann, following the work of Gerard Genette, refers to as "paratexts"—textual features "that surround the central text: like prefaces, dedications, notebooks, advertisements, footnotes, and so forth"—which McGann states are "consistently regarded as only quasi-textual, ancillary to the main textual event."[7] The case for treating this paratext seriously is furthered by Menikoff, who recognizes that "[f]ew modern authors were more attentive to their dedication pages than Robert Louis Stevenson" and notes that with *Kidnapped* and *David Balfour*, "For the first time, the dedication served as a preface to the text itself—even as it was so veiled and deprecating as to pass unnoticed."[8] The paratexts of the first U.K. edition of *Catriona* would also include the subtitle that is placed immediately underneath the title, in bold print: "A Sequel to *Kidnapped*" and continues "Being Memoirs of the *Further Adventures* of David Balfour at Home and Abroad." These headings, which occupy a prominent place on the title page, help to construct the text as a supplement to an original work and as the conclusion of an ongoing story.[9]

This effect of continuity is enhanced, in terms of its narrative beginning, by the fact that *David Balfour* apparently opens exactly where *Kidnapped* left off, with David emerging from the doors of the Edinburgh bank: "The 25th day of August, 1751, about two in the afternoon, I, David Balfour, came forth of the British Linen Company, a porter attending me with a bag of money, and some of the chief of these merchants bowing me from their doors" (*K*, 215). In its sentence structure, the transition is almost seamless, an invisible edit that sutures the new adventures of David with the old. What this paratextual construction of the novel as a sequel disguises, of course, is the complete transformation of David's material circumstances, reflected in his possession of "a bag of money." In the narrative ellipsis between *Kidnapped* and *David Balfour*, David has entered the bank and acquired his fortune. This transformation also reflects Stevenson's economic status as a world-famous author.

Yet the city into which David emerges from the bank at the opening of *David Balfour* is not the same as the one at which he arrived at the end of *Kid-*

*napped*. As David's destination in *Kidnapped,* Edinburgh is a beacon of hope, a familiar landmark with its "castle on the hill" (*K,* 207), to which David is brought by "the hand of Providence" (208). At the opening of *David Balfour,* this has transformed into "the tall, black city" (215), a fragmented "rabbit-warren" inhabited by "a brotherhood of spies" (216), and a site of political intrigue. This altered portrayal of the city reflects a change in the material history of the urban environment and its institutions, which Jameson characterizes as "a fatal trajectory from the traditional to the rationalized, passing through a crucial transitional stage which is the moment—the vanishing mediation—of so-called charisma."[10] In Stevenson's narrative, this transitional stage occurs in the hiatus or ellipsis between the two novels, in which the situations of author and protagonist are alike transformed. Though David appears to be the same at the beginning of *David Balfour,* he is not, as his language of contrast discloses: "Two days before, and even so late as yester-morning, I was like a beggar-man by the wayside, clad in rags, brought down to my last shillings, my companion a condemned traitor, a price set on my own head for a crime with the news of which the country rang. To-day I was served heir to my position in life, a landed laird, a bank porter by me carrying my gold" (215).

Embodied in "the mechanical animation of late Victorian city life, with all the smoke and conveyance inherent in new living conditions," urban rationalization is also reflected in "the reorganization of operations in terms of the binary system of means and ends," a process in which "the book or printed text is wrenched from its concrete position . . . and becomes a free-floating object," a commodity in a system of market relations.[11] The urban focus of *David Balfour* contrasts sharply with the Highland setting of much of *Kidnapped,* which focuses on the traditional clan system that is being eradicated by the spread of market relations.

Whereas the transformed material circumstances of Stevenson and his society are repressed, buried deeply in the narrative, the metamorphosis of David into a man of property is highlighted in the opening paragraph, cited above. Yet, though he may be possessed of new wealth and dressed in "new clothes" (*K,* 231), David Balfour shows few signs of having become more single-minded: he is again caught in a political conflict that he is powerless to influence; is again kidnapped and held in captivity, this time on the Bass Rock; and is again unable to control the course of his "adventures." Indeed, David makes an explicit comparison between the two episodes of captivity, stating that "the 21st, the day set for the trial, I passed in such misery of mind as I can scarce recall to have endured, save perhaps upon [the] Isle of Earraid" (338). The political duality of Whig and Jacobite that appears in the relationship between Alan and David in the earlier novel is displaced in *David Balfour* into a romantic dilemma, as David wavers between the attractions of Barbara Grant (daughter of the lord chief advocate) and Catriona Drummond, child of a disgraced Jacobite. Yet perhaps the most telling sign of his lingering indeterminacy occurs in chapter 12, in which Alan Breck returns, providing David's "first sight of my friend since we were parted" (302). In trying to elicit a description of a possible foe, Alan asks if this red -headed man was moving "fast or slow." David's reply is "Betwixt and Between" (309)—a remark that echoes their first conversation on the *Covenant* when David refuses to commit himself politically. Alan's reply then may still apply now: "And that's naething" (53). To be "betwixt and between" is to be "stuck about the middle," a narrative impasse that Stevenson seeks in vain to overcome by means of the long-deferred sequel.

The critical tendency to view *David Balfour* as a simplistic exercise in adventure narrative was illustrated by Robert Kiely, who argues, "Like *Treasure Island* and *Kidnapped,* its basic impulse is play. Its incidents are without serious moral implications, its characters without psyches, its politics without issue, and its history without consequence."[12] While I disagree fundamentally with Kiely's assessment of the novel, I concur that David is politically ineffective as a protagonist. Since Kiely's analysis, critics have recognized the historical substance of Stevenson's project in *Kidnapped* and *David Balfour* and the close links between them: as Menikoff argues, "*Kidnapped* and *David Balfour* are two parts of an epic novel, impelled by a studied reading of the past and an inventive manipulation of narrative art. That Stevenson managed for more than a century to deceive readers as to the origin and purpose of this work is a testament to his artistry."[13] Unlike Kiely, Barry Menikoff emphasizes the political substance of the novel in stating that "[w]hile *Kidnapped* and *David Balfour* have always been read together, as a single story of comradeship, courage, and adventure, behind the written texts stand[s] a political allegory of colonial dominance, of the subjugation of a native people by an alien and aggrandizing foreign culture." However, Menikoff does not explicitly identify this allegory with the colonial situation in which Stevenson was involved on Samoa.[14]

The Jacobite plot of *Kidnapped*—which extends into *David Balfour*—is a strategy of containment that deflects the reader's attention to a fictionalized version of the past rather than the material conditions in which the novel was produced. Yet (as I argue in chapter 4) the novel's form contains contradictions, most notably between the plot of inheritance with which it begins and the Jacobite/political plot that emerges after the shipwreck. Ideologically, these contradictions replay the tension between the bourgeois class, with its investment in property and social status, and the aristocracy, with its emphasis on ancestry, reputation, and honor. As I have argued, the failure of narrative closure in *Kidnapped*—the abrupt ending that leaves David stranded at the doors of the bank—is symptomatic of these unresolved ideological contradictions. Unable to contain both the bourgeois inheritance plot and the Jacobite political plot, the narrative resolves neither. The novel does not so much conclude as terminate: in Henry James's phrase, it "stops without ending."[15] In this respect, the novel fails as a strategy of containment, being unable to produce an imagined resolution to real contradictions.

If the narrative of *Kidnapped* is symptomatic of the ideological conditions of its production, what makes *David Balfour* any different? First, in terms of the representation of political turmoil on Samoa, the novel's status as a sequel is itself a strategy of containment, seeking to direct attention to the narrative's continuity with a previous historical romance and away from its engagement with the contemporary political crisis. This provides another layer to the "ideological mirage" generated by the fiction, namely, that historical novels disclose facts about the period in which they are set rather than that in which they are written. Second, Stevenson's ideological position on imperialism had shifted dramatically since 1887 as a result of his travels and habitation in the South Seas and his material investment in Samoan culture. In 1886 Stevenson self-identified as a Briton—referring to himself on different occasions as "English" or "Scottish" in his letters and essays—and largely shared the ideology of British imperialism, with its assumptions of racial superiority and its expansionist agenda. By 1893, when *David Balfour* was published, he had become "R.L.S., known throughout the English-speaking world simply by his initials," and he used this fame to influence the colonized race of Samoans and portray the European and American powers as oppressors of native peoples.[16] This is neither to deny the actual material privilege of Stevenson's position at Vailima nor to ignore how deeply he was still invested in British and American interests through his literary, publishing, and social networks in those countries. As Colley observes, "When Stevenson sailed through the islands and finally landed in Upolu, he arrived, whether he intended to or not, as a representative of the British Empire, and, therefore, as a person of consequence."[17] Yet clearly he identified politically with the Samoan people and adopted an explicitly critical position toward European colonization in the South Seas.

Given this shift in Stevenson's political attitudes—especially his commitment to Samoan independence—it is perhaps surprising that his protagonist, despite the intervening period, shows few signs of having become more politically effective in *David Balfour.* David's political hesitancy and vacillation remain in evidence, as he becomes involved against his will in the trial of James of the Glens for the Appin murder. At a crucial point in the trial, where David's testimony as an eyewitness of the Appin murder is needed to save James from the gallows, David is again kidnapped and forcibly removed from the scene of the trial.

David's chief concern is with his effectiveness as a narrator, the threat to his "credit" as a storyteller having "screwed me up to fighting point" (*K*, 324). Yet in other respects this delay and enforced absence suits David's interests, ensuring his removal from a dangerous scene and "low dirty intrigue" (325), while absolving him of any direct guilt for his nonappearance. The fear of "arriving too late" on the scene, which David attributes to his captivity, is also expressed by Stevenson about the publication of *David Balfour* which Stevenson felt had been left too long unwritten, such that it did not smoothly follow its predecessor: "The join is bad; I have not thought to strain too much for continuity. . . . [T]here's no doubt David seems to have changed his style. . . . [M]uch I care, if the tale travel!"[18]

Stevenson's concern about the inconsistencies of David's "style"—presumably his manner as a narrator—was overridden by a desire for literary success. Hoping that the tale would "travel"—that is, find readers and achieve success with audiences across the world—Stevenson also hinted at the central role of travel within his tale, as it shifts locations from Edinburgh to the Bass

Rock and later to Holland. David's concern that his return to Edinburgh would be too late also echoes Stevenson's worry that his account of Samoan conflict in *A Footnote to History* "would come just too late to be of any service," while he shared David's anxiety about the high cost of speaking one's mind: "[I]f my plain speaking shall cost me any of the friends that I still count, I shall be sorry."[19] Hence, Stevenson's concerns about deferral, tardiness, incompletion, and the consequences of narration are mirrored by his protagonist's attempts to exert a historical influence on the aftermath of the Appin murder: as, for example, when David states to a kinsman, "My trouble is to have become dipped in a political complication" (*K*, 236).

Yet one might argue that it is precisely because he is involved in a "political complication" that David is able to narrate the events of the story. Had David not been (fortuitously?) present at the Appin murder, an inadvertent witness to a political assassination, there would have been no basis for his narrative. Although David's implication in the crime is mysteriously waived, as James becomes the chief suspect, he has enough of a stake in the process—because of his potential role as witness—to bring authenticity to his narrative. The novel's grounding in historical detail and political intrigue is key to its effect.[20] If David's travels construct him as an eyewitness to history, one of the questions raised by *Kidnapped* and *David Balfour* is, to what extent is a witness of historical events implicated in those events and their outcomes? Is a witness simply a detached observer or a kind of participant in historical action?

In fact, following David's failure to appear and testify at the trial of James, storytelling is his only compensation for a lack of direct political influence: only following his release could he inform the reader, "I made a short narration of my seizure and captivity and . . . upon the circumstances of the murder . . . this was the first time I had had my say out" (*K*, 346). Paradoxically, David is empowered by the act of narrating that reveals his exclusion from history: as Stewart the writer remarks, "Sirs, this is a tale to make the world ring with!" (347).

This indeterminacy of David's position "betwixt and between" opposing historical forces, which enables his narration, also presents a narrative problem concerning the function of *David Balfour* as a sequel, the purpose of which is to resolve the plot left unfinished at the end of *Kidnapped*. Such narrative closure cannot occur while David remains "betwixt and between," uncommitted to either side. He is threatened with another extended period of limbo, unable to resolve contradictions between his identification as a Whig and his attraction to Jacobitism, particularly his connection to Alan Breck. In the case of David Balfour, the political dilemma he faces is also represented in the form of a romantic duality. It is valuable to recall here Jameson's point that the nineteenth-century novel is a strategy of containment that seeks to "contain" critical insight within the boundaries or the narrative or argument, thereby repressing the "unthinkable" that lies outside those boundaries. Specifically, the realist novel imposes a formal unity on inchoate experience, seeking to enforce meaning on the narrative.[21] One such resolution is, of course, the marriage plot, which is introduced in an attempt to avoid the kind of narrative impasse that brought *Kidnapped* to a premature end.

Indeed, one key insight to be gleaned from *David Balfour* is that the indeterminacy of the narrator is not ideologically neutral. In his wavering between conflicting parties, his lack of clear commitment to either side, David (as narrator, as historical subject) effectively supports the status quo. David's priority remains the restoration of his property under the existing (Hanoverian) regime, a privilege in which Alan, as an outlawed Highlander, can by no means expect to share. David's partnership with Alan therefore involves no ideological commitment to the rebels' cause and indeed may be a strategy to further his own material advantage (Alan, of course, is instrumental in trapping both the uncle and James More into acting in David's interests).

Decrying the corruption of the government and the legal system, David is unable or unwilling to change the course of the trial or avert the scapegoating of the Jacobite. He admits the futility of his protests in an important passage that reports the execution of James of the Glens: "So there was the final upshot of my politics! Innocent men have perished before James, and are like to keep on perishing (in spite of all our wisdom) till the end of time. And till the end of time young folk (who are not yet used with the duplicity of life and men) will struggle as I did, and make heroical resolves, and take long risks; and the course of events will push them upon the one side and go on like a marching army" (382).[22] One might even argue that David benefits from this miscarriage of justice, as it exculpates both Alan and himself from criminal charges. David's narrative, while arguably antigovernment, is never pro-Jacobite. In this sense, his indeterminate narrative allows history to continue on its projected course, from which he will emerge as a propertied gentleman.

The representation of political corruption and intrigue, as well as the damaging effects of clan rivalry on Scottish civil life, is, as I have suggested, reflective of Stevenson's altered material circumstances and ideological position on political authority and colonialism. Certainly, David is no longer naive about the political motives behind the Appin murder or of those seeking to convict James. Moreover, the shift from "open-air adventure" and romantic incident (in *Kidnapped*) to a close, almost claustrophobic atmosphere defined by conspiracy and stratagem is connected to Stevenson's immersion in Samoan politics. Yet to suggest that David is aware of this atmosphere of menace and intrigue is far from claiming that he is able to alter it or remedy the clan warfare that fuels the plot. Indeed, David's narration is punctuated with reminders of its futility, much as Stevenson feared that his account of the war in Samoa would have no effect on the outcome. The narrator, although seeming to be in command of his destiny at the opening of *Kidnapped,* is thus condemned to indeterminacy and impotence.

The parallels that I am pointing to between David and Stevenson, as narrators and as political subjects, opens up the intertextual relationship between *David Balfour* and *A Footnote to History.* While the thematic and plot parallels between David's adventures in *Kidnapped* and *David Balfour* cannot be ignored, there is less continuity between the two novels than the designation of "sequel" suggests. Rather, Stevenson's involvement with Samoan politics found its dual expression in a fictional political allegory, *David Balfour,* and his nonfictional account *A Footnote to History,* published in 1892. Referred to by Stevenson as "Samoa" or "the Samoan history," the latter book confirmed his investment in trying to protect his adopted country from complete domination by European and American interests. With its harsh portrayal of German, American, and British commercial intrigue in Samoa and attacks on the widespread manipulation of and brutality against native people by Europeans, *A Footnote* was a nonfictional counterpart to the scathing representations of colonialists in the South Sea stories "The Beach of Falesá" and *The Ebb-Tide.* Yet the project of writing a Samoan history that was critical of European colonialism presented unique problems for Stevenson as a storyteller and as a writer for a popular market. Stevenson faced the dilemma of trying to reconcile his political and historical commitments with the need to support his family and household at Vailima.

A second and perhaps more significant challenge was writing a Samoan history for an audience that scarcely knew of the island's existence, for whom Samoa was, literally, off the map. Roslyn Jolly writes that "this deafness of European readers to all that lay outside the modern 'Roman' culture of the West was the greatest problem confronting Stevenson as he set out to tell the story of Samoa."[23] One might also describe it as a blindness to Samoa's strategic importance in an imperial struggle that culminated in the Great War of 1914–18.[24] I argue that the problem of writing Samoan history surfaces in the symptomatic duality of Stevenson's literary labor during the period, a doubling to be explored in terms of the intertextual parallels between *A Footnote to History* and the novel written concurrently with it, *David Balfour.* Pivotal to this intertextual reading is the paradox that Stevenson could most effectively narrate what he called "contemporary history" (*F,* 1) by delving into the Scottish past.

In his correspondence from Samoa, Stevenson portrays fiction writing during this period as a pleasurable release from the burden of history, as when he writes to Colvin, "I have a confession to make. When I was sick I tried to get to work to finish that Samoa thing; wouldn't go; and at last . . . I slid off into *David Balfour,* some 50 pp. of which are drafted, and like me well."[25] Yet this discourse of imaginary escape should not be allowed to mask the extent to which *David Balfour* and *A Footnote* occupy the same territory in being ideologically related. Indeed, *David Balfour,* far from being an "escape" from Samoa, presents a parallel version of the historical conflict addressed in *A Footnote;* while ostensibly a historical novel about eighteenth-century Scotland, *David Balfour* tells us a great deal about the political climate of Samoa in the 1890s.[26]

Why, though, having launched on his Samoan (his)story in *A Footnote,* would Stevenson want or need to revisit the same events and conflicts in *David Balfour?* If he viewed fiction as his escape from Samoan history, why would he sacrifice the imaginative pleasurableness of his Scottish novel to continue his engagement with Polynesian politics? I suggest that there are two answers to this question. First, Stevenson sought to assuage doubts about the historical significance of Samoan affairs—doubts inscribed in the very title of his work—by developing his narrative in tandem with Scottish Jacobite history, which was widely recognized as being of importance. Second, Stevenson, as a professional storyteller, was eager to produce a more successful narration of Samoan history: "success" being measured in both popular reception and commercial appeal. In both respects, the duality of *David Balfour* and *A Footnote* runs deeper than their generic differences would suggest. Stevenson's Samoan history, to employ the words of Henry Jekyll, "is not truly one but truly two."[27]

## Footnoting Samoa

The kind of duality that I have been discussing in Stevenson's *Footnote to History* and *David Balfour* is, according to Hayden White, central to the very possibility of historical narration. Asserting that history "belongs to the category of what might be called 'the discourse of the real,' as against the 'discourse of the imaginary' or 'the discourse of desire'"—to which, presumably, works of fiction belong—White articulates a dilemma at the heart of historical storytelling: namely, that the same narrativizing of historical events that allows them to serve as "tokens of reality" within a story also potentially subverts their authority as "facts." White explains that "[i]n order to qualify as historical, an event must be susceptible *to at least two narrations of its occurrence.* Unless at least two versions of the same set of events can be imagined, there is no reason for the historian to take upon himself the authority of giving the true account of what really happened. The authority of the historical narrative is the authority of reality itself; the historical account endows this reality with form and *thereby makes it desirable* by the imposition upon its processes of the formal coherency that only stories possess."[28]

This feature of narrative desire is central to White's overall argument that history, as a narrative form, participates in plot structures and stylistic features that are indistinguishable from those deployed by the novelist. Without such apparatuses of plot, history would revert to the earlier forms of annals or chronicle, presenting historical events without narrative form or direction. To be readable, that is, history must also be "desirable," and such readerly desire can only (or best) be stimulated by plot structures that White acknowledges are an "imposition" and—more revealingly—"an embarrassment" in a work of history.[29]

If we agree that history shares modes of emplotment with fiction, however, why should it follow that plot is an embarrassment for the historian? White, interestingly, uses an eroticized terminology to explore the textual seduction of history, defining it as a discourse that "[m]akes the real desirable, makes the real into an object of desire." The embarrassment created by such desire is, presumably, that it is inappropriate to a "discourse of the real," such as history, belonging more properly to an "imaginary" discourse, such as fiction, that has as its aim the stimulation of desire, with no necessary commitment to factuality. Yet the embarrassment also registers something more complex: despite its claims to represent truth, history is in practice dependent on plot and "but for its story form, would have no appeal at all." The only way to counter such embarrassment is the ruse of feigning that such formal coherency is inherent to the events, so that plot "has to be presented as 'found' in the events rather than put there by narrative techniques."[30] Such a subterfuge is clearly facilitated by the existence of previous accounts of a given set of events, from which an author may claim to have inherited a formal structure, rather than having to create it and put it there. If, as White claims, "every narrative, however seemingly 'full' is constructed on the basis of a set of events that might have been included but were left out," then there is always a space, or a lack, in a historical account that a competing narrative may expose and/or supplement.[31]

This brings into sharper focus the labor of writing Samoan history, for, as suggested at the beginning of this chapter, a large part of "that grind" that Stevenson endured while writing *A Footnote* derived from the lack of alternative versions of the events on which to base his narrative or to which he might respond.[32] In the preface to the book, he writes, "Truth, in the midst of conflicting rumours and *in the dearth of printed material,* was often hard to ascertain" (*F,* xvii; emphasis added). The lack of printed records in what was still, in the 1890s, a predominantly oral Polynesian culture is perhaps not surprising. In the absence of these sources, Stevenson depended for information on anecdotal evidence from those, such as H. J. Moors, who had lived in Samoa for a longer period than Stevenson had. In the preface, Stevenson reveals the subjective nature of his perspective on the history he recounts, stating that "most of those engaged were of my personal acquaintance" (xvii). The combination of oral sources and personal familiarity with the characters brings into his narrative a disturbing resemblance to the genre of the fictional tale, a point that Stevenson acknowledges in referring to *A Footnote* as "my sickening yarn." Describing the events on Samoa as "not to be written of—and I should think scarce to be read without a thrill," Stevenson tacitly acknowledges that such a thrill might be inappropriate for a work of "actuality" and might cause a blurring of generic boundaries that would arouse suspicions of fabrication.[33]

The claims of *A Footnote* as a historical narrative are further undercut by the opening sentence of the text: "The story I have to tell is still going on as I write; the characters are alive and active; it is a piece of contemporary history in the most exact sense" (*F*, 1). Significantly, these references to "the story" and "the characters" invite us to link the narrative, as a literary artifact, with the novelist's art.[34] Stevenson had previously called into question the formal distinction between fiction and nonfiction, writing in "A Humble Remonstrance" that the "art of narrative, in fact, is the same, whether it is applied to the selection and illustration of a real series of events or of an imaginary series" and further emphasizes this commonality between novelist and historian by observing that "in Tacitus, in Carlyle, in Michelet, in Macaulay . . . the novelist will find many of his own methods most conspicuously and adroitly handled." Yet Stevenson also undercuts the claims to veracity of the historian, asserting that "truth will seem a word of very debateable propriety, not only for the labours of the novelist, but for those of the historian."[35] These comments in an essay of 1884 suggest the appeal for Stevenson of telling the history of Samoa in fictional form, as he does in *David Balfour:* if truth is not the defining purpose of history, then it becomes a matter of using the material—or series of events—to tell the most compelling story.

However, in the case of *A Footnote,* the narrative problem facing Stevenson as a historian resides not only in the fact that (as White observes) the events "can be shown to display the formal coherency of a story" but also in Stevenson's claim that this story "is still going on as I write" (*F*, 1) and therefore lacks both the temporal distance and the formal closure expected of history. For, as White points out, one of the distinguishing formal features of historical discourse is "the turn in the narrative that permits it to come to an end." By contrast, White observes, "the chronicle, like the annals but unlike the history, does not so much conclude as simply terminate; typically it lacks closure, that summing up of the 'meaning' of the chain of events with which it deals that we normally expect from the well-made story."[36]

In writing *A Footnote to History,* Stevenson tried to make Samoan history both legible and appealing to British and American readers by highlighting the motifs of adventure that it suggested. From the opening pages, Stevenson indicates that this will be a story of war, replete with drama and action, emphasizing "the part played in it by mails and telegraphs and iron warships" (1). As Colley states, *A Footnote* resembles fictional tales such as *The Ebb-Tide,* which "explore the diverse forms of encounter among traders, sailors, missionaries, beachcombers, Chinese servants, 'black boys' . . . German, British, and American officers, and the indigenous populations."[37] As part of this strategy of creating popular appeal, parallels between Samoan and Highland cultures are developed: for example, in explaining the causes of the Samoan chieftain's precarious status, Stevenson asks the reader to "compare the case of a highland chief: born one of the great ones of his clan, he was sometimes appointed its chief officer and conventional father; was loved and respected and served and fed and died for implicitly, if he gave loyalty a chance; and yet, if he sufficiently outraged clan sentiment, was liable to deposition" (2). As Stevenson makes clear, the resemblance between two clan systems forms the foundation of this cross-cultural comparison. Indeed, Stevenson uses the term *clan* interchangeably for Samoans and Highlanders, stating of the former that "even a small minority will often strike a clan or a province impotent" (2).

Readers of the South Seas letters would have been familiar with this comparative technique, which Stevenson outlines as follows: "When I desired any detail of savage custom, or of superstitious belief, I cast back in the story of my fathers, and fished for what I wanted with some trait of equal barbarism. . . . [W]hat I knew of the Cluny Macphersons, or the Appin Stewarts, enabled me to learn, and helped me to understand, about the Tevas of Tahiti. . . . It is this sense of kinship that the traveler must rouse and share."[38] Stevenson assumes that his reader will share in or approve of this culturally comparative approach to his travels. However, pointing to the kinship between white European and "savage" Polynesian was a controversial gesture, especially as Stevenson's narrative delves into taboo Polynesian practices such as cannibalism and head hunting. Yet it is essential to Stevenson's strategy in *A Footnote* of overcoming the "otherness" of Polynesia and establishing its history as an "object of desire" that would be legible within Western narrative and cultural conventions.[39]

As part of this strategy, Stevenson examines the conflict in Samoa in terms that explicitly echo the political divisions of eighteenth-century Scotland: "Two royal lines; some cloudy idea of alternation between the two; an electorate in which the vote of each province is immediately effectual, as regards itself, so that every candidate who attains one name becomes a perpetual and dangerous competitor for the other four" (3–4). The long-standing political rivalry means that "war was imminent" (3) between competing chiefs and clans, even more so as two provinces met "and elected their own two princes, Tamasese and Mataafa, to an alternate monarchy" (3).[40] Expanding the legibility of Samoan politics, Stevenson uses clannish imagery to define the commercial culture of the island, referring to Moors and MacArthur as "the two rival chiefs of the firm" (42).

To further the readerly appeal of *A Footnote,* Stevenson also develops an atmosphere of intrigue with narrative techniques of suspense. For example: "the land is full of war and rumours of war. Scarce a year goes by but some province is in arms, or sits sulky and menacing, holding parliaments, disregarding the king's proclamations" (4). Describing "the first step of military preparation" (4), Stevenson portrays rumor as one of the chief obstacles to peace. Equally, linguistic divisions reflect the dangerous political situation: "To address these demigods is quite a branch of knowledge, and he who goes to visit a high chief does well to make sure of the competence of his interpreter" (2). In contrast to Stevenson's freedom of communication while cruising the South Seas (when "the impediment of tongues was one that I particularly over-estimated"), differences of language prove highly problematic in "these distracted islands" (3), reflecting both the rivalry of the native chiefs and the competition between the "Great Powers" as "the beach twinkled with the flags of nations" (60).[41]

Siding with the ousted yet popular Samoan chief Mataafa, Stevenson portrays Mataafa's chief rivals, Laupepa and Tamasese, as incompetent leaders—"Laupepa and Tamasese were both heavy, well-meaning, inconclusive men. . . . Impossible to conceive two less dashing champions for a threatened race" (23). In elsewhere referring to the chiefs as "childish" (*F,* 24), Stevenson apparently deploys a stereotype of native behavior as fundamentally immature. Yet this occurs within the "plot" of a struggle for succession that mirrors the Jacobite uprising of 1745, in which Stevenson's preferred leader emerges in the heroic role: "There was one thing requisite to the intrigue—a native pretender; and the very man, you would have said, stood waiting: Mataafa, titular of Atua, descended from both the royal lines . . . a chief with a strong following" (24–25). In explaining the "elements of discord" in Samoa, Stevenson portrays Apia as a divided city, "the seat of the political sickness of Samoa" (10). Like the Highland line in Scotland, which was portrayed as a boundary between competing cultures, the divide in Apia is symbolic of the rival powers competing for influence on Samoa: "The bridge which crosses here . . . is a frontier; behind is Matafele; beyond, Apia proper; behind, Germans are supreme; beyond, with but few exceptions, all is Anglo-Saxon" (11). Stevenson frequently refers to the cultural sources of the "sickness" of Samoa—writing, for example, "Everyone tells everything he knows; that is our country sickness. Nearly everyone has been betrayed at times, and told a trifle more; the way our sickness takes the predisposed" (13).

Stevenson perhaps unsurprisingly attributes the cause of this disease to German commercial influence. Indeed, he directly asserts German culpability for the Samoan troubles: "But the true center of trouble, the head of the boil of which Samoa languishes, is the German firm" (14). Certainly this is the interpretation of C. Brunsdon Fletcher in his book *Stevenson's Germany,* which "concludes the argument against Germany begun in 'The New Pacific'" and seeks "to place Robert Louis Stevenson before the world *as an important witness* in the case." However, the author concedes that "to get Stevenson into the witness box the history of Germany's thirty years of intrigue and tergiversation, before he reached Samoa, has to be told." Yet in seeking to secure "merited punishment for the abominable crimes committed by Germany"—such punishment being that "Germany cannot be allowed to return as master of her late possessions"—Fletcher distorts Stevenson's role.[42] His role as narrator of *A Footnote* is less that of a witness and more like an advocate—reflecting his legal training in Edinburgh—marshalling evidence to support his case for Samoan autonomy and ending with a petition to the judge and jury: the latter his readers, the former "the sovereign of the wise Stuebel and the loyal Brandeis—[to whom] I make my appeal" (155). Clearly, Stevenson's chief purpose was not to condemn Germany—as Fletcher suggested—but to advance the claims for Samoan independence, which necessarily involved securing German sympathy. Indeed, the parallels between colonialism and sickness are a recurring motif throughout the South Seas writings, as when, in *In the South Seas,* Stevenson attributes the decimation of the Marquesans ("the approaching extinction of his race") to European influence ("the coming of the whites"), with its "introduction of new maladies and vices."[43]

John Kucich argues, in a provocative essay, that Stevenson attributed this decline of the race to Polynesian masochism rather than European imperialism. In *A Footnote to History,* Kucich argues, Stevenson returns to an earlier fragmentation of the masochistic subject between magical potency and melancholy suffering, realized most dramatically in the Durie brothers, James and Henry, in *The Master of Ballantrae* (1889). Claiming that Stevenson, following his move to Samoa, "suddenly stopped writing about magical and melancholic doubles," Kucich soon contradicts this point by invoking Stevenson's "relegation of masochistic splitting—of the kind we have seen in *The Master of Ballantrae*—entirely to the realm of racial otherness." Rather than continuing his technique of masochistic splitting in his fiction, Kucich argues, Stevenson displaced it into his historical narration, especially *A Footnote,* in which "Stevenson maps the masochistic polarities of James and Henry Durie onto warring Germans and Samoans." In particular, Kucich relates German delusions of omnipotence in Samoa to the "magical" fantasies of masochism embodied by James Durie, while Samoan "self-sacrifice" and "reticence" are the counterparts of the melancholy passivity of Henry Durie. More broadly, Kucich argues, Stevenson's portrayal of Samoans "conforms to his general attribution of melancholia to Polynesians."[44]

Despite the obvious force of Kucich's argument—especially in its ingenious exploration of narrative techniques shared by fictional and nonfictional texts—his reading of *A Footnote* is flawed by his failure to recognize the political roots of Stevenson's representation of duality. As I have argued, Stevenson establishes numerous parallels between Scotland and Samoa in both *A Footnote* and *In the South Seas.* Yet Kucich's only reference to Scottish Jacobite history occurs in describing James Durie "impetuously joining the doomed cause of Bonnie Prince Charlie." Hence, Kucich overlooks the profound ongoing duality of

Whig and Jacobite in Stevenson's fiction and, more generally, in Scottish history. Impressively, Kucich seeks to challenge "the conventional view of masochism as eroticized submission," preferring instead "to better understand the *political dynamics* of late-Victorian masochism." Paradoxically, however, a significant political source of the "splitting" in Stevenson's narratives explored by Kucich remains unaddressed.[45]

*A Footnote* presents a more pervasive linguistic symptom of disease in the prevalence of intrigue: "Should Apia ever choose a coat of arms, I have a motto ready: 'Enter Rumour painted full of tongues' . . . gossip is the common resource of all" (*F,* 13). A discourse that exercises potent influence and spreads like a virus, evading control, gossip threatens both the political stability on Samoa and the coherency of the narrative. We recall that Stevenson cited the existence of conflicting rumors among the chief reasons that writing the book was "a task of difficulty" (xvii). Insecurity about his sources contributed to a contagion of uncertainty surrounding *A Footnote,* reflected even in Stevenson's indecision about how much of the text he composed during 1892.[46] As we shall see, a more serious assertion of corruption both in and of his text soon brought Stevenson to the brink of deportation and financial ruin.[47]

Stevenson's dual purpose in *A Footnote*—to narrate Samoan history while also attracting readers—resulted in mixed textual signals. Despite his claim that "I have my facts pretty correct," Stevenson was less concerned with the historical accuracy of his book than with its probable allure for readers. Telling Colvin that "of course, this book is not written for honour and glory, and the few who will read it may not know the difference," Stevenson made telling references to his ambivalence about provoking readerly pleasure. For example, Stevenson admitted that in writing the hurricane chapter, he was "tempted . . . to be literary" and continued, "I felt sure the less of that there is in my little handbook, the more chance it has of some utility." Explaining that "*I had but one desire,* to get the thing as right as might be, and avoid false concords," Stevenson consoled himself for (temporary) popular failure with the thought that he had produced an enduring historical work: "[I]f Samoa turns up again, my book has to be counted with, being *the only narrative extant.*"[48] Yet this assertion of the book's importance is undercut by the connotation of his title, *A Footnote to History,* with its self-declaration as a paratext that is supplementary or marginal to the main textual event. In contrast to history proper, which was of central concern to British and European readers—what Colvin termed "the main currents of human affairs"—the troubles on Samoa are relegated to a footnote, which may be bypassed by readers.[49]

Stevenson elaborates on this marginal status in his preface, which tends to diminish the significance of what follows: "[A]n affair, which might be deemed worthy of a note of a few lines in any general history, has been here expanded to the size of a volume or large pamphlet. The smallness of the scale and the singularity of the characters considered, it is hoped that, in spite of its outlandish subject, the sketch may find readers" (xvii). Words such as *pamphlet, smallness, singularity,* and *outlandish* all tend to undermine the scope of the work as a historical account. Yet Stevenson's pose of humility is indeed just that: his narrative shows how the apparently minor squabbles between Samoan chiefs have in fact brought the world's three "Great Powers"—Britain, Germany, and the United States—to "the brink of war . . . view[ing] each other with looks of hatred" (120).

This atmosphere of intrigue, secrecy, and disease that Stevenson depicts in late-nineteenth-century Samoa also surfaces in the portrayal of Edinburgh in *David Balfour,* where David Balfour describes the treacherous and fractured landscape of "this old black city, which was for all the world like a rabbit-warren, not only by the number of its indwellers, but the complication of its passages and holes. It was indeed a place where no stranger had a chance to find a friend, let be another stranger" (216). Even the city's guides, or "caddies," are not to be trusted, as they "had grown to form a brotherhood of spies; and I knew from tales . . . how they communicated one with another, what a rage of curiosity they conceived as to their employer's business, and how they were like eyes and fingers to the police" (216). With its "black" appearance, its "noise" and "throng" (215), and its "treason and traitors" (229), the city—which seemed a beacon of civilization and hope in *Kidnapped*—is a place of danger and corruption in *David Balfour.*[50]

Compromised by what he terms "the whole Jacobitical side of my business" (217), David is advised that "this is not a case, ye see, it's a conspiracy" (283), and he becomes enmeshed in a tangled web of guilt and deceit: "Not only was the visit to Appin's agent, in the midst of the cry about the Appin murder, dangerous in itself, but it was highly inconsistent with the other" (217). Moreover, his noble intention to prove that Alan—viewed as "a forfeited rebel and an accused murderer"—has been "wrongfully accused" (225) sucks him into what is described as a "conspiracy" and "a great scandal" (347).

In both works, therefore, Stevenson conveys a mood of paranoia and surveillance that is reflected in the political divisions and topographies of the cities themselves. As with the first impression of island life in *In the South Seas,* the reality of Edinburgh proves to be far more disturbing. The dramatically altered atmosphere of *David Balfour* stems from Stevenson's observations of Samoan colonial politics, in which the German chief, Becker, "while . . . thus outwardly straining decency in the interest of Tamasese . . . was privately intriguing or pretending to intrigue with Mataafa" (*F,* 68). Stating that "Becker was preparing to change sides," Stevenson ironically notes that the German's portrayal of Mataafa as "very dark and artful" (68) is surely a projection of his own duplicitous practices onto the native chief. David Balfour likewise portrays those in authority in ambivalent terms, especially Lord Prestongrange, who acts as a "father" to him yet also plays a double game, as when he arranges the "escape" of Catriona from prison and residence with a family "quite at the Advocate's disposition. . . . Thus Prestongrange obtained and used his instrument; nor did there leak out the smallest word of his acquaintance with the daughter of James More" (*K,* 379–80).

To compensate for his narrative's emphasis on the temporal immediacy of contemporary "actuality" (*F,* 1), Stevenson shores up the historical claims of his narrative by foregrounding the cultural and developmental difference of modern (that is, nineteenth-century) Samoans, calling them "the contemporaries of our tattooed ancestors who drove their chariots on the wrong side of the Roman wall. We have passed the feudal system; they are not yet clear of the patriarchal. We are in the thick of the age of finance; they are in a period of communism" (1). As Roslyn Jolly argues, "Stevenson saw the European 'invasion' of the Pacific as an expansion of the frontiers of Roman civilization, which he identified with modernity and the west." Jolly reminds us that "comparisons between Scotland and Polynesia were much on Stevenson's mind when he first entered the Pacific. Both regions had experienced the repression of their indigenous culture under an imperial regime."[51] By projecting historical difference onto a contemporaneous culture, Stevenson perhaps falls into the trap of appearing to condescend to Samoan culture as "primitive" and to assume a posture of European cultural superiority. However, I argue that this construction of difference strategically identifies the Samoan troubles as a suitable subject for history, about which moral and political judgments can be made.[52]

In addition to the desire for a wide audience, economic pressures demanded that Stevenson find a commercially viable outlet for his Samoan material. Writing hopefully in August 1892 that "this should be rather a profitable year," Stevenson made a mournful exception: "[N]ot to mention, as quite hopeless, *The History of Samoa*."[53] Attention to issues such as head hunting, which he admitted revolted his readers, jeopardized the appeal of his Samoan history in Britain and the United States. Lamenting both the depreciated market value of his South Seas writings and the lack of desire they sparked in his readers, Stevenson admitted, "I know there is a frost: the *Samoa* book can only increase that—I can't help it . . . but I mean to break that frost inside two years, and pull off a big success." Alluding, it seems, to the anticipated success of *David Balfour*, with its links to the ever-popular *Kidnapped*, Stevenson hoped that this return to one of his most popular protagonists would restore his favor with the public. Yet another anxiety affecting the irresolute novelist appears later in the letter: "If I had not recopied *Davie* he would now be done and dead and buried; and here I am stuck about the middle, with an immediate publication threatened and the fear before me of having after all to scamp *the essential business of the end*." The closure of the novel is here equated with the specter of death and burial: attached as he was to his hero—"I love my *Davy*"—Stevenson was reluctant to terminate David's adventures, preferring to be "stuck about the middle" than to confront mortality, which is inevitably part of "the essential business of the end."[54] With his fragile health, Stevenson no doubt recognized that each novel he completed might be his last, and he was understandably concerned that David would be the death of him.[55]

Tellingly, however, the threat that produced fear in Stevenson was not that of sudden death but of immediate publication, with its commitment to satisfy the readership that he had referred to as "that great, hulking, bullering whale, the public."[56] Henry James complained of a lack of enjoyment in Stevenson's South Seas writings, spotlighting their failure to stimulate the visual imagination:

"I missed the visible in them—I mean as regards people, things, objects, faces, bodies, costumes, features, gestures, manners, the introductory, the *personal* painter-touch. . . . No theory is kind to us that cheats us of seeing."[57] James invokes visual pleasure as an erotic stimulant, a desired sensual immersion in the material diversity of Samoan bodies and culture. To be cheated of this pleasure, as he would explain in a later comment on *David Balfour,* subjected him "to an almost painful underfeeding." James's complaint of undernourishment contrasts with Stevenson's assessment of the South Sea letters, which he conveyed to Colvin on September 8, 1891: "The mistake is all through that I have told too much; I had not sufficient confidence in the reader, and have overfed him."[58]

The role of fiction in historical narration is further exposed by an additional parallel between Stevenson and his protagonist David Balfour: their viability as historical storytellers is undercut by their exclusion from the crucial historical events on which their narrations are founded. Stevenson's absence from the key events narrated in *A Footnote to History,* in particular, embroiled him in a controversy that arose directly from his attempt to be both an advocate and a spectator.

## The Missing Witness

One of the turning points of *David Balfour* occurs when David is again kidnapped and removed from Edinburgh to the Bass Rock. Because of his abduction, David is identified as "the missing witness"—a label of absence and impotence that haunts his narrative. This impotence is apparent in the scene of his abduction, which is at once a condensation and a displacement of the plot of *Kidnapped.* As in the earlier novel, David's association with Alan Breck gets him in trouble with the government, for it is while parting from Alan on Gillane Sands that David is lured into a trap and abducted (*K,* 312–13). In contrast to the earlier occurrence in *Kidnapped,* however, this one does not come as a surprise to David: he has already been warned by Stewart the writer, "I'm in bitter error if ye're not to be kidnapped and carried away like the Lady Grange" (285).[59]

Despite this forewarning, David puts up little resistance to being abducted, never even drawing his sword against his captors. Significantly, he justifies this passive acceptance of his capture by alluding to the absence of his former protector, stating, "I am no Alan to fall upon so many" (321). Surrendering without fuss, David states, "I shut my eyes and prayed. . . . I held out my hands empty" (316). When David is asked if he will submit to his captors, he answers, "Under protest . . . if ye ken what that means" (316). Certainly the reader has difficulty in understanding what the statement means, given the lack of any visible struggle with his captors. As he is taken away, David regrets that "there was no second Alan" (318), a statement that reiterates his inadequacy without the reinforcements of Alan's martial prowess, in a world where violent action is needed. Moreover, once he is imprisoned on the Bass Rock, he makes no effort to escape. Indeed, he admits that he is quite comfortable in his captivity and is treated well by his guards: "It seemed to me a safe place, as though I was escaped there out of my troubles. . . . I had my life safe and my honour safe" (323). David's emphasis on being safe indicates his unheroic traits, as distinguished from Alan Breck.

David's enforced absence is in some ways convenient, preventing him from participating in a historical event that threatens his destruction: for if James is acquitted, the glare of suspicion falls once again on Alan and his "accomplice" (*K*, 110), David. Lacking any strong political commitment, David cannot be a historical agent, his ambivalent status of "betwixt and between" guaranteeing a political impotence. Instead, David is a spectator of the historical action. Yet he is a "missing witness," as the chapter states, as David objects to the "insidious" plan by his captors—clearly sponsored by the government—to release him from the Bass "precisely in time to be too late" (*K*, 324), which would thereby "cast the more discredit on my tale" (324).

David's role as storyteller is suspended while on the Bass, as he instead becomes a listener enjoying the narrative skills of another. While imprisoned on the Bass, and removed from the scene of historical action, David hears "The Tale of Tod Lapraik," told by the Lowlander Black Andie, who David says has "a natural genius for narration, so that the people seemed to speak and the things to be done before your face" (323). David's bond with Andie is based on storytelling, for "this gift of his and my assiduity to listen brought us the more close together" (323). David's eagerness to listen derives from both his need for a distraction and the fact that Andie provides David with a model of powerful narration that he will seek to exploit for the conclusion of his own story. "The Tale of Tod Lapraik," like others of Andie's tales, focuses on aspects of Highland superstition, such as "bogles" and "warlocks," and it stands out from the main narrative in being told in Scots dialect. It points to the relative absence of such dialect in David's discourse and to his skepticism about superstition: "[T]here can be no bogles here, Neil; for it's not likely they would fash themselves to frighten solan geese" (*K*, 328). Yet Andie's tale also offers a striking allegory of colonialism that parallels both the English dominance of Scotland and the interference of the "Great Powers" in Samoa. Two Highlanders, Tam Dale and Tod Lapraik, are in competition for custodianship of an island, the Bass Rock, and use of its precious natural resources (solan geese). The rivalry between these two men mirrors the competition for control of Samoa's natural resources and strategic significance by the "Great Powers," while the supernatural aspects of the story—Tod is demonically possessed and shot with a silver bullet—reflects the Samoans' belief that they required supernatural intervention to counter the ascendancy of foreign interference, as with the chief Malietoa Laupepa, who "departed with the halo of a saint, and men thought of him as of some King Arthur snatched into Avillion" (*F*, 38). It also recalls the stratagems of Case in "The Beach of Falesá," because he "worked upon the natives' fears" to secure his dominance on the island.[60]

During Black Andie's narrative, David is effectively removed from the plot, being allowed to return only when he "can see for himself it is too late to meddle" (*K*, 338). As the narrator of this episode of history, David is rendered helpless to affect its course, a failure that leads to political disillusionment: "I had had my view of that detestable business they call politics—I had seen it from behind, when it is all bones and blackness; and I was cured for life of any temptations to take part in it again. . . . [W]ith the greatest possible amount of big speech and preparation, [I] had accomplished nothing" (383). Following the failure of his "big speech," the only power remaining to David is to narrate, as his "story," if "properly handled and carefully redd out" would mean that "[t]he whole administration of justice, from its highest officer downward, would be totally discredited" (348–49). Yet this empowering view of the consequences of storytelling is never realized, as David comes to assess the futility of resistance to historical necessity: David opts instead for a romantic resolution to his plot, with his marriage to Catriona Drummond, and it is significant that his interest in marriage arises after the failure of his political ideals. Although the novel is set in the eighteenth century, David's disillusionment represents "the melancholy of disbelief, the nostalgia of the nineteenth-century intellectual for the 'wholeness' of a faith that is no longer possible."[61] Marriage emerges only as a compensatory form of closure.

Stevenson, like David in *David Balfour,* also emerges as a "missing witness" to the history that he narrates in *A Footnote.* Stevenson is up-front about the hampering of his efforts by rumor and lack of printed resources—thereby implying his dependence on oral accounts—but is far more reticent about an equally important problem: almost all of the events he recounts had taken place prior to his settlement on Samoa. Indeed, the climactic event of the narrative—"The Hurricane of March 1889," which forms the penultimate chapter—had occurred six months prior to his first landfall on the island. This is not to claim that Stevenson was posing as a long-term resident on the island. Rather, one should recognize that Stevenson was dependent on secondhand accounts for his history and—like David—arrived too late to influence the central events of the story. Indeed, Stevenson complained to Colvin, in a letter of September 1891, "The sense of my helplessness here has been rather bitter. I feel it wretched to see this dance of folly and injustice and unconscious rapacity go forward from day to day, and to be impotent."[62]

Stevenson's absence from the central events brings into focus an anxiety about his exclusion from and tardy arrival on the historical scene. In particular, it reveals the fragility of his claims as a historian, as his account hovers close to the indeterminacy of the chronicle as defined by White: "The chronicle often seems to wish to tell a story, aspires to narrativity, but typically fails to achieve it. More specifically, the chronicle usually is marked by a failure to achieve narrative closure. It does not so much conclude as simply terminate. It starts out to tell a story but breaks off *in medias res,* in the chronicler's own present; it leaves things unresolved, or rather, it leaves them unresolved in a story-like way."[63] Stevenson refers to himself at one point as a "chronicler" (*F,* 125) in the context of complaining about "his . . . abhorrent task" (125) of narrating the Samoan troubles. By foregrounding the present actuality of events—with phrases such as "As I write these words, three miles in the mountains . . . the sound of that vexed harbour hums in my ears" (118)—Stevenson benefits from the immediacy of his account. Yet he also imperils the historical status of his narrative, depending as it does on achieving narrative closure. As such, these allusions to the ongoing status of Samoan conflict bring *A Footnote* into the realm of the chronicle.[64]

Stevenson frequently alludes to his personal role in the events he writes of, and he comments on "all the strange doings I have to narrate" (96). At times this is reflected in distaste for the duties of narration, as when he remarks during his account of Becker, the German consul, "There falls one more incident to be narrated, and then I can close with this ungracious chapter" (80). Indeed, Becker's characterization of Mataafa as "very dark and artful" (68) applies more aptly, in Stevenson's account, to Becker himself, who is described as behaving "artfully" (67) and "privately intriguing or pretending to intrigue with Mataafa" (68). It is striking that, in a literary work, "artful" takes on this negative connotation. Yet Becker comes to represent the doubt and uncertainty throughout the narrative, as at key points Stevenson highlights his duplicity: "Becker was preparing to change sides . . . the hopes held secretly forth to Mataafa and secretly reported to his government at home, trenchantly contrast with his [Becker's] external conduct" (68). Becker indeed illustrates Stevenson's point that the "tissue of my story is one of rapacity, intrigue, and the triumphs of temper" (82), and in seeking an explanation for "the progressive decivilisation of the town" (82), Stevenson holds the German personally responsible: the capital of Samoa, "not by any fault of the inhabitants, rather by the act of Becker, had fallen back in civilization about a thousand years" (80).

Stevenson admits, "I have not been able to conceal my distaste" (92) for Becker, yet he is no more able to conceal his admiration for Mataafa, the Samoan chief who emerges as the heroic figure of the story. Stevenson's support for Mataafa hinges on the chief's opposition to control by white colonial interests, his independence, and his honesty: "Mataafa is besides an exceptional native. . . . [H]e seems distinctly and consistently averse to lying" (143). This association of Mataafa with truth contrasts him with the duplicitous Becker and thus reverses a racial stereotype about the dishonesty of natives that Stevenson elsewhere participates in, as when he remarks that "the natives . . . might be trusted to lie like schoolboys, or (if the reader prefer it) like Samoans" (107–8) and "I would scarce dare say of any Samoan that he is truthful" (143). To a large extent, Stevenson's narrative focuses less on European conflict with Samoans than on what he terms "the animosity between whites" (97), a phrase that echoes the shifting meaning of the "White Man's Quarrel" in "The Beach of Falesá." Repeatedly calling into question the right of the British, Germans, and Americans to occupy Samoa, at times Stevenson explicitly challenges British imperialism, as when he states, "The British flags were of course fired upon; and I hear that one of them was struck down, but I think everyone must be privately of the mind that it was fired upon and fell, in a place where it had little business to be shown" (107). There is of course no such questioning of the right of the British flag to be shown on Treasure Island.

Stevenson's admiration for Mataafa is reflected in parallels between the Samoan chief and the Jacobites, whom he portrays sympathetically in both *Kidnapped* and *David Balfour:* in the latter case portraying Jacobites (especially Alan Breck and James of the Glens) as innocent victims of governmental guile and political malice. Stevenson here participates in a literary tradition of romantic Jacobitism that hit its zenith with Sir Walter Scott's Edward Waverley and continued well into the twentieth century.[65] In practice, Stevenson splits the positive, Jacobite-influenced representation between the two rivals for Samoan kingship: Stevenson refers to Mataafa as "the pretender," a term that links the Samoan both to the exiled James, son of James II (the Old Pretender), and more significantly to his son, Bonnie Prince Charlie (the Young Pretender). Yet the exiled Laupepa is the one who comes back to his native land and "returned (November 1889) to a changed world" (131), the poignancy of his having "returned from the dead of exile to find himself replaced" (132) echoing the fate of the Stuarts in their failed attempt to wrest back the British monarchy. Mataafa, however, is portrayed as the people's choice, like the Young Pretender, as "an ominous cry for Mataafa began to arise in the islands" (135), while "Laupepa seems never to have been a popular king" (135).

Mataafa's stalwart resistance to the domination of whites further illustrates his heroic status, as when Stevenson narrates, "White travelers, to their indescribable irritation, are (on his approach) waved from his path by his armed guards" (151). This dismissal of white presence is reminiscent of another charismatic Polynesian king, Tembinok' of Apemama in the Gilberts, whom

Stevenson portrayed in *In the South Seas.* Indeed, Stevenson compares Mataafa with Tembinok' in *A Footnote,* writing, "About himself and all his surroundings there breathes a striking sense of order, tranquility and native plenty. . . . I have visited and dwelt in almost every seat of the Polynesian race, and have met but one man who gave me a stronger impression of character and parts" (151); readers of the South Seas letters, which had been serialized in Britain and America the previous year (1891), would have had no trouble in recognizing Tembinok', whom Neil Rennie terms "a powerful character around whom all the material naturally revolves."[66]

The dilemmas facing Stevenson as a historian of contemporary events are revealed through various narrative cruces in which he reflects on the role of the historian in making history. In the "Hurricane" chapter, Stevenson attempts to present the cataclysmic event as nature's vengeance on imperial hubris, in which "the sword-arm of each of the two angry powers [America and Germany] was broken" (128). Departing from his practice of treating the events as marginal, no more than a footnote, Stevenson insists that "the so-called hurricane of March 16th made thus a marking epoch in world history" (129). Stevenson no sooner claims a position from which to judge the impact of the Samoan troubles on world history, however, than he immediately concedes that "coming years and other historians will declare the influence of that" (129). Unable to determine the influence of the events he has narrated, Stevenson in effect fails to meet "the demand for closure in the history, for the want of which the chronicle form is adjudged to be deficient."[67]

Indeed, chief among the trials of writing "contemporary history" in *A Footnote* is that the effects of the narrative cannot be enclosed within its pages but puncture the text, as it were, and rebound upon the author. Another incident from the final chapter demonstrates that, even as he attempts to translate the "real" events into what White terms a "discourse of desire," Stevenson is painfully reminded of the difference between the two. Toward the end of *A Footnote,* Stevenson narrates a story that he heard from the American consul-general on Samoa, Harold Sewall, of a plot to kidnap and remove the popular Samoan chief Mataafa, whom Stevenson supported in the civil strife. According to the account in *A Footnote*—which withholds the names of the participants—"A [Sewall] was a gentleman who had long been an intimate of Mataafa's, and had recently . . . more or less completely broken off relations. To him came one whom I shall call B with a dastardly proposition. . . . It was proposed that A should simulate a renewal of friendship, decoy Mataafa to a suitable place, and have him there arrested" (142). When A objects to the plan, B assures him, "You will have no discredit. The Germans are to take the blame of the arrest" (142). The episode not only reveals the intrigue surrounding the American-German rivalry in Samoa, but also suggests striking parallels with the kidnapping of David Balfour on Gillane Sands and his confinement on the Bass Rock in *David Balfour,* a capture that also takes advantage of a friendship (with Alan Breck) and removes "a most uncomfortable witness" (*K,* 347). Unlike David, Stevenson, of course, is not the victim of the "plot" but only its reporter. Yet while David eventually escapes unharmed, Stevenson fears that "in the end RLS must pay the piper" for his textual indiscretion, being "unguarded enough to show a copy of it to one of the man's colleagues."[68]

The man referred to here, and identified as "B" in the *Footnote,* was the Reverend Arthur E. Claxton (who, in an ironic twist of fate, had translated Stevenson's story "The Bottle Imp" into Samoan). Claxton, an English missionary with the London Missionary Society (LMS), recognized himself in the narrative, despite the removal of his name, and threatened to prosecute Stevenson for libel. The case was a long-running one, in which Stevenson and others gave evidence before a missionary committee in Apia. Claxton was ultimately declared innocent by the LMS in London. As Colley remarks, "Stevenson had lost, but he had succeeded in avoiding a libel suit and ridding Samoa of Claxton's presence."[69]

Evidently, Stevenson misunderstood the power of his "sketch" to provoke, rather than assuage or simply represent, political turmoil. As a narrator of contemporary history, Stevenson had no position of distance from which to construct the unfolding story. Hence, as McLynn observes, "RLS was personally plunged into the maelstrom when he again crossed swords with a Protestant missionary" on Samoa, as the episode showed the power of the text to produce new conflicts rather than simply narrate the history of Samoa.[70] The episode, which Stevenson oddly termed "a pleasing anecdote" in his correspondence, spilled over to threaten the very possibility of authorship. Stevenson indeed apparently confused the trials of storytelling with the pains of history, a confusion evident in his insistence in a letter to Baxter that "the truth of the story can be proved and proved again." If a story's truth needs to be "proved again," one might suggest, then it probably cannot be proved at all. More to the point, Stevenson's criterion for a "good story" or "pleasing anecdote" was apparently not its truth but its desirability as support of his thesis. Yet Stevenson's textual indiscretion is exposed in his confessed lack of knowledge of his own text: "I *suppose* it is on that issue he means to attack. I have never yet received any copy of the book and seem to have lost the proofs of that part; so that I cannot be certain of what words I used" (emphasis in original). Even lacking his "proofs," however, Stevenson was confident that he had his proof and had "a good chance to come scatheless."[71]

Like the German consul Brandeis, whom he admired, Stevenson "had a double task" (*F,* 42) in telling his Samoan history, even though this duality threatened his narrative project with "ultimate failure" (42). For, like Buridan's donkey, Stevenson seemed unable to choose between two equally appealing objects of desire, two similarly alluring discourses for the representation of the events. Ultimately, this very indecision discloses the fictitious basis of *both* discourses, as both the "footnote" and the "further adventures" of David Balfour propose a deferred supplement to an original, authoritative text that, as Stevenson knew better than most, would never be completed.

# PART FOUR

## Rewriting the Imperial Romance

# SEVEN

## "The White Man's Quarrel"

### Sexuality, Travel, and Colonialism in Stevenson's South Sea Tales

IN THE PREVIOUS CHAPTER, I explore the intertextuality of *A Footnote to History,* a nonfictional narrative of the civil war on Samoa, and *David Balfour,* which proclaims itself the sequel to *Kidnapped.* Though *David Balfour* was set in eighteenth-century Scotland, I argue that it reflects the turmoil of contemporary Samoa, on which Stevenson was living. In this chapter, I examine fictional works in which Stevenson develops his critique of colonialism more directly. Following his decision to settle on Samoa, Stevenson came to question the distinction that he had originally made between his fictional accounts of Polynesia, or "yarns," and his nonfictional writings on the people, culture, and manners of the islands. He sought to produce a hybrid form that would combine fictional form with documentary style. As he wrote to Sidney Colvin in May 1892 (with reference to "The Beach of Falesá"), "you scarce do justice to the fact that this is a piece of realism *à outrance* nothing extenuated or adorned. Looked at so, is it not, with all its tragic features, wonderfully idyllic, with great beauty of scene and circumstance?"[1]

Yet Stevenson's claim to be offering realistic portrayals of the South Seas did not impress his critics. As Nicholas Daly argues, "there has been considerable critical reluctance to see the late Victorian romance as a modern form at all. Just as the critics of the 1880s sought to assimilate the apparent novelty of the romance as a 'revival' of an older literature, present-day critics have interpreted the romance as a revenant, as the ghost of eighteenth-century Gothic fiction."[2] In this view, the capacity of romance to comment on contemporary political reality was extremely limited. Arthur Johnstone, for example, would call into question the veracity of Stevenson's observations on the South Seas, referring to the limitations of the romance: "Stevenson's analysis failed, and in consequence he reached theoretical conclusions without considering all the factors of the case. The view that he took of Polynesian character and nationality would have formed a splendid mosaic in a South-Sea romance; but by the earnest practical pioneers in the Pacific, the existing social and political conditions were more strictly construed under a riper experience." The purpose of Johnstone's account is to discredit Stevenson's judgment of the character of Polynesians and to accuse him of blindness to the real situation in the South Seas: "[H]is love for the natives, and his pity for their helplessness under the conditions in which he found them, seemed to obscure his keener realization, shown elsewhere, of their precocious faults and unvarying instability."[3]

Arguing that Stevenson failed to grasp the reality of the South Seas, Johnstone condemns the author for having abandoned the imaginative realm of "South-Sea romance" in favor of a more realistic mode of fiction. Yet "The Beach of Falesá" is the exception among Stevenson's yarns, forgoing the use of symbolic and even supernatural devices or methods that he deployed elsewhere in his South Seas fiction. On the surface, "The Isle of Voices," for example, seems to depart dramatically from the narrative model of "The Beach of Falesá" by abandoning the realistic technique of a white trader as narrator and adapting the conventions of the Polynesian folktale, with its cast of native characters and atmosphere of folklore. Stevenson wrote to Charles Baxter on August 11, 1892, strenuously protesting against the publication of "The Beach of Falesá" in the same volume as "The Bottle Imp" and "The Isle of Voices," as being "a story of a totally different scope and intention."[4] In the end, the three stories were published together under the title *Island Nights' Entertainments* (1893).

Yet while recognizing the formal and stylistic differences between "The Isle of Voices" and "The Beach of Falesá," I believe that Stevenson exaggerated the dissimilarity of their scope and intention. "The Isle of Voices" not only is concerned with encounters between white and Polynesian cultures but also can be understood as an allegory of colonialism, and the story centrally places issues of labor and commercial exploitation that are Stevenson's concern in "The Beach of Falesá." Indeed, the problem of how one society's values—both cultural and economic—may be translated into the terms of another culture is one of the tale's chief interests. In this respect, the absence of white characters from the story may be viewed as a way to cloak its subtle critique of colonial exploitation and cross-cultural encounters in manifest form of "the original Polynesian tale or legend." According to Johnstone, Stevenson, by seeking to represent "the extremes of native and foreign island life," had recourse to write "sometimes in an allegory or fable."[5]

Among critics who have considered the critique of colonial culture in Stevenson's South Seas fiction, Rod Edmond offers one of the most perceptive readings, asserting of "The Isle of Voices" and "The Bottle Imp" that "it is interesting to try and read these tales as colonial allegories." Edmond does indeed map out some important aspects of the tales' relation to imperial ideology; for example, he observes that "in both these tales magic is modern rather than traditional, and associated with material greed" and, in the case of "The Isle of Voices," points to the "consistent identification of supernatural with economic power." In an argument to which I am sympathetic, Edmond points out that "the making of dollars from sea-shells suggests western economic exploitation of the Pacific islands, here particularly . . . the activity of pearl-fishing." Yet despite offering these insights, Edmond believes that the colonial reading "cannot be wholly sustained," giving as his objections the narration of the story from Keola's point of view, and he states that "against the logic of the imperial allegory, the tale ends happily with Keola restored to his wife."[6] I argue, to the contrary, that the representation of Keola's point of view is essential to the colonial allegory, revealing as it does the split subjectivity of the colonized subject. In addition, I read the story's conclusion in a different way than

Edmond does: the residual threat of "discipline and punishment" with which the narrative concludes reinscribes the central couple as colonial subjects.

## "Beset with invisible devils": Magic, Money, and Discipline in "The Isle of Voices"

To recognize the colonial allegory of "The Isle of Voices," one must remember the context in which Stevenson wrote it. During 1892, he became more deeply involved in Samoan politics, writing regular letters to the *Times* on the Samoan judicial and political situation and trying to serve as a peacemaker between the rival kings Mataafa and Laupepa.[7] As a result of this involvement, Stevenson was threatened by deportation by the British high commissioner. In addition, his friends in England became increasingly disenchanted with his apparent fixation on Samoan affairs. The failure of Stevenson's attempts at peacemaking became evident when war broke out between the two rival kings in July 1893, resulting in defeat for Mataafa, whom Stevenson had supported. Meanwhile, in Hawaii, American commercial and political interests had established hegemony, culminating in the American-backed revolution of 1893 that ended the native monarchy of Kalakaua and prepared the way for annexation by the United States in 1898. Hence, both in Samoa and in Hawaii, the intervention of foreign powers at once provoked and exploited civil strife between native leaders.

"The Isle of Voices," first published in February 1893, anticipates a speech that Stevenson made to the Samoan chiefs at Vailima, following their construction of the Road of the Loving Hearts, in October 1894. In this powerful speech, Stevenson warned the chiefs of the dangers of neglecting their land: "And I repeat to you that thing which is sure, if you do not use your talent, if you do not occupy and use your country, others will." To authenticate his argument about the perils of colonialism, Stevenson drew on his firsthand experience of the effects of English imperialism in Scotland and Ireland: "I who speak to you have seen these things. I have seen them with my eyes, these judgements of God. I have seen them in Ireland, and I have seen them in the mountains of my own country in Scotland, and my heart was sad." Speaking as the fellow subject of a colonized country, he applied the lessons of his native country to his adopted one, using the example of Hawaii and its loss of independence:

> The *other people* that I tell you of have come upon them like a fog in the night, and these are the other-people's sheep who browse upon the foundations of their houses. To come nearer hand I have seen this judgement in Oahu also, I have ridden there a whole day along the coast of an island. Hour after hour went by and I saw the face of no living man except the guide who rode with me. . . . All along that desolate coast, in one bay after another, we saw still standing the churches that had been built by the Hawaiians of old. There must have been many hundreds, many thousands, dwelling there in old times, and worshipping God in these now empty churches. For today they were empty, the doors were closed, the villages had disappeared, the people were dead and gone, only the church stood on like a tombstone over a grave, in the midst of the white men's sugar fields. The *other people* had come and used that country, and the [<farmer men>] {Hawaiians} who occupied it for nothing had been swept away, where is weeping and gnashing of teeth.[8]

Stevenson's use of biblical language evokes the specter of colonialism as a plague that will devastate Polynesia. In the context of the speech, the "other people" evidently refers to white men, as when he refers to the "white men's sugar fields." However, his examples of Scotland and Ireland indicate a more general, less racially specific colonial enemy, one that takes on an almost supernatural power of exploitation ("come upon them like a fog in the night"). This speech demonstrates Stevenson's separation of the colonizer from a specific racial category, a disconnection that also occurs in "The Isle of Voices," where, as in "The Tale of Tod Lapraik," Stevenson uses the supernatural—specifically, the figure of the warlock—to represent colonial struggle for the spoils of an island. In his speech to the Samoan chiefs, Stevenson moves from Ireland and Scotland to the physically and culturally closer example of Hawaii to illustrate the dangers of surrendering independence. Similarly, by setting "The Isle of Voices" on Hawaii—as he had done with "The Bottle Imp"—Stevenson registered the fact that the Eight Islands furnished the most flagrant instance of colonial usurpation of a Polynesian territory.

The greed and materialism that motivate the central characters of "The Isle of Voices"—both Keola and his father-in-law, the warlock-figure Kalamake—

are clearly linked to the influence of American colonialism, represented by the measurement of wealth in U.S. currency: "[F]or all he paid in bright new dollars. 'Bright as Kalamake's dollars' was another saying in the Eight Isles."[9] Yet "The Isle of Voices" takes its title from a distinct fictional space, which provides the site of the key colonial encounters. The identification of this isle with spoken language marks it as a location where linguistic difference is articulated as part of an ongoing commercial system of exchange. The magical aspects of the island (specifically, the invisibility of the warlocks) suggest an uncanny potency of the economic practices of colonialism, practices that silence the native voices in the cacophony of trade.

Johnstone reports an interview in which Stevenson raised "the question of the introduction of the white element being necessary in successful work about the South Seas, which he again took up by saying: 'From what I have now said you will see why it is that "The Isle of Voices" is not up to the mark—I left out too much of the civilized ingredient.'"[10] Aside from the question of whether "The Isle of Voices" contains a "civilized" element, it would be incorrect to state that the tale is lacking in white characters. When Keola flees from his father-in-law, he takes refuge on board a trading ship with a white crew, at which point the story significantly shifts from the viewpoint of white anti-"kanaka" prejudice (as in "The Beach of Falesá," where Wiltshire defines himself as "[a] white man, and a British subject. . . . I've come here to do them good, and bring them civilization" [*SST*, 23]) to that of Polynesian prejudice against whites: Keola views the trading ship's crew as "no worse than other whites" and neatly inverts the European judgment of Polynesians as unreliable and untrustworthy in stating that "it was the trouble with these white men, and above all with the mate, that you could never be sure of them" (112, 113). This ship's mate is later described as "a fool of a white man" who, because he "would believe no stories but his own," ignores the warnings and dies from eating a poisoned fish (116).

Yet the story goes further than simply inverting the racial stereotypes of "white" and "kanaka" by adopting the Polynesian point of view. It calls into question the distinction itself, in particular challenging the idea that colonial exploitation is restricted to the practice of whites. This racial ambivalence in the story is introduced in the description of Kalamake (whose name translates into English as "make money") as "a strange man to see. He was come of the best blood in Molokai and Maui, of a pure descent; and yet he was more white to look upon than any foreigner" (103).[11] As Edmond remarks, "This helps identify him with European economic power. It is as if he has been bleached by his taste for western goods and the need to have the dollars to support his habit."[12] Indeed, the sentence—both designating and calling into question a racial purity—suggests that Kalamake represents a hybridity in the story, identifying him with the "other people" who, at the time, were taking over Hawaii. This is in part associated with his supernatural powers and status as a warlock.

But more pertinently, the description of Kalamake as racially ambiguous suggests that greed and authoritarian control are not exclusive to Hawaiian or white but are applicable to all races. I have argued earlier in this volume that Stevenson establishes a parallel between Tembinok', the king of Apemama in the South Seas letters, and Attwater in *The Ebb-Tide* to question the simplistic distinction between European colonialist and native subject. The allegory of the "The Isle of Voices" again blurs boundaries of racial identity, representing the warlocks or wizards—rather than the whites—as the agents of colonial manipulation and acquisitiveness.

The key to the power of these warlocks, who come to the isle from all parts of the globe—"the French, the Dutch, the Russian, the Tamil, the Chinese" (119)—is their invisibility, their ability to extract wealth from the island without being detected: from Keola's point of view, "the beach was thick as a cried fair, yet no man seen; and as he walked he saw the shells vanish before him, and no man to pick them up" (119). The warlocks thus resemble the "other people," who descend on a beautiful land like an invisible plague and strip away its beauty. The shells (a representation of dollars, of course) vanish miraculously in an immediate translation of natural resources into currency. With this supernatural device, the story depicts the colonial profit-making operation as a magical trick, devised by an invisible agency that whisks away the assets of Polynesia without labor and without consent.

The only trace of the presence of the colonizer is language (and linguistic difference). The invisible power of the warlocks is undermined by their audibility, as Kalamake explains: "Yet they hear us; and therefore it is well to speak softly as I do" (107). Keola experiences this linguistic trace of the colonizer's presence as he listens to the Babel-like cacophony of "the beach," on which "all tongues of the earth were spoken" (119). Colonialism is here depicted as a hybrid practice composed of many languages and cultures, a state of mutual unintelligibility that can be resolved only by a shared language, or "beach de mar."

The story goes on to destabilize the opposition between colonizer and colonized still further. Having presented a Hawaiian man, Kalamake, as the worst oppressor, the narrative indicates the futility of attempting to escape such oppression by stating that Keola "had left home and wife and all his friends for no other cause but to escape his enemy, and the place he had come to was that wizard's hunting ground, and the shore where he walked invisible" (115). However, another layer of complexity is added to the allegory with Keola's discovery that he is living among cannibals and is to be their next victim. The belief of the native people in the isle as a protection against colonial oppression is thereby dissolved, as Keola learns that he faces a greater menace from within the native community: the irony of Keola's statement about the island that "I am dying to leave it" is brought out by his wife's reply, "You will never leave it alive" (117). The warning is reminiscent of Stevenson's observation at the beginning of *In the South Seas* that "few men who come to the islands leave them": the island is a seductive prison.[13] Having learned their secret, Keola immediately reinterprets the friendliness of the natives in a sinister light by observing that "when they are in a mind to eat a man, they cherish and fondle him like a mother with a favourite baby" (118). Similarly, the cultured demeanor of the islanders that initially impressed him has come to repel him, as he imagines himself providing their next meal: "[T]hey were elegant speakers, and they made beautiful poetry, and jested at meals . . . [yet] all he saw was the white teeth shining in their mouths" (118).

Keola's point of view dramatizes the split identity of the colonized subject, unable to completely identify either with his oppressor or with his fellow natives. Indeed, Keola's statement of his dilemma—"I am between the devil and the deep sea" (118)—reveals that in being caught between the colonial oppression of the warlocks and the murderous intentions of the natives, Keola has no alternative but to appropriate the magic of the warlocks.

Edmond believes that "the tale ends happily with Keola restored to his wife," suggesting a reproductive future that would depart from Stevenson's grim prognosis of Polynesian culture elsewhere, which Stevenson refers to as "the approaching extinction of his race" (*ISS*, 25).[14] However, the conclusion of the story is less optimistic than Edmond claims. Though Keola seems to have been restored to his former identity at the end of "The Isle of Voices"—"there were Keola and Lehua in the room at home. . . . Keola could see his wife at last" (121)—there is a significant disruption of this closure, with the suggestion that he is still in limbo: "[H]e was out of the body with pleasure to be clean escaped out of the hands of the eaters of men" (121). To be "out of the body" is to be transported, a state in which identity is in dissolution. Clearly, Keola has not been able to return to his prior self, as his identity is left in suspension at the end of the tale. Having been empowered, like Dr. Jekyll, by a magical transformation, he is unable to return to his previous subject-position. Moreover, Keola has lost his state of innocence as to the magical source of Kalamake's wealth, based on no obvious labor: "[H]e neither sold, nor planted, nor took hire . . . and there was no source conceivable for so much silver coin" (103–4). Recognizing the magic of money, Keola is aware that the sources of wealth are derived from colonial exploitation, and he is canny about the deceptions of the domestic economy: "[T]o think they have fooled me with their talk of mints . . . [when] it is clear that all the new coin in all the world is gathered on these sands!" (119). Finally, Keola has learned that this colonial trade is international, involving "all tongues of the earth."

Moreover, the tale ends with a significant menace still hanging over Keola and Lehua. Ironically, this is not the possibility that Kalamake will return and punish them.[15] Rather, the threat comes from the white missionary whom they consult precisely to ward off the danger of Kalamake's revenge. The missionary's responses are threefold, each of which involves an aspect of colonial authority and judgment. First, using his moral authority, he condemns Keola "for taking the second wife in the low island" (122), thereby illustrating that the missionary fails to interpret the true import of the story, focusing instead on a marginal event that fits his own moral judgment on Keola's sexual choices. In so judging, the missionary displays an urge to control and regulate the sexuality of native peoples, imposing his standards of what constitutes a "proper" marriage. Second, the missionary advises Keola to donate some of the money to "the lepers and some to the missionary fund" (122), thereby enriching his own cause and implying that the "dirty" money can be laundered by good use.[16]

Most significant, however, is the missionary's third response to Keola's confession: "[H]e warned the police at Honolulu that, by all he could make out, Kalamake and Keola had been coining false money, and it would not be amiss to watch them" (122). The missionary obviously violates the secrecy of the confessional act; moreover, unlike Keola, he has not learned that the sources of wealth are colonial territories rather than mints. Aside from the obvious hypocrisy of the missionary—accepting the money from Keola, while warning the police that it is false—the missionary's warning also displays the complicity of the various offices of colonial rule. The missionary is the religious arm of colonialism, as the police are the legal and disciplinary arm: the two work in league to protect their class interests, subjecting the native populace to surveillance and discipline. Specifically, the warning that "it would not be amiss to watch them" reveals a system of colonial oversight and punishment. This surveillance, rather than the return of Kalamake, is what the Hawaiian couple must fear, and they keep it at bay only by succumbing to blackmail: "Keola and Lehua took his advice, and gave many dollars to the lepers and the fund" (122). The colonized subjects, Stevenson suggests, have to pay and pay to maintain their precarious hold on liberty and land against the authority of "other people."

Notwithstanding Johnstone's account, it seems clear that Stevenson does not exclude what he terms the "civilized" element from "The Isle of Voices," nor does he omit whites from the tale. Rather, the tale dramatizes an encounter between Polynesian and white cultures and allegorizes the appropriation of Polynesian land and resources by whites, both in the legend of the isle of voices and in its limitless supply of wealth. Defusing any simplistic opposition between "white" and "native," the tale demonstrates the misprision of each race by the other, while also demonstrating that colonialism is a system of exploitation that involves all races and all tongues. Rather than deploying the tactic of using a white trader as his narrator, as he did in "The Beach of Falesá" (with its ideological blind spots), Stevenson in "The Isle of Voices" depicts the white point of view in fragments: in the crew of the trading ship and the white missionary. This fragmentation of the white viewpoint diffuses its authority and is also balanced by a portrayal of the negative native views of whites, illustrating the reversibility of racial prejudices. One might say that Stevenson conceals or disguises the "civilized element" within the folktale form, constructing a narrative that both draws on Polynesian legend and allegorizes the encounters and fluctuating identities of colonialism. Reflecting what Stevenson described as "the extremes of native and foreign life," "The Isle of Voices" is a textual site in which colonial encounters take place, identities are destabilized, and languages and cultures mingle.[17] Quite distinct in location from Hawaii—the narrative insists on this difference at several points—the isle of voices is nevertheless the fictional space in which the fate of the Eight Islands is implied and anticipated. For 1893—the year in which the tale was first published and the year before Stevenson's death—would see the end of native rule of the Hawaiian islands. Even if, to quote Kokua in "The Bottle Imp," "all the world is not American" (92), a significant part of Polynesia was about to become so.

## "Dreaming England": Race, Desire, and Nostalgia in "The Beach of Falesá"

A significant change in Stevenson's relation to the South Seas occurred when, "after nearly three years of cruising in the South Seas, he settled at Vailima in late 1890."[18] Prior to settling on Samoa, Stevenson had already set out his intentions for the group of stories he called his "South Sea Yarns," writing to Sidney Colvin in September 1889 about the "strange ways of life, I think, they set forth: things that I can scarce touch upon, or even not at all, in my travel book; and the yarns are good, I do believe."[19] Significantly, Stevenson suggests that the yarns offer an alternative outlet to the travel book for his materials. Neil Rennie argues that "the 'scientific' South Seas of the projected book was already, in the early months at Vailima, taking second place in Stevenson's mind to the romantic South Seas of fiction."[20] Yet the actual form that the yarns took was determined as much by the experience of settlement as by the pleasures of cruising. Stevenson's portrayal of the South Seas, in stories such as "The Beach of Falesá" and *The Ebb-Tide,* is less "romantic" than Rennie suggests. In particular, nostalgia for Britain and a realistic grasp of the problems of life in the South Seas informed Stevenson's fictional portrayal of the islands.

Stevenson had ambitious plans for some of his yarns, having been influenced not only by other writers on the South Seas, such as Melville, but also by previous masters of romance, especially Alexandre Dumas.[21] Stevenson wrote of *The Pearl Fisher* (an early title for the tale that eventually became *The Ebb-Tide*) that "the yarn is a kind of *Monte Cristo* one. *The Wrecker* is the least good as a story, I think; but the characters seem to me good."[22] By contrast, Stevenson thought highly of "The Beach of Falesá" from the time he began writing it in 1891. Stevenson wrote to Colvin in September 1891, "I never did a better piece of work, horrid, and pleasing, and extraordinarily *true:* it's sixteen pages of the South Seas: their essence." Yet the story also presented him with a dilemma over how to proceed with his other South Seas yarns, in which he had little faith: "What am I to do? Lose this little gem—for I'll be bold, and that's what I think it—or go on with the rest which I don't believe in, and don't like, and which can never make aught but a silly yarn?"[23]

Rennie argues that the yarns were an attempt to find consolation for Stevenson's aborted plan to write a "big book" on the South Seas: "Stevenson's little tale was no substitute for his failure to transcribe the South Sea facts in his projected *The South Seas,* but 'the beach' he had observed in the Gilberts did contribute to the realism of *The Beach of Falesá.*"[24] Yet Stevenson's experience of living on Samoa was at least as influential on the story as were his cruising adventures, and shaped its realist style. Because of this realism, evidently Stevenson did not include "The Beach of Falesá" with his other yarns but kept it in a category apart, attempting something more ambitious. While the South Seas letters were a source of aggravation to Stevenson, he was delighted that his story had combined the romance of the South Seas with the realism that he sought in his nonfiction: in another letter to Colvin, in September 1891, Stevenson described "The Beach of Falesá" as "the first realistic South Sea story; I mean with real South Sea character and details of life; everybody else who has tried, that I have seen, got carried away by the romance and ended in a kind of sugar candy sham epic. . . . You will know more about the South Seas after you have read my little tale, than if you had read a library."[25] Stevenson offers his story as an antidote to the romance of South Seas fiction, not an example of it.

The realism of "The Beach of Falesá" is largely influenced by its protagonist and narrator, John Wiltshire, a British trader who arrives "at the village of

Falesá on an imaginary South Sea island."[26] At the prompting of Case, another trader, Wiltshire participates in a fraudulent marriage to Uma, an island girl, and as a result comes under taboo by the natives. Unable to conduct trade for copra, Wiltshire traces the source of the taboo to the manipulations of Case, who uses his knowledge of local superstitions to control the islanders and establish a monopoly on the copra trade. Wiltshire pursues Case to his secret lair in the "High Woods" and engages in a fatal struggle with his antagonist, being seriously wounded before eventually stabbing Case to death. After being "properly" married to Uma by the missionary, Tarleton, Wiltshire settles with her on the island and has a family.

As Rennie points out, the tale displaces the conflict between European traders and the native peoples onto a struggle between white men. Yet Rennie implies that Stevenson, in so doing, ignores a more important conflict in the South Seas: "The conflict between islanders and missionaries is thus made into a conflict between traders and missionaries, which is to recognize the new realities of power in the Pacific, but to pass over the continuing and more fundamental conflict between the indigenous cultures and civilization in all its manifestations."[27] The tale does indeed challenge Western views of the South Seas as a site of struggle between islanders and missionaries, but I disagree with Rennie's claim that Stevenson overlooks the conflict between native and European colonialists. Rather, Stevenson shows that what he terms the "White Man's Quarrel" has devastating consequences for indigenous people and culture.

Ann Colley's focus is on the missionary rivalries, arguing that "[i]n the telling of his tale, Stevenson enlists the rivalries and frictions attending and sometimes sullying an island's missionary culture. To begin with he draws on the conflict between the traders and the missionaries—a hostility . . . that Stevenson thought counterproductive and unnecessary."[28] Of course, this conflict is present in "The Beach of Falesá," but Stevenson, I argue, shows that the primary and decisive conflict is between white traders, not between traders and missionaries. In so doing, Stevenson exposes the clash between white colonial interests as a direct cause of the oppression of indigenous people. This, as I discuss in chapter 6, was the case on Samoa, where the rivalry of German, British, and American representatives (the "Great Powers") exacerbated and exploited the rivalry between indigenous chiefs, such as Laupepa and Mataafa, and their respective clans. In other words, the "conflict between indigenous cultures and civilization" cannot be separated from hostilities between whites. As Stevenson spelled out in a letter to Colvin concerning "The Beach of Falesá," "almost all that is ugly is in the whites."[29]

This "ugly" quality is the result of greed, as Stevenson makes clear that the chief motive for white presence in the South Seas is the extraction of profit. "Trade" is a kind of euphemism for commercial exploitation, and Case's dubious methods are initially admired by Wiltshire: "There was no smarter trader, and none dodgier, in the islands. I thought Falesá seemed to be the right kind of a place" (*SST*, 6). The narrative suggests Wiltshire's initial attraction to Case, who "used me like a gentleman and like a friend, made me welcome to Falesá, and put his services at my disposal" (5). Wiltshire's approval of Falesá is exclusively based on its being a lucrative trading station: "I . . . saw the cocoanuts waving and posted up the tons of copra, and over the village green and saw the island dandies and reckoned up the yards of print they wanted for their kilts and dresses, I felt as if I was in the right place to make a fortune" (17).

Fearing that there would be problems of "translating" his new material for an audience unfamiliar with it and that "the very trades and hopes and fears of the characters, are all novel and may be found unwelcome to . . . the public," Stevenson created a narrator, John Wiltshire, who could mediate between the life and culture of the South Seas and the trader's discourse that would be familiar to English and American readers. Stevenson's satisfaction with his narrator is evident in a letter he wrote to Colvin: "Mr Wiltshire (the narrator) is a huge lark, though I say it. But there is always the exotic question." By "the exotic question," Stevenson referred to the various alien elements that might be hard to assimilate into a story for English-speaking readers: "[T]he life, the place, the dialects—traders' talk, which is a strange conglomerate of literary expressions and English and American slang, and Beach de Mar, or native English."[30]

Colley argues that the missionary, Tarleton, is a key figure in providing resolution for the story, transcending the conflicts that mar relations between the traders. For example, she states, "Tarleton helps Wiltshire understand Case's viciousness, the history and terrible fate of his predecessors, the weaknesses of the native preacher. . . . Later, Tarleton intercedes to bring an end to the ostracism of Uma and Wiltshire. . . . With this deed, Tarleton rises above the rivalries dividing the religious sects and momentarily unites them to help heal a wounded island." Indeed, Colley's argument represents Tarleton as the protagonist of "The Beach of Falesá," the key figure in the story's realism: "The complexity of Tarleton's responses toward his work, himself, and others (white and native), as well as their complicated reactions to him, are what fascinated Stevenson and keep the realism within the pages of *The Beach of Falesá* outside the margins of the earlier adventure stories."[31] Colley's strategy of bringing an apparently marginal figure into the limelight is intriguing, yet I believe she exaggerates Tarleton's importance to the story. Stevenson's tale remains focused throughout on the narrator, Wiltshire, and his changing point of view as he becomes more immersed in Polynesian culture.

Moreover, I would argue that Stevenson exposes the significant limits of the missionary's influence and competence. Colley seeks to heroize Tarleton, arguing that he "steps out of the darkness in time to bury Case and carry out a wounded Wiltshire. He continues his healing vocation when he then sets Wiltshire's injured leg (but, as Wiltshire points out, it was a missionary splice, so he limps to this day)."[32] Colley's parentheses suggest that the ineptitude of Tarleton's leg-setting is less significant than his intention to do good, his "healing vocation." However, the phrase "missionary splice" calls into question Tarleton's ability to heal, suggesting that he may do more harm than good. Like Colley, Rennie ascribes great significance to the missionary, arguing that Stevenson's tale achieves "much the same conclusion" as *Coral Island,* with "the victory of Christianity, marked by the arrival of the missionary, the marriage of the Christian island girl, and the burning of the false gods."[33] As I argue, however, "The Beach of Falesá" opens up disturbing issues of power and conflict that cannot be resolved as neatly as Rennie claims. What brings about a transformation on the island is not the arrival of the missionary but the arrival of Wiltshire, who is the first to successfully challenge the tyranny of the corrupt trader.

As with earlier adventure stories such as *Treasure Island* and *Kidnapped,* Stevenson uses the first-person narrator as a device for attracting the reader, fashioning an accessible figure with whom the reader might identify. Also, as in those earlier stories, the narrator's persona becomes an important part of the story, with his prejudices, emotions, and traits coloring every dimension of the narrative.

But whereas Stevenson had used juvenile narrators in earlier romances, for "The Beach of Falesá" he developed an adult male persona, a seasoned traveler and trader in the South Seas. Having been "for years on a low island near the line, living for the most part solitary among natives" (*SST*, 3), Wiltshire longs for the company of members of his own race, hence his initial enthusiasm for Case. Yet Wiltshire emulates neither Jim's romantic enthusiasm for adventure nor David's sense of ethical caution and justice. A pragmatist, Wiltshire never forgets that he is there for "the business of . . . my trade" or that he represents "the firm" (6). This characteristic is necessary for the combination of romance and realism that Stevenson sought, for "The Beach of Falesá," unlike its predecessors, is set in the present, and the narrator has therefore to reflect modern attitudes toward and trends in colonial expansion.

Wiltshire's perspective, in the first place, is resolutely British: he is named after an English county and so suggests a center from which he (like the empire) had radiated outward and to which he plans to eventually return. Indeed, his great ambition is to return to England and open a public house: a plan that he has abandoned by the end of the narrative.[34] Wiltshire's nostalgia for England is apparent in many statements, as when he remarks, on walking home with Uma, "I felt for all the world as though she were some girl at home in the Old Country, and, forgetting myself for the minute, took her hand to walk with" (12). Wiltshire is able to take Uma's hand—a token of affectionate respect—only by deluding himself that she is an English girl, whom he might view as his equal. Clearly, Wiltshire has some problems of adaptation, and homesickness might be termed the prevailing tone of the opening chapters, as Wiltshire finds himself constantly returning imaginatively to his native country: "There was I sitting in that veranda, in as handsome a piece of scenery as you could find, a splendid sun, and a fine fresh healthy trade that stirred up a man's blood like sea-bathing; and the whole thing was clean gone from me, and I was dreaming England, which is, after all, a nasty, cold muddy hole, with not enough light to see to read by; and dreaming the looks of my public, by a cant of a broad high-road like an avenue, and with the sign on a green tree" (17).

Though Wiltshire should not be mistaken for Stevenson, Wiltshire's nostalgia for his home country does recall that of the author, who also dreamed of Scotland while living in the South Seas.[35] To Colvin he wrote in September 1891,

"You ask me if I am ever homesick for the Highlands and the Isles. Conceive that for the last month I have been living there between 1786 and 1850, in my grandfather's diaries and letters. . . . Now imagine if I have been homesick for Barra-head and Island Glass, and Kirkwall, and Cape Wrath, and the Wells of the Pentland Firth; I could have wept."[36] This emotional reaction to being separated from his native country is translated into Wiltshire's "dreaming England." Yet aside from its sentimental resonance, nostalgia has an economic value attached to it, as Wiltshire's practice of "dreaming England" soon translates into "dreaming the looks of my public"—the public house that drives his wish "to make a fortune, and go home again" (17). The allusion to "my public" also evokes Stevenson imagining his distant "literary public," on whose "looks" (or approval) he was dependent for his income. And Stevenson, too, would turn his nostalgia for Scotland into commercial benefit, specifically, the sequel to *Kidnapped.*

Yet Wiltshire's initial perception that he has "the best station in the South Pacific" (3) is modified by the realization that it "stood in a bad place" (9). At first believing, like his predecessor Adams, "I've dropped into a soft thing here" (3), Wiltshire soon learns that he has actually been caught between a rock and a hard place: a fraudulent marriage that has brought him under taboo and cutthroat competition, characterized by deception, swindling, and manipulation. Though Wiltshire goes along with the deceit of Uma, he is "ashamed" of his trick (11), showing an ambivalence that will make him vulnerable to Case's stratagems. Rather than accept full responsibility for his abuse of Uma, Wiltshire displaces it onto others: "[I]t was the practice in these parts, and (as I told myself) not the least the fault of us white men, but of the missionaries. If they had let the natives be, I had never needed this deception" (11).

Wiltshire's Englishness becomes more pronounced during his residence in the South Seas. A strong component of this identity, notwithstanding, is his belief in the racial superiority of whites. His experience of "living for the most part solitary among natives" (3) has left him "sick for white neighbours after my four years at the line, which I always counted years of prison" (4). His desire for white company causes him to embrace Case as a friend and ally and blinds him to Case's machinations against him. If Wiltshire's identification as "English" is strong, his self-image as a "white man" is even more visible as an influence on his narrative.

In this context, it is significant that Wiltshire makes a sharp distinction between "white men" and "missionaries"—the latter, though they may be racially white, do not count as "white men" in Wiltshire's code, for reasons that he explains in commenting on the missionary, Tarleton: "I didn't like the lot [missionaries], no trader does; they look down upon us, and make no concealment; and besides, they're partly Kanakaized, and suck up with natives instead of with other white men like themselves" (34). Tainted by their close contact with the natives, the missionaries are excluded from the privileged category of "white man," which demands unwavering loyalty to the idea of white superiority.[37] Ironically, when this missionary arrives, he appears like a vision of the colonial official rather than a man of the church: Tarleton is dressed in "the regular uniform, white duck clothes, pith helmet, white shirt and tie, and yellow boots to his feet" (34). Hence the missionary is far more formally dressed than Wiltshire, who "had on a rig of clean striped pajamas" (34).[38] Colley argues that Wiltshire responds positively to Tarleton's spruce appearance: "Wiltshire describes Tarleton's entrances and exits, . . . as if—in spite of his prejudices—he is gazing at someone who is extraordinary, if not almost magnificent. Watching the missionary boat approach the shores of Falesá, the trader enviously observes Tarleton, dressed smartly in white clothes, commanding a white vessel shooting for the mouth of the river."[39] The focus on the missionary's white clothing might seem an index of his "white race." Yet Wiltshire considers the missionary his inferior because Tartleton is "partly Kanakaized." In other words, Wiltshire is not envious but scornful and believes that Tarleton has "gone native," abandoning his innate superiority as a white man to gain the trust of the natives: as Wiltshire points out in his criticism of missionaries, "they can always find civility for a Kanaka, it's us white men they lord it over" (36). Rather than reflecting his race, Tarleton's outfit disguises his absorption into native culture. Moreover, his dandified appearance, while presumably preferable to "the frightening darkness of Case's folly and the putrid dinginess of Captain Randall's filthy body," seems effeminate in the world of masculine traders.[40]

However, if missionaries are excluded from Wiltshire's category of "white men," there remains the problem of who exactly is included, given the racial diversity of the South Seas. Most obviously, Case, as a fellow trader, asserts his identity as a "white man," even though he is first introduced as "yellow and smallish, [and] had a hawk's nose" (5). There is some ambiguity surrounding Case's background: "No man knew his country, beyond he was of English speech," while his language is also ambivalent in that "when he chose he could blaspheme worse than a Yankee boatswain, and talk smart to sicken a Kanaka" (5). The racial signifiers surrounding Case are multiple, as though he is a figure for the heterogeneity of "traders' talk." He is indeed a "Strange Case."[41] Racial boundaries are further blurred with the role of "Black Jack," Case's accomplice, who plays the role of "chaplain" at Wiltshire's marriage to Uma. As they approach "the house of these three white men," Wiltshire explains that "a negro is counted a white man, and so is a Chinese! A strange idea, but common in the islands" (7). The crucial binary is between "white" and "kanaka," with all other racial identities being placed on one side or another of "the line." Hence, Wiltshire's racial categories will be confounded by his own offspring, whom he calls "half-castes."

The tendency is to view those of nonwhite origin, or of mixed race, as inferior or even subhuman: as Jennifer DeVere Brody has written of the distancing of the racial "other," "one way in which this distancing occurred was the analogical labeling of low others as animalistic. The analogies made between the poor and pigs, between enslaved black bodies and unruly beasts, between apes and the Irish . . . served to protect certain (mostly white male) individuals from contamination." Given the urge to resist "contamination," colonialists "frowned . . . on 'brute' miscegenation as evil, as untamed nature mixed too promiscuously. Only white Englishmen were able to strike the proportionate balance between variation and stability."[42]

Yet in Stevenson's tale, it is the white man who descends to the level of the animalistic. Case, besides his "hawk's nose," had "the courage of a lion and the cunning of a rat" (5). Captain Randall, the nominal "father of the beach" (6), has descended into piglike squalor in his hut, "squatting on the floor native fashion, fat and pale, naked to the waist, grey as a badger, and his eyes set with drink. His body was covered with grey hair and crawled over by flies; . . . the mosquitoes hummed about the man like bees. Any clean-minded man would have had the creature out at once and buried him" (8). Stevenson emphasizes the corruption of the "white man" and exposes the fiction that specimens such as Randall are racially superior or pure. Randall, labeled a "creature," in his grotesque physicality alerts Wiltshire to the inversion of hierarchies on the island. Randall's ownership of "trade and station" meant nothing, as "Case and the negro were parasites; they crawled and fed upon him like the flies, he none the wiser" (9).

Yet it is with Case that Wiltshire forms the closest racial bond, as his colleague vociferously asserts the superiority of "whites" to "Kanakas." When Wiltshire reports that he has been placed under a taboo and that no native will do business at his store, Case professes outrage at "the impudence of these Kanakas . . . they seem to have lost all idea of respect for whites" (22). Wiltshire mimics this phrase when he reports of Uma, "I must say she was always well brought up, and had a great respect for whites" (27). Case further expresses approval for the use of military force by the white man in suppressing native insurgency, stating that "what we want is a man-of-war—a German, if we could—they know how to manage Kanakas" (22).[43] Like Wiltshire, Case invariably links the quality of "whiteness" with that of masculinity, his response to the taboo being one of white racial solidarity and male bonding: "I'll stand by you, Wiltshire, man to man. . . . Understand me, Wiltshire; I don't count this your quarrel. . . . I count it all of our quarrel, I count it the White Man's Quarrel." Wiltshire is at first "well pleased with [Case's] attitude" (22) and reinforces the ideology of white superiority in asking Case to address the native chiefs on his behalf: "You tell them who I am. I'm a white man and a British subject, and no end of a big chief at home; and I've come here to do them good, and bring them civilization" (23). Wiltshire's combination of race, masculinity, and national identity (with its almost ironic recitation of imperial certainties) depends on the support of Case, as a fellow white man, in negotiations with the native chiefs. Acting on the assumption that Case is overriding the local taboo, Wiltshire offers an apt summation of the racial bias of imperial ideology: "They haven't any real government or any real law, that's what you've got to knock into their heads; and even if they had, it would be a good joke if it was to apply to a white man. It would be a strange thing if we came all this way and couldn't do what we pleased" (24). Wiltshire's attitude exemplifies what Edward Said calls "the *continuity* of British imperial policy throughout the nineteenth century," which is "accompanied by this novelistic process, whose main purpose is not to raise more questions, not to disturb or otherwise preoccupy attention, but to keep the empire more or less in place" (emphasis in original). For Wiltshire, "British dominance . . . is a sort of norm" that he believes his alliance with Case will maintain.[44]

Significantly, commercial interests cause this bond of the white men to unravel, as Case reminds Wiltshire "I'm a trader myself" and so must protect his own interests: "I'll go as far as I dare for another white man; but when I find I'm in the scrape myself, I think first of my own bacon" (26). In response to Case's "every man for himself" philosophy, Wiltshire turns Case's terminology against him, objecting sarcastically that "you're a nice kind of a white man!" (27). In fact, Case's betrayal goes far deeper than Wiltshire at this point suspects: his greatest treachery is not that he fails to support Wiltshire in the tabooing crisis, but that he has engineered the crisis by marrying Wiltshire to Uma, knowing that she was under taboo and that the stigma would attach to her husband. Indeed, as Wiltshire learns from Tarleton the missionary, Case has made it his goal to drive all other rival traders from the island.[45] As a trader, Case carries out ruthless campaigns against his rivals, even killing them when necessary: "Mr Vigours had evidently been driven out of Falesá by the machinations of Case and with something not very unlike the collusion of my pastor" (39). Tarleton further reports that Case had one of his predecessors, Underhill, buried alive. Tarleton's most alarming warning, however, is that "there is no question but he [Case] has now made up his mind to rid himself of you" (42).

Stevenson's text exposes the intrigue between the colonial power of Case and native leaders: "[W]ith a certain following among the chiefs, and the pastor in his pocket, the man was as good as master of the village" (40). Case's pledge of solidarity (the "White Man's Quarrel") is a masquerade, designed to conceal Case's vendetta against all rival white traders. Hence, the phrase "White Man's Quarrel" ceases to refer to the union of Case and Wiltshire against the "kanakas" and designates instead the battle for supremacy between white traders.

Wiltshire's marriage to a native woman may entail a loss of status, but his revenge on Case is to thoroughly discredit Case as a "white man." Wiltshire's actions against Case are not only violent but also serve to disfigure Case's whiteness: after Wiltshire punches him, "he only looked up white and blank, and the blood spread upon his face like wine upon a napkin" (34). Case's whiteness has become a blank or enigma, which is stained by the blood and so loses its purity. This reflects the marring of Wiltshire's idealized image of Case, and he later rejoices to see the trace of his violence: "[W]hat pleased me mightily, he had still my trade mark on his brow" (47). Wiltshire's play on words, the reference to the scar as a "trade mark," reminds us of the convergence of violence and commerce on the island, such that Wiltshire's brand is inscribed upon the face of his rival.

As he becomes estranged from Case, Wiltshire turns for support to Uma, and their relationship reflects his changing attitudes toward the natives. Initially treating Uma as a sexual object, Wiltshire comes to represent her as "a powerful . . . woman" (70). As Katherine Linehan argues, "Stevenson's critique of colonialism incorporates a remarkable dimension of feminist insight into the parallel workings of racial and sexual domination."[46] Wiltshire's initially exploitative relationship to Uma parallels his design of exploiting profit from the islanders, and as he grows to love and trust Uma, his attitudes toward the indigenous people also change. On entering the woods (the original title of the story was "The High Woods of Ulufanua") in search of Case's hidden lair, for example, Wiltshire reflects on some important parallels between races: "[W]e laugh at the natives and their superstitions; but see how many traders take them up, splendidly educated white men" (52). Indeed, Wiltshire admits that he himself is not immune to these superstitions: "It's my belief a superstition grows up in a place like the different kinds of weeds; as I stood there and listened to that wailing I twittered in my shoes" (52). Wiltshire's point is key to the representation of race and culture in "The Beach of Falesá": if superstitions, like other cultural practices and beliefs, are intrinsically local ("grows up in a place"), then the outsider will inevitably adapt to and absorb them regardless of one's racial background. It is also while looking for "my enemy's head office" (53) (a commercial metaphor that shows how Wiltshire keeps their business rivalry in the foreground) that he comments on the native "rite of passage" of going into the woods, observing that "a young man scarce reckoned himself grown till he had got his breech tattooed, for one thing, and seen Case's devils for another. This is mighty like Kanakas: but, if you look at it in another way, it's mighty like white folks too" (54). This willingness to "look at it in another way," or to recognize the kinship between whites and kanakas rather than ascribing each a place in a binary opposition, is a direct result of his enmity with Case and affiliation with Uma.

Indeed, the racial hierarchy to which Wiltshire has subscribed is turned upside down in the woods. In addition, his initial attraction to Case is explosively transformed into murderous violence. Case had been his "protector" and had set him up with Uma, whose contamination by taboo Wiltshire felt was the cause of his troubles. In the woods, Case—the white man—is identified as the source of evil: as Rennie observes, Stevenson "has made the false gods of Falesá the creation, not of the islanders, but of Case, a white man, 'a good forger of island curiosities.'"[47] Meanwhile, Uma becomes the protector that Case has patently failed to be, literally throwing herself between Wiltshire and Case's bullet: "[A]s soon as she heard me sing out, she ran forward. The Winchester cracked again, and down she went" (66). Wiltshire, in searching for Case as an enemy, states, "I looked all round for his white face, you may be sure; but there was not a sign of him" (66). Case's "white face" has become an emblem of the adversary, a trademark that identifies the man whom Wiltshire wishes to eliminate.

Wiltshire's climactic stabbing of Case—a killing that can be seen as self-defense—repeats the motif of staining, a discoloring of Case's whiteness, as Wiltshire recalls that "the blood came over my hands . . . hot as tea" (68). The word "came" also suggests an orgasmic moment, as the scene is the consummation of Case and Wiltshire's sexual rivalry, for the two have been rivals for Uma as well as for trade (30–31). By passing Uma onto Wiltshire, Case has participated in a "traffic in women" that also serves to mediate desire between men, as when Case touches Wiltshire to draw his attention to Uma's beauty. The climactic violence between the men suggests a sexual assault, a symptom of pent-up desire. Fixing his knife "in the place," Wiltshire asks, "Do you feel the point of that?" and "gave him the cold steel for all I was worth. His body kicked under me like a spring sofa; he gave a dreadful kind of a long moan, and lay still" (67). Wiltshire's violence mimics sexual penetration, and his final posture suggests their quasi-gothic eroticized union: "I fainted clean away, and fell with my head on the man's mouth" (68).[48]

The killing not only finally ends Wiltshire's commercial rivalry with Case but also breaks their homoerotic bond, allowing for the final transference of

Wiltshire's desire to Uma. Having regained consciousness, Wiltshire stabs Case again: "'I bet you're dead now,' I said, and then I called to Uma" (68). This language suggests that Uma is Case's erotic replacement, as she arrives to fill the void left by Case's death. Yet the physical traces of his encounter with Case remain with Wiltshire, as he carries the marks of violence on his body: "[T]hey made me a litter of poles and carried me down to the station. Mr Tarleton set my leg, and made a regular missionary splice of it, so that I limp to this day" (69). Ironically, it was also Tarleton who presided as Uma and Wiltshire "were spliced in our own house," obeying Wiltshire's desire "to be married to her right" (36). The first marriage to Uma was "wrong" and had to be erased, not only because Uma was tricked with a false certificate but also because the union formed an erotic triangle between Case, Wiltshire, and Uma. Only Case's elimination, and the ceremony performed by a missionary, can create a "proper name of a man's wife" (36), a legitimate heterosexual union.

Hence, racial and commercial relations both are transformed by Wiltshire's journey into the woods. When he emerges from the High Woods, he is the sole trader on the island, "left alone in my glory at Falesá" (70). Yet he is also "partly Kanakaized," having adapted to island customs and being committed to a marriage with Uma, for whom he gives up his dream of returning to England: "[M]y public-house? Not a bit of it, nor ever likely. I'm stuck here, I fancy" (71). Indeed, on looking closely at the story, one can see that racial categories have been ambiguous throughout. When Wiltshire arrives, he is delighted to be met by two white men—"I was pleased with the looks of them at once. . . . I was sick for white neighbours" (4)—yet he then plays a trick upon the reader by confounding the very categories he has invoked: "One was a negro to be sure; but they were both rigged out smart" (5). Having established a binary between "white" and "natives" (or later, "kanakas"), the narrative introduces a "third term"—"negro"—that disrupts the entire system. Despite the claim that "a negro is counted a white man" (7), Wiltshire certainly does not treat Black Jack as his equal when Black Jack's arrival at the store leads Wiltshire to address him scornfully: "Here, you nigger!" (44). Wiltshire then threatens him with assault, using terms that allude to his violent chastisement of Case: he asks Black Jack, "[D]id you see Case's figure-head about a week ago? . . . I'll show you the own brother to it, only black, in the inside of about two minutes"

(44–45). Wiltshire's allusion to the "own brother" invokes a notion of interracial solidarity that his threat contradicts. Case also looks down on blacks as inferior: he uses Black Jack as his puppet in the marriage ceremony, even forging Black Jack's signature, and says scornfully to Wiltshire when the latter is forced to operate without native labor, "You haven't got one pound of copra but what you made with your own hands, like a negro slave" (56).

Though Wiltshire claims that the negro "counts" as a white man, there is little evidence of this in the narrative, as both Wiltshire and Case treat the negro as inferior. Moreover the Chinese, who also "counts" as a white man, is wholly invisible in the story. Yet these racial categories serve to expose the identity of "white man" as a fiction, or rather a racial fantasy of purity in a racially diverse culture, in which ethnic distinctions are always tenuous and fragile. Eventually rejecting Case's claim to be a "white man," Wiltshire finds himself the sole occupant of this category. However, it is a position that cannot be sustained without support, the "White Man's Quarrel" requiring a male bond for its successful pursuit.

The position of Wiltshire at the end of the story is therefore ambiguous. The position of the white man having been exposed as a fiction, an artifice dependent on the kind of unity spuriously proposed by Case, Wiltshire's status as a white man is called into question by his marriage to Uma. His final concern is for his daughters, whom he describes as "only half-castes," adding that "nobody thinks less of half-castes than I do" (71). The "half-caste" further blurs racial categories, occupying a liminal space between "white" and "kanaka," precisely the space that must be disavowed for the binary opposition of races to function. As we have seen, the "problem" of other racial categories (i.e., neither white nor "kanaka") has been solved by including the "negro" and "Chinese" as "white men": a purely nominal concession that brings no preferential treatment. The "half-caste" presents a more serious transgression of Wiltshire's racial classification, however, not least because his daughters spring from his own loins and so are of his own blood. Unlike "negro," "half-caste" is not a "third term" but a hybrid between already-existing categories. As such, it calls into question the validity (or purity) of those categories. Wiltshire is faced with a conflict: as a father, he is duty-bound to love and protect his daughters, as he admits "they're mine and about all I've got" (71). In effect, Wiltshire's "line" or posterity is dependent for its transmission on his "half-castes," whom he views as part of his property. But as a "white man," he is distanced from the half-caste as a threat to his racial purity.

The island is associated throughout with the blurring of distinctions, as we recall the opening line of the story: "I saw that island first when it was neither night nor morning" (3). Wiltshire's portrayal of the island is thus characterized, from its opening page, by ambiguity, the undoing of positive attributes. Wiltshire has arrived from a place of clear-cut distinctions, where he was "solitary among natives" (3). One should note the oxymoron: to be "among" other people is not to be solitary. Hence, Wiltshire's "solitary" state can be explained only if he considers the natives as not people, or at least not his equals. Hence, his admission that "I was sick for white neighbours" (4) can be interpreted as a need to share the "white man's burden" (or, as Case puts it, the "White Man's Quarrel") with those whom he considers his equals. Wiltshire's eagerness to accept the false solidarity offered by Case can thus be explained by his investment in racial distinctions.

A further ambiguity is indicated by Wiltshire's residence "near the line" (3)—referring to the equator—which positions him between the Northern and Southern hemispheres, the boundary between the tropics and the European countries. Hence Wiltshire occupies a space between regions, fully identified with neither. As such, he is positioned to move between races and identities rather than sit squarely or comfortably within one. Such ambiguity may be hazardous for those seeking to trade in the islands. For example, the captain who sets Wiltshire on the island issues a warning that his predecessor, "old Adams," failed there because he "couldn't get on with the natives, or the whites, or something" (3). The ambivalent syntax of this utterance by the captain may conceal the crucial difference it makes as to which group Adams "couldn't get on with." For Wiltshire does not expect to "get on with the natives," except insofar as he needs them for commercial purposes. However, he eagerly desires "white neighbours," and Adams's failure to bond with the whites would indicate a fissure in the structure of white identity—a fissure that may have been fatal to Adams, as the captain discloses that "the next time we came round there he was dead and buried" (3–4).

Wiltshire's dislike of missionaries derives from his assertion that they confused racial boundaries, "suck[ed] up to the natives" and were "partly Kanakaized." The irony of the narrative is that Wiltshire eventually accepts his dislocation from "white neighbours." Not only are his "kids . . . better here than what they would be in a white man's country" (71), but also Wiltshire has "gone native" to the extent that he can never be comfortable returning to England. Wiltshire's decision to remain on the island reflects Stevenson's realization that he had settled in the South Seas: as he wrote to Henry James in August 1890, "I do not think I shall come to England more than once, and then it'll be to die. Health I enjoy in the tropics."[49]

Wiltshire's final dilemma is how best to handle the mixed-race offspring he has produced. His lingering desire for racial purity causes him to fear the further dilution of his "whiteness," as he states, "I can't reconcile my mind to their taking up with Kanakas" (71), even though he has married a "kanaka." Yet the narrative's most insoluble problem is produced by the practical issue faced by Wiltshire: how can he find white men willing to marry his half-caste daughters, a match implicitly less desirable than his own union with a native woman? The problem reflects more broadly on the residual racial prejudice in the story: a prejudice that inevitably invokes the colonial world outside the story, figured in the references to England and Auckland.

Wiltshire's conclusion that his children are better off on the island than in "a white man's country" (71) discloses the extent to which he has come to view the world of the "white man" as "other," a space in which he can no longer imagine settling. In this sense, Wiltshire's prejudice is a faint reflection of the wider thinking about race, an ideology that his own conversion has not wholly erased. Notably, Stevenson's manuscript of "The Beach of Falesá" originally phrased the question as "where I'm to find *them* whites?" emphasizing the practical problem of "where can I find white husbands for them?" (270n). The revised, published story substitutes the definite article, thereby foregrounding the broader racial issues at stake: "I'd like to know where I'm to find the whites?" (71). Wiltshire's concluding question might now be paraphrased as "where can I find whites who will view half-castes as marriageable?" This is less an admission of paternal failure on his part than a recognition of the wider racism of the "white man's country." Indeed, Wiltshire—having abandoned his plan for a public house and his dreams of England—would himself be viewed as having "gone native" and become, at least in cultural terms, a hybrid or half-caste.

Having spent much of his time on the island "dreaming England," Wiltshire finally recognizes that England, and the vision of racial purity and insularity it promises and promotes, is nothing but a dream.[50]

## Conclusion

In his South Seas fiction, Stevenson sought to combine a realistic portrayal of Polynesian society with sufficient elements of romance to appeal to the reading public. As such, the tales indicate Stevenson's dual literary heritage. As Nicholas Daly writes, "realism was often represented as essentially a noxious weed of foreign growth, deriving from the school of Zola and the Goncourts, and imported into Britain by American expatriates like James and Howells; romance, on the other hand, often strived to establish links to Scott . . . and to imagine a grand tradition of native British fiction. Stevenson was perceived by some to be a new Scott, and like his fellow-countryman was given credit for changing the course of the English novel."[51] Yet Stevenson was also a close friend and admirer of James and, despite their disagreement over the purposes of the novel, was clearly proud of the realistic elements in "The Beach of Falesá."

One may conclude, then, that Stevenson developed a hybrid form in the South Sea tales, blending techniques of realism with elements of the imperial romance, while giving unique literary representation to the South Seas. Arthur Johnstone records an interview that Stevenson gave to the editor of the *Pacific Commercial Advertiser* in Honolulu in 1893, in which Stevenson responds to the editor's suggestion of "the unfitness of many South Sea subjects for literary elaboration." Asked by Stevenson to elaborate, the editor explains this was because "while the folklore and legends of the Pacific Islands were admirably adapted for sketches, short essays, or poetry, they would be found largely unsuited for romance proper, or even short stories." The editor goes on to claim that the success of these materials required "the introduction of the civilized element, with certain other foreign and native local phases. This in turn necessitated a transformation of the original Polynesian tale or legend to make the inter-racial or composite story, like 'The Beach of Falesá.'"[52]

This description of "The Beach of Falesá" aptly discloses the hybridity of the tale, its mingling of cultural and linguistic elements from British, American, and Polynesian sources. Stevenson's response illustrates both the problem that he faced in adapting South Seas material for a Western audience and his solution to that problem: "[T]o my chagrin I found my matter would not work up even into readable travels (from the public's point of view). It seems to me that you have put the difficulty into a line—everything in the Pacific must be first translated into terms of civilization before being written. I am pleased that you speak well of 'The Beach of Falesá,' for I have a sneaking liking for it myself, and think it a pretty good story. But mind it was an experiment to see if such difficulties as those you mentioned . . . could be successfully overborne."[53]

Stevenson's reference to the fiasco over his South Seas letters—the difficulty of creating "readable travels" out of his "quarry of materials"—reminds us of the challenge he faced in fashioning his "farrago" of the tropics into readable and popular narratives. His recognition that "The Beach of Falesá" was a kind of composite is reflected in his futile plea that the story not be included in the same volume as "The Bottle Imp" and "The Isle of Voices" (the stories were in fact published all together in *Island Nights' Entertainments* [1893]). Stevenson passionately defended his original conception of "The Beach of Falesá" in arranging for the story's publication in volume form: "I will not allow it to be called *Uma* in book form, that is not the logical name of the story. Nor can I have the marriage contract omitted; and the thing is full of misprints abominable."[54] Stevenson's dismay that editorial interference had made his tale "abominable" was furthered by the dismemberment of his story in its serial publication: in a letter to J. M. Barrie of November 1, 1892, he described it as "a little tale of mine, the slashed and gaping ruins of which appeared recently in the *Illustrated London News*" and related that "a perfect synod of appalled editors and apologetic friends had sat and wrangled over the thing in private with astonishing results." Stevenson's conclusion—"I wish we could afford to do without serial publication altogether"—reflects the economic dilemma of the author in the late-nineteenth-century literary marketplace.[55]

In discussing his South Seas material, Stevenson added his opinion of "the introduction of the white element being necessary in successful work about the South Seas," which he again took up by saying, "From what I have now said you will see why it is that 'The Isle of Voices' is not up to the mark—I left out too much of the civilized ingredient.'"[56] The "white element" is thus for

Stevenson less a statement about civilization or cultural superiority than a strategic device. The key to his approach in "The Beach of Falesá" is his insight that "everything in the Pacific must be first translated into terms of civilization." What Stevenson refers to here is not literal translation from one language to another but a cultural translation whereby the exotic and alien facets of Polynesian life are adapted into familiar equivalents. Wiltshire is the ideal narrator for this purpose: put simply, Wiltshire's style relates everything new or threatening that he encounters into accessible and familiar language. One might say that he is a surrogate for the reader, for despite having lived in the South Seas, he arrives on Falesá as a newcomer, a perspective made clear in the opening paragraph: "Here was a fresh experience: . . . the look of these woods and mountains and the rare smell of them, renewed my blood" (*SST,* 3).

This combination of unfamiliarity and experience makes Wiltshire a suitable guide for the distant reader and "fireside travelers" whom Stevenson sought to address "from the uttermost parts of the sea."[57] The lack of such a guide, Stevenson believed, was what prevented "The Isle of Voices" from appealing to a British and American readership. The absence of such a figure also compromised the success of the South Seas letters, which failed to connect with readers who wished for more of Stevenson himself. In effect, Wiltshire serves as the translator, his position at the cultural hinterland between Britain, America, and the South Seas qualifying him to mediate between them. By employing this ambiguous narrator, Stevenson is able to expose the shabbiness of European civilization and the commercial ruthlessness of the "White Man's Quarrel." Yet even the realism of "The Beach of Falesá" would pale by comparison with the grim indictment of European colonialism in *The Ebb-Tide.*

# EIGHT

## "There's an end to it"
### Disease and Partnership in *The Ebb-Tide*

In fact the mythology of Empire and of Apocalypse are very closely related.

—Frank Kermode, *The Sense of an Ending*[1]

IN HIS NOW-CLASSIC STUDY of endings in fiction, Frank Kermode observes that "there are famous *saecula,* Ends of which everyone is aware, and in which we may take a complex comfort, as in the nineteenth-century *fin-de-siècle,* where all the elements of the apocalyptic paradigm clearly co-exist."[2] For the final chapter of this study, I turn to the last book published by Stevenson during his lifetime, a work that reflects his awareness of the approaching end of the nineteenth century and of the British Empire. Published in 1894, the final year of Stevenson's life, *The Ebb-Tide* directly resulted from Stevenson's cruising and settlement in the South Seas. Yet compared to "Beach of Falesá," *The Ebb-Tide* represents a far more bleak portrait of the possibilities and consequences of European settlement in the South Seas. Wiltshire, of course, has unrealistic expectations of his island and naïve faith in his fellow "white man," Case. Yet by shifting his alliance and affection to a native woman, Uma, he is able to become absorbed in a multiracial Polynesian society. By contrast, Herrick—the

British protagonist of *The Ebb-Tide*—is destitute and despairing at the outset of the narrative and is unable to gain a foothold in his new surroundings.[3]

In chapter 5, I examine how Stevenson drew on his South Seas journal and letters to construct his portrayal of Attwater, the English colonialist in *The Ebb-Tide.* The parallels between Tembinok' and Attwater, I argue, demonstrate the extent to which Stevenson views tyrannical rule and colonial domination as crossing boundaries of race and nation. Though Attwater is an English settler, he represents various traits of the native ruler. My focus in this chapter is, by contrast, how *The Ebb-Tide* reflects Stevenson's sense of the impending demise of European colonialism. Stevenson attempts in *The Ebb-Tide* to delineate the extinction of the "shabby civilization" to which he attributed the impending "extinction of the Polynesian Islanders."[4] Wiltshire, the narrator of "Beach of Falesá," proclaims himself "sick for white neighbours" but learns from the captain that the island is "a healthy place" (*SST,* 4); in *The Ebb-Tide,* sickness is attributed to the whites, while Attwater's island is ravaged by disease. Indeed, Stevenson not only uses disease as a metaphor for colonial expansion but also shows how the disease may afflict the colonizers as well as the colonized. Bringing to an end his fictional treatment of the South Seas, *The Ebb-Tide* depicts the exhaustion of the energies of travel and adventure that Stevenson exploited in his narratives of cruising.

Stevenson's indictment of European colonialism begins with the very opening of his final work. Frank Kermode, in discussing peripeteia, or sudden narrative reversal, theorizes the possibility of a novel "in which the departure from a basic paradigm, the peripeteia in the sense I am now giving it, seems to begin with the first sentence."[5] One could hardly find a better example of such immediate peripeteia than the opening sentence of *The Ebb-Tide:* "Throughout the island world of the Pacific, scattered men of many European races and from almost every grade of society carry activity and disseminate disease."[6]

This opening exemplifies how "the schematic expectations of the reader are discouraged immediately."[7] Anticipating a narrative of romance, adventure, and imperial action, the reader is immediately forced to abandon such expectations with the damning reference to corrupting European influence in the South Seas. As the reference to disease suggests, imperialism and its "activity" is represented as a kind of plague that is "carried" by Europeans and lays native cultures and peoples to waste. The reference sets the tone for the novel, as every location in the text—whether on land or at sea—is infected or contaminated. The threat of extinction that Stevenson associated with Polynesians in *In the South Seas*—writing of "the wide-spread depression and acceptance of the national end"—is transferred to the white man in *The Ebb-Tide.*[8] The presence of white men in the islands derives not from missionary zeal or commercial ambition but from "sheer idleness," as they "sprawl in palm-leaf verandahs and entertain an island audience with memoirs of the music-hall" (123).[9]

Like Wiltshire, Robert Herrick, the British protagonist of *The Ebb-Tide,* returns in imagination to his native country: "[V]isions of England at least would throng upon the exile's memory: the busy schoolroom, the green playing-fields, holidays at home, and the perennial roar of London, and the fireside, and the white head of his father" (125). Yet this Dickensian nostalgia contains no practical purpose, instead being a temporary escape from and contrast to his "career . . . of unbroken shame" (125) in the South Seas. Herrick, who has adopted an alias and abandoned his family, is in the South Seas to escape "life's battle and his own immediate duty" (126), not to achieve success.

At the story's beginning, the members of the trio are described as "the three most miserable English-speaking creatures in Tahiti" (124), and Herrick's companions are "two creatures equally outcast with himself" (127). From the outset, therefore, the debased state of the three men and their hopeless situation suggest that their story has ended before it has begun. Faced with poverty and disgrace in Tahiti, Captain Davis announces, "This thing's got to come to an end," to which the Cockney Huish replies, "Looks like signs of an end, don't it?" (138). This comment indicates that the narrative itself has nowhere to go, having ground to a halt in its opening scene on Tahiti. Stevenson writes that "each had made a long apprenticeship in going downward" (124), and indeed they have reached rock bottom by the time "this tale begins" (126). To some extent, the narrative reflects Stevenson's disillusionment with the motives of the European presence and, indeed, his own role and domestic situation on Samoa. The protagonist of the story is also named Robert, and some of Herrick's disenchantment with his lot in the South Seas reflects the author's discontent.

Yet Stevenson takes these "signs of an end" and creates a new beginning, launching his debased trio on a cruise that engenders new narrative possibilities and insights into the complex fabric of colonialism in the South Seas. Both the aborted journey of the *Farallone* and the arrival on Attwater's island that results provide the context for Stevenson's most powerful and incisive critique of colonial ideology and practice. Indeed, Stevenson's tale discloses the "signs of an end" to Britain's empire, which has gone into an ebb by the late nineteenth century. As a representative of Britain's upper middle class—intelligent, highly educated, with "talent and taste" (125)—Herrick has descended into a "moral bankruptcy" (126) that reflects the collapse of the imperial society to which he belonged.

*The Ebb-Tide* was also the third and last work of fiction coauthored by Stevenson and his stepson, Lloyd Osbourne. The literary collaboration between Stevenson and Osbourne arguably dates back to the composition of *Treasure Island.*[10] Significantly, the works that Stevenson coauthored with Osbourne are among the most neglected and/or underrated texts in his canon. This adverse reaction (as I argue in chapter 1) reflects a more general anxiety about the confusion of authorship that is involved in a collaborative work.[11] Part of my purpose in this chapter, therefore, is to argue that collaboration was an important ingredient of Stevenson's narrative cruising. Anxiety concerning inappropriate "sharing"—whether textual or sexual—was among the inhibitions that Stevenson challenged when he "escaped out of the shadow of the Roman empire."[12] Travel, especially with a companion, tended to relax the boundaries of authorship, making possible new kinds of creative combination. This later shared adventure of Stevenson and Osbourne while cruising in Polynesia provided the context for their collaboration on both *The Wrecker* (1892) and *The Ebb-Tide* (1894). The trajectory of the latter novel follows the course plotted by Stevenson and Osborne in their cruises on the *Casco* and *Equator. The Ebb-Tide* opens in Tahiti, where the Stevensons remained stranded for several months in 1889, following Stevenson's physical collapse at the village of Tautira. The second half, opening with the trio's arrival at an "undiscovered . . . scarce believed in" (*SST,* 187) island, reflects the Stevensons' initial excitement at making landfall in the South Seas and also draws upon their visit to the pearl island of Penrhyn while cruising on the *Janet Nicoll* in May 1890.

While the details and techniques of this literary collaboration are not the central focus of this chapter, it is an important context for the theme of partnership that I examine in the narrative. As Stephen Arata observes in a recent essay on *The Wrecker,* "texts are, to a limited but discernable degree, autonomous from their 'authors.' They signify in ways that are not in the control of any one individual. Their signification is instead a function of all those various interchanges, those collaborations. . . . Lloyd Osbourne is the name we give to one such collaboration, but it is only one among many."[13] I am taken with Arata's nuanced approach to the specific literary collaboration between Stevenson and Osbourne, which remains sensitive to broader issues of collaboration within Stevenson's texts and, more generally, in critical discourse about literary production. In this respect, all of Stevenson's texts—even those published exclusively under his own name—are collaborative in that they emerge from contexts not wholly determined by the author and take shape in part through the responses and contributions of others. Collaboration, like cruising, multiplies the possibilities of authorship, creating new contexts in which narrative energies emerge and circulate. Using an image that suggests the duality of Jekyll and Hyde, Jerome McGann argues, "Every text has variants of itself screaming to get out, or antithetical texts waiting to make themselves known. These variants and antitheses appear (and multiply) over time, as the hidden features of the textual media are developed and made explicit."[14] In this regard, the text—whether written by a single author or by collaborators—is always "other" than itself.

Cruising as a narrative practice is conducive to the emergence of alternative versions of texts: for example, revisions (of journals) or serialized editions that are succeeded—yet never wholly supplanted—by publication in volume form. Cruising tends to dissolve the isolation, if not the singularity, of the individual author and to promote the merging of textual forms such as drafts, variants, and fragments. In the case of the literary collaborations between Stevenson and Osbourne, their shared experience of travel in the South Seas led to their merger as authorial figures. All three of their joint-authored volumes were produced following Stevenson's final departure from Britain in 1887. Lloyd was a member of the group that set off on the *Casco* from San Francisco in June 1888, and he accompanied Stevenson on all his cruises except the cruise of the *Janet Nicoll,* which left Sydney en route to Samoa in April 1890. Wherever Stevenson lived or stayed, Osbourne was there also. This partnership of travel in close, often-uncomfortable quarters and adverse situations was vital to the formation of their shared literary enterprise. Writing became, in a quite literal sense, a domestic "cottage industry" in which "Stevenson and Son" were the two partners. The roles of the two women, "Fanny and Daughter," were comparatively minor, with Fanny acting as reader and critic and Belle as amanuensis. During a temporary separation, Stevenson complained that Osbourne was "half the world away," a reproach that reverses the laments of Stevenson's friends when he left Britain and settled in the South Seas, thereby forestalling any possibility of literary community with him.[15] Stevenson's letter to Osbourne from Vailima also reveals intriguing aspects of their method: evidently each writer was responsible for specific chapters, as Stevenson was anxious to avoid conflicts between their sections of the narrative. However, Stevenson apparently took overall responsibility for the structure of the novel, for he wrote to Lloyd, "If yours should be already written, leave it; and this Old Parliamentary Hand will find a way to patch it up."[16] Stevenson here asserts his greater experience at fiction writing (he is the "old . . . hand") while respectfully according Lloyd independence in writing his own chapters. This method is significantly different from that employed on *The Wrong Box,* in which Lloyd had drafted a narrative (variously called "A Game of Bluff" and "The Finsbury Tontine") that was then entirely rewritten by Stevenson.

Aside from the questions about the extent of Stevenson's authorship of *The Ebb-Tide* and the difference that collaboration makes to the creative process, there is another way in which the book's inclusion in this section on Stevenson's South Seas writing might seem contentious. Unlike the stories collected in *Island Nights' Entertainments, The Ebb-Tide* (1894) does not contain "native" Polynesian characters in any central or prominent roles. Rather, South Sea islanders are reduced to cameo and background figures, such as "Sally Day," a crew member on the *Farallone* (based on a Melanesian crew member on board the *Janet Nicoll*), and the natives "Obsequious" and "Sullens," whose grisly fates Attwater narrates. However, *The Ebb-Tide* is firmly located in the South Seas, with its settings on Tahiti and New Island, and it does explore interracial encounters, including the exploitation of native labor by European colonizers.[17] Moreover, the journey by sea to a South Sea island is of pivotal significance in the narrative, representing a turning point in the plot (or, arguably, the termination of one plot and the beginning of another). The power of the journey or cruise to both disrupt the generic conventions and expectations and renew the narrative energies of the novel is nowhere more apparent than in this text.

The novel also develops critiques of the mercenary motives for South Seas exploration and colonization. The prospect of acquiring vast wealth illegally is, of course, the driving motive of the trio of beachcombers in *The Ebb-Tide.* Just as the beachcombers seek to leave behind complications of their past by "the adoption of an *alias*" (*SST,* 124) and to escape scandal at their port of origin by boarding the *Farallone,* so too does the novel attempt to jettison the baggage of a plot that cannot be concluded, by making a fresh start with the cruise. What is compelling is the engagement with the dual significance of the cruise, as at once a "fresh start" and adventure (from the point of view of the Europeans and the authors) and a corrupt invasion of foreign territory and property. In this respect, the name of the island destination is significant: the trio in *The Ebb-Tide* head for "New Island," which they mistakenly believe to be "undiscovered" (187). Yet although the island proves to be inhabited, they remain convinced that it holds the key to their redemption, and the narrative takes on new life with the appearance of Attwater.[18] In this novel, the partnerships that are formed with enthusiasm and promise in the first half are brought into crisis in the second and tend toward collapse.[19] The fluidity and fragility of partnership, its tendency to disruption and dissolution, is one of the key concerns of the narrative and involves the effects on identity of the cruise in an alien environment.

One of the strikingly ironic moments of *The Ebb-Tide* occurs at the beginning of the second part, "A Quartette," when the trio arrives at New Island in possession of the stolen schooner and its fraudulent cargo. On entering the lagoon of New Island, the *Farallone* is mistaken by the resident colonist, Attwater, for his own trading ship, *The Trinity Hall.* In fact, Attwater's first words in the story indicate his overriding concern with trade and commerce, in particular the fate of his own trading vessel: "Is the doctor on board . . . Dr Symonds, I mean? You never heard of him? Nor yet of the *Trinity Hall?* Ah" (192). Attwater's interest in the new arrivals is initially that of economic profit: he eyes them with "curiosity that was almost savage" (192) once his hopes of Symonds's arrival have been thwarted. The irony, of course, is that not only is Dr. Symonds *not* on board, but the trio of men on the *Farallone* have arrived not to enrich

Attwater with the spoils of trade but to seek a transaction far less advantageous for the English colonialist: to strip him of his collection of pearls. Having stolen a ship with its counterfeit cargo of champagne, Captain Davis has sought New Island from desperation at their depleted provisions and aims to "fill up with fish, and cocoanuts, and native stuff" (185).[20] Yet Davis also holds out a more attractive prospect to his crewmates, interpreting the language from *Findlay's Directory*—"this island, which from private interests would remain unknown" (185)—to "mean pearls. . . . A pearling island the government don't know about? That sounds like real estate" (185). Attwater's "private interests" are thus construed as an invitation to plunder the island's resources, in a repetition of the exploitation of the native peoples. Before they even reach the lagoon, the narrative suggests that the men have a definite intention to despoil this "pearling island" of its riches.[21]

As is the case with *Kidnapped*, *The Ebb-Tide* takes a new direction following an aborted journey. Whereas the plot of *Kidnapped* is completely rerouted by the shipwreck of the *Covenant*, the plot of *The Ebb-Tide* is the outcome of two plans—and two voyages—that fail.[22] The trio's original intention of selling the stolen champagne in Peru (148) is abandoned when they discover that the wine is fraudulent and that they have "stolen a cargo of spring water" (178); their subsequent plan of sailing to Samoa so that they may sink the ship and claim the insurance money (181) is foiled by their urgent need for supplies. This change of plan intersects coincidentally with the delayed arrival of the *Trinity Hall*, which, Attwater informs Davis, is "thirty-three days overdue at noon today" (195). The speed with which Attwater comes out to greet them—"a boat put suddenly and briskly out, and a voice hailed" (191)—reflects his expectancy at a profitable return of his ship. Surely one may infer that Attwater's greeting would have been far less eager had he not been expecting his own vessel: it is doubtful, in that case, that the trio would ever have made it onto the island. These two deferrals cross paths, as it were, such that the *Farallone* arrives instead of and substitutes for the missing trading ship, which makes voyages according to pattern "every four months; three trips a year" (195).[23] The location of the missing ship is a mystery that even Attwater, whom Herrick states "knows all . . . sees through all" (222) is unable to explain; as he asks Huish in mock-Cockney, "if you could tell me where the *Trinity 'All* was, you would confer a favour, Mr Whish!" (214).

In commenting on a scene from *The Wrecker* that takes place at a different port, San Francisco, Stephen Arata has astutely pointed to "error's unexpected yet undeniable productivity in intellectual life." Arata's observation specifically illuminates "how critical insight gets entangled with critical blindness"; one can also identify this productive role of error in the development of plot in Stevenson's fiction, especially that coauthored with Osbourne.[24] The trio erroneously believe they have captured a cargo of champagne, until on further investigation "the fraud was manifest" (177) as the bottles are discovered to contain water. The arrival of the *Farallone* is described by Attwater as "some *small mistake,* no doubt" (192; emphasis added), yet this mistake generates the plot of the novel, bringing its central characters into contact and producing the decisive conflicts. As such, it compounds other errors, mistakes, and accidents, such as the crew's "discovery" of the island despite the fact that it is nowhere marked on the chart (according to which they are located "in the midst of a white field of paper" [184]). Stevenson's narratives are unusually replete with such fertile, random mishaps, which would include the wreck of the Bournemouth train in *The Wrong Box,* the wreck of the *Covenant* in *Kidnapped,* and the loss of the father's money in "The Misadventures of John Nicholson."

The trio, however, interpret the accident of their discovery of the island as a kind of providence guiding them in the right direction. Indeed, they assume that the island is destined to be their property: on reading the details in the directory, Davis pronounces, "That's our place, and don't you make any mistake" (185). In particular, the name "New Island" suggests a departure from the previous part of the text, an antidote to the trio's sense of being "done with life" (172). A new beginning, the island also promises renewed hope for profit, with its reference to "private interests." As such, the transition from the "trio" to the "quartette"—alluding to the beginning of a new movement in a musical piece—is associated with a change of location, from the corrupt ship to the "strange and delicate" (187) island. The language suggests new hope, as "a brightening came in the east" until "the hollow of heaven was filled with the daylight" (187). This scene replays Stevenson's rapturous account of the "first landfall" in Polynesia, from *In the South Seas.* However, the scene occurs not at the beginning of *The Ebb-Tide* but halfway through. Given the narrative's rejection of the conventions of romance, its multiplication of the "signs of an end," the scene suggests that the narrative is delicately poised between the "end" and the "new," leaving the reader divided "between credulity and skepticism." As Kermode argues, "peripeteia depends on our confidence of the end [that] it is a disconfirmation followed by a consonance." No reader is "indifferent to all conventional expectations," which "must be there to be defeated."[25] At this turning point in *The Ebb-Tide,* the reader is unsure as to what future the narrative offers. The possibility of a new beginning for the trio, like the isle itself, is "scarce-believed in" (187).

Identifying the island as "our place," Davis effectively lays claim to all the resources of the island as though they were divinely appointed. Yet the text continues to suggest that the island may be a mirage or a fantasy of the trio's, that their perceptions are erroneous. The text of *Findlay's Directory* indeed questions "if such an island exists, which is very doubtful, and totally disbelieved in by South Sea traders" (185). Even as the narrative offers the possibility for a new beginning, then, it suggests that this hope may be fictitious.[26] The text refers to the possible island as "that elusive glimmer in the sky," which began to "diminish in size, as the stain of breath vanishes from a window pane" (185). At the beginning of the second part, it is referred to as "the invisible isle" (187), then as "the isle—the undiscovered, the scarce-believed in" (187). Stevenson here evokes the isle as a magical place, reminiscent of the island in *The Tempest* where Prospero rules with supernatural powers. Yet he also suggests that while the isle turns out not to be an illusion—it physically exists and is inhabited—it is deceptive and elusive, perhaps unknowable. The reference to the isle as "undiscovered" reflects the men's fantasy that they are the first—at least the first white men—to arrive there, reinforced by their observation that "still there was *no mark* of habitation" (189; emphasis added). The island is a kind of text that the three beachcombers are compelled to interpret and onto which they project their fantasies.[27] Stating that "to the expert eye the isle itself was to be inferred from a certain string of blots," Stevenson represents the cruiser as a kind of reader, inferring meanings from visible signs on the horizon or landscape. Yet the text also suggests that the "expert eye" may be clouded by more emotional responses, driven by desire and fear: Herrick "in the gratified lust of his eye . . . forgot the past and the present; forgot that he was menaced by a prison on the one hand and starvation on the other" (189). Like the island of lotos-eaters, this island brings forgetfulness, while also provoking lust.

In this way, Stevenson's plot replays the arrival of Europeans in the South Seas, attracted by the island's natural beauty while seeking to extract native commodities by trade if possible, by force if necessary. Not believing that the native islanders had any rights to their land, the Europeans felt entitled to appropriate any desirable resources; as Edward Said argues, "at some very basic level, imperialism means thinking about, settling on, controlling land that you do not possess, that is distant, that is lived on and owned by others."[28] The irony of *The Ebb-Tide* is that the new colonialists, Davis and company, discover that the island is occupied not by indigenous people but by an English settler. The idea of "origin" present in native inhabitation is one of the colonial fantasies dispelled by the tale: the isle proves not to be "new" at all, but thoroughly colonized. After their illusion that the island is uninhabited is dispelled, Davis's idealized view is supplanted by the theory that Attwater's presence is exclusively for commercial reasons: "[W]hat's he here upon this beastly island for? . . . *He's* not here collecting eggs. . . . He's been doing good business here, then. . . . It's pearl and shell, of course . . . no doubt the shell goes off regularly by this *Trinity Hall,* and the money for it straight into the bank" (197; original emphasis).[29] This reasoning leads to the important conclusion that the most valuable hoard—"pearls—a ten years' collection of them" (198)—remains on the island and may be plundered by the new arrivals (Davis advises Herrick that "if you get him and his pearls aboard, I'll spare him. If you don't, there's going to be a funeral" [198]). Even as the three men learn that Attwater has preceded them, they seek to replay the original appropriation of land by European settlers. That they are dealing not with an unarmed native people but a British colonialist who combines traits of the "savage" with modern technology, marksmanship, and guile does not deter Davis.[30] As parasites, the trio expect to feed on Attwater's accumulated fortune as easily as they consume his "island dinner" (212). They assume that their "partnership" and bond—they are like a debased parody of the *Three Musketeers*—will overcome the resistance of a single man.[31]

In *The Ebb-Tide,* Stevenson examines and critiques several crucial aspects of trade in the tropics, some of which I have already touched on in this chapter. In the first place, each trader is a replacement for a predecessor or belongs to a succession of white men who have already colonized the island and, in many cases, died in the process. The fantasy of the trio that they are the first white men to arrive on the island is exposed as a common imperial delusion. Yet there is a duality in the men's responses, as Herrick idealizes the island's miraculous beauty—"the beach was excellently white, the continuous barrier of trees inimitably green . . . so frail and pretty, he would scarce have wondered to see it sink and disappear" (188)—while Davis is more the practical colonizer: "the captain was in the four cross-trees, glass in hand, his eyes in every quarter, spying for an entrance, spying for signs of tenancy" (188). The island appears uninhabited ("there was neither house nor man, nor the smoke of fire" [188]) until they enter the lagoon, when "suddenly the curtain was raised; they began to open out a haven, snugly elbowed there, and beheld, with an astonishment beyond words, the roofs of men" (189).

Stevenson here replays the excitement of the first landfall (as he described in the South Seas letters), with its prospects of wealth and pleasure, despite the fact that the island has already been colonized. This delusion of discovery is repeated by Davis to Attwater: "I allow we are about the first white men upon this island, sir" (213), upon which Attwater immediately reminds him of his error: "Myself and Dr Symonds excepted, I should say the only ones" (213). Attwater's genteel response is actually a warning, informing his guests that he has already claimed the island as his property. Yet even as he lays claim to the island, reinforcing his dominance as a colonizer, Attwater implies that there have been others before him: "In the course of the ages some one may have lived here, and we sometimes think that some one must. The cocoa-palms grow all round the island, which is scarce like nature's planting. We found besides, when we landed, an unmistakable cairn upon the beach" (213). Attwater assumes that these traces of prior civilized activity are signs of prior white inhabitants—"some thick-witted gentry whose bones are lost" (214)—never entertaining the idea that the island may have been cultivated by indigenous South Sea islanders. The cruise to the South Seas in search of undiscovered islands is doomed to disappointment, as Stevenson shows that every location has a history of settlement, with the various problems that this entails.

Although the narrative leads us to share the three men's view of the island as a new beginning, there are clear signs that they have not left behind their past: "[A]ll the while the excitement of the three adventurers glowed about their bones like a fever" (188). The reference to fever suggests that the men may be sick and reminds us that they have been traveling on an infected ship. In their eagerness to escape Tahiti, the three took the opportunity to board the *Farallone,* despite the ominous signs: "Captain, mate, and one hand all died of the small-pox, same as they had round in the Paumotus" (146). Only Davis (alias Brown) is desperate enough to accept the berth, all other captains being "scared of small-pox" (147). The reference to the *Farallone* as "the forbidden ship" (152) informs the reader that it is still infected, and Davis clearly believes so as he refuses to berth in the stateroom, in which the previous captain and mate had died: "I don't know as I'm afraid, but I've no immediate use for confluent smallpox" (154). Herrick agrees, saying that "the thought of these two men sticks in my throat; that captain and mate dying here, one opposite to the other. It's grim" (154).

In his portrayal of the infected ship, Stevenson deploys contemporary understandings of disease. Timothy Mitchell has argued that "the miasmic theory of contagion . . . in nineteenth-century Europe had temporarily superseded the rival germ theory as an explanation of the transmission of diseases. Contagion would not be checked, it was now thought, by quarantine and confinement."[32] Stevenson suggests the ineffectiveness of quarantine, for although the ship flies a "hospital flag" (146) and "the effects of the dead men had been disinfected and conveyed on shore" (153), the three new crew members are aware of an atmosphere of contagion. The ship is referred to as "the outcast *Farallone*" and is "flaunting the plague-flag as she rolled" (152), as though boasting of its infected state.

In the course of the voyage, Herrick learns in more detail the fate of the previous captain and mate, Wiseman and Wishart. The prefix of "Wise" is singularly inappropriate, given the sheer folly of their actions, as "the captain and mate had entered on a career of drunkenness, which was scarcely interrupted by their malady and only closed by death" (169). From one of the native crew members, Taveeta (first called "Uncle Ned"), Herrick learns the details of Wiseman's and Wishart's demise. Taveeta had "heard the sounds of island lamentation" (169) and recognized that the low island on which they proposed to make landfall was diseased. However, the white men ignored his warning ("too many people die here!") and went in pursuit of food, drink, and women. Entering a house, they witnessed "the sick man raising from his mat a head already defeatured by disease" (169); a week later, the two white men were dead.[33]

Herrick believes that the island where Wiseman and Wishart were infected was among the Paumotus, "for the Dangerous Archipelago had been swept that year from east to west by devastating smallpox" (169–70). The story prepares the reader for the possibility that any island in the region may be similarly infected. In Tahiti, "a ship from Peru had brought an influenza" (128); the disease is thus linked with trade and with the trio's plan to sell the champagne in Peru. From the opening of the story, disease is presented as endemic to the South Seas, a thoroughly sick society suffering the ravages of colonialism. In Tahiti, the influenza "now raged in the island, and particularly in Papeete. From all round the *purao* arose and fell a dismal sound of men coughing, and strangling as they coughed" (128). Huish in particular is afflicted ("the disease shook him to the vitals"), while his companions experience "[t]he disgust attendant on so ugly a sickness" (128). Yet in their efforts to escape the disease, they enter the sphere of a more deadly one. Most important is that Herrick recognizes that they are trapped on the *Farallone* in a repetitive cycle, condemned to recapitulate the downward journey of their predecessors: "Sickness fell upon him at the image thus called up; and when he compared it with the scene in which himself was acting, and considered the doom that seemed to brood upon the schooner, a horror that was almost superstitious fell upon him" (170). The term *sickness* refers both to physical disease and a moral contagion that Herrick feels he has contracted from knowledge of the "prolonged, sordid, sodden sensuality" (170) of Wiseman and Wishart, as well as contact with Davis and Huish. What had seemed like "Destiny knocking at the door" (145), an opportunity to escape their hopeless situation in Tahiti, proves to be an extension of the diseased condition. In persuading Herrick to join him, Davis presented a grim specter of the alternative, a penal colony: "It's either this for you; or else it's Caledonia. I bet you never were there, and saw those white, shaved men, in their dust clothes and straw hats, prowling around in gangs in the lamplight at Noumea; they look like wolves, and they look like preachers, and they look like the sick" (150). Yet Herrick is unable to escape "the sick," finding constant reminders of death and disease on board the *Farallone.*

Similarly, the idyllic appearance of New Island promises an escape from the corrupted atmosphere of the ship. Yet no sooner have they landed than Attwater reveals the grim truth: "[B]y the by, here is a question I should have asked you when I came on board: have you had smallpox? . . . [I]t is a dreadful sickness" (193). Attwater explains they have had "twenty-nine deaths and thirty-one cases out of thirty-three souls upon the island . . . that is why the house is empty and the graveyard full" (194). The three adventurers discover that they have arrived at an even worse place than they left, in which disease has decimated the population. Rather than conveying a sense of progress, the narrative displays repetition, a cycle of disease and corruption from which the men cannot escape.

Cruising, in other words, does not enable the characters in *The Ebb-Tide* to escape the past or embark on a new phase of experience. Rather, the cruise is itself a source of disease, as trading ships and their crews help to spread the contagion, whether influenza or smallpox. In their attempt to avoid the penal colony of Noumea, the three men have been lured to a more fatal spot, ominously greeted by the figurehead with "its leprous whiteness" (190). As they approach, the narrative refers to a "tall grove of palms, which had masked the settlement in the beginning" (190); the natural beauty of the island is indeed a mask that covers its infected condition.

In *Colonising Egypt,* Timothy Mitchell argues that the rise of colonial power was accomplished by means of disciplinary systems that involved establishing institutions and practices of control in the colonized country. Crucially, however, these systems were exported from the metropolitan "center," having been developed there, and applied to the colonized country. In practices such as "model housing," the "model village" and the "model school," European structures of civic society and order became the basis for colonial settlements based on surveillance. The meticulous plan of such structures, Mitchell argues, "introduce space as something apparently abstract and neutral, a series of inert frames or containers." When exported overseas, these plans could be enormously effective when reproduced, as "French administrators drew up similar plans for the reconstruction of villages in Algeria. . . . Enormous numbers of Algerians had their villages destroyed and were moved to the new settlements, in order to depopulate areas where it was proving difficult to establish colonial control, and to bring the population under closer surveillance."[34]

According to Mitchell, the colonial society brings with it a need for continual maintenance of order: "This kind of order must be continually reestablished, and so appears precarious, negotiated, and continually in flux." Noting that colonial societies were based on the extension of the idea of an "exhibition"—everywhere visitors went "they seemed to encounter this rendering up the world as a picture"—Mitchell suggests that the continuity between society "at home" and "abroad" was crucial to sustaining colonial power.[35] In like manner, Stevenson's *The Ebb-Tide* reflects how the establishment of colonial society by whites in the tropics was carried out under the influence of nostalgia for British culture. Like Wiltshire with his "dreaming England," Attwater seeks to reproduce the culture and customs of his native land in the tropics. The dwellings seen by the trio on their arrival are described as "a substantial country farm with its attendant hamlet: a long line of sheds and store-houses" (189), imagery that suggests an English rustic scene. The national allegiance of the settlement is soon disclosed, as "from a flagstaff at the pierhead, the red ensign of England was displayed" (190).[36] Though he is not an official representative of England, Attwater wears his national identity on his sleeve.[37]

Attwater's nostalgia for England is also apparent in his immediate questioning of Herrick as to whether he is a "University man" (193) and, on discovering Herrick's Oxford educational background, his admission that "I am of the other lot. . . . Trinity Hall, Cambridge, I called my schooner after the old shop" (193). Attwater's designation of his alma mater as a "shop" indicates that his commercial practices derived from its influence; naming his ship after the college might suggest his talismanic faith in the tradition of Cambridge to produce wealth. Moreover, the bond between Attwater and Herrick indicates that English class structures remained intact despite the vast geographic and cultural distance from "home"; Attwater's contemptuous treatment of the working-class Cockney, Huish, reveals the exclusivity of such class identity. Herrick's ambivalent reaction is significant: "Herrick was embarrassed; the silken brutality of their visitor made him blush; that he should be accepted as an equal, and the others thus pointedly ignored, pleased him in spite of himself, and then ran through his veins in a recoil of anger" (193). Herrick's negative reaction to being thus recognized cannot be ascribed to concern for his partners. Rather, it is, as Attwater observes, sparked by shame at having betrayed his class: "I saw the blood come into your face today when you remembered Oxford. And I could have blushed for you myself, to see a man, a gentleman, with these two vulgar wolves" (205). Both men are conscious of their status as upper-class gentlemen.[38] Davis immediately identifies their host as "the real article . . . the real first-rate, copper-bottomed aristocrat . . . a man got to be born to that, and notice!" (197). Yet Davis also states, "I don't like it" (197), expressing his own class antagonism to Attwater's patrician behavior.

Attwater's affection for his college seems to transfer to Dr. Symonds, his partner, whose absence he repeatedly laments ("Pity Symonds isn't here! He is full of yarns" [215]). Though there is no reference to the two having been college friends, and although Symonds never appears in the story, he is a significant figure, not least because he is the exception to Attwater's general misanthropy: "I dislike men, and hate women" (205), he informs Herrick while the two visit the graveyard. Disappointed that Symonds is not on board the ship, Attwater describes his partner as "a dear fellow" (214) and repeatedly speaks for them both in the first-person plural, as when Davis asks about the difficulty of obtaining labor: "And of course, in our case, as we could name no destination, we had to go far and wide and do the best we could" (215). Dr. Symonds, in fact, represents a class bond with Attwater that is never directly represented in the novel. As such, the absent Dr. Symonds represents a crucial missing piece of what French social theorist Pierre Bourdieu calls "class habitus." For Bourdieu, the habitus is a vital aspect of the class condition, in that it identifies a "unity hidden under the diversity and multiplicity of the set of practices" that one might term "distinctive life-styles." A key factor of this habitus is what Bourdieu terms "dispositions," which produce the individual's response to specific products and practices. Interested in "the economic conditions of the production of the dispositions demanded by the economy," Bourdieu identifies "taste" as a crucial component of consumption and also a form of labor.[39]

Clearly, taste is a central part of Attwater's "class habitus, the internalized form of class condition and of the conditionings it entails." Taste is used to reproduce the conditions and class habitus of home in an alien environment. Yet, as Mitchell argues in his application of Bourdieu's ideas to colonial society, the hierarchy between the "original" society and the colonial "imitation" is dissolved: "Where everything occurs as the trace of what precedes and follows it, nothing is determined as the original. . . . There is no hierarchical order of the imitator and the imitated. . . . Everything both imitates and is imitated."[40] Attwater's island dinner is significant as a place where social habitus is represented, for as Bourdieu argues, "nothing, perhaps, more directly depends on early learning . . . than the dispositions and knowledge that are invested in clothing, furnishing, and cooking." Bourdieu designates this "the maternal world," claiming that "it is probably in tastes in *food* that one would find the strongest and most indelible mark of infant learning, the lessons which longest withstand the distancing or collapse of the native world and most durably maintain nostalgia for it."[41] While Bourdieu refers to the "native world" as the environment into which one is born, it suggests an interesting parallel with the "native world" in the form of the island that has "collapsed" because of the epidemic of smallpox but which Attwater attempts to recreate with his "island dinner."

Lurking in the background of this description of the "island dinner" is the specter of cannibalism, the communal consumption of "long pig" that Stevenson examines in *In the South Seas.* Writing that "cannibalism is traced from end to end of the Pacific," Stevenson is perplexed by "the universality of the practice over so vast an area, among people of such varying civilisation, and . . . such different blood." He recognizes how deeply interwoven the practice is with Polynesian culture and observes that "the Marquesans intertwined man-eating with the whole texture of their lives; the long-pig was in a sense their currency and sacrament." One of the striking features of Stevenson's approach to cannibalism is his refusal to condemn the practice. Indeed, he makes parallels between the consumption of "long pig" and the carnivorous habits of his readers: "We consume the carcases of creatures of like appetites, passions, and organs with ourselves; we feed on babes, though not our own; and the slaughter-house resounds daily with screams of pain and fear. We distinguish indeed; but the unwillingness of many nations to eat the dog . . . shows how precariously the distinction is grounded."[42]

Hence Stevenson argues that "we see some ground of indulgence for the island cannibal."[43] Stevenson displays some of this indulgence, although not altogether favorably, in his portrayal of Attwater. For the cannibal, the "island dinner" would of course consist of "long pig," and Attwater's table is furnished with "a sucking pig" (212). Stevenson blurs the distinction between them in *In the South Seas,* describing the pig in human terms: "[T]he island pig is a fellow of activity, enterprise, and sense. He husks his own cocoa-nuts, and (I am told) rolls them into the sun to burst; he is the terror of the sheperd"

(*ISS*, 69). Additionally, while Attwater is a gracious host, the narrative suggests something predatory in his demeanor: "To a cat he might be likened himself, as he lolled at the head of his table, dealing out attentions and innuendoes, and using the velvet and the claw indifferently" (212). The population of Attwater's island has of course been decimated, but while he claims that smallpox is the cause, his evasiveness about the fate of the native bodies (stating that he "buried them" in the lagoon [194]) suggests that there may have been a still more sinister explanation of why "the house is empty" and "everything's deserted" (194). His account of their disappearance is scarcely more satisfactory: "I was making a new people here, and behold, the angel of the Lord smote them and they were not!" (204). Stevenson makes a connection between disease and cannibalism in the South Seas, both being causes of the depopulation of the islands ("the annals of the past are gloomy with famine and cannibalism"). The outlawing of cannibalism, moreover, falls under "the decay or proscription of ancient pleasures" to which Stevenson attributes the fatal melancholy of Polynesia. In describing the widespread impact of cannibalism, Stevenson evokes the imagery of epidemic disease, writing that "all Melanesia appears tainted."[44]

If Attwater appears to preside over a sacrificial banquet, the narrative suggests that he may also be the object of a cannibalistic appetite, as Herrick's vision of Attwater suggests the sacrifice prior to a cannibal feast: "[H]e had before him the image of that great mass of man stricken down in varying attitudes and with varying wounds; fallen prone, fallen supine, fallen on his side; or clinging to a doorpost with the changing face and the relaxing fingers of the death-agony. He heard the click of the trigger, the thud of the ball, the cry of the victim; he saw the blood flow" (208). This emphasis on Attwater's physical size suggests the desire to consume him, an implication even more evident in Davis's response as "his eyes drank in the huge proportions of the other with delight" (216).

The island dinner also illustrates the collapse of the native world through the absence of native people from the occasion, apart from the "two brown natives" (214) who wait on Attwater and his guests. The nostalgia for and imitation of this lost native world is represented by the menu, which consists of "turtle-soup and steak, fish, fowls, a sucking pig, a cocoanut salad, and sprouting cocoanut roasted for dessert. Not a tin had been opened; and . . . not even the condiments were European" (212). If the reliance on indigenous ingredients suggests that Attwater has "gone native," his function is to give and receive pleasure: "Attwater had a dash of the epicure. For such characters it is softening to eat well; doubly so to have designed and had prepared an excellent meal for others" (212). As a colonial ruler, Attwater's habitus is thus a complex mix of British upper-class manners and snobbery (as in his discourse on wine) with native "primordial" pleasure-giving. He has combined his English upper-class habitus with the native material surroundings and cultural influences.

Yet there is an important qualification to Attwater's demeanor of upper-class civility and his generosity as a host. This occurs with his practice of colonial discipline in relation to the native islanders. The first description of Attwater notes "his sinews . . . dissolved in a listlessness that was more than languor" (191); however, he has "an eye that bid you beware of the man's devastating anger" (192). The significance of the eye as betokening Attwater's anger is that he runs his colony by a system of surveillance, in which every move of the natives, and of any visitors, is watched. This power of surveillance is what "betrayed the European" (192) in Attwater. The trio, on arriving at the island, felt "a sense of being watched and played with, and of a blow impending, that was hardly bearable" (190–91), and this ominous surveillance is attributed to Attwater. Indeed, the invisibility of this system is key to its effectiveness: as Mitchell argues about colonial power, "techniques of order and surveillance" may be compared "to the uniform and invisible force of a magnetic fluid." Mitchell goes on to argue, "The appearance of order means the disappearance of power. Power is to operate more and more in a manner that is slow, uninterrupted and without external manifestation."[45]

Attwater's system of discipline is best revealed by the story he tells during the island dinner of the two natives whom he dubs "Obsequiousness" and "Sullens"; this tale has broader application to his use of power. The intentions and character of the natives are read by Attwater in terms of the "eye," hence Sullens "rolled a dull eye upon me, with a spark in it" (*SST*, 217) and later "Obsequiousness" "looked at one with a trouble in his eye" (218). Attwater presents the spectacle of the two natives as a warning to the trio. One of the natives hangs himself, while the other, sent to retrieve the body, is shot by Attwater, and "they came to ground together" (219). This vivid image of disciplinary power is intended to warn the interlopers of what happens when "my justice had been made a fool of" (218). Presented as an anecdote in the midst of Attwater's apparently civilized dinner party, the tale actually offers an allegory of his system of tyranny.

Attwater appears to be a solitary ruler, who has "got the law with you" (216) and so is able to make the natives "jump" without assistance. During the dinner, however, Attwater refers frequently to Dr. Symonds, representing them as cruising partners who have traveled widely in search of wealth: "[W]e had to go far and wide and do the best we could. We have gone as far west as the Kingsmills and as far south as Rapa-iti" (215). Like Stevenson and his party, Attwater and Symonds have cruised widely even though they could "name no destination" (215). In terms of the narrative, however, Symonds is a sleeping partner, taking no share in the work of defending the settlement and its treasure from the invaders. Yet Attwater's claim that he "ran" the natives "single-handed . . . because there was nobody to help one" (216) follows a key disclosure about Dr. Symonds's role in acquiring labor: "That was his part, to collect them" (215). The absent Symonds is in fact crucial to the trading operation, raiding neighboring islands to obtain native laborers, a practice of which Roslyn Jolly comments, "As most of the natives were taken by fraud or simply kidnapped, the term 'labour trade' was a euphemism for an effective slave trade" (261n). As slavers, Attwater and Symonds view native labor merely as a commodity, which is why Attwater is able to describe the corpses as so much refuse, "empty bottles" to be thrown into the lagoon when they are of no more use to him (194). Symonds is also responsible for exporting the pearl shell and importing necessary commodities; hence, he is a vital (though invisible) figure in the partnership.

Even as the *Farallone* is mistaken by Attwater for the *Trinity Hall*, however, Attwater suggests on its arrival that he may put this mistake to good use and find a new partner": "It may suit me, your coming here. . . . My own schooner is overdue, and I may put something in your way in the meantime. Are you open to a charter?" (192). The bond between him and Dr. Symonds is ultimately a pragmatic one, based on the acquisition of wealth. As a practical "man of the world" (204), Attwater cannot allow sentiment to stand in the way of business, and so he offers to recruit Davis as a temporary trading associate.

Indeed, in spite of Attwater's class habitus, revealed in the acknowledgment of the Oxford-educated Herrick as a social equal, his more significant observation might be his question to Davis: "You, I presume, are the captain?" (192). By recognizing the captain as the one who holds authority, Attwater identifies Davis as the man with whom he must do business, his equal as a trader. As Vanessa Smith observes, "the more resourceful plotting of Davis . . . meets its match in Attwater."[46] When Davis remarks, "Your own schooner is overdue, I understand?" (195), Attwater's flattering response, "You understand perfectly, Captain Brown" (195), illuminates their understanding as a bond between crafty men of business, which anticipates Davis's final role as "Attwater's spoiled darling and pet penitent" (252).

The practice of trade as a free exchange of goods and commodities entails a pattern of displacement and substitution that runs rampant through the narrative at large. People, no less than objects, are commodities to be traded in *The Ebb-Tide,* meaning that all relationships are temporary and commodified. Indeed, there are several indications that Attwater seeks a substitute for Symonds, both in his business and in his affections. While it is never explained how Attwater and Symonds came to found their partnership, it is certainly possible—given Attwater's "interest in missions" (203)—that Symonds was one of his previous converts, or "penitents." Attwater's zeal for conversions shows no signs of abatement in the story. Seeking to bring Herrick over to Christ—"Why not the grace of your Maker and Redeemer, He who died for you, He who upholds you, He whom you daily crucify afresh" (203)—Attwater also suggests an erotic interest in his guest: "'I am fanciful,' he added, looking hard at Herrick, 'and I take fads. I like you'" (205). There is a perceptible slippage between Attwater's attempt to convert Herrick and a seduction of him. Asserting that "you are attractive, very attractive" (205), Attwater is aroused by his own pursuit. Following Herrick's rejection, "The rapture was all gone from Attwater's countenance; the dark apostle had disappeared" (207). The attraction is reciprocated, as Herrick experiences "an immense temptation to go up, to touch him" (207). The complex reactions of Herrick to his host—"Attwater intrigued, puzzled, dazzled, enchanted and revolted him" (207–8)—registers what McLynn calls the "fearsome power and charisma" that this character projects and the mix of desire and disgust that he provokes. Ann Colley describes Attwater as "a hybrid of the worst elements delineating a destructive colonial presence," while for Smith he represents "the dominant authorial presence within the narrative," featuring "a regime of absolute power based on insufficient perception."[47] Certainly Attwater's treatment of the natives—whom he blithely refers to as "brown innocents" (206)—is a failure to recognize their humanity: as Davis remarks, "you must be a holy terror" (216). Yet what critics have not recognized is that Attwater, in dealing with other whites, prefers to use seduction rather than force, a seduction that is clearly coded with erotic meaning and contains an intoxicating power. Even the hard-headed Davis "drank in" Attwater's presence and is "flushed" with "admiration" as a result, addressing him approvingly, "You're a man" (216). Only Colley recognizes that Attwater "more or less seduces the last of the three, Robert Herrick," although she focuses on the class bond between them rather than the sexual attraction.[48] Yet given the ambiguity of the term *partner*—covering the romantic, sexual, and commercial forms of union—Attwater's special attention to Herrick is clearly an invitation to fill the vacant space left by Symonds, while the offer to examine his collection of pearls (210) is an attempt to interest Herrick in the spoils of the colony.

Like "The Beach of Falesá," *The Ebb-Tide* illustrates the convergence of desire, exploitation, and violence in the commercial ventures of Europeans in the South Seas. In both narratives, the pursuit of colonial trade establishes partnerships between white male traders, missionaries, and beachcombers: partnerships dedicated to the plundering of resources and the appropriation of native labor. These bonds are founded on a shared habitus, featuring nostalgia for British or European culture and society. Yet they also are jeopardized by rivalries in which outbreaks of violence threaten to dismantle the professed solidarity of "white men." Moreover, *The Ebb-Tide* goes beyond "The Beach of Falesá" to demonstrate what Smith calls "a general failure of enterprise," in which the commercial exploits of colonial traders and adventurers are devastated by conflict, disease, and/or native resistance. This commercial failure is also a striking distinction between the South Seas narratives and the earlier romances of Stevenson, in which the protagonists gain economic wealth even though it may be ambivalently portrayed. Given the "failure of enterprise" in the South Seas fiction, Smith argues, "the common product of these ventures is narrative": as the failure to produce profit brings an end to the commercial partnership, it yields another commodity, the "yarn" itself.[49]

Certainly there is little sense of spatial progression in *The Ebb-Tide,* which rather suggests the pattern of a circular journey. Each of the destinations and locations is contingent rather than planned by the travelers. Moreover, the three beachcombers are left no better off, in terms of their material circumstances, at the end of the novel than they were at the beginning: one of them (Huish) is dead at Attwater's hands; another (Davis) has become his abject "true penitent" (*SST,* 249); while the third, Herrick, is still "on the beach," an outcast with no clear social role or purpose. In economic and social terms, their partnership has failed; yet their misadventures have borne fruit in narrative, the production of a yarn that may be consumed by those willing to face its squalor. As though to foreground the narrative's circularity, the novel ends with the arrival of the *Trinity Hall,* a deferral that has provided the pretext for the second half of the story. Ironically, by the time it arrives, the trading ship has become insignificant because of the conversion or failure of the three men. Davis remarks, concerning its arrival, "Well, it don't amount to a hill of beans" (251). Davis has abandoned his trading venture for a different kind of partnership between himself and Attwater or indeed between himself and Christ (as he asks Herrick, "why not come to Jesus right away, and let's meet in yon beautiful land?" [252]). While New Island has failed to yield the treasure trove of pearls that Davis originally desired, it has delivered something that he now values more highly, faith: "I'd most rather stay here upon this island. I found peace here, peace in believing" (251–52).

The cruise has ended for Davis, as for Stevenson, when he finds an island that seems to offer peace, a salve for his body and soul. The termination of his journey is signified by the fate of the *Farallone,* the cursed and contaminated ship on which he sailed wide of the law and which, in a final act of purification, Herrick sets on fire: "[H]is visit was followed by a coil of smoke; and he had scarce entered his boat again and shoved off, before flames broke forth upon the schooner" (*SST,* 250). Besides disposing of the evidence of their shared crime and plot, in burning the ship Herrick also destroys the traces of colonial corruption embodied by the spreading of disease and plundering of resources (from its first appearance "flaunting the plague-flag" [152], the ship's role in "disseminat[ing] disease" [123] is explicit). In so doing, Herrick effectively dissolves the corrupt partnership and brings closure to the yarn, with final confirmation of Davis's earlier point that "the bottom is out of this *Farallone* speculation" (197).

Herrick's verdict about the fate of the previous partners, Wiseman and Wishart, was simply, "It's grim" (*SST*, 154). Stevenson represents this grim quality to the narrative in a letter to Henry James dated June 17, 1893, describing *The Ebb-Tide:* "My dear man the grimness of that story is not to be depicted in words. There are only four characters to be sure, but they are such a troop of swine! And their behavior is really so deeply beneath any possible standard, that on a retrospect I wonder I have been able to endure them myself until the yarn was finished." Stevenson here dissociates himself from his characters, in stark contrast to his affection for David Balfour and Alan Breck. Being "beneath any possible standard," the men's conduct is outside the realm of the human, linked instead to the behavior of beasts (swine). Comparing the novel to the works of Zola, Stevenson identifies the "pertinent ugliness and pessimism" of his tale, which he would refer to as "the ever-to-be-execrated *Ebb-Tide,* or Stevenson's Blooming Error."[50] The "error"—like the errors in the narrative—is of course productive of the yarn. Yet there is a strong suggestion that Stevenson recognized that this would be his last work: "It seems as if literature were coming to a stand. I am sure it is with me; and I am sure everybody will say so when they have the privilege of reading *The Ebb-Tide.*"[51] So concerned was Stevenson with the likely reception of the work that he felt his partner should be spared the disgrace: "I propose, if it be not too late, to delete Lloyd's name. He has nothing to do with the last half. . . . I think it rather unfair on the young man to couple his name with so infamous a work."[52] Writing from Vailima in the year before his death, Stevenson seemed to realize that with this tale his cruise was over and that the time had come to dissolve his own partnership.

# NOTES

## Introduction

1. Robert Louis Stevenson, "My First Book: *Treasure Island*," in *The Lantern-Bearers and Other Essays*, ed. Jeremy Treglown (New York: Cooper Square, 1999), 277.

2. Stevenson's first four books, in order of publication, were *An Inland Voyage* (1878), *Edinburgh: Picturesque Notes* (1878), *Travels with a Donkey in the Cevennes* (1879), and *Virginibus Puerisque* (1881). See J. R. Hammond, *A Robert Louis Stevenson Chronology* (New York: St. Martin's, 1997), 91. I do not include here the publication of *Deacon Brodie* (1880), a play that Stevenson coauthored with W. E. Henley.

3. Whereas his father's side of the family was firmly grounded in Scotland, his mother's "Brother John, high in the medical service of the East India Company, was last man out of Delhi when the Mutiny broke; Brother James was engineer to the Crown Colony of New Zealand." See J. C. Furnas, *Voyage to Windward: The Life of Robert Louis Stevenson* (New York: William Sloane, 1951), 4–5.

4. Robert Louis Stevenson, *Travels with a Donkey in the Cevennes and Selected Travel Writings*, ed. Emma Letley (New York: Oxford University Press, 1992), 163. Subsequent references to this edition, which also contains *An Inland Voyage*, will be cited as *Travels with a Donkey*, or *An Inland Voyage*, as appropriate.

5. According to James Buzard, "Steam vessels began crossing the English channel in 1821: estimates suggest that as many as 100,000 people a year were availing themselves of the service by 1840." Buzard, "The Grand Tour and after (1660–1840)," in *The Cambridge Companion to Travel Writing*, ed. Peter Hulme and Tim Youngs (New York: Cambridge University Press, 2002), 47. Buzard goes on to argue that "the same period (roughly 1825–40) that witnessed the rise and initial effects of steam transport also saw other developments that greased the wheels on which travel was heading into the domain of mass tourism" (48).

6. Helen Carr has identified a cultural shift in travel writing after 1880 that relates to Stevenson's experience: "There was a move—as in imaginative literature—from the detailed, realist text, often with an overtly didactic or at any rate moral purpose, to a more impressionistic style with the interest focused as much on the travellers' responses or consciousness as their travels." Carr, "Modernism and Travel (1880–1940)," in *Hulme and Youngs,* eds., *The Cambridge Companion to Travel Writing,* 74. The "purpose" of the realist text is related to the purpose of travel, the renunciation of this narrative purpose being comparable to the journey as an open-ended process.

7. This illustrates Michel Bérubé's point that writers "travel in order to write, they travel while writing, because for them, travel *is* writing" (Carr, "Modernism and Travel," 74)

8. Roger G. Swearingen, *The Prose Writings of Robert Louis Stevenson: A Guide* (Hamden, CT: Archon, 1980), 29, 34, 42–43.

9. Frank McLynn, *Robert Louis Stevenson: A Biography* (London: Pimlico, 1994), 147, 141.

10. Charles Dickens, *Pictures from Italy,* ed. Kate Flint (New York: Penguin, 1998), 6.

11. Formally, this change of location sometimes results in breaks or fissures in the narrative, as, for example, in the sixteenth chapter of *Treasure Island:* where Stevenson resumes the novel after his "block," he not only introduces a new section but also changes the narrative point of view from Jim Hawkins to Dr. Livesey, such that the change of location is accompanied by a change of narrator.

12. James, of course, was himself an expatriate, one of the early modernist writers experiencing what Peter Nicholls describes as "the shock of 'exile' and cultural contrast" (cited in Carr, "Modernism and Travel," 74).

13. Henry James, "The Art of Fiction," 1884, in *Victorian Criticism of the Novel,* ed. Edwin M. Eigner and George J. Worth (Cambridge: Cambridge University Press, 1985), 196.

14. Robert Louis Stevenson, "A Humble Remonstrance," 1884, in *Victorian Criticism of the Novel,* ed. Edwin M. Eigner and George J. Worth (Cambridge: Cambridge University Press, 1985), 217, 215.

15. *An Inland Voyage* ends with "the travelers telling their misadventure in the dining-room at Siron's" (120), whereas *Travels with a Donkey* ends with Stevenson's emotional reaction to selling the donkey (231).

16. Fredric Jameson, *The Political Unconscious: Narrative as a Socially Symbolic Act* (Ithaca, NY: Cornell University Press, 1981), 54, 266.

17. I would note in passing that Stevenson constructs the historical trauma as the result of an arrested journey: it is at the moment when David interrupts the progress of Colin Roy, or "The Red Fox," that the fatal shot is fired. David's decision "to go through with my adventure" involves the disrupted journey: "He stopped and looked at me, as I thought, a little oddly." When the shot is fired, "with the very sound of it, Glenure fell upon the road," reminding us that the journey will never be completed. Robert Louis Stevenson, *Kidnapped, or the Lad with the Silver Button,* ed. Barry Menikoff (New York: Modern Library, 2001), 147, 148.

18. The *Shorter OED* also defines *cruiser* as "one who drives around looking for amusement, a sexual partner."

19. Lee Wallace, *Sexual Encounters: Pacific Texts, Modern Sexualities* (Ithaca, NY: Cornell University Press, 2003), 17. Wallace's book contains an outstanding analysis of Gauguin's painting *Manoa Tupapau* (109–37).

20. Robert Louis Stevenson, *In the South Seas,* ed. Neil Rennie (New York: Penguin, 1998), 5. Subsequent references to this edition will be cited parenthetically as *ISS.*

21. Certainly, his journey to America in 1879 was motivated by the sexual desire he felt for Fanny Osbourne, and this journey changed the course of Stevenson's sexual history no less than it altered his professional path (McLynn, *Robert Louis Stevenson,* 143–48). His most significant journeys thereafter were made in Fanny's company, including his cruises in the South Seas. Traveling with his wife, mother, and stepson—a family group that departed Britain following the death of Stevenson's father—Stevenson would hardly have expected the level of sexual freedom attained by Gauguin. For an interesting study of Gauguin's erotic and creative responses to the South Seas, see Eckhard Hollmann, *Paul Gauguin: Images from the South Seas* (New York: Prestel, 1996).

22. One striking example of such an enticement occurs in *Treasure Island,* when Squire Trelawney proposes a cruise for treasure in response to Dr. Livesey's excited opening of Jim's "oilskin packet"—an offer that prompts the doctor to pledge secrecy: "I'll be as silent as the grave." Robert Louis Stevenson, *Treasure Island,* ed. Wendy R. Katz (Edinburgh: Edinburgh University Press, 1998), 41, 44. Subsequent references to this edition will be cited parenthetically in the text.

23. For two of the most influential "queer" readings of *Strange Case,* see Elaine Showalter, *Sexual Anarchy: Gender and Culture at the Fin-de-Siècle* (New York: Viking, 1990), and Wayne Koestenbaum, "The Shadow on the Bed: Dr. Jekyll, Mr. Hyde, and the Labouchère Amendment," *Critical Matrix,* special issue, no. 1 (Spring 1988): 31–55. Eve Kosofsky Sedgwick's *Epistemology of the Closet* (Berkeley: University of

California Press, 1991) makes only fleeting reference to Stevenson, despite the fact that he belongs in the late-Victorian culture of homophobia and the emergence of the modern sexual classifications explored in her analysis.

24. In an interesting example of "cruising" in a homosexual context, Roland Barthes envisages textual production as a same-sex encounter: "Does writing in pleasure guarantee—guarantee me, the writer—my reader's pleasure? Not at all. I must seek out this reader, (must 'cruise him') *without knowing where he is.* A site of bliss is then created" (original emphasis). Barthes, *The Pleasure of the Text,* trans. Richard Miller (New York: Hill and Wang, 1975), 4. Writing of the textual signs of Barthes's homosexuality, D. A. Miller observes, "However intimately Barthes's writing proved its connection with gay sexuality, the link was so discreet that it seemed to emerge only in the coy or hapless intermittences of what under the circumstances I could hardly pretend to reduce to just his repression. What might it mean for me, lifting the repression, to notice and articulate this link for him?" Miller goes on to re-create the textual encounter between author and reader, Barthes and himself: "What I most sought, or what I most seek now, in the evidence of Roland Barthes's gayness is the opportunity it affords for staging this imaginary relation between us, between those lines on which we each in writing them may be thought to have put our bodies—for fashioning thus an intimacy with the writer whom (above all when it comes to writing) I otherwise can't touch." Miller, *Bringing Out Roland Barthes* (Berkeley: University of California Press, 1992), 6, 7. This sense of textuality as a form of imaginary relation that nonetheless brings the body of author and reader into an intimacy is relevant to my use of the term *cruising* in a context that bridges narrative drives and same-sex desire.

25. Claire Harman, *Robert Louis Stevenson: A Biography* (London: HarperCollins, 2005), 212. Harman's recent biography gives the fullest treatment of Stevenson's sexual ambiguity among the numerous accounts of his life. Among other interesting assertions, Harman notes that "Stevenson's personal manner and habits of dress had long constituted a standing challenge to bourgeois assumptions, social *and* sexual: what better way to rile fogeys than to go around looking almost like a caricature of the limp-wrested [*sic*] 'Uranian' of popular myth?" (211).

26. Symonds, *The Letters of John Addington Symonds,* vol. 3, ed. Herbert M. Schueller and Robert L. Peters (Detroit: Wayne State University Press, 1969), 121. Though Harman believes that "no trace of secret knowledge or special understanding enters the documented relations of the two men, and there was, presumably, no physical attraction between them" (*Robert Louis Stevenson,* 212), one can recognize a kinship between the two writers.

27. Robert Louis Stevenson, *The Letters of Robert Louis Stevenson,* 8 vols., ed. Bradford A. Booth and Ernest Mehew (New Haven, CT: Yale University Press, 1994–95), 5:220. Subsequently cited as *Letters,* with volume and page number.

28. Nicholas Daly, *Modernism, Romance and the Fin de Siècle: Popular Fiction and British Culture, 1880–1914* (Cambridge, UK: Cambridge University Press, 1999), 18, 19.

29. Henry James, "Robert Louis Stevenson," in *Literary Criticism: Essays on Literature, American Writers, English Writers,* ed. Leon Edel (New York: Library of America, 1984), 1233.

30. In particular, the association of anality with primitive cultures, Wallace suggests, is a construction of European fantasy, "the projection of a particular modern subjectivity onto 'the primitive,'" allowing "the primitivist projection of anality onto the racially marked other" (*Sexual Encounters,* 122).

31. Joseph Allan Boone, *Libidinal Currents: Sexuality and the Shaping of Modernism* (Chicago: University of Chicago Press, 1998).

32. Robert Louis Stevenson, *Strange Case of Dr. Jekyll and Mr. Hyde,* ed. Richard Dury (Edinburgh: Edinburgh University Press, 2004), 22, 19.

33. A particular motif that recurs in Stevenson's narratives is a male friendship or bond that erupts into savage violence: Frank Cassilis and Northmour in "Pavilion on the Links"; James and Henry Durie in *Master of Ballantrae;* Case and Wiltshire in "Beach of Falesá"; Archie Weir and Frank Innes in *Weir of Hermiston.* All these pairs illustrate this pattern of male friendship or kinship that transforms to murderous violence.

34. Eve Kosofsky Sedgwick, *Between Men: English Literature and Male Homosocial Desire* (New York: Columbia University Press, 1985).

35. Daly, *Modernism,* 12. Arguing against this tradition, Daly asserts that "once we recognize the romance and modernism as part of the same moment, we can begin to understand the serious cultural function of the romance," which "actually possesses a theoretical backbone" (24). A key component of this backbone, for Daly, is the defense of romance by Stevenson in his debate with Henry James (17–18).

36. Stevenson, *An Inland Voyage,* 5, 6. Using Grindlay's code name "Cigarette" (referring to the name of his canoe), Stevenson invokes him as a travel partner who has shared the pleasures and trials of their adventures. Yet Stevenson also refers to another, failed "cruise," the product of a fantasy or daydream of extended male intimacy aboard a boat: he writes of a barge that the two men had contemplated purchasing together (and we recall that the life of a bargee was idealized by Stevenson in the text), yet "The 'Eleven Thousand Virgins of Cologne' rotted in the stream where she was beautified. She felt not the impulse of the breeze; she was never harnessed to the patient track-horse" (5).

37. Stevenson describes how one man haunted their enclosure, remarking that "his white, handsome face (which I beheld with loathing) looked in upon us at all hours across the fence" (*ISS*, 171). The notice of the man's handsomeness seems incongruous given Stevenson's emphasis on his negative reaction to it ("loathing"), yet it reveals his tendency to dwell on masculine beauty in the South Seas.

38. Wallace, *Sexual Encounters*, 25–26. As a witness to Polynesian culture, Stevenson at times reveals the same criticism of whites in his nonfiction as he does in his stories; for example, he writes of "one black sheep," a white beachcomber in the Gilberts who is "typical of a class of ruffians that once disgraced the whole field of the South Seas" (*ISS*, 170). This man seems to resemble Case in "The Beach of Falesá" with his recurring complaint, "What is the matter with this island is the want of respect for whites" (170). This comment resembles Case's remark in reference to the "kanakas" in "The Beach of Falesá" that "they seem to have lost all idea of respect for whites." Robert Louis Stevenson, *South Sea Tales*, ed. Roslyn Jolly (New York: Oxford University Press, 1996), 22. Subsequent references to this edition will be cited parenthetically as *SST*.

39. The patriarchal power of Tembinok' is not, it seems, diminished by his masquerade: Stevenson writes that "something effeminate and courtly distinguishes the islanders of Apemama" (*ISS*, 237), in contrast to "[t]he king, with his manly and plain bearing," who "stood out alone" (237). Hence, the king ultimately conforms to Victorian stereotypes of gender, especially in his brutal treatment of his wives.

40. Significantly, Stevenson retains a certain distance from the couple in describing them as "this funny household" whose "attention to ourselves was surprising" (*ISS*, 205). Yet his attention to the couple exemplifies how Stevenson's experience of cruising in the South Seas offers alternatives to patriarchal Victorian gender conventions.

41. In the final chapter of Symonds's *Memoirs*, he celebrates the beauty of a Venetian gondolier named Angelo Fusato, dwelling on his "short blond moustache; dazzling teeth; skin bronzed, but showing white and delicate through open front and sleeves of lilac shirt." Symonds, *The Memoirs of John Addington Symonds*, ed. Phyllis Grosskurth (Chicago: University of Chicago Press, 1986), 271. For Symonds, the appeal of Angelo is irresistible: "He took hold of me by a hundred subtle threads of feeling, in which the powerful and radiant manhood of the splendid animal was intertwined with sentiment for Venice, a keen delight in the landscape of the lagoons" (272).

42. In Stevenson's account, Te Kop confesses, "I like you too much!" (*ISS*, 239) and addresses Stevenson with "gentle ecstasy" (239). Curiously, their intimacy is threatened not by Victorian prohibition or law but by the local tyrant Tembinok': Te Kop's "terror of the king" leads him "to speak guardedly" (239), and Stevenson seems regretful at the abrupt disappearance of his beautiful friend, remarking, "In any other island in the whole South Seas, if I had advanced half as far with any native, he would have been at my door next morning, bringing and expecting gifts" (239).

43. Boone, *Libidinal Currents,* 67.

44. Joan Pau Rubiés, "Travel Writing and Ethnography," in Hulme and Youngs, eds., *The Cambridge Companion to Travel Writing,* 258,

45. Wallace, *Sexual Encounters,* 7, 19, 21, 22. As Wallace writes of Pacific texts, "even as . . . these writers and artists, map identity more and more ferociously onto the known grid of gender, the horizon of sexual certainty seems to recede further and further" (36).

46. Daly, *Modernism,* 63–64. An unresolved contradiction also appears in Stevenson's nonfictional account of same-sex attraction. It is significant that he encounters Te Kop while he is out wandering alone. Admitting that he "was haunted and troubled by a problem," Stevenson's meeting with Te Kop seems to assuage this anxiety that leads him away from home. Yet the interracial relationship can exist only outside the domestic, familial space: *"My house, of course, was unapproachable,* but he knew where to find me on the ocean beach, where I went daily" (*ISS,* 238, 239; emphasis added).

47. Stevenson, *Letters,* 7:140–41 (emphasis added).

48. Colleen Lamos, *Deviant Modernism: Sexual and Textual Errancy in T. S. Eliot, James Joyce, and Marcel Proust* (Cambridge: Cambridge University Press, 1998), 6.

49. Wallace, *Sexual Encounters,* 36, 56.

50. Stevenson, *Letters,* 7:141.

51. Lamos, *Deviant Modernism,* 6, 10.

52. Stevenson's texts not only express admiration for male Polynesian bodies but also represent the South Sea islands as a location where homoerotic attraction between white men may be explored. According to Wallace, "it is the male body—*whether native or European*—not the female which . . . structures many Pacific narratives," and Stevenson's texts are an apt illustration of this point (*Sexual Encounters,* 56; emphasis added). In *The Ebb-Tide,* for example, the English colonialist Attwater declares his misogyny ("I hate women") prior to admitting that "I am fanciful" while "looking hard at Herrick," and "I take fads. I like you" (*The Ebb-Tide,* in *South Sea Tales,* ed. Jolly, 205).

53. Bill Ashcroft, Gareth Griffiths, and Helen Tiffin, *Post-Colonial Studies: The Key Concepts* (New York: Routledge, 2000), 42.

54. Edward W. Said, *Culture and Imperialism* (New York: Vintage, 1994), 56, 59.

55. Carr, "Modernism and Travel," 71, 73, 82.

56. Stevenson, *Letters,* 6:209.

57. Carr, "Modernism and Travel," 73, 71. Carr remarks that "travelling in ostentatious discomfort was not new—Robert Louis Stevenson had, one could argue, invented that kind of European traveller much earlier" (78–79).

58. Stevenson, *Letters,* 6:209, 312, 327; 7:282.

59. Said, *Culture and Imperialism,* 132, 74.

60. Arthur Johnstone, *Recollections of Robert Louis Stevenson in the Pacific* (London: Chatto, 1905), 102–3 (emphasis added).

61. Carr, "Modernism and Travel," 83.

62. Vanessa Smith, *Literary Culture and the Pacific: Nineteenth-Century Textual Encounters* (Cambridge, UK: Cambridge University Press, 1998), 112, 113.

63. Carr, "Modernism and Travel," 83; Said, *Culture and Imperialism,* 147. Bernard Porter has written of popular Victorian perceptions of the barbaric practices of the South Seas: "South Sea islanders . . . indulged in cannibalism. . . . Replace these, and the South Sea islanders . . . would soon be on the right 'progressive' track." Bernard Porter, *The Absent-Minded Imperialists: Empire, Society, and Culture in Britain* (New York: Oxford University Press, 2004), 100. Even as the empire was supposed to provide an outlet for energies that might otherwise result in sexual deviation, it could allow the expression of homosexual desires not admissible at home. As Porter writes of the Wilde trials, "Presumably his persecutors were unaware of the homosexual propensities of some of their imperial heroes," listing Gordon, Rhodes, Baden-Powell, and Kitchener as examples (412). Said also acknowledges that "critics have speculated on a hidden homosexual motif in these [imperial] relationships" (*Culture and Imperialism,* 138), a reading he counters with the idea that such romances "celebrates the friendship of two men," because "in the field or on the open road, two men can travel together more easily, and they can come to each other's rescue more credibly than if a woman were along" (138)—as though a pair of men traveling together could not function as a "homosexual motif"!

64. Stevenson, *Letters,* 8:279n.

65. Johnstone, *Recollections,* 7, 9.

66. Said, *Culture and Imperialism,* 136, 133.

67. Ann C. Colley, *Robert Louis Stevenson and the Colonial Imagination* (Burlington, VT: Ashgate, 2004), 54.

68. Ashcroft, Griffiths, and Tiffin, *Post-Colonial Studies,* 115, 119, 118, 120.

69. Said, *Culture and Imperialism,* 140; Colley, *Robert Louis Stevenson,* 54, 55.

70. Stevenson, *Travels with a Donkey,* 163, 188.

71. Colley, *Robert Louis Stevenson,* 60.

72. Colley, *Robert Louis Stevenson,* 54.

73. Cited in Said, *Culture and Imperialism,* 141.

74. For Stevenson's expression of interest in this position, see *Letters,* 7:310–11. The material emoluments and the likelihood of amusement rather than a desire for political power, appear to have been the chief sources of his interest. Ironically, it was later reported, erroneously, that Stevenson had been made consul on Samoa (7:386–87).

75. Lloyd Osbourne, *An Intimate Portrait of R.L.S.* (New York: Scribner's, 1924), 124.

76. Ann Colley has shown that Stevenson was more closely involved with missionary culture than has been previously recognized. In some ways, Stevenson's mediating role, as storyteller, resembles that of the missionary who seeks to convert the native to accept European cultural norms. Stevenson was aided by one missionary, Arthur Claxton, in reaching a Samoan audience, as Claxton translated Stevenson's tale "The Bottle Imp" into Samoan. Yet the fragility of this alliance is reflected in the bitter conflict between the two over an alleged plot to kidnap the chief Mataafa. Colley describes this episode (*Robert Louis Stevenson,* 161–71), and I examine it in more detail in chapter 6.

77. Wilde, *The Complete Letters of Oscar Wilde,* ed. Merlin Holland and Rupert Hart-Davis (New York: Holt, 2000), 789.

78. See Stevenson's letter to Henry James dated December 5, 1892 (*Letters,* 7:449), and Colley, *Robert Louis Stevenson,* 151–53.

79. Said, *Culture and Imperialism,* 9.

80. Stevenson, *Kidnapped and Catriona,* 350.

81. Stevenson, *Kidnapped, or the Lad with the Silver Button,* ed. Barry Menikoff (New York: Modern Library, 2001), 73–74. Although Alan does not wear the proscribed tartan, his clothes clearly mark him as a Jacobite, as Hoseason remarks: "Y'eve a French soldier's coat upon your back and a Scotch tongue in your head" (74). Alan's "vanity in dress" (127) is used by Stevenson as one of the markers of his Highland identity, and dramatizes how pivotal his clothes are to his sense of identity.

82. Wallace, *Sexual Encounters,* 72, 86. This marking of the body of the "native"—whether Scottish Highlander or Polynesian—as "other" is reminiscent of the inscription of sexual difference on the body of the homosexual, as analyzed by Lee

Edelman, who observes that "homosexuals themselves have been seen as producing—and, by some medical 'experts,' as being produced by—bodies that bore a distinct, and therefore legible, anatomical code . . . thus allowing the nineteenth century's medicalization of sexual discourse to serve more efficiently the purposes of criminology and the law. As a result, John Addington Symonds would be able to invoke the received idea of the homosexual as a man with 'lusts written on his face.'" Lee Edelman, *Homographesis: Essays in Gay Literary and Cultural Theory* (New York: Routledge, 1994), 5. Given that tattoo is sometimes referred to as "punctuation," a kind of writing on the body, it is perhaps inevitable that the Marquesan body becomes textualized, such that "male figures must be read as sexual texts in their own right" (Wallace, *Sexual Encounters,* 68). Wallace's use of "must" is significant here, indicating the kind of obligatory reading of difference onto the body that Edelman refers to as the "inherently textual" (Edelman, *Homographesis,* 6).

83. The Highlander's tartan indicated his clan, and also designated specific occasions for wear. As John Prebble argues, the Highlands "was still a warrior society, tribal at the bottom and quasi-feudal at the top, dressed in tartan swagger." John Prebble, *The Lion in the North: One Thousand Years of Scotland's History* (Harmondsworth: Penguin, 1973), 290.

84. Edmund Burt, cited in Barry Menikoff, *Narrating Scotland: The Imagination of Robert Louis Stevenson* (Columbus: University of South Carolina Press, 2005), 42.

85. Wallace, *Sexual Encounters,* 85; Said, *Culture and Imperialism,* 31–32.

86. Timothy Mitchell, *Colonising Egypt* (Berkeley: University of California Press, 1991), 167. It is perhaps not surprising that the author of *Strange Case of Dr. Jekyll and Mr. Hyde* should display the presence of an "other" within, given that text's famous assertions that "man is not truly one but truly two" and that "man will be ultimately known for a mere polity of multifarious, incongruous and independent denizens" (*Strange Case,* 59). Significantly, an influential anthropologist "identifies one of the functions of Marquesan tattoo as an apotropaic 'doubling' or 'multiplication' of the person" (Wallace, *Sexual Encounters,* 78).

87. Boone, *Libidinal Currents,* 83.

88. Stevenson, *Letters,* 7:140.

89. Similarly, his own body and persona refused to conform to the stereotype of the British colonialist: whereas the colonial masculinity of Attwater is revealed in his "huge . . . proportionally strong" build and his "eye of unimpaired health and virility" (*SST,* 191), Stevenson's emaciated, ailing corpus was far from the ideal.

90. Stevenson, *Letters,* 3:113.

91. In February 1884, Gladstone's Liberal government dispatched General Charles Gordon to Khartoum to defend the Egyptian-led government in the Sudan. Gordon's death at the fall of Khartoum in January 1885 led to a public outcry against the failure of Gladstone's government to defend its empire. Stevenson voiced his hostility towards Gladstone in his correspondence, writing to his parents, "I would rather be a louse this day than W.E. Gladstone. I give up this government. I think they should be ranged against a wall and shot" (*Letters,* 4:239). Clearly Stevenson felt that the abandonment of Gordon was a betrayal of Britain's imperial role, a hostility that Gladstone's reported admiration for *Treasure Island* did nothing to assuage: "It appears Gladstone talks all the time about *Treasure Island;* he would do better to attend to the imperial affairs of England" (5:80–81, 49).

92. Barry Menikoff, introduction to *The Complete Stories of Robert Louis Stevenson* (New York: Modern Library, 2002), xlii, xliii.

93. *Letters,* 5:365; emphasis added.

94. Significantly, the anticolonialism of *The Ebb-Tide* (Stevenson's last work published in his lifetime) corresponds to the end of Stevenson's travels, as he settled in his final home at Vailima and disavowed any intention to return to Europe. Around this time, Stevenson wrote to Sidney Colvin that "so long as I cruise in the South Seas, I shall be well and happy—. . . I mean that, so soon as I cease from cruising, the nerves are strained, the decline commences, and I steer slowly but surely back to bedward" (*Letters,* 6:388). Hence, it is perhaps not surprising that the currents of pleasure and desire associated with travel began to ebb with Stevenson's settlement on Samoa. Nicholas Daly writes that "in the romance the line between the team and its surroundings must be maintained. . . . [T]he explorers must never become part of that landscape" (*Modernism,* 64). Stevenson's eroticized response to landscape began a process by which he became part of that landscape, a settler rather than an explorer. As a result, the pleasures of cruising—which even in the region of "blue water and a ship" (*Letters,* 6:403) required constant motion and unanchored desire—were dissipated by Stevenson's settlement on Samoa.

95. Wendy R. Katz, introduction to *Treasure Island,* xix.

## Chapter 1

1. The biographies are by Ian Bell, *Dreams of Exile: Robert Louis Stevenson, A Biography* (New York: Holt, 1992); McLynn, *Robert Louis Stevenson;* and Claire Harman, *Robert Louis Stevenson.* Alan Sandison's 1996 study of Stevenson was the most extensive and

important critical discussion to have appeared in many years; Sandison, *Robert Louis Stevenson and the Appearance of Modernism* (New York: St. Martin's, 1996). Since then, there have been book-length studies of Stevenson by Ann Colley (*Robert Louis Stevenson and the Colonial Imagination*) and Barry Menikoff (*Narrating Scotland*), as well as a collection of critical essays edited bv William B. Jones Jr.: *Robert Louis Stevenson Reconsidered: New Critical Perspectives* ( Jefferson, NC: McFarland, 2003).

2. Robert Kiely, *Robert Louis Stevenson and the Fiction of Adventure* (Cambridge, MA: Harvard University Press, 1964), 11.

3. The concept of reanimation is central to the fictional masterpieces of Wilde and Haggard, *The Picture of Dorian Gray* (1891) and *She* (1887), respectively. Dorian's painting is animated by the wish that Dorian should be able to indulge his desires without penalty, and the aesthetic object thereafter takes on the degenerative aspects of the corpse. In Haggard's romance, Ayesha, or She-Who-Must-Be-Obeyed, preserves the corpse of her ancient lover, Kallikrates, while awaiting his reincarnation. The character of Leo is, of course, just such a reanimated version of Kallikrates, while Ayesha is a reanimated corpse, endlessly renewed by the "pillar of life."

4. Paul Maixner, ed., *Robert Louis Stevenson: The Critical Heritage* (London: Routledge and Kegan Paul, 1981), 337. Subsequently cited as *Critical Heritage.*

5. Wayne Koestenbaum, "Shadow on the Bed". Koestenbaum argues that Stevenson's most famous gothic story is an example of "bachelor" literature of the fin-de-siècle, which excludes women and concentrates instead on the production of erotic and violent energies between men. This focus on male desire is read by Koestenbaum as a response to the Labouchère Amendment, which made any act of "gross indecency" between men, whether in public or private, punishable by a maximum sentence of two years' imprisonment with hard labor. The effect of the amendment, certainly apparent before the trials of Wilde in 1895, was to consolidate the association of male homosexuality with secrecy, since concealment was the only effective defense against prosecution. See also Jeffrey Weeks, *Coming Out: Homosexual Politics in Britain from the Nineteenth Century to the Present,* rev. ed. (London: Quartet, 1990), 14–20.

6. Koestenbaum, "Shadow on the Bed," 52.

7. For Fredric Jameson's use of this concept of "containment strategies"—which may have both ideological and formal applications—see *The Political Unconscious: Narrative as a Socially Symbolic Act* (Ithaca: Cornell University Press, 1981), 53–54. The relevant insight for my argument, is that a strategy of containment "allows what can be thought to seem internally coherent in its own terms, while repressing the unthinkable . . . which lies beyond its boundaries" (53).

8. Joseph Bristow, *Sexuality* (London: Routledge, 1997), 174.

9. Stevenson's narrative representation of the reanimated corpse participates in a Scottish gothic tradition in fiction originating with James Hogg's *Confessions of a Justified Sinner* (1824), which uses the corpse to dramatize a concern with the continuing vitality of an oral tradition and to expose the deathly powers of narrative. At the conclusion of Hogg's novel, the "editor"—who first narrates the series of events that are retold in Robert Wringhim's narrative—descends into the grave in a search for the corpse that will also disclose the origin of the narrative of Wringhim. This descent produces a dizzying circularity in the narrative, characteristic of the gothic mode, in which, as Fiona Robertson argues, "narrative and historical processes are repeatedly figured as tortuous approaches through hidden subterranean passageways to a secret which may finally be revealed, but which can never be an adequate recompense for the terrors of the quest." Robertson, *Legitimate Histories: Scott, Gothic, and the Authorities of Fiction* (Oxford: Clarendon Press, 1994), 17.

10. Magdalene Redekop, "Beyond Closure: Buried Alive with Hogg's *Justified Sinner*," *ELH* 52 (1985): 159–60.

11. Robert Louis Stevenson, "A Note on Realism," in *Selected Essays*, ed. George Scott-Moncrieff (Washington, DC: Regnery Gateway, 1988), 264, 262, 269.

12. M. M. Bakhtin, *The Dialogic Imagination*, ed. Michael Holquist, trans. Caryl Emerson and Michael Holquist (Austin: University of Texas Press, 1981), 7.

13. Michael Holquist, introduction to *The Dialogic Imagination*, by M. M. Bakhtin (Austin: University of Texas Press, 1981), xxxi.

14. Stevenson, *The Lantern-Bearers*, 178.

15. Christine Quigley, *The Corpse: A History* (Jefferson, NC: McFarland, 1996), 15.

16. Guy Hocquenghem, *Homosexual Desire*, trans. Daniella Dangoor (Durham, NC: Duke University Press, 1993), 100.

17. Koestenbaum, "Shadow on the Bed," 48, 39, 41.

18. Maixner, *Critical Heritage*, 31, 337.

19. Stevenson, *Letters*, 6:138, 15.

20. Robert Louis Stevenson and Lloyd Osbourne, *The Wrong Box* (New York: Oxford University Press, 1995), 67. Subsequent references to this edition will be cited parenthetically in the text.

21. Stevenson, *Letters*, 6:263, 264 (emphasis added).

22. Bernard Darwin, introduction to *The Wrong Box*, by Robert Louis Stevenson and Lloyd Osbourne (London: Oxford University Press, 1954), xi, xii.

23. Maixner, *Critical Heritage*, 360. Significantly, modern judgments about the novel also reveal anxiety about the contaminating effects of joint authorship on Stevenson's reputation. McLynn dismisses *The Wrong Box* as "a truly calamitous apology for a

novel" (*Robert Louis Stevenson,* 284) and remarks that "it was a great pity he ever saw fit to put his name on the title page—which was assuredly the only reason the work was ever published" (285).

24. Maixner, *Critical Heritage,* 336–37.

25. Patrick Brantlinger, "What Is 'Sensational' about the Sensation Novel?" *Nineteenth-Century Fiction* 37 (1982), 12.

26. Although I dwell at length on the negative reactions to the novel, *The Wrong Box* did have its admirers. Rudyard Kipling wrote to Edmonia Hill in September 1889, "I have got RL Stevenson's 'In the Wrong Box' [*sic*] and laughed over it dementedly when I read it." Kipling, *Something of Myself and Other Autobiographical Writings,* ed. Thomas Pinney (Cambridge, UK: Cambridge University Press, 1990), 241n. In his autobiography, Kipling declared himself "Eminent Past Master R.L.S. Even to-day I would back myself to take seventy-five percent marks in written or viva voce on The Wrong Box which, as the Initiated know, is the Test Volume of that Degree. I read it first in a small hotel in Boston in '89, when the negro waiter nearly turned me out of the dining-room for spluttering over my meal" (60). Clearly, Stevenson was not the only one who "split" over the novel.

27. The point of origin of the train is significant in that Stevenson, Fanny, and Lloyd had lived in Bournemouth for three years, 1884–87: RLS, like the fragile Joseph Finsbury, was staying at this seaside resort in an attempt to restore his health (McLynn, *Robert Louis Stevenson,* 232–53).

28. John Sutherland, *The Stanford Companion to Victorian Fiction* (Stanford, CA: Stanford University Press, 1989), 519.

29. Stevenson, *An Inland Voyage,* 3–4. Subsequent references are cited parenthetically.

30. Peter Brooks, *Reading for the Plot: Design and Intention in Narrative* (New York: Knopf, 1984), 44. Brooks's focus on the plot of the novel as an engine—"these emblematic motors and engines invented by novelists"—motivates his critique of the rigid formalism that examines narrative as a structure rather than a dynamic process. Brooks seeks to develop a reading strategy "that would be more adequate to our experience of reading narrative as a dynamic operation—what makes plot move us forward to the end, to put it in simplest terms" (47).

31. Brooks, *Reading for the Plot,* 52, 43.

32. Stevenson related his ambivalent response to his father's death, and Thomas's unstable identity, in a letter to Sidney Colvin: "I . . . can but say that I am glad. If we could have had my father, that would have been a different thing. But to keep

that changeling—suffering changeling—any longer, could better none and nothing. Now he rests: it is more significant, it is more like himself" (*Letters,* 5:411).

33. D. A. Miller, *The Novel and the Police* (Berkeley: University of California Press, 1988), 241n6.

34. See Christopher Craft's insightful reading of the sodomitical significance of "Bunburying" in Wilde's *Importance of Being Earnest;* Craft traces in the play's deployment of the "alias" of Bunbury a displaced desire for anal penetration—"to bury in the bun." Craft, *Another Kind of Love: Male Homosexual Desire in English Discourse, 1850–1920* (Berkeley: University of California Press, 1994), 118.

35. Leo Bersani, "Is the Rectum a Grave?" *October* 43 (Winter 1987): 220.

36. Bersani, "Is the Rectum a Grave?" 222.

37. Jameson, *Political Unconscious,* 266.

38. Miller, *Novel and the Police,* 200.

39. Maixner, *Critical Heritage,* 337.

40. Robert Louis Stevenson, "The Suicide Club," in *The Complete Stories of Robert Louis Stevenson,* ed. Barry Menikoff (New York: Modern Library, 2002), 40. Subsequent references to this edition will be cited parenthetically in the text as "Suicide Club."

41. Stevenson, *Treasure Island,* 148.

42. Robert Louis Stevenson, *Kidnapped, or The Lad with the Silver Button,* ed. Barry Menikoff (New York: Modern Library, 2001), 37. Subsequent references to this edition will be cited parenthetically as *Kidnapped.*

43. According to Penny Fielding, the generic disharmony of *The Master* has gendered implications, as "James [Durie] is associated with an irrational, female, and subversive orality which threatens the male romance." Fielding, *Writing and Orality* (Oxford: Clarendon Press, 1996), 165.

44. Stevenson, *Letters,* 6:105. Stevenson links the fates of the two works in a letter to Sidney Colvin dated August 22, 1889: "I wonder what has befallen me too, that flimsy part of me that lives (or dwindles) in the public mind; and what has befallen *The Master,* and what kind of a Box *The Wrong Box* has been found? It is odd to know nothing of all this" (6:329).

45. Maixner, *Critical Heritage,* 360.

46. Maixner, *Critical Heritage,* 341, 343.

47. Maixner, *Critical Heritage,* 349.

48. Stevenson, *The Master of Ballantrae,* ed. Adrian Poole (Harmondsworth: Penguin, 1996), 94. Subsequent references to this edition will be cited parenthetically in the text.

49. As Maggie Kilgour has commented on the double effect of this technique, "by reviving the dead, recalling to life an idealized past, the gothic tries to heal the ruptures of rapid change, and preserve continuity"; yet this desire can be undermined by the spectre of repetition when "the past comes back not to critique or reform the present, but to deform and destroy it." Kilgour, *The Rise of the Gothic Novel* (London: Routledge, 1995), 30–31.

50. As Stevenson wrote to Sidney Colvin on Christmas Eve 1887, "the Master is all I know of the devil; I have known hints of him, in the world, but always cowards; he is as bold as a lion, but with the same deadly, causeless duplicity" (*Letters,* 6:87).

51. Apparently recognizing the novel's hybridity, Stevenson wondered whether "I have not gone too far with the fantastic," warning Henry James that "the third supposed death and the manner of the third reappearance is steep; steep, sir" even as he boasted "how daring is the design" (*Letters,* 6:105).

52. Stevenson, *Letters,* 6:301–2.

53. For Stevenson's nonfictional accounts of his experiences in the South Seas, see in particular *A Footnote to History: Eight Years of Trouble in Samoa* (Honolulu: University of Hawai'i Press, 1996) and *In the South Seas.* For a fuller account of Stevenson's changing opinions and moods about Samoan society and politics, see McLynn, *Robert Louis Stevenson,* 366–505. Volumes 7 and 8 of the *Letters* are also a valuable source of information on Stevenson's experience of living on Samoa.

54. Robert Louis Stevenson and Lloyd Osbourne, *The Ebb-Tide: A Trio and Quartette,* in Stevenson, *South Sea Tales,* ed. Roslyn Jolly (New York: Oxford University Press, 1996), 204.

55. Colley, *Robert Louis Stevenson,* 39.

56. Smith, *Literary Culture,* 164.

57. In a letter of April 25, 1889, Stevenson asks Baxter to "register the title *The Pearlfisher* for me. It is for a story Lloyd and I are on; the gaudiest yarn; and I have a dreadful fear someone will hook the name" (*Letters* 6:289). Booth and Mehew note that this story was "[l]ater, in truncated form, to provide the basis for *The Ebb-Tide*" (6:289n).

58. Smith, *Literary Culture,* 156.

59. Maixner, *Critical Heritage,* 458. Wayne Koestenbaum offers an interesting discussion of the potentially homosexual associations of *fag* in the late-Victorian period, which he terms "the fag-end of the nineteenth century, when fears of degeneration abounded." Koestenbaum, "Shadow on the Bed," 54.

60. Maixner, *Critical Heritage,* 459. The situation with respect to the two writers is thus a curiously inverted one as compared to *The Wrong Box.* Smith writes of the

collaboration on *The Ebb-Tide* that "adverse reviews lead Stevenson to consider deleting Osbourne's name from the book's cover: erasure, rather than signature of authorship seemed in this instance more likely to serve Osbourne's literary reputation" (*Literary Culture,* 156).

61. Roslyn Jolly, introduction to *South Sea Tales,* by Robert Louis Stevenson (New York: Oxford University Press, 1996), xxx.

62. Quigley, *Corpse,* 12.

## Chapter 2

1. Robert Louis Stevenson, *An Inland Voyage,* 43.

2. Harman, *Robert Louis Stevenson,* 161. Interestingly, Harman summarizes *Travels with a Donkey* as "a cautionary tale of how much effort and artifice were involved if the middle-class Victorian wished to get 'back to nature'" (162). This reading strikes me as somewhat superficial. Certainly, there are passages in which Stevenson indicates that he wishes to get back to nature, or at least to a simpler mode of living. Yet the quest of *Travels with a Donkey* is somewhat more complex—that of reaching a reconciliation with the physical body, its desires and materiality, while at the same time struggling against control by the "feminine," both without and within.

3. For an account of this reception, see McLynn, *Robert Louis Stevenson,* 106.

4. McLynn has argued, with reference to *An Inland Voyage,* that "some of RLS's asides show an almost Freudian appreciation of journey as a metaphor for self-realisation" (*Robert Louis Stevenson,* 107). I argue that the relevance of Freudian interpretation is even more apparent in *Travels with a Donkey;* however, the journey becomes a metaphor for the obstacles to such realization.

5. Of course, any writer on the donkey must sooner or later reference Aesop, whose fable about the father and son who travel with an ass—each being reproached for allowing the other to walk, until finally they carry the ass—is one of the most famous literary representations of the animal. Stevenson does allude to the fable in writing, "What the devil was the good of a she-ass if she could not carry a sleeping-bag and a few necessaries? I saw the end of the fable rapidly approaching, when I should have to carry Modestine. Aesop was the man to know the world!" (*Travels with a Donkey,* 162).

6. Richard Holmes argues that the true purpose of Stevenson's journey was a preparation for the longer, more arduous trip that he would make to California the next year: "For Stevenson himself . . . the whole Cevennes experience was a kind

of initiation ceremony: a grappling with physical hardships, loneliness, religious doubts, the influence of his parents, and the overwhelming question of whether he should take the enormous risk of traveling to America and throwing his life in with Fanny's. . . . So the pilgrimage begun at Le Monastier ended six thousand miles away in a honeymoon on the wooded hills of the Pacific coast of California." Richard Holmes, *Footsteps: Adventures of a Romantic Biographer* (New York: Vintage, 1996), 5. Yet the narrative was also part of a literary pilgrimage, a journey towards the elusive literary success to which Stevenson was committed.

7. Nicholas Daly has examined the mummy fiction of the late-Victorian period in terms of its construction of an "intimate relation to the mummy [which] is displaced into fiction." Daly, *Modernism,* 89. Daly follows Allon White in observing that "the other of the bourgeois self-image, the 'grotesque body,' summoned up in carnival, is not so much forgotten as it is banished into the realms of literary culture and privatized consciousness" (89). Modestine, as the grotesque body, is a significant example of this "attenuation and marginalization of the culture of carnival" (89) in nineteenth-century literature.

8. The title of Stevenson's next proposed book of travels was *The Amateur Emigrant,* though this was withheld from publication at Thomas Stevenson's insistence (see McLynn, *Robert Louis Stevenson,* 196–97); indeed, one wonders whether this pattern or theme of the traveler-ingénue—a "green" or amateur voyager—is a key part of Stevenson's persona, a pose or self-representation that strengthens the random, incidental dimension of the travels.

9. In *An Inland Voyage,* Stevenson suggests that the donkey might achieve posthumous revenge for its harsh treatment in life: writing of the use of asses' skin for military drums, he asks whether "there [is] not something in the nature of a revenge upon the donkey's persecutors? Of old, he might say, you drubbed me up hill and down dale and I must endure; but now that I am dead those dull thwacks that were scarcely audible in country lanes have become stirring music in front of the brigade, and for every blow that you lay on my old great-coat, you will see a comrade stumble and fall" (43).

10. Stevenson, *Letters,* 2:313.

11. Holmes, *Footsteps,* 20.

12. Harman, *Robert Louis Stevenson,* 149. Later in life, Bob Stevenson would emerge as an antagonist in a more sinister context: his role as exacerbator of the conflict between Stevenson and W. E. Henley over Fanny's plagiarism of "The Nixie," a story by Stevenson's cousin Katherine de Mattos. Harman writes, "Bob's is a silent but potent presence throughout the whole affair, his handwriting on archive drafts

of letters from both Henley and Katherine proof of his complicity, his very concealment behind the others a mark of deep-seated resentments and jealousies against his cousin" (349). This rather Hyde-like portrait of Bob belongs, however, to 1888, many years after Stevenson's courtship of Fanny.

13. Harman, *Robert Louis Stevenson,* 88. Harman, while admitting that "the triangular pattern usually suggests strife and rivalry" (87), argues that the triangle of Stevenson, Colvin, and Sitwell was an exception: "Stevenson met two friends who were separately very important to him and whose relationship with each other was strengthened, possibly cemented, by their mutual concern for him" (87).

14. Holmes, *Footsteps,* 20.

15. Harman, *Robert Louis Stevenson,* 163.

16. Harman comments that Stevenson's "confusion at the auberge in Bouchet-Saint-Nicholas at being so near someone else's semi-naked wife is surely made worse because the situation reminds him of his new position relative to the reunited Osbournes" (*Robert Louis Stevenson,* 163).

17. Daly, *Modernism,* 39.

18. Interestingly, Richard Holmes seems to share Stevenson's enjoyment in the violent exploits of the beast. In recounting several explanations for the beast's return, Holmes writes, "My favourite had a sinister simplicity. It proposed . . . a rogue family of three wolves (like the Three Bears) who, ostracized from the main pack, had tasted the delights of human flesh, and thereafter attacked in combination. Hence the inexplicable ferocity of the Beast; and also its ability to be in two places at once. This theory had the great attraction of leaving *one wolf still unaccounted for.* I liked this very much" (*Footsteps,* 25; original emphasis).

19. Stevenson, *Strange Case,* 72.

20. It is tempting here to read a prefiguring of a later female icon, that of the "naval sculpture" in *The Ebb-Tide* (1894). An underlying claim of my argument is that Stevenson returns to and recycles various scenes, objects, and images throughout his travel writing. In this latter case, the purity of the female is compromised by the fact that the appearance of the figurehead is described as "leprous whiteness" (Stevenson, *South Sea Tales,* 190)—indicating a diseased condition. Yet both statues are instances of the "return of the repressed," a material representation of the femininity that is denied or disavowed in the narratives as a whole.

21. I am grateful to Stephen Arata for drawing my attention to this point that Stevenson moves from one version of femininity to another at this juncture of the narrative.

22. Harman, *Robert Louis Stevenson,* 160.

23. Stevenson, *Strange Case,* 60.

24. Stevenson, *Letters,* 7:280. So closely intertwined has this phrase become with Stevenson's physical decline during the Bournemouth years that both Jenni Calder and Claire Harman use it as the title for the relevant chapters of their biographies. A precedent was set by Graham Balfour, who quotes the phrase at the beginning of volume 2 of his biography of Stevenson, the chapter covering the Bournemouth years: "Looking back on this period in after days, he cries out: 'Remember the pallid brute that lived in Skerryvore like a weevil in a biscuit.'" Balfour, *The Life of Robert Louis Stevenson,* 2 vols. (London: Methuen, 1901), 2:2. Stevenson had used the phrase earlier in *Treasure Island,* where Blind Pew urges his piratical associates to pursue Jim and his mother, who have absconded with the map: "If you had the pluck of a weevil in a biscuit you would catch them still" (37).

25. Stevenson, *Letters,* 5:23.

26. Stevenson and Osbourne, *The Wrong Box,* 59.

27. Stevenson, *Letters,* 5:23.

28. Stevenson, *Letters,* 5:21, 24, 25.

29. For an account of Stevenson's loss of religious faith and conflict with his father over this lapse, see McLynn, *Robert Louis Stevenson,* 60–73.

30. Stevenson, *The Lantern-Bearers,* 279.

31. Significantly, Stevenson makes no mention in *The Amateur Emigrant,* the whole of which was never published during his lifetime, that the chief purpose of his trip to the United States was to pursue Fanny and induce her to marry him. Such an admission might have compromised Stevenson's persona as a rugged traveler renouncing his middle-class life for the hardships of steerage. Harman comments, rather unkindly, that "Stevenson's identification with steerage was snobbism, too, but inverted. . . . They [the ladies and gentlemen from first-class to whom Stevenson objected] were class-tourists but he was a class-imposter, traveling rough to make a book of its novelty" (*Robert Louis Stevenson,* 172). Harman seems to forget that Stevenson had left his parents without notifying them—parents on whom he was still dependent for his income and the comforts of his middle-class life.

32. McLynn, *Robert Louis Stevenson,* 82. McLynn comments that notwithstanding Stevenson's pleasure at being elected to the club, "the real magnet in London continued to be Fanny Sitwell" (82). However, Sitwell and Colvin were always associated in Stevenson's mind, and Colvin had sponsored his election to the Savile.

33. Stevenson, *Strange Case,* 12. In this regard, Hyde is like a waste product or excrement that is discharged by Jekyll's bourgeois identity and cannot be contained

by it. This is furthered by descriptions of Hyde as "not only hellish but inorganic . . . the slime of the pit . . . the amorphous dust . . . what was dead, and had no shape, should usurp the offices of life" (*Strange Case,* 72). The "offices of life" relate to the genitalia as the site of reproductive sexuality, whereas the anus usurps these as a zone of pleasure, a pleasure that is associated (through nonreproductive sterility) with death. For an examination of the cultural interconnections between the anus and death, see Bersani, "Is the Rectum a Grave?"

34. *Strange Case,* 61, 59.

35. *Strange Case,* 64, 63.

36. *Strange Case,* 60, 61, 64.

37. *Strange Case,* 62.

38. *Strange Case,* 59.

39. Initially representing Modestine as a substitute for Fanny, a desired woman, Stevenson transforms her with Jekyll-like rapidity into Fanny's opposite, the "ever memorable BEAST" (*Travels with a Donkey,* 150), who is finally exposed as "a common wolf, and even small for that" (150), mirroring Modestine's diminutive state. Similarly, Hyde appears diminished in death, "dressed in clothes far too large for him, clothes of the doctor's bigness" (*Strange Case,* 48).

40. *Strange Case,* 65.

41. *Strange Case,* 67.

42. *Strange Case,* 66.

43. *Strange Case,* 63.

## Chapter 3

1. Said, *Culture and Imperialism,* 58–59 (original emphasis).

2. Stevenson, *Travels with a Donkey,* 230, 122, 230.

3. Daly, *Modernism,* 8–9.

4. Daly, *Modernism,* 21, 22.

5. Daly, *Modernism,* 85.

6. Katz, introduction to *Treasure Island,* xix.

7. Grant Allen's review of *Travels with a Donkey* in the *Fortnightly Review,* cited in Emma Letley, introduction to *Travels with a Donkey,* xiii. Allen pointed to continuities of style between Stevenson's first two works of travel writing: "His *Inland Voyage* struck the keynote of his literary gamut; and the new volume of travel with which he now favours us, has the self-same happy ring, the self-same light and graceful

touch, as if Mr Stevenson were rather a Frenchman born out of due place, than a Scotsman of the Scots" (xii–xiii).

8. Stevenson, "My First Book," 277 (emphasis added). Subsequent references will be cited parenthetically in the text.

9. Maixner, *Critical Heritage,* 8.

10. The word "success" buried within "succession" not only balances the "defeats" but also anticipates the eventual success that this succession would produce. The early abortive fictional efforts can thus be recuperated as early steps on this eventually remunerative path of novel writing, their ineptitude redeemed by the ultimately successful "first novel" that Stevenson claimed he "was bound to write." The definition of *defeat,* however, had by 1894 come to take on an exclusively economic dimension—in hindsight, Stevenson's "little books" were failures in his mind because he made no money from them. He relates that he suffered from "the futility . . . that I should spend a man's energy upon this business, and yet could not earn a livelihood" (Stevenson, "My First Book," 277).

11. Both the character and the characters of the book were thus foreseen by Stevenson. Lloyd Osbourne's account of this episode differs significantly from Stevenson's, as Katz points out: "Osbourne claims that on that afternoon when RLS joined him, he was already painting the map of an island he had drawn. It was the imagination of his stepfather, however, that created 'the thrill of "Skeleton Island, Spy-Glass Hill"'" (Katz, introduction to *Treasure Island,* xxiv).

12. Stevenson, *Letters,* 3:229.

13. Japp wrote his own account of the episode in which he emphasizes his role in bringing Stevenson's text to the attention of a profitable juvenile audience: "When I left Braemar, I carried with me a considerable portion of the MS. of *Treasure Island,* with an outline of the rest of the story. It originally bore the odd title of *The Sea-Cook,* and . . . I showed it to Mr Henderson, the proprietor of the *Young Folks' Paper,* who came to an arrangement with Mr Stevenson, and the story duly appeared in its pages, as well as the two which succeeded it." Alexander H. Japp, *Robert Louis Stevenson: A Record, an Estimate, and a Memorial* (London: T. Werner Laurie, 1905), 15.

14. N. N. Feltes, *Modes of Production of Victorian Novels* (Chicago: University of Chicago Press, 1986), 9–10. In this context, the dispute between versions of the composition of *Treasure Island,* as surveyed by Katz, is especially interesting insofar as it touches on the issue of whether Stevenson was self-consciously—or rather, calculatedly—producing a text for consumption by an audience of children, specifically

the readers of *Young Folks.* Katz states that the editor of the journal later claimed that its owner, James Henderson, "gave RLS copies of YF in which a serial entitled 'Billy Bo's'n' by Charles E. Pearse was then running and from which, Leighton alleges, RLS was able to get certain suggestions for TI" (Katz, introduction to *Treasure Island,* xxiv). However, both Henderson and Alexander Japp, who acted as an intermediary between author and publisher, "categorically denie[d] that Henderson primed RLS with material indicating what he wanted" (xxiv).

15. Feltes, *Modes of Production,* 9, 64.

16. Daly, *Modernism,* 53, 60, 89.

17. Daly, *Modernism,* 118.

18. James, "Robert Louis Stevenson," in Edel, ed., *Literary Criticism,* 1236. It is interesting to see how James changed his opinion on this matter: in his earlier "The Art of Fiction" (1884), he appeared to refuse to participate in this "game" of treasure hunting (see my discussion below). If Stevenson had converted James to the juvenile adventure story, is it a coincidence, one wonders, that the title of James's autobiography is *A Small Boy and Others*?

19. Stevenson, *An Inland Voyage,* in *Travels with a Donkey,* 6. Subsequent references will be cited parenthetically in the text. Lloyd Osbourne recalled first meeting Stevenson as a traveler in France, one who was defined by his romantic mode of transport: "[W]e all trooped down to the riverside to see the *Cigarette* and the *Arethusa*—the two canoes that had just finished the 'Inland Voyage'—the stranger allowed me to sit in his, and even went to the trouble of setting up the little masts and sails for my amusement" (Osbourne, *Intimate Portrait,* 1). Osbourne would also emphasize Stevenson's affinity for France, stating that "the time he spent in Hyeres was the happiest in his life" (45) and concluding that "it was a mistake he ever left Hyeres; it was so entirely congenial and suited him so well" (49). Of course, Lloyd's connection with Stevenson was the result of Stevenson's controversial relationship with Lloyd's mother, Fanny Osbourne; hence, it is interesting to discover Lloyd's opinion that what Stevenson "praised most in the French as a national trait was their universal indulgence towards all sexual problems—their clear-sighted toleration of everything affecting the relations of men and women. He often said that in this the French were the most civilized people in Europe." Osbourne, cited in Nicholas Rankin, *Dead Man's Chest: Travels after Robert Louis Stevenson* (London: Phoenix, 2001), 86.

20. Robert Louis Stevenson, *The Silverado Squatters* (San Francisco: Mercury House, 1996), 20.

21. For a richly detailed account of the Stevenson family's role in building lighthouses at some of the most inaccessible points of the Scottish coast, see Bella Bathurst, *The Lighthouse Stevensons* (London: Flamingo, 2000). Bathurst argues, deploying a commercial image, that "Louis alchemised his experiences around the ragged coasts of the north into the gold of his best fiction. *Treasure Island* and *Kidnapped* both contain salvaged traces of his early career. The further he grew away from engineering, the more he felt towards it" (xiv).

22. For an overview of the critical reception of *An Inland Voyage,* see Letley, introduction to *Travels with a Donkey,* xii–xviii.

23. Indeed, Stevenson soon abandoned any pretense of civilized decorum as, suffering from the misadventure of being refused a lodging under suspicion of vagrancy, he wrote with feeling of being an outcast: "Six hours of police surveillance . . . or one brutal rejection from an inn-door change your views upon the subject. . . . I will give most respectable men a fortnight of such a life, and then I will offer them twopence for what remains of their morality" (*An Inland Voyage,* 73).

24. Stevenson makes the analogy between architect and author—one that would resonate throughout his career—in the preface to the first edition of *An Inland Voyage.* See *An Inland Voyage,* 3–4.

25. Maixner, *Critical Heritage,* 52, 54, 53, 51, 56, 9.

26. Letley, introduction to *Travels with a Donkey,* xii.

27. Stevenson, *Letters,* 2:313.

28. Maixner, *Critical Heritage,* 64. Thomas informed Louis that the account of his voyage by ship and train from Edinburgh to California was unworthy of him and paid £100 to have the manuscript withdrawn from the publisher. See McLynn, *Robert Louis Stevenson,* 197–98.

29. Maixner, *Critical Heritage,* 66. In a similar vein, the reviewer for *Fraser's* commented acerbically on Stevenson's voluntary encounter with adversity: "[H]e is at the same time, we presume, one of those darlings of fortune, who, having no natural hardships of their own, find a piquant gratification in inventing a few artificial ones, that they may know how it feels to be weary, and cold, and footsore, and belated, with the option at any moment of returning to their ordinary life" (67). Perhaps the most telling criticism was this reviewer's "doubt . . . as to whether the graceful art of writing about nothing will suffice to build a great and permanent reputation upon." A review in *The Spectator* pointed to a lack of substance, and especially a lack of incident, in the narrative: "Seldom has any book of the kind

been woven out of slighter materials. No adventures happened to our traveler, no exciting incidents fell to his lot. His journeying was as peaceful as the country he traveled over" (72).

30. Robert Louis Stevenson, "A Gossip on Romance," in Treglown, ed., *The Lantern-Bearers,* 175.

31. Daly, *Modernism,* 90, 19.

32. H. Rider Haggard, *King Solomon's Mines* (London: Cassell, 1887), 1. In the frontispiece of this edition of the novel, Cassell advertises its leading works of fiction ("Price 5s. each") the first three of which are *King Solomon's Mines, Kidnapped,* and *Treasure Island.* This is an apt illustration of the commercial viability of Stevenson's and Haggard's names in the late-Victorian marketplace.

33. Stevenson, "A Gossip on Romance," 172.

34. Stevenson, *Treasure Island,* 31. Subsequent references will be cited parenthetically in the text.

35. Stevenson, "A Gossip on Romance," 174.

36. Significantly, the map did not appear in the serial version of *Treasure Island* in *Young Folks.* In addition, Stevenson used a nom de plume, Captain George North, in the serial version. Hence, Stevenson's name as author and the map belong together as guarantors of the commodity-text.

37. Maixner, *Critical Heritage,* 142. So important was the map in thus addressing the adult reader as boy that when H. Rider Haggard wrote *King Solomon's Mines* in 1885—a work he produced in direct competition with *Treasure Island* and one that was also published by Cassell—he also included a map leading to the treasure, in this case the diamond mines of King Solomon (*King Solomon's Mines,* 27). Like the map in *Treasure Island,* King Solomon's map is concealed in pouches and is identified as a secret document. Where Stevenson has the three crosses indicating the treasure drawn in red ink, Haggard goes a step further, describing the map as "drawn by the dying hand of the old Dom [Jose Da Silvestra] with his blood for ink" (29). Both maps thus illustrate what Benedict Anderson terms the "pink red dye of the British Colonies." Benedict Anderson, *Imagined Communities: Reflections on the Origin and Spread of Nationalism,* rev. ed. (London: Verso, 1991), 175. Thus the human cost of the treasure, as well as the imperial pretensions of the journey, is made manifest from the outset of Haggard's narrative. The original edition, moreover, included a large map folded into the front cover, with the caption "Fac-simile of the Map of Route to King Solomon's Mines, Now in the Possession of Allan Quatermain, Esq, Drawn by the Dom Jose Da Silvestra, in his Own Blood, Upon

a Fragment of Linen, in the Year 1590" (*King Solomon's Mines*). The facsimile reproduces the red color of the map's script.

38. Martin Green, *Dreams of Adventure, Deeds of Empire* (New York: Basic, 1979), 228.

39. Daly, *Modernism*, 21, 27.

40. Sutherland, *Stanford Companion*, 79.

41. Jacqueline Rose, *The Case of Peter Pan, or the Impossibility of Children's Fiction* (Philadelphia: University of Pennsylvania Press, 1993), 105, 106, 88, 87. In light of this argument, N. N. Feltes's observation that "[t]he writer's work was produced in a journal within relations of production analogous to those prevailing in a textile mill" (*Modes of Production*, 63), which Daly characterizes as "gloomy" (*Modernism*, 21), invokes the specter of child labor, the exploitation of childhood for commercial profit.

42. Maixner, *Critical Heritage*, 131, 132.

43. Stevenson, "A Gossip on Romance," 173.

44. Ashcroft, Griffiths, and Tiffin, *Post-Colonial Studies*, 31–32.

45. Green, *Dreams of Adventure*, 3.

46. Stevenson, *The Silverado Squatters*, 29.

47. Anderson, *Imagined Communities*, 163, 173.

48. Anderson, *Imagined Communities*, 175.

49. It is certainly true that, after the disappearance of Jim's mother at the beginning of part 2, *Treasure Island* contains no significant female characters. What seems buried here, however, is an allusion in this opening portrait of the mother to Fanny Stevenson, the mother of Lloyd, the "boy at hand." Stevenson previously referred to Fanny as a collaborator on "a joint volume of bogey stories," which was also discarded from the literary lineage that Stevenson constructs in "My First Book." Rather, the limelight there is given to a different kind of collaboration, one with his stepson, Lloyd.

50. Koestenbaum, "Shadow on the Bed," 32–33. As Koestenbaum writes, "Male writers revered Stevenson's 'books for boys' because they omitted women. Henry James, in particular, celebrated the absence of women from Stevenson's fiction" and claimed that Stevenson had "given to the world the romance of boyhood" (36).

51. In his avowed preference for the techniques of romance—such as the emphasis on incident and adventure and the secondary role played by character—Stevenson sought to reanimate the corpse of Victorian realism by unshackling the novel from the burden of the heterosexual romance and projecting it on an incom-

plete journey founded on male camaraderie and action. Such reanimation was seized on by critics such as Henry James, who praised "the delightful story of Treasure Island" (James, "The Art of Fiction," 209), and Oscar Wilde, who, even while objecting to *The Black Arrow*'s realism ("so inartistic as not to contain a single anachronism"), praises Stevenson as "that delightful master of delicate and fanciful prose" (Wilde, *The Artist as Critic*, 295). That both critics used the word "delightful" in their praise suggests that, for the aesthetic movement to which both Wilde and James adhered, the ultimate value of literature was to be a source of pleasure. The delight that both critics derived from Stevenson was thus the key to his success as a writer, far more so than his occasional forays into realism. That James—whose "Art of Fiction" is one of the classic defenses of literary realism—was a capacious enough critic to admire Stevenson's gifts is a testament to the power of romance to appeal to "boys of all ages."

52. Maixner, *Critical Heritage*, 132, 138.

53. Henry James, "The Art of Fiction," in *Victorian Criticism*, 209.

54. Stevenson, "A Humble Remonstrance," in *Victorian Criticism*, 218–19.

55. Stevenson, *An Inland Voyage*, 3.

56. Thus, although "A Humble Remonstrance" is ostensibly a defense of the art of romance against the superior aesthetic claims of Jamesian realism, this aesthetic difference reveals Stevenson's practice of tailoring his literary output to the demands of a popular and profitable audience of boys. Fiction, Stevenson insists in response to James' now-famous phrase, should not try to "compete with life" but rather should be selective, with the duty of artists being to "turn away their eyes from the gross, coloured and mobile nature at our feet, and regard instead a certain figmentary abstraction" ("A Humble Remonstrance," 216).

57. Green, *Dreams of Adventure*, 228.

58. Recognizing a certain overlapping in *Treasure Island* between morality and adventure, Rose disputes the view that the story is "a major breakthrough against the earlier moral and ideological constraint" of children's fiction (Rose, *Case of Peter Pan*, 79). The breakthrough of *Treasure Island* is, she claims, a technical one, involving the adaptation of travel writing for a reader interested in "colonialist venture" (80). Thus, she notes, "*Treasure Island* is remarkable for the way it perfects this form for the child reader" and "conceals the slide between nature study and suspense. In this sense, verisimilitude is no more than a way of closing the reader's eyes to the mechanisms of the book by dissolving what is in fact a very sophisticated writing strategy into the objects of the visible world" (80). Rose's only error is to be

overly literal in identifying the implicitly naive "child reader" as the target of this technique.

59. Stevenson, "Note on Realism," 267.

60. There is surely a play on words here that suggests the actual location of the treasure: "gone" echoes "Gunn," in whose cave the money now resides.

61. Stevenson, *Letters,* 3:224.

62. Green, *Dreams of Adventure,* 228.

63. Stevenson, *Letters,* 3:229.

64. Stevenson, "A Humble Remonstrance," 219.

65. Green, *Dreams of Adventure,* 228.

66. Interestingly, Japp portrays Osbourne as "Stevenson's trusted companion and collaborator—clearly with a touch of genius," emphasizing *Treasure Island* as a collaborative venture (Japp, *Robert Louis Stevenson,* 11).

67. Maixner, *Critical Heritage,* 128.

68. Stevenson, *Letters,* 3:229; 4:119, 120.

69. Maixner, *Critical Heritage,* 142, 6.

70. Stevenson, *Letters,* 5:171. In this letter to Edmund Gosse, dated January 2, 1886, Stevenson writes antagonistically of the public, asserting that they "are shamed into silence or affection. I do not write for the public; I do write for money, a nobler deity" (171).

71. Maixner, *Critical Heritage,* 139.

72. Daly, *Modernism,* 22.

73. Maixner, *Critical Heritage,* 141.

## Chapter 4

1. Stevenson, *Letters,* 5:89–90.

2. Barry Menikoff, editor's preface to *Kidnapped, or the Lad with the Silver Button,* by Robert Louis Stevenson (New York: Modern Library, 2001), xxxiii.

3. Menikoff, *Narrating Scotland,* 48.

4. Menikoff, *Narrating Scotland,* 29, 47.

5. Stevenson, "My First Book," 281.

6. In addition to the problems with *Treasure Island,* several of Stevenson's later novels, such as *The Master of Ballantrae* and *The Ebb-Tide,* proved even more resistant to closure (see chapters 1 and 8 for discussions of problems of closure with *The Master* and *The Ebb-Tide,* respectively).

7. Stevenson gave permission both for the change of title to *Catriona* and to the publication of a two-volume edition of both novels under the general title *The Adventures of David Balfour.* He stipulated to Colvin, "About *David Balfour* in two volumes: do see that they make it a decent looking book" (*Letters,* 8:187). It was published posthumously in 1895. A further complication is produced by the division of *Catriona* into two parts, "The Lord Advocate" and "Father and Daughter," which suggests another narrative break and change of focus, signaled by a change of location (the first part is set in Scotland, while the second is set in Holland).

8. Robert Louis Stevenson, *Catriona* (London: Cassell, 1893), v. In chapter 6, I discuss the sequel, *David Balfour/Catriona,* as a product of Stevenson's ambitious voyage to the South Seas. The political landscape of Samoa, I argue there, dramatically reshaped the conclusion of a narrative that he had deferred for seven years. Yet the duality of the sequel's title—*Catriona* and *David Balfour*—only added to the sense that David, like another of Stevenson's protagonists who debuted in 1886, was "not truly one, but truly two" (Stevenson, *Strange Case,* 59).

9. Stevenson, *Letters,* 5:94. His confidence remained into 1886, as a letter to his father in January indicates: "I think David is on his feet, and (to my mind) a far better story and far sounder at heart than *Treasure Island*" (5:182).

10. Stevenson, *Letters,* 5:186. The reviews of the novel detected a similar duality, repeating Stevenson's tendency to think of the narrative in two parts. However, the hierarchy between the two portions was reversed: Theodore Watts-Duncan, for example, claimed that "the story passes through two stages" and argued that "of *Kidnapped* the Highland portions alone are imagined" (5:313–14n). Stevenson responded by claiming the economic pressure to publish: "[T]here was the cursed beginning, and a cursed end must be appended. . . . So it had to go into the world, one part . . . alive, one part mere galvanized" (5:313–14).

11. Menikoff, *Narrating Scotland,* 27.

12. Stevenson, *Letters,* 5:214, 249. He added later the same month, "I keep grinding out David at the rate of a page a day, with the least conceivable pleasure; but he's got to be ground out" (5:215). In early May, he wrote to Henley that his novel was "advancing at the rate of less than a page a day; this with infinite labour and poor results as to merit" (5:248).

13. Stevenson, *Letters,* 5:187, 255. Elaborating on this point, Stevenson wrote to his father on May 23, "I had to give up *David Balfour,* but by Colvin's suggestion, left the end for a sequel, which, if the first part is successful, I should be able to do with both pleasure and effect" (5:256–57).

14. Robert Louis Stevenson, *Kidnapped, or The Lad with the Silver Button,* ed. Barry Menikoff (New York: Modern Library, 2001), 277. Subsequent references to this edition will be cited parenthetically as *Kidnapped.* The postscript occupies a kind of narrative no-man's land: it is neither part of what Fredric Jameson terms the central fiction of a "concrete social situation" (Jameson, *Political Unconscious,* 220)—that is, it is not "spoken" by David—nor is it an authorial intervention. Rather, it is an utterance by the "editor" of the work, who mediates between David (as narrator of his story) and the public (which consumes it), and thus plays a role closer to an agent, representing his client's interests in negotiating with the public. This postscript appeared in the 1886 edition but not in the Edinburgh edition of the novel—presumably because it advertised too flagrantly the novel's incompletion and dependence on a supplement.

15. Stevenson referred elsewhere to violence against his texts, but it was usually described as being perpetrated by others. For example, he wrote to J. M. Barrie in 1892 about "a little tale of mine, the slashed and gaping ruins of which appeared recently in the *Illustrated London News*" (*Letters,* 7:413). In referring to his South Seas letters—which were drawn from material that he hoped to use for a "big book" on the South Seas—Stevenson wrote to Henry James of the pain he suffered "seeing the most finely finished portions of my work come part by part in pieces" (7:66). Here it is as though the material were fragmenting itself: a process of textual decomposing, as it were.

16. Jameson, *Political Unconscious,* 53, 221.

17. Jameson, *Political Unconscious,* 59. One might speculate how far this suppression of ideological conflict is a function of the novel's original place of publication: in the pages of *Young Folks,* a magazine for boys. Jerome McGann reminds us of the importance of the material conditions of a text's publication, noting that "serial publication of one kind of another was the rule. . . . Writers worked within those particular sets of circulatory conventions . . . and the literary results—the books issued—are coded for meaning accordingly." Jerome J. McGann, *The Textual Condition* (Princeton, NJ: Princeton University Press, 1991), 81.

18. Jameson, *Political Unconscious,* 206, 210.

19. Joseph Conrad, *Lord Jim* (New York: Oxford University Press, 2000), 5.

20. Daly, *Modernism,* 9.

21. For example, Conrad sets the scene of Marlow's narration as follows: "Perhaps it would be after dinner, on a verandah draped in motionless foliage and crowned with flowers, in the deep dusk speckled by fiery cigar-ends. The elongated

bulk of each cane-chair harboured a silent listener. Now and then a small red glow would move abruptly, and expanding light up the fingers of a languid hand, part of a face in profound repose" (Conrad, *Lord Jim,* 24–25).

22. Jameson, *Political Unconscious,* 219, 220.

23. Menikoff, *Narrating Scotland,* 125.

24. Eric Hobsbawm, *The Age of Empire: 1875–1914* (New York: Vintage, 1989), 9.

25. Daly, *Modernism,* 36.

26. Jameson, *Political Unconscious,* 220.

27. Menikoff, *Narrating Scotland,* 32.

28. Stevenson, "My First Book," 282.

29. Stevenson, *Travels with a Donkey,* 163.

30. Robert Louis Stevenson, *Kidnapped and Catriona,* ed. Emma Letley (New York: Oxford University Press, 1986), 210. This map did not appear in the first U.K. edition of *Catriona* (published by Cassell in 1893), which instead included text entitled "Summary of the Earlier Adventures of David Balfour as Set Forth in *Kidnapped*" to offer a narrative link with the earlier novel.

31. Significantly, given this Scott-influenced historical context, Stevenson refers to David's "acquaintance with . . . the sons of the notorious *Rob Roy*" in his early description of *Kidnapped* to Henley (*Letters,* 5:89).

32. Early reviews of the latter novel tended to view *Kidnapped* and *David Balfour (Catriona)* as a single work, as was the case with Arthur Quiller-Couch's review in the *Speaker,* entitled "First Thoughts on *Catriona.*" He considered the two works together "a very big feat—a gay and gallant tale" (Stevenson, *Letters,* 8:187n). This union of the novels is continued in modern times by their publication in a single volume as part of the Oxford World's Classics series.

33. Stevenson, "A Gossip on Romance," 176, 173. In this essay, Stevenson famously refers to the characters in romance as "no more than puppets. . . . The bony fist of the showman visibly propels them; their springs are an open secret" (178), a description that aptly fits David Balfour, whose strings are flagrantly manipulated by others.

34. Stevenson, *Treasure Island,* 11, 208, 33.

35. Though David does not marry Alan, Alan does eventually bring about David's marriage to someone else. As John Sutherland remarks of David Balfour's eventual union with Catriona, "the match is finally brought about by the vigorous intervention of Alan Breck" (Sutherland, *Stanford Guide,* 352), and this intervention results in the marriage as the means of narrative closure.

36. For an account of the influence of the Labouchère Amendment on Stevenson's fiction, in particular *Strange Case of Dr. Jekyll and Mr. Hyde,* see Koestenbaum, "Shadow on the Bed."

37. Daly, *Modernism,* 62.

38. Stevenson, "Walt Whitman," in *The Lantern-Bearers,* 78.

39. Stevenson, "Walt Whitman," 79.

40. Stevenson, "Walt Whitman," 79, 85, 86.

41. Stevenson, *Strange Case,* 38, 39.

42. James, "Robert Louis Stevenson," in Edel, ed., *Literary Criticism,* 1233, 1236, 1237.

43. James, "Robert Louis Stevenson," 1238, 1239, 1247, 1243.

44. Stevenson, *Letters,* 7:284.

45. James, "Robert Louis Stevenson," 1244, 1254.

46. James, "Robert Louis Stevenson," 1254.

47. James, "Robert Louis Stevenson," 1253.

48. Stevenson, "Walt Whitman," 73.

49. Stephen Arata, "Observing *The Wrecker,*" plenary paper delivered at the 2nd Biennial International Conference on Stevenson, "Stevenson and Conrad: Writers of Land and Sea," Edinburgh, Scotland (July 7–9, 2004).

50. Stevenson, *Silverado Squatters,* 29; James, "Robert Louis Stevenson," 1254.

51. Stevenson, "A Gossip on Romance," 175.

52. Stevenson, *Treasure Island,* 208.

53. James, "Robert Louis Stevenson," 1248.

54. One can ascribe this reaction of David's to guilt at his good fortune, as compared to that of Alan, who must flee the country as an outlaw. Yet it also registers the impossibility of concluding the narrative in the absence of its chief driving force. Ironically, Alan has taken a false name—Mr. Thomson—with the aim of concealing his identity from the authorities. Yet David's status as "Mr. Betwixt-and-Between" is what proves the shipwreck of the novel, which can conclude only with his "drifting to the very doors of the British Linen Company's bank" (*Kidnapped,* 277). The shipwreck of the *Covenant* is of course an earlier point at which the novel dramatically changes course.

55. James, "Robert Louis Stevenson," 1242.

56. The dialog between Alan and David is an example of what Bakhtin terms the "double-voicedness" of the novel, which "makes its presence felt by the novelist in the living heteroglossia of language, and in the multi-languagedness surrounding and nourishing his own consciousness" (*Dialogic Imagination,* 326–27). More broadly,

Bakhtin defines the novel as "a diversity of social speech types (sometimes even diversity of languages) and a diversity of individual voices, artistically organized" (262). Through the juxtaposition of these voices, the novel achieves "its dialogization . . . the basic distinguishing feature of the stylistics of the novel" (263). Hence, David's voice as narrator is dependent on Alan's Highland speech for the "novelization" and "combination of its styles" (262).

57. Stevenson, *Letters,* 8:38. Stevenson then termed the novel "a very pretty piece of workmanship" (8:38).

## Chapter 5

1. Edmund Gosse, cited in McLynn, *Robert Louis Stevenson,* 408.

2. Stevenson, letter to Will Low, *Letters,* 8:235. To his chief confidant, Sidney Colvin, Stevenson expressed regrets in a still franker manner: "Were it not for my health, which made it impossible, I could not find it in my heart to forgive myself that I did not stick to an honest, commonplace trade, when I was young, which might have now supported me during these ill years" (8:371). Stevenson added, "I cannot take myself seriously as an artist; the limitations are so obvious. I did take myself seriously as a workman of old, but my practice has fallen off. I am now an idler and cumberer of the ground" (8:372).

3. McLynn, *Robert Louis Stevenson,* 313.

4. For Gosse's phrase about London's "literary atmosphere," see above. Stevenson often described the South Sea Islands as attractive precisely because they were conducive to leisure and possessed a salubrious climate. In the first of his South Seas letters, Stevenson portrays himself as an invalid in search of health: "For nearly ten years my health had been declining; and for some while before I set forth upon my voyage, I believed I was come to the afterpiece of life and had only the nurse and undertaker to expect. It was suggested that I should try the South Seas." *ISS,* 5.

5. Stevenson, *Letters,* 6:401.

6. Johnstone, *Recollections,* 103.

7. Stevenson, *Letters,* 6:388. Stevenson's linking of cruising with happiness and well-being echoes that of his grandfather, Robert Stevenson, who looked forward to his annual cruise of the Scottish lighthouses, which became the highlight of his life and key to staying alive. When Robert was finally prohibited from taking the cruise, in old age, his death soon followed.

8. In a letter to James, Stevenson refuted his English critics, claiming that "my exile to the place of schooners and islands can be in no sense regarded as a calamity" (*Letters,* 6:403). He also gave a powerful account of cruising as an end in itself, pursued for pleasure: "The sea, islands, the islanders, the island life and climate, make and keep me truly happier. These last two years I have been much at sea, and I have *never wearied,* sometimes I have indeed grown impatient for some destination; more often I was sorry that the voyage drew so early to an end" (6:403; original emphasis).

9. Stevenson, *Letters,* 6:192n, 256. In the frontispiece of his private copy of the 1890 *South Seas* edition, Will H. Low wrote, "This copy was given me by S. S. McClure, whose generous scale of payment for the series of letters ($10000) enabled Stevenson to make the voyage. It served for the first publication of the letters through a newspaper syndicate" (copy in the Huntington Library, HM 285157). Low's note goes on to observe that Stevenson's material was in fact suppressed: "[I]t is significant that in the table of contents two of the letters (chapters) are marked for suppression, making their number not fifteen but fourteen."

10. Samuel McClure to Robert Louis Stevenson, March 9, 1889, Balfour Papers, MS 9891, 21–23.

11. McLynn, *Robert Louis Stevenson,* 329, 406. It should be pointed out that the title *In the South Seas* was not used during the serial publication of the letters or in the 1890 copyright edition. Rather, the title was adopted (and the preposition added) for the 1896 Edinburgh edition, edited by Colvin and published after Stevenson's death. Hence, McLynn's reference to the "*In the South Seas* letters" is misleading, as the full title was not used until after Stevenson's death.

12. Stevenson, *Letters,* 7:157n. Stevenson angrily responded by rejecting Colvin's request for more details of his journeys: "A man upwards of forty cannot waste his time in communicating matter of that degree of indifference. The Letters, it appears, are tedious; by God, they would be more tedious still if I wasted my time upon such infantile and sucking-bottle details" (*Letters,* 7:157). Interestingly, Stevenson went on to suggest that a map—the uses of which he had discovered with Treasure Island—might solve certain problems of narration that he encountered in *In the South Seas:* "O, Colvin! Suppose it had made a book, all such information is given to one glance of an eye by a map with a little dotted line upon it" (7:157).

13. By contrast, the letters as they appeared in *Black and White* in London were subtitled "A Record of Three Cruises," suggesting a documentary purpose and organized itinerary, as opposed to the leisurely traveler of the *New York Sun.* This

documentary quality to the letters was also enhanced by the high-quality, almost photographic illustrations in *Black and White*, which reinforced the literary realism of the text with a visual realism. The illustrations in the *Sun* were more sketchlike.

14. Indeed, Stevenson shared some of his critics' opinions that his South Seas letters, in their serial form, were unsatisfactory—being the result of a professional duty rather than a literary pleasure. As he wrote to his mother in January 1891, "I believe the grisly Letters have begun; the cart is at my heels; but I have a good start. . . . I have now sent, as well as I remember twenty-seven, or one more than the half, and the year of publication began only yesterday" (*Letters*, 7:68–69).

15. Henry James, cited in Stevenson, *ISS*, xxi. As Gosse later pointed out (in his introduction to the Pentland edition of *In the South Seas*), the subtitle of this copyright edition promised "a record of three cruises," whereas the volume only actually delivered a record of one: the cruise of the *Casco* through the Marquesas.

16. A second part of the journal, which deals with Samoa and formed the basis for *A Footnote to History* (1892), is in the collection of the Beinecke Library at Yale University.

17. Gosse's assertion that Stevenson had only begun to write the South Seas letters while cruising on the *Janet Nicoll*, from Sydney to Apia, apparently takes its cue from the opening chapter of *The South Seas* (1890), entitled "An Island Landfall," in which Stevenson writes, "I *begin to prepare these pages* at sea on a third cruise, in the trading steamer *Janet Nicoll.* If more days are granted me, they shall be passed where I have found life most pleasant and man most interesting" (emphasis added). Stevenson, *The South Seas: A Record of Three Cruises* (London: Cassell, 1890), 2. Stevenson's use of the present tense suggests that he was in the process of arranging the volume while writing the introduction. More to the point, it suggests that he was cruising while writing at the same time. In the 1896 Edinburgh edition, also used as the basis for the Scribner's U.S. edition and the modern Penguin edition, the present tense is dropped and the introduction reads, "I began to prepare these pages at sea, on a third cruise, in the trading steamer *Janet Nicoll*" (*ISS*, 2). This indeed seems to support Gosse's interpretation that the pages were written during the *Janet Nicoll* cruise. What is clear, in any case, is that the journal Stevenson kept during the cruises of the *Casco* and the *Equator*—a journal of 242 manuscript pages in the Huntington Library—formed the quarry of materials from which he would draw both his letters and his South Seas stories. Indeed, this journal follows the same four-part structure as *In the South Seas* and contains many passages that, when rewritten, would form the basis of the work's chapters. Yet there is some further

ambiguity in the phrase "prepare these pages": Gosse apparently took this to mean that Stevenson actually started writing while cruising on the *Janet Nicoll.* A more likely construction, however, is that he began to prepare them for publication—to make revisions and selections from the journal for the purpose of the letters. Given that the printed pages of *The South Seas* (in 1890) formed the proofs for the serial publication in *Black and White* and the *New York Sun* (which did not begin until February 1891), Stevenson had to have been arranging the material (i.e., the dated entries) into chapters before he formed them into letters. Additionally, the serialized letters would follow the structure of the volume, with each "letter" comprising one or two chapters.

18. Stevenson to Samuel McClure, July 19, 1890, Balfour Papers, MS 9891 (emphasis added).

19. Stevenson to Samuel McClure, Balfour Papers. Ironically, as Low notes, while some chapters from the 1890 edition were indeed "marked for suppression" and never appeared in serial form, Stevenson himself suppressed a significant portion of the material from his plans for the published book.

20. Stevenson to Samuel McClure, Balfour Papers.

21. Stevenson, *Letters,* 7:65–66.

22. McClure, unsurprisingly, was dejected when the "letters" began to appear on his desk and he discovered that "the letters did not come as letters are supposed to come. They were not a correspondence from the South Seas, they were not dated and . . . in no way did the matter . . . fulfil [*sic*] the definition of the word 'letter,' as used in newspaper correspondence" (McClure, cited in Stevenson, *ISS,* xx–xxi).

23. Robert Irwin Hillier, *The South Seas Fiction of Robert Louis Stevenson* (New York: Peter Lang, 1989), 34.

24. Stevenson, *Letters,* 7:115 (emphasis added).

25. Stevenson, *Letters,* 6:312. In November 1890, Stevenson revealed more about his actual intentions to Colvin: "I have got in a better vein with the South Sea book as I think you will see: I think these chapters will do for the volume without much change" (7:21).

26. McLynn, *Robert Louis Stevenson,* 329.

27. Stevenson, "My First Book," 277.

28. Stevenson, "The South Seas: A Record of Three Cruises," *Black and White: A Weekly Illustrated Record and Review* [London], February 6–December 19, 1891. Stevenson 1083, Beinecke Library.

29. Stevenson, *Letters,* 6:256.

30. Green, *Dreams of Adventure,* 228.

31. Robert Louis Stevenson, *Memories and Portraits* (New York: Scribner's, 1898), 120.

32. Stevenson recalled the transformation of the island between his first and second visits, witnessing a process that might now be viewed as less a process of "civilization" than of "colonization," involving stripping the island of its natural resources: "[T]here was now a pier of stone, there were rows of sheds, railways, traveling-cranes, a street of cottages, an iron house for the resident engineer, wooden bothies for the men, a stage where the courses of the tower were put together experimentally, and behind the settlement a great gash in the hillside where granite was quarried" (*Memories and Portraits,* 124–25).

33. Smith, *Literary Culture,* 117.

34. Smith, *Literary Culture,* 22.

35. Barthes, *Pleasure of the Text,* 4.

36. Stevenson, *SST,* 3. There is an ongoing tension in Stevenson's South Seas writing between the pleasure and sensual stimulation of cruising—allowing for a distant and superficial or partial perception of the beauty of sea and islands—and the realities of labor, disease, exploitation, and conflict that descend on the cruiser when s/he disembarks and settles. In part, this tension results from the contrast between myths and stereotypes of South Sea islanders as peace-loving "children" and the reality of civil war taking place on Samoa.

37. Fanny Vandegrift Stevenson, *Cruise of the "Janet Nichol"* (London: Chatto, 1915), 64. The identical U.S. edition was published by Scribner's in 1914. This incident was undoubtedly inspired by Ben Hird's anecdote, recorded by Fanny. However, Stevenson was fascinated by the idea of the living dead throughout his career (see chapter 1). An early story, "The Body Snatcher," features a supposed corpse coming back to life at the end of the story. At the end of the *Master of Ballantrae* (1889), the master is buried alive and returns to life.

38. Hillier, *South Seas Fiction,* 24–25.

39. Smith, *Literary Culture,* 160, 162.

40. McLynn, *Robert Louis Stevenson,* 466, 467.

41. Robert Louis Stevenson, "The Free Island," Balfour Papers, MS 9892, 50–51.

42. Stevenson, "A Pearl Island: Penrhyn." Words in < > are authorial additions to the manuscript; words in { } are authorial deletions from the manuscript. Balfour Papers, MS 9892, 20–21.

43. Fanny Vandegrift Stevenson, *The Cruise of the "Janet Nichol,"* 55, 56.

44. *The Ebb-Tide* was published in 1894 under the joint authorship of Robert Louis Stevenson and Lloyd Osbourne. However, for convenience I shall refer to the novel as by Stevenson for the remainder of this chapter.

45. McLynn, *Robert Louis Stevenson,* 466.

46. Stevenson, "Leprosy on Penrhyn," Balfour Papers, MS 9892, 26. A note in pencil in this typescript states, "Printed in the Swanston Edition of RLS but not previously." This is a reminder that the Penrhyn and Hawaiian chapters were not included in the early editions of *In the South Seas*—partly because Stevenson was dissatisfied with them. A passage from the chapter called "The Lazaretto of To-Day" indicates Stevenson's strong sympathetic response to those suffering from leprosy: "It would be easy in this place to gratify the curiosity of readers, to heap up moving detail, and communicate a lively and erroneous impression. But sometimes that which is the most vivid is merely the commonplace and the external; the significance lies sometimes inconspicuous; and to convey truth it becomes needful to alleviate the colours. The need may arise not only from the nature of the particular subject, but from the existence of a particular bias in the writer, or from both. The lazaretto is beyond question such a subject, and acquaintance with my own infirmities inclines me to believe I am such a writer. The ideas of deformity and living decay have been burthensome to my imagination since the nightmares of childhood; and when I at last beheld, lying athwart the sunrise, the leper promontory and the bare town of Kalaupapa—when the first boat set forth laden with patients—when it was my turn to follow in the second, seated by two sisters on the way to their brave employment—when we drew near the landing stairs and saw them thronged with the dishonoured images of god—honour and cowardice worked in the marrow of my bones" ("The Lazaretto of To-Day," Balfour Papers, MS 9892, 33). It is striking that Stevenson refers to the lepers as "images of god," suggesting not only the presence of divine will in such figures of suffering but also the transformation of the leprous body into the figurehead.

47. McLynn, *Robert Louis Stevenson,* 467.

48. Rennie, introduction to *ISS,* xxx.

49. Ironically, the section of *The South Seas* dealing with Apemama gained more influential admirers than any other portion of the narrative, as a typescript note in the original manuscript of 'The King of Apemama' (held in the Beinecke Library, MS Vault 6433) indicates: "In Sidney Colvin's editorial note to the Edinburgh Edition of *The South Seas,* he says that The King of Apemama was one of the two parts of the work that Stevenson himself liked best; and in his *Memories and Notes* he adds:

'I thought the series of papers afterwards arranged into the volume of *The South Seas* . . . disappointingly lacking in the thrill and romance one expected of him in relating experiences which had realized the dream of his youth. (I ought to mention that a far better qualified judge, Mr Joseph Conrad, differs from me in this, and even prefers *In The South Seas* to *Treasure Island,* principally for the sake of what he regards as a very masterpiece of native portraiture in the character of Tembinok, King of Apemama).'"

50. Smith, *Literary Culture,* 130.

51. Robert Louis Stevenson, "Journal of Two Visits to the South Seas," HM 2412, 229, Huntington Library (subsequently cited as "Journal," HM 2412).

52. Stevenson, "Journal," HM 2412, 229–30.

53. Stevenson, "Journal," HM 2412. Words in < > are authorial additions to the manuscript; words in { } are authorial deletions from the manuscript.

54. Stevenson, "Journal," HM 2412.

55. Smith, *Literary Culture,* 135.

56. Hillier, *South Seas Fiction,* 21.

57. Stevenson, "Journal," HM 2412.

58. Of course, Stevenson had encountered problems with his portrayals of native characters (specifically, Uma in "The Beach of Falesá") because of the prudishness of English editors who objected to the erotic themes of the story. This reaction might have discouraged him from again placing a native South Seas character at the center of one of his fictions.

59. Smith, *Literary Culture,* 62.

60. Robert Louis Stevenson, *In the South Seas,* ed. Sidney Colvin (Edinburgh, 1896), vi.

61. McLynn, *Robert Louis Stevenson,* 329.

62. Stevenson, *Letters,* 6:330; 7:180–81.

63. Stevenson, *Letters,* 7:157.

## Chapter 6

1. Stevenson, *Letters,* 7:412.

2. Colley, *Robert Louis Stevenson,* 4.

3. Stevenson, *Letters,* 7:182. In the background, of course, is the status of the donkey as a beast of burden, whose fate is to carry the load of its owners. A much-maligned animal, "proverbially regarded as the type of clumsiness, ignorance, and

stupidity" (*Shorter OED*), the donkey, as we know, was a significant animal to Stevenson. Stevenson had previously used a similar figure of ambivalence in a letter to Colvin dated October 26, 1891, addressing a dilemma over whether to pursue his "Historia Samoae" or other projects, in the discussion of which he writes, "Buridan's Ass! Whither to go; what to attack" (7:183).

4. The fact that the novel was published under two separate titles inevitably creates the problem of how to refer to the text in this chapter. I have chosen to follow Stevenson's practice of calling the novel *David Balfour,* except in cases where *Catriona* is used as part of a quotation. In March 1892, he wrote to Colvin, "Is it not characteristic of my broken tenacity of mind, that I should have left Davie Balfour some five years in the British Linen Company's office, and then fall on him at last with such vivacity? But I leave you again; the last (fifteenth) chapter ought to be rewrote, or part of it" (*Letters,* 7:246).

5. Robert Louis Stevenson, *Kidnapped and Catriona,* ed. Emma Letley (New York: Oxford University Press, 1986), 208. Subsequent references to this edition, which contains the full texts of both *Kidnapped* and *David Balfour,* are cited parenthetically as *K.*

6. Colley, *Robert Louis Stevenson,* 4.

7. McGann, *Textual Condition,* 13.

8. Menikoff, *Narrating Scotland,* 5.

9. Robert Louis Stevenson, *Catriona* (London: Cassell, 1893), iii (emphasis added). The placement of such materials contributes to what McGann terms the "bibliographical codes" of the text, which, he argues, contain their own "hidden ideological histories" (*Textual Condition,* 85). Equally significant is Stevenson's reminder in the dedication to Baxter of the physical and temporal distance that he has traveled from his Scottish birthplace—"the venerable city which I must always think of as my home" (*K,* 211)—and assertion of continuity with that past. Despite his residence "on these ultimate islands," Stevenson is connected to "the whole stream of lives flowing down there far in the north" (211). Yet his description of having been "cast out . . . in the end" (211) reflects his exile, a severing from his past that the new novel seeks to repair.

10. Jameson, *Political Unconscious,* 249.

11. Jameson, *Political Unconscious,* 251, 250, 220. Crucially, this "depersonalization of the text" is accompanied by alienation between author and audience, "the disappearance from the horizon of its readership, which will become the *public introuvable* of modernism" (*Political Unconscious,* 221). Stevenson referred to his readership

in "My First Book" (1894) as "my paymaster" (*Lantern-Bearers,* 277), specifying a commercial relationship that became increasingly oppressive.

12. Kiely, *Robert Louis Stevenson,* 90.

13. Menikoff, *Narrating Scotland,* 28.

14. Menikoff, *Narrating Scotland,* 3.

15. James, "Robert Louis Stevenson," 1253.

16. Menikoff, *Narrating Scotland,* 206.

17. Colley, *Robert Louis Stevenson,* 4.

18. Stevenson, *Letters,* 7:241.

19. Robert Louis Stevenson, *A Footnote to History: Eight Years of Trouble in Samoa* (Honolulu: University of Hawai'i Press, 1996), xvii. Subsequent references to this edition will be cited parenthetically as *F.*

20. Menikoff points out that Burt's letters were "a wonderful source for Stevenson, providing him with an authentic eyewitness account of life in the Highlands at a particular historical moment" (*Narrating Scotland,* 29) and notes that "David's journey would not have been possible" (32) without them.

21. Jameson, *Political Unconscious,* 53. As "absent cause," history, in Jameson's argument, cannot be directly represented. History is not a text or a narrative, yet it can only be approached in textual form: "Lukacs' conception of totality may here be said to rejoin the Althusserian notion of History or the Real as an 'absent cause.' Totality is not available for representation, any more than it is accessible in the form of some ultimate truth" (*Political Unconscious,* 54–55). However, the presence of "history" in a text is found not in the manifest content but in the text's unconscious, which Jameson defines as "nodal points." The function of the narrative plot is thus to provide an imaginary resolution to real contradictions, "by way of attention to those narrative frames or containment strategies which seek to endow their objects of representation with formal unity" (*Political Unconscious,* 54).

22. One should note here that David's reference to "young folk" invokes the material context in which *Kidnapped* first appeared, the journal *Young Folks.* In so doing, Stevenson establishes a kind of bond with the juvenile reader, which he hopes will carry over to the new venue in which David Balfour appears, the journal *Atlanta.*

23. Roslyn Jolly, "Robert Louis Stevenson and Samoan History: Crossing the Roman Wall," in *Crossing Cultures: Essays on Literature and Culture of the Asia-Pacific,* ed. Bruce Bennett, Jeff Doyle, et al. (London: Skoob, 1996), 113.

24. It is striking that accounts of Stevenson's opposition to European colonialism changed dramatically in tone after the war. Whereas Arthur Johnstone (1905),

for example, saw Stevenson as a defector, a betrayer of white interests in the South Seas, making little distinction between his critique of British versus German colonialism (Johnstone, *Recollections*), Fletcher, writing in 1920, presented Stevenson as prophetic in his opposition to German interference and used *A Footnote* to support Fletcher's claim that Germany's foreign possessions should not be returned. C. Brunsdon Fletcher, *Stevenson's Germany: The Case against Germany in the Pacific* (New York: Scribner's, 1920).

25. Stevenson, *Letters,* 7:241. Stevenson made a corollary between the pleasure he took in writing a work and its aesthetic value: explaining why he did not include *Master of Ballantrae* in his examples of "what I mean by fiction," he stated that it "lacked all pleasureableness, and hence was imperfect in essence" (7:384). Of course, Stevenson might have been referring to the pleasure it provided to readers, but clearly he believed that his pleasure-in-writing translated into both aesthetic merit and pleasure-in-reading.

26. Further emphasizing the dutiful aspect of his history writing, contrasted with the pleasure of fiction, Stevenson indicates, in the above-cited letter, that his preference is to continue working on *David Balfour,* "But I can't I fear; I shall have some belated material arriving by next mail, and must go again at the *History* [i.e., *Footnote*]" (*Letters,* 7:246).

27. Stevenson, *Strange Case,* 59.

28. Hayden White, *The Content of the Form: Narrative Discourse and Historical Representation* (Baltimore, MD: Johns Hopkins University Press, 1987), 20 (emphasis added).

29. White, *Content of the Form,* 21.

30. White, *Content of the Form,* 20, 21. The earliest English meaning of *embarrass* recorded by the *Shorter OED* is "hamper, impede (a person, movement, or action)," followed by "perplex, thrown into doubt or difficulty." In this sense, Stevenson was clearly embarrassed in writing *David Balfour,* having "come to a collapse." Equally, Stevenson was embarrassed, or thrown into difficulty, in writing *A Footnote,* a work over which he struggled even more than *David Balfour* and complained that "there ought to be a future state to reward me for that grind!" (*Letters,* 7:283).

31. White, *Content of the Form,* 10. White returns to the question of desire in historical narrative in comparing the "narrative coherency" of the annals and the chronicle: "Suppose we grant not that the chronicle is a 'higher' or more sophisticated representation of reality than the annals, but that it is merely a different kind of representation, marked by a desire for a kind of order and fullness in an account of reality that remains theoretically unjustified, a desire that is, until shown

otherwise, purely gratuitous" (16–17). White's discourse leads one to ask, what would it mean to talk of a desire that is not gratuitous—that is, excessive, nonutilitarian, and (in economic terms) free? Can desire be shown to be otherwise than gratuitous?

32. Stevenson, *Letters,* 7:283.

33. Stevenson, *Letters,* 7:251, 252. He would deploy the narrative frame of the oral story, or yarn, to good effect in another novel written during this period, *The Wrecker* (published in June 1892, two months before *A Footnote*). In the prologue to this novel, the central narrator, Loudon Dodd, arrives in the Marquesas and is welcomed by an old friend, Havens. The two men retire to Havens's house, and after dinner, Dodd tells his host "a queer yarn" that is, substantially, the plot of *The Wrecker.* Stevenson here invokes the context of the oral story in a way that anticipates Conrad's narrator Marlow in *Heart of Darkness* (1899) and *Lord Jim* (1901).

34. As Hayden White reminds us, "what distinguishes 'historical' from 'fictional' stories is first and foremost their content, rather than their form" (*Content of the Form,* 27).

35. Stevenson, "A Humble Remonstrance," 215, 216. These comments, it seems to me, offer a striking anticipation of Oscar Wilde's observation in "The Decay of Lying" that "[t]ruth is entirely and absolutely a matter of style." Oscar Wilde, *The Artist as Critic: Critical Writings of Oscar Wilde,* ed. Richard Ellmann (Chicago: University of Chicago Press, 1969), 305. In this essay, Wilde (or Vivian) refers to "Robert Louis Stevenson, that delightful master of delicate and fanciful prose [who] is tainted with this modern vice" (295) of "truth-telling" (294).

36. White, *Content of the Form,* 4, 23, 16. The abrupt and arbitrary technique of chronicling events is revealed in Stevenson's narration, for example, in recounting the termination of the rule of a German official whom Stevenson admired: "So through an ill-timed skirmish, two severed heads, and a dead body, the rule of Brandeis came to a sudden end. . . . [H]is government, take it for all in all, the most promising that has ever been in these unlucky islands, was from that hour *a piece of history*" (A *Footnote,* 55; emphasis added). The creation of "history" is here determined by a spontaneous outburst of violence rather than what White terms the "moralizing judgments" that are needed for history to attain "narrative closure." Stevenson's account discloses "the anarchy of the current social situation" producing corpses and consigning leaders to "history" without presenting "the passage from one moral order to another" (White, *Content of the Form,* 24, 23).

37. Colley, *Robert Louis Stevenson,* 93.

38. Stevenson, *ISS,* 13.

39. White, *Content of the Form,* 21.

40. Frank McLynn, in his biography of Stevenson, represents the Scottish/Samoan parallels as explicit, observing that "for Stevenson, Mataafa was 'Charlie over the water,' Laupepa and his minions the Campbells, and the Germans in Samoa the equivalent of the Hanoverians in London one hundred and fifty years earlier" (McLynn, *Robert Louis Stevenson,* 426).

41. Stevenson, *ISS,* 10. Language differences are a key factor in the encounters between European and Polynesian in Stevenson's South Seas fiction as well. One might think here of Wiltshire, in "Beach of Falesá," who trusts in the competence of Case as his interpreter to the chiefs and is betrayed as a result.

42. Fletcher, *Stevenson's Germany,* vii, 3, 4 (emphasis added).

43. Stevenson, *ISS,* 25, 31.

44. John Kucich, "Melancholy Magic: Masochism, Stevenson, Anti-Imperialism," *Nineteenth-Century Literature* 56, no. 3 (2001), 383, 387–88, 389.

45. Kucich, "Melancholy Magic," 378, 376 (emphasis added).

46. In a letter to Henry James incorrectly dated December 5, 1891 (actually 1892), Stevenson originally wrote that he had composed "all" of *A Footnote* in the last year, then substituted "almost all," and finally added "(well much of )" (*Letters,* 7:449 and note). By contrast, Stevenson displayed no such hesitancy concerning the amount of fiction he wrote, stating that he "began And Finished *David Balfour* [*sic*]" within the year (7:449). In pointing out Stevenson's dating error, James referred to him as "my dear time-deluded islander" (7:448n).

47. I am referring both to the Claxton affair, discussed below, and Stevenson's report that "[o]n the hot water side, it may entertain you to know that I have been actually sentenced to deportation by my friends on Mulinuu, C.J. Cedercrantz and Baron Senfft von Pilsach" as a result of *A Footnote* (*Letters,* 7:449).

48. Stevenson, *Letters,* 7:251, 252, 251, 283 (emphasis added). This idea of utility suggests that his intention was to produce a practical work or piece of propaganda, as he worried that "the book, with my best expedition, may come just too late to be of use" (*Letters,* 7:252), a point reiterated in the preface: "[S]peed was essential, or it might come too late to be of any service to a distracted country" (*A Footnote,* xvii). White observes, "No more vexed—and mystifying—notion appears in the theory of historical writing than that of the historian's 'style.' It is a problem because insofar as the historian's discourse is conceived to have style, it is also conceived to be literary. But insofar as a historian's discourse is literary, it seems to be rhetorical, which is anathema for those who wish to claim for historical discourse

the status of objective representation" (*Content of the Form,* 227n19). Stevenson likewise perceived a potential conflict between literary style and practical effect, not because he lacked the leisure to invest in stylistic flourishes but because he felt that the work's practical value would be diminished were it to be classed as "literary."

49. Like other paratexts, the footnote is a marginal textual feature that is deemed unworthy of serious critical attention. Yet such paratextual features, as McGann argues, play a formative role in "the text's bibliographic codes" (*Textual Condition,* 16) and hence inform its impact as a material artifact (12, 16).

50. Stevenson's portrayal of his native city in an earlier work, *Edinburgh: Picturesque Notes* (1878), contains the observation that "the whole city leads a double existence." Stevenson then comments on the topography of the city in terms that anticipate the division of *David Balfour:* "You go under dark arches, and down dark stairs and alleys. The way is so narrow that you can lay a hand on either wall; so steep that, in greasy winter weather, the pavement is almost as treacherous as ice."Stevenson also hints at the surveillance and voyeurism that surfaces in the novel in commenting that "Edinburgh is not so much a small city as the largest of small towns. It is scarce possible to avoid observing your neighbours; and I never yet heard of anyone who tried." *Edinburgh: Picturesque Notes* (Edinburgh: Salamander Press, 1983), 11, 23, 24.

51. Jolly, "Robert Louis Stevenson and Samoan History," 113, 114.

52. White asserts that "only a moral authority could justify the turn in the narrative that permits it to come to an end" and asks a question that has direct significance to the narrativizing impulse in *A Footnote:* "What else could narrative closure consist of than the passage from one moral order to another?" (*Content of the Form,* 23).

53. Stevenson, *Letters,* 7:344.

54. Stevenson, *Letters,* 7:287, 344 (emphasis added).

55. In fact, when Stevenson died, he was working on *Weir of Hermiston,* a novel (posthumously published in 1896) whose incompletion resulted directly from the author's sudden demise.

56. Stevenson, *Letters,* 7:161. Indeed, the difficulty with stimulating readerly pleasure and commercial profit was endemic to Stevenson's South Seas writings in general. Menikoff writes of the "general consensus that *In the South Seas* . . . was a complete departure from Stevenson's habitual style and method, and it would have been better had he never written it." Barry Menikoff, "'These Problematic Shores': Robert Louis Stevenson in the South Seas," in *English Literature and the Wider World,*

vol. 4, *1876–1918: The Ends of the Earth,* ed. Simon Gatrell (London: Ashfield, 1992), 143. Colvin, for example, complained to Baxter that the "South Sea Islands book . . . is the very devil for dullness, confusion, and ineffective,—even incompetent workmanship: and all because he would insist in laying aside personality, incident, adventure, and humour" (cited in Menikoff, "These Problematic Shores," 145). Ironically, Colvin used Stevenson's own credo of incident and adventure to demean his South Seas work.

57. Henry James to Stevenson, cited in *ISS,* xxi (original emphasis).

58. Stevenson, *Letters,* 8:193, 7:157. Interestingly, James made his latter remark in a critique of *David Balfour,* of which Stevenson told Meredith, "I am sometimes tempted to think [it] is about my best work" (8:163), and which he hoped would delight his readers. In his generally favorable response to the novel, James noted, "The one thing I miss in the book is the note of visibility—it subjects my visual sense, my seeing imagination, to an almost painful underfeeding. The hearing imagination, as it were, is nourished like an alderman, . . . so that I seem to myself . . . in the presence of voices in the darkness—voices the more distinct and vivid, the more brave and sonorous, as voices always are (but also the more tormenting and confounding) by reason of these bandaged eyes" (8:193n). Stevenson's reply states his "two aims" as "War to the adjective" and "Death to the optic nerve" (8:193). Certainly some of the reviews of *David Balfour* were favorable, such as the *Saturday Review*'s, which praised "this very delightful book" (8:187n). However, Stevenson's conclusion was, "I thought the reviews of *Catriona* beastly" (8:184).

59. It is striking that Stewart uses another historical example of a politically motivated kidnapping: the imprisonment of Rachel Grange by her husband, James Erskine, on St. Kilda, which changes the emphasis from the personally motivated occurrence in *Kidnapped* (*K,* 485n).

60. Stevenson, *South Sea Tales,* 40.

61. Jameson, *Political Unconscious,* 252.

62. Stevenson, *Letters,* 7:153.

63. White, *Content of the Form,* 5.

64. White extends his analysis of the formal and conceptual differences between chronicle and narrative in a later essay, writing, "A chronicle, however, is not a narrative, even if it contains the same set of facts as its informational content, because a narrative discourse performs differently from a chronicle. Chronology is no doubt a code shared by both chronicle and narrative, but narrative utilizes other codes as well and produces a meaning quite different from that of any chronicle"

(*Content of the Form,* 42). Hence, Stevenson's indeterminacy between "chronicle" and "narrative" reflects an indecision about the kind of meaning he wants to produce, with regard to this set of historical events.

65. A twentieth-century instance of such romantic Jacobitism occurs in John Buchan's 1922 novel *Huntingtower,* which contains the following description of the protagonist, Dickson McCunn: "He was a Jacobite not because he had any views on Divine Right, but because he had always before his eyes a picture of a knot of adventurers in cloaks, new landed from France among the western heather." John Buchan, *Huntingtower,* ed. Ann F. Stonehouse (New York: Oxford University Press, 1996), 14. An adventure writer very much in Stevenson's mold, Buchan clearly participates in the same sympathies with Jacobitism that are literary and romantic rather than political. As Ann Stonehouse remarks, the enthusiasts for Jacobitism were especially attracted to "the lost cause of Prince Charles Edward Stuart" (*Huntingtower,* 215n).

66. Rennie, "Introduction," xxx.

67. White, *Content of the Form,* 21.

68. Stevenson, *Letters,* 7:396. This incident was related in the same letter in which Stevenson informed Baxter that he was sending the final chapters of *David Balfour.*

69. Colley, *Robert Louis Stevenson,* 170.

70. McLynn, *Robert Louis Stevenson,* 428.

71. Stevenson, *Letters,* 7:395, 396. In an 1891 letter to Colvin, Stevenson referred to this plot "to kidnap and deport Mataafa" as evidence that "the natives have been scurvily used by all the white Powers without exception" (7:142). As proof of the venality of white officialdom, the story suits Stevenson's narrative needs perfectly.

## Chapter 7

1. Stevenson, *Letters,* 7:282.

2. Daly, *Modernism,* 12.

3. Johnstone, *Recollections,* 8–9, 7. One can only speculate as to how far Johnstone's thesis, broadly antagonistic towards Stevenson's role in Samoa, led him to cite selectively from the interview, to distort Stevenson's position by claiming that "Isle of Voices" was inferior because it was lacking in "civilized" elements, and to finesse the substitution of *white* for *civilized* so that it passes almost without notice.

4. Stevenson, *Letters,* 7:350.

5. Johnstone, *Recollections,* 101, 102.

6. Rod Edmond, *Representing the South Pacific: Colonial Discourse from Cook to Gauguin* (Cambridge, UK: Cambridge University Press, 1997), 189, 190.

7. McLynn, *Robert Louis Stevenson,* 430, 434, 481.

8. Robert Louis Stevenson, "Address to the Samoan Chiefs," Beinecke MS Vault 5942 (original emphasis). The Beinecke Library has in its collection two versions of Stevenson's speech to the Samoan chiefs. The first draft, MS Vault 5941, is in the hand of Stevenson and bears numerous additions and corrections. The second draft, MS Vault 5942, is in the hand of Belle Strong, Stevenson's stepdaughter and amanuensis, with corrections in the hand of Stevenson. The second is clearly the later of the two drafts, containing the extended comparison between Samoa and colonialism in Ireland and Scotland. Stevenson refers, in the later draft, to colonial invaders as "the other people," a phrase not used in the preliminary draft. Deletions from the manuscript are bracketed by < >. Corrections and additions in the manuscript are bracketed by { }.

9. Robert Louis Stevenson, "The Isle of Voices," in *SST,* 102. This edition also contains "The Beach of Falesá."

10. Johnstone, *Recollections,* 103.

11. Stevenson's interest in racial hybridity may also be seen in his formation of the "Half-Caste Club" on Samoa: "Stevenson, his mother, Fanny, and Belle held weekly gatherings at which the half-castes were supposed to learn European manners and customs" (Colley, *Robert Louis Stevenson,* 60). The assumption of this project seems to be that half-castes were more susceptible to European influence than those of unmixed Polynesian race; yet, as Colley writes, "the half-caste woman is not allowed the plunging necklines and corseted waist of the European woman. . . . Her attire . . . makes sure that no matter how thoroughly she absorbs Western ways and no matter how much her features and skin color resemble those of a white person, she is not to be misread and mistaken for something other than herself" (*Robert Louis Stevenson,* 61). I discuss the significance of the "half-caste" in "The Beach of Falesá" later in this chapter.

12. Edmond, *Representing the South Pacific,* 190.

13. Stevenson, *ISS,* 5. Stevenson writes that, in preferring the South Seas to Europe, he "reversed the verdict of Lord Tennyson's hero" (*ISS,* 5), apparently referring to the narrator of "Locksley Hall." However, Stevenson's portrayal of an alluring island from which men have no desire to leave also invokes Tennyson's "Lotos-Eaters."

14. Edmond, *Representing the South Pacific,* 190.

15. The disappearance of the danger represented by Kalamake is confirmed when we are told that his location "seemed a far way for an old gentleman to walk" and that "Kalamake has never more been heard of" (*SST,* 122).

16. Ann Colley has made a generally persuasive case for Stevenson's indebtedness to missionaries on Samoa and his personal friendships with individual missionaries. However, this does not alter the fact that missionaries are at times portrayed in a negative light in his South Seas fiction. See Colley, *Robert Louis Stevenson,* 10–48.

17. Johnstone, *Recollections,* 102.

18. Neil Rennie, *Far-Fetched Facts: The Literature of Travel and the Idea of the South Seas* (Oxford: Clarendon Press, 1995), 213.

19. Stevenson, *Letters,* 6:330.

20. Rennie, *Far-Fetched Facts,* 215.

21. In June 1884, Stevenson had written to Henley, "I do desire a book of adventure—a romance—and no man will get or write me one. Dumas I have read and re-read too often; Scott, too, and I am short. I want to hear swords clash. I want a book to begin in a good way; a book, I guess, like *Treasure Island*" (*Letters,* 4:307). Stevenson's admiration for Dumas lasted throughout his career, and in "A Gossip on Romance" (after lavishly praising the *Arabian Nights*), Stevenson wrote, "Dumas approaches perhaps nearest of any modern to these Arabian authors in the purely material charm of some of his romances. The early part of *Monte Cristo,* down to the finding of the treasure, is a piece of perfect story-telling" (*The Lantern-Bearers,* 177).

22. Stevenson, *Letters,* 6:330.

23. Stevenson, *Letters,* 7:155 (original emphasis).

24. Rennie, *Far-Fetched Facts,* 215.

25. Stevenson, *Letters,* 7:161. Stevenson's confidence in the documentary authenticity of his tale sets it apart from *The Wrecker,* coauthored with Lloyd Osbourne, about which he wrote to Colvin that "of course it don't set up to be a book—only a long tough yarn with some pictures of the manners of today in the greater world" (*Letters,* 7:180–81).

26. Rennie, *Far-Fetched Facts,* 215.

27. Rennie, *Far-Fetched Facts,* 216.

28. Colley, *Robert Louis Stevenson,* 36.

29. Stevenson, *Letters,* 7:282.

30. Stevenson, *Letters,* 7:161.

31. Colley, *Robert Louis Stevenson,* 42, 44.

32. Colley, *Robert Louis Stevenson,* 42.

33. Rennie, *Far-Fetched Facts,* 216.

34. The text suggests another origin of Wiltshire's name, as he informs Tarleton, "I'm mostly called Welsher" (*SST,* 35). As a slang name for a cheat or swindler, "Welsher" is, as Roslyn Jolly points out, "an unflattering one for a trader" (265n). However, given the geographical resonance of the name "Wiltshire," the narrative suggests a link between England and shady trading practices. Another resonance of the name not noted by Jolly is "Welsh," a Welshman, which would conflict with Wiltshire's proclaimed "Englishness." In particular, the fact that Wales is a neighboring country to England means that national boundaries are difficult to classify and that Wiltshire's national identity is less stable than he claims.

35. For a parallel passage in Stevenson's correspondence, see his letter to J. M. Barrie, cited at the beginning of chapter 6. In both passages, Stevenson dwells on the hostility of the British climate, which he evocatively described in *Edinburgh: Picturesque Notes:* "[T]o none but those who have themselves suffered the thing in the body, can the gloom and depression of our Edinburgh winter be brought home. . . . [T]he wind whistles through the town as if it were an open meadow; and if you lie awake all night, you hear it shrieking and raving overhead" (80–81).

36. Stevenson, *Letters,* 7:152. Even the unsentimental Attwater, who "do[es] not take the romantic view of marriage," is motivated in his pearl farming by the wish "to make an excellent marriage when I go home," a match that will be easier given that, as he tells Herrick, "I am rich" (*SST,* 210).

37. Although Wiltshire's use of the term "white man" occurs in the context of a multiracial society—and therefore has a specific discriminatory edge—such a context is not necessary for the deployment of the phrase. For example, in John Buchan's *The Thirty-Nine Steps* (1915), Franklin Scudder, a white American, enlists the help of Richard Hannay, a white South African, in trying to foil a "Jewish" plot. When Hannay agrees to help, Scudder responds, "I haven't the privilege of your name, sir, but let me tell you that you're a white man." *The Thirty-Nine Steps* (London: Penguin, 1991), 21. Even without the identity of the individual's name, the privileged status of "white man" is ensured by Hannay's conduct in the imperial struggle against Germany.

38. For an excellent analysis of the sartorial codes of the South Seas, and the Stevensons' transgressions of them, see Colley, *Robert Louis Stevenson,* 49–72. It is noteworthy that in terms of dress the missionary is closer to Attwater in *The Ebb-Tide* wearing "white drill" and a tie (*SST,* 192).

39. Colley, *Robert Louis Stevenson,* 41.

40. Colley, *Robert Louis Stevenson,* 41.

41. With this reference to *Strange Case of Dr. Jekyll and Mr. Hyde,* I mean to invoke the duality, even multiplicity, in Case's character as representative of the Stevenson antihero. Not only is Case a combination of different racial and ethnic ingredients, but he is also morally ambivalent. Despite asserting Case's evil nature, stating that "if he's not in hell today, there's no such place" (*SST,* 5), Wiltshire makes an exception: "I know but one good point to the man: that he was fond of his wife, and kind to her. . . . [W]hen he came to die . . . they found one strange thing—that he had made a will, like a Christian, and the widow got the lot" (5). The "strange thing," like the "Strange Case," indicates the presence of moral contradiction and self-division. Henry Jekyll, likewise, displays his surprising fondness for his friend, to whom he is "knit closer than a wife," in the form of a bequest, which provided "that, in the case of the decease of Henry Jekyll . . . all his possessions were to pass into the hands of his 'friend and benefactor Edward Hyde'" (Stevenson, *Strange Case,* 13).

42. Jennifer DeVere Brody, *Impossible Purities: Blackness, Femininity, and Victorian Culture* (Durham, NC: Duke University Press, 1998), 138, 137.

43. As Roslyn Jolly observes, Case's comment alludes to "the Samoan war of December 1888, when German men-of-war fired several times on native villages" (*SST,* 263n). However, although Wiltshire makes no objection, Case's "statement represent[s] an attitude of belligerence and high-handedness towards the natives that Stevenson deplored" (263).

44. Said, *Culture and Imperialism* (New York: Vintage, 1994), 74.

45. As Roslyn Jolly observes, the pronunciation of Case's name as "Ese," in relation to "the verb 'Esi' meaning 'to drive away,' . . . seems the meaning most appropriate to Case, who drives all other white men away from Falesá" (*SST,* 264n).

46. Katherine Linehan, "Taking Up with Kanakas: Stevenson's Complex Social Criticism in 'The Beach of Falesá,'" *ELT* 33, no. 4 (1990): 407.

47. Rennie, *Far-Fetched Facts,* 216.

48. The scene also recalls the climactic scene of *The Master of Ballantrae,* in which the brothers James and Henry Durie die at the same time and lie together in the same grave.

49. Stevenson, *Letters,* 6:402.

50. Henry James conveyed the opposition of Stevenson's friends to his settlement on Samoa in a letter in March 1890, in which James wrote of the "long howl

of horror" from Stevenson's friends "on the question of Samoa and expatriation" (Stevenson, *Letters,* 6:403n).

51. Daly, *Modernism,* 17.

52. Johnstone, *Recollections,* 100–101.

53. Johnstone, *Recollections,* 101.

54. Stevenson, *Letters,* 7:363.

55. Stevenson, *Letters,* 7:413.

56. Johnstone, *Recollections,* 103.

57. Stevenson, *ISS,* 5.

## Chapter 8

1. Frank Kermode, *The Sense of an Ending: Studies in the Theory of Fiction* (New York: Oxford University Press, 2000), 10. Kermode offers an insight into the need for, and corresponding fear of, an end that has striking relevance for Stevenson at the end of his career: people "need fictive concords with origins and ends, such as give meaning to lives and to poems. The End they imagine will reflect their irreducibly intermediary preoccupations. They fear it. . . . [T]he End is a figure for their own deaths" (7).

2. Kermode, *Sense of an Ending,* 11.

3. I use the word *protagonist,* for want of a better one, to describe Herrick. Certainly there is no hero in the novel, nor does the narrative focus primarily on a single character. However, it is through Herrick's consciousness that much of the story is told.

4. Johnstone, *Recollections,* 103.

5. Kermode, *Sense of an Ending,* 19.

6. Robert Louis Stevenson and Lloyd Osbourne, *The Ebb-Tide: A Trio and Quartette,* in *SST,* 123.

7. Kermode, *Sense of an Ending,* 19.

8. Stevenson, *ISS,* 27.

9. What Kermode terms "the desire for consonance" (*Sense of an Ending,* 17) involves "the invention of new end-fictions" by the reader, whose "need [for] fictive concords with origins and ends"(7) will require a strategy that finds meaning in the "ends in fiction" (7). By beginning at the end—with an exhausted protagonist who participates in a debased subculture of European exiles—Stevenson seems to close the door on any possibility of narrative renewal. Yet, as I argue below, the

introduction of a new location (the aptly named "New Island") and a key character (the colonialist Attwater) invites the reader to construct new "ends in fiction."

10. Wayne Koestenbaum has written of the collaboration that Stevenson was concerned "that his love for Lloyd, if not checked, would make him the subject of a medical 'case' like Jekyll-and-Hyde's" ("Shadow on the Bed," 40). Koestenbaum's reading of the collaboration, which included "three substantial tales, *The Ebb Tide, The Wrecker,* and *The Wrong Box*" (39), is that it involved "the metaphorically sexual conception of . . . a 'romance of boyhood'" within the context of "men fleeing to exotic places for sexual freedom" (41). Whether or not one agrees with Koestenbaum that the collaboration was erotic in nature—with a doubly prohibited desire (between both men and father-son) being channeled into literary production, "a primal scene which excluded Fanny Osborne[*sic*]-Stevenson—Lloyd's mother and Robert Louis Stevenson's wife" (41)—we can concur that the persistence of this coauthorship over a long period of time deserves serious critical attention. Certainly, the close familial relationship between Stevenson and Osbourne allowed an intimate cohabitation between an older and a younger man that might otherwise have raised eyebrows.

11. Maixner, *Critical Heritage,* 31, 337.

12. Stevenson, *ISS,* 9.

13. Arata, "Observing *The Wrecker,*" 25.

14. McGann, *Textual Condition,* 10.

15. Stevenson, *Letters,* 7:9. This interesting letter written by Stevenson (in Vailima) to Lloyd (then traveling in Paris) makes clear the problems that their physical distance caused for their coauthorship of *The Wrecker,* as they attempted to combine the sections of the narrative into a single work: "I wish I had your narrative to help me just now for XVI ('Light from the Man of War'). I would fain put in some traits; but fear to be in conflict with something good in yours. This is the hell of collaboration half the world away. I think I must take my chance, and if I have time, I will send a note of that to which I have committed you" (7:9).

16. Stevenson, *Letters,* 7:9–10.

17. In *The Wrecker,* by contrast, the very status of the novel as a "South Seas" story is open for critical discussion. Yet in both novels, the relationships of male "partners" are linked to voyages to and commercial exploitation of the South Seas.

18. In *The Wrecker,* the *Flying Scud* is wrecked near Midway Island; thus, almost exactly midway through the novel is where Dodd's cruise to the island begins, serving as a dramatic twist of the plot that is necessary to reenergize the novel, which,

as Arata notes, is "full, overfull, of action" (Arata, "Observing *The Wrecker,*" 4) and has difficulty reconciling its "three main plot lines . . . one having to do with art, one having to do with business, and one having to do with adventure and romance" (6). The journey to Midway, then, attempts to bring all three "lines" into productive partnership.

19. Chapter 6 of *The Ebb-Tide* is titled "The Partners"—describing the trio in their fraudulent projects, while also anticipating the partnership of Attwater and Symonds. Chapter 11 is titled "David and Goliath," indicating not collaboration but antagonism.

20. This motive for seeking refuge at an out-of-the-way island and then attempting to displace an existing British settler would be appropriated by Conrad for the final chapters of *Lord Jim,* in which Gentlemen Brown—a "pirate" who shares some traits with Davis—arrives at Patusan and engages in a fatal conflict with Jim. Conrad's debt to Stevenson is evident in the resemblances between these two novels (see Conrad, *Lord Jim,* 250–305).

21. An obvious source for the setting of New Island is Penrhyn, the "pearl island" in the South Seas visited by Stevenson and Fanny on the *Janet Nicoll* in May 1890 (see chapter 5).

22. As I discuss in chapter 4, David's initial intended fate of being kidnapped and sold into slavery in the Carolinas is transformed, following the wreck of the *Covenant* and the arrival of Alan Breck, to pursuit by the English army as an accomplice in the Appin murder.

23. One is reminded, by this recurring pattern, not only of Stevenson's regular trips between Samoa and other islands and Australia but also of the structured publication of work in serial form, which occurred at regular intervals throughout the year (in the case of *The Ebb-Tide,* between November 11, 1893, and February 3, 1894, in *To-Day*).

24. Arata, "Observing *The Wrecker,*" 10–11. In a previous collaboration, the mistaking of an anonymous corpse for the body of Joseph Finsbury is productive of the ensuing plot of *The Wrong Box,* the very title of which inscribes error as a central issue.

25. Kermode, *Sense of an Ending,* 18, 20. Kermode goes on to describe the reader's experience of the text in terms that invoke a journey: "[T]he interest of having our expectations falsified is obviously related to our wish to reach the discovery or recognition by an unexpected and instructive route" (18).

26. In a letter to Baxter, Stevenson described *Findlay's Directory* as "the best of reading . . . [which] may almost count as fiction" (*SST,* 284n). Stevenson thereby sug-

gested both the pleasure of the *Findlay's* text and its possible inaccuracies—for a directory to be likened to fiction may call into question its reliability as a source of information about the South Seas.

27. One of the many ways in which Stevenson anticipates Conrad in *The Ebb-Tide* is in this suggestion that the life of the seaman is founded on an illusion about the romance of the sea and of adventure, which involves the projection of a man's own desires onto a natural surface or landscape. Conrad has Marlow state in *Lord Jim*, "Surely in no other craft as in that of the sea do the hearts of those already launched to sink or swim go out so much to the youth on the brink, looking with shining eyes upon that glitter of the vast surface which is only a reflection of his own glances full of fire. There is such magnificent vagueness in the expectations that had driven each of us to sea, such a glorious indefiniteness, such a beautiful greed of adventures that are their own and only reward!" (94). Like Marlow and Jim, Davis and company are deceived by their fantasies about the island.

28. Said, *Culture and Imperialism*, 7.

29. This reference to Attwater's banking his wealth recalls a manuscript passage that was omitted from the serial and book publication of "The Beach of Falesá," in which Case advises Wiltshire about how to maximize his profits by saying that "whenever you get hold of any money . . . any Christian money I mean—the first thing to do is to fire it up to Sydney to the bank. . . . [T]he name of the man that buys copra with gold is Damfool" (*SST*, 260n).

30. For a discussion of the signs that suggest Attwater has "gone native," see chapter 5.

31. Stevenson, of course, was a great admirer of Alexandre Dumas père and had his works in mind while writing "The Pearl Fisher" (the original title of *The Ebb-Tide*). As Stevenson wrote to Marcel Schwob, "I love Dumas and I love Shakespeare. . . . [I]f by any sacrifice of my own literary baggage I could clear *Le Vicomte de Bragelonne* of Porthos, *Jekyll* might go" (*Letters*, 6:401).

32. Mitchell, *Colonising Egypt*, 67.

33. Roslyn Jolly remarks that Taveeta is the "Polynesian pronounciation of David" (*SST*, 284n).

34. Mitchell, *Colonising Egypt*, 45.

35. Mitchell, *Colonising Egypt*, 82, 6.

36. This reference seems to replay, in a different key, the scene in *Treasure Island* when Jim, having arrived on the island, "beheld the Union Jack flutter in the air above a wood" (96). In the subsequent narrative, Dr. Livesey recounts how Captain

Smollett, who came prepared with "a great many various stores," including "the British colours" (109), had climbed on the roof of the enclosure "and run up the colours" (110) that Jim sees. The British or English flag, it seems, was an essential piece of equipment for those preparing to trade with or plunder an island. Ironically, the British flag becomes a target for the pirates, but when the squire suggests taking it down, the captain replies, "Strike my colours! . . . No, sir, not I" (110–11). As a Scot, of course, Stevenson was thoroughly aware of the difference between an "ensign of England" and the "Union Jack": the latter being a flag that proclaims the colonization of the "British Isles," in addition to its overseas territories.

37. Similarly, Stevenson had no official colonial function on Samoa, though he apparently hoped at one point to be appointed British consul. In one of his long "Vailima Letters" to Sidney Colvin (begun May 29, 1892), he wrote that "supposing a vacancy to occur, I would condescend to accept the office of H.B.M.'s Consul with parts, pendicles and appurtenances" (*Letters,* 7:310). Apart from the attractions of the income, Stevenson listed his motives as the "possibility of being able to do some good" and "[l]arks for the family who seem filled with childish avidity for the kudos" (7:311). Stevenson does not suggest that his desire for prestige might be a factor, and Booth and Mayhew remark that "Colvin misleadingly states that the idea of the Consulship was 'only a passing notion of the part of RLS'" (7:311n). Though this hope of an official post never came to fruition, Stevenson clearly retained a strong affinity for England as well as Scotland. Indeed, in writing of the events following Stevenson's death in December 1894, Lloyd Osbourne observed, "Placing the body on our big table, we drew over it the red English ensign, twelve feet long and proportionately broad, that we habitually flew over the house" (Osbourne, *Intimate Portrait,* 148–49).

38. It is perhaps apt, given his emphasis on his university training, that Attwater describes his function with the native laborers as "the educational" (*SST,* 215), which Davis immediately interprets in disciplinary terms: "'You mean to run them?' . . . 'Ay! To run them,' said Attwater" (216).

39. Pierre Bourdieu, *Distinction: A Social Critique of the Judgement of Taste,* trans. Richard Nice (Cambridge, MA: Harvard University Press, 1984), 101.

40. Bourdieu, *Distinction,* 101; Mitchell, *Colonising Egypt,* 61.

41. Bourdieu, *Distinction,* 78, 79.

42. Stevenson, *ISS,* 70, 71, 68.

43. Stevenson, *ISS,* 71.

44. Stevenson, *ISS,* 29, 33, 70.

45. Mitchell, *Colonising Egypt,* 79.

46. Smith, *Literary Culture,* 161.

47. McLynn, *Robert Louis Stevenson,* 466; Colley, *Robert Louis Stevenson,* 39; Smith, *Literary Culture,* 162, 164.

48. Colley, *Robert Louis Stevenson,* 39.

49. Smith, *Literary Culture,* 160.

50. Stevenson, *Letters,* 8:107; Robert Louis Stevenson, *Selected Letters of Robert Louis Stevenson,* ed. Ernest Mehew (New Haven, CT: Yale University Press, 1998), 545n.

51. Stevenson, *Letters,* 8:107.

52. Stevenson, *Letters,* 8:107.

# BIBLIOGRAPHY

## Manuscript Collections

Balfour Papers. National Library of Scotland, Edinburgh.

Huntington Library, San Marino, CA.

Mitchell Library, State Library of New South Wales, Sydney, Australia.

Robert Louis Stevenson Collection. Beinecke Library, Yale University, New Haven, CT.

## Individual Editions of Works by Robert Louis Stevenson (and collaborators)

Stevenson, Robert Louis. *Catriona.* London: Cassell, 1893.

———. *The Complete Stories of Robert Louis Stevenson.* Edited by Barry Menikoff. New York: Modern Library, 2002.

———. *Edinburgh: Picturesque Notes.* 1878. Edinburgh: Salamander Press, 1983.

———. *A Footnote to History: Eight Years of Trouble in Samoa.* 1892. Honolulu: University of Hawai'i Press, 1996.

———. "The Free Island." Balfour Papers, MS 9892. National Library of Scotland, Edinburgh.

———. *From Scotland to Silverado.* Edited by James D. Hart. Cambridge, MA: Harvard University Press, 1966.

———. "A Gossip on Romance." In *The Lantern-Bearers and Other Essays,* edited by Jeremy Treglown, 172–82.

———. "A Humble Remonstrance." In *Victorian Criticism of the Novel,* edited by Edwin M. Eigner and George J. Worth, 213–22. Cambridge: Cambridge University Press, 1985.

———. *An Inland Voyage.* In *Travels with a Donkey in the Cevennes and Selected Travel Writings,* edited by Emma Letley, 1–170.

———. *In the South Seas.* Edited by Sidney Colvin. Edinburgh, 1896.

———. *In the South Seas.* 1896. Edited by Neil Rennie. New York: Penguin, 1998.

———. "Journal of Two Visits to the South Seas." HM 2412. Huntington Library, San Marino, CA.

———. *Kidnapped, or The Lad with the Silver Button.* Edited by Barry Menikoff. New York: Modern Library, 2001.

———. *Kidnapped and Catriona.* Edited by Emma Letley. New York: Oxford University Press, 1986.

———. *The Lantern-Bearers and Other Essays.* Edited by Jeremy Treglown. New York: Cooper Square, 1999.

———. "The Lazaretto of To-Day." Balfour Papers, MS 9892. National Library of Scotland, Edinburgh.

———. "Leprosy on Penrhyn." Balfour Papers, MS 9892. National Library of Scotland, Edinburgh.

———. *The Letters of Robert Louis Stevenson.* Edited by Bradford A. Booth and Ernest Mehew. 8 vols. New Haven, CT: Yale University Press, 1994–95.

———. "Letter to Samuel McClure." July 19, 1890. Typescript. Balfour Papers, MS 9891. National Library of Scotland, Edinburgh.

———. *The Master of Ballantrae.* Edited by Adrian Poole. Harmondsworth: Penguin, 1996.

———. *Memories and Portraits.* New York: Scribner's, 1898.

———. "My First Book: *Treasure Island.*" In *The Lantern Bearers and Other Essays,* edited by Jeremy Treglown, 277–84.

———. "A Note on Realism." In *Selected Essays,* edited by George Scott-Moncrieff, 262–70. Washington, DC: Regnery Gateway, 1988.

———. "A Pearl Island: Penrhyn." Balfour Papers, MS 9892. National Library of Scotland, Edinburgh.

———. *Selected Letters of Robert Louis Stevenson.* Edited by Ernest Mehew. New Haven, CT: Yale University Press, 1998.

———. *The Silverado Squatters.* 1883. San Francisco: Mercury House, 1996.

———. "The South Seas: A Record of Three Cruises." *Black and White: A Weekly Illustrated Record and Review* [London], February 6–December 19, 1891. Stevenson 1083. Beinecke Library, Yale University, New Haven, CT.

———. *The South Seas: A Record of Three Cruises.* London: Cassell, 1890.

———. "The South Seas: Letters from a Leisurely Traveller." *New York Sun,* February 1–December 3, 1891.

———. *South Sea Tales.* Edited by Roslyn Jolly. New York: Oxford University Press, 1996.

———. *Strange Case of Dr. Jekyll and Mr. Hyde.* Edited by Richard Dury. Edinburgh: Edinburgh University Press, 2004.

———. *Travels with a Donkey in the Cevennes and Selected Travel Writings.* Edited by Emma Letley. New York: Oxford University Press, 1992.

———. *Treasure Island.* Edited by Wendy R. Katz. Edinburgh: Edinburgh University Press, 1998.

———. *Vailima Letters: Being Correspondence Addressed by Robert Louis Stevenson to Sidney Colvin, November 1890–October 1894.* 2 vols. 1895. New York: Greenwood, 1969.

———. *Weir of Hermiston.* Edited by Catherine Kerrigan. Edinburgh: Edinburgh University Press, 1995.

Stevenson, Robert Louis, and Lloyd Osbourne. *The Ebb-Tide: A Trio and Quartette.* London: Heinemann, 1894.

———. *The Wrecker.* 1892. London: Cassell, 1914.

———. *The Wrong Box.* 1889. New York: Oxford University Press, 1995.

## Biographies, Letters, and Other Biographical Material

Balfour, Graham. *The Life of Robert Louis Stevenson.* 2 vols. London: Methuen, 1901.

Bathurst, Bella. *The Lighthouse Stevensons.* London: Flamingo, 2000.

Bell, Ian. *Dreams of Exile: Robert Louis Stevenson, A Biography.* New York: Holt, 1992.

Calder, Jenni. *Robert Louis Stevenson: A Life Study.* New York: Oxford University Press, 1980.

Furnas, J. C. *Voyage to Windward: The Life of Robert Louis Stevenson.* New York: William Sloane, 1951.

Hammond, J. R. *A Robert Louis Stevenson Chronology.* New York: St. Martin's, 1997.

Harman, Claire. *Robert Louis Stevenson: A Biography.* London: HarperCollins, 2005.

Holmes, Richard. *Footsteps: Adventures of a Romantic Biographer.* New York: Vintage, 1996.

Japp, Alexander H. *Robert Louis Stevenson: A Record, an Estimate, and a Memorial.* London: T. Werner Laurie, 1905.

Johnstone, Arthur. *Recollections of Robert Louis Stevenson in the Pacific.* London: Chatto, 1905.

Low, Will H. Note in private copy of *The South Seas* (1890). HM 285157. Huntington Library, San Marino, CA.

McClure, Samuel. "Letter to Robert Louis Stevenson." March 9, 1889. Balfour Papers, MS 9891. National Library of Scotland, Edinburgh.

McLynn, Frank. *Robert Louis Stevenson: A Biography.* London: Pimlico, 1994.

Osbourne, Lloyd. *An Intimate Portrait of R.L.S.* New York: Scribner's, 1924.

Pope Hennessy, James. *Robert Louis Stevenson.* New York: Simon and Schuster, 1974.

Stevenson, Fanny Vandegrift. *The Cruise of the "Janet Nichol."* London: Chatto, 1915.

———. *The Cruise of the Janet Nichol among the South Sea Islands.* Edited by Roslyn Jolly. Seattle: University of Washington Press, 2004.

## Works of Criticism, Theory, History, and Fiction

Anderson, Benedict. *Imagined Communities: Reflections on the Origin and Spread of Nationalism.* Rev. ed. London: Verso, 1991.

Arata, Stephen. "Observing *The Wrecker.*" Plenary paper delivered at the 2nd Biennial International Conference on Stevenson, "Stevenson and Conrad: Writers of Land and Sea." Edinburgh, Scotland, July 7–9, 2004.

Arnold, Matthew. *Culture and Anarchy and Other Writings.* Edited by Stefan Collini. Cambridge: Cambridge University Press, 1993.

Ashcroft, Bill, Gareth Griffiths, and Helen Tiffin. *Post-Colonial Studies: The Key Concepts.* London: Routledge, 1998.

Bakhtin, M. M. *The Dialogic Imagination.* Edited by Michael Holquist. Translated by Caryl Emerson and Michael Holquist. Austin: University of Texas Press, 1981.

Barthes, Roland. *The Pleasure of the Text.* Translated by Richard Miller. New York: Hill and Wang, 1975.

Bersani, Leo. "Is the Rectum a Grave?" *October* 43 (Winter 1987): 197–122.

Bhaba, Homi K. *The Location of Culture.* New York: Routledge, 1994.

Boone, Joseph Allen. *Libidinal Currents: Sexuality and the Shaping of Modernism.* Chicago: University of Chicago Press, 1998.

Bourdieu, Pierre. *Distinction: A Social Critique of the Judgement of Taste.* Translated by Richard Nice. Cambridge, MA: Harvard University Press, 1984.

Brantlinger, Patrick. "What Is 'Sensational' about the Sensation Novel?" *Nineteenth-Century Fiction* 37 (1982): 1–28.

Bristow, Joseph. *Sexuality.* London: Routledge, 1997.

Brody, Jennifer DeVere. *Impossible Purities: Blackness, Femininity, and Victorian Culture.* Durham, NC: Duke University Press, 1998.

Brooks, Peter. *Reading for the Plot: Design and Intention in Narrative.* New York: Knopf, 1984.

Buchan, John. *Huntingtower.* 1922. Edited by Ann F. Stonehouse. New York: Oxford University Press, 1996.

———. *The Thirty-Nine Steps.* 1915. London: Penguin, 1991.

Buckton, Oliver S. "Reanimating Stevenson's Corpus." In *Robert Louis Stevenson Reconsidered: New Critical Perspectives,* edited by William B. Jones Jr., 37–67. Jefferson, NC: McFarland, 2003.

Buzard, James. "The Grand Tour and after (1660–1840)." In *The Cambridge Companion to Travel Writing,* edited by Peter Hulme and Tim Youngs, 37–52. New York: Cambridge University Press, 2002.

Carney, Seamus. *The Appin Murder: The Killing of the Red Fox.* Edinburgh: Birlinn, 1994.

Carr, Helen. "Modernism and Travel (1880–1940)." In *The Cambridge Companion to Travel Writing,* edited by Peter Hulme and Tim Youngs, 70–86. New York: Cambridge University Press, 2002.

Colley, Ann C. *Robert Louis Stevenson and the Colonial Imagination.* Burlington, VT: Ashgate, 2004.

Conrad, Joseph. *Lord Jim.* New York: Oxford University Press, 2000.

Craft, Christopher. *Another Kind of Love: Male Homosexual Desire in English Discourse, 1850–1920.* Berkeley: University of California Press, 1994.

Daly, Nicholas. *Modernism, Romance and the Fin de Siècle: Popular Fiction and British Culture, 1880–1914.* Cambridge: Cambridge University Press, 1999.

Dickens, Charles. *Pictures from Italy.* Edited by Kate Flint. New York: Penguin, 1998.

Edelman, Lee. *Homographesis: Essays in Gay Literary and Cultural Theory.* New York: Routledge, 1994.

———. *No Future: Queer Theory and the Death Drive.* Durham, NC: Duke University Press, 2004.

Edmond, Rod. *Representing the South Pacific: Colonial Discourse from Cook to Gauguin.* Cambridge: Cambridge University Press, 1997.

Feltes, N. N. *Modes of Production of Victorian Novels.* Chicago: University of Chicago Press, 1986.

Fielding, Penny. *Writing and Orality.* Oxford: Clarendon Press, 1996.

Fletcher, C. Brunsdon. *Stevenson's Germany: The Case against Germany in the Pacific.* New York: Scribner's, 1920.

Foucault, Michel. *Discipline and Punish: The Birth of the Modern Prison.* Translated by Alan Sheridan. New York: Vintage, 1979.

———. "What Is an Author?" In *The Norton Anthology of Theory and Criticism,* edited by Vincent B. Leitch, 1622–36. New York: Norton, 2001.

Goodman, Jonathan. *The Oscar Wilde File.* London: Allison and Busby, 1988.

Green, Martin. *Dreams of Adventure, Deeds of Empire.* New York: Basic, 1979.

Greenslade, William. *Degeneration, Culture, and the Novel, 1880–1940.* Cambridge: Cambridge University Press, 1994.

Haggard, H. Rider. *King Solomon's Mines.* London: Cassell, 1887.

Hillier, Robert Irwin. *The South Seas Fiction of Robert Louis Stevenson.* New York: Peter Lang, 1989.

Hobsbawm, Eric. *The Age of Empire, 1875–1914.* New York: Vintage, 1989.

Hocquenghem, Guy. *Homosexual Desire.* Translated by Daniella Dangoor. Durham, NC: Duke University Press, 1993.

Hollmann, Eckhard. *Paul Gauguin: Images from the South Seas.* New York: Prestel, 1996.

Holquist, Michael. Introduction to *The Dialogic Imagination,* by M. M. Bakhtin, xv–xxxiv. Austin: University of Texas Press, 1981.

Hyde, H. Montgomery. *The Trials of Oscar Wilde.* 1962. New York: Dover, 1973.

James, Henry. *Literary Criticism: Essays on Literature, American Writers, English Writers.* Edited by Leon Edel. New York: Library of America, 1984.

Jameson, Fredric. *The Political Unconscious: Narrative as a Socially Symbolic Act.* Ithaca, NY: Cornell University Press, 1981.

Jolly, Roslyn. Introduction to *South Sea Tales,* by Robert Louis Stevenson. New York: Oxford University Press, 1996.

———. "Robert Louis Stevenson and Samoan History: Crossing the Roman Wall." In *Crossing Cultures: Essays on Literature and Culture of the Asia-Pacific,* edited by Bruce Bennett, Jeff Doyle, et al., 113–20. London: Skoob, 1996.

Jones, William B., Jr., ed. *Robert Louis Stevenson Reconsidered: New Critical Perspectives.* Jefferson, NC: McFarland, 2003.

Katz, Wendy. Introduction to Stevenson, *Treasure Island.*

Kermode, Frank. *The Sense of an Ending: Studies in the Theory of Fiction.* New York: Oxford University Press, 2000.

Kiely, Robert. *Robert Louis Stevenson and the Fiction of Adventure.* Cambridge, MA: Harvard University Press, 1964.

Kilgour, Maggie. *The Rise of the Gothic Novel.* London: Routledge, 1995.

Kipling, Rudyard. *Something of Myself and Other Autobiographical Writings.* Edited by Thomas Pinney. Cambridge: Cambridge University Press, 1990.

Koestenbaum, Wayne. "The Shadow on the Bed: Dr. Jekyll, Mr. Hyde, and the Labouchere Amendment." *Critical Matrix,* Special Issue, no. 1 (1988): 31–55.

Kucich, John. "Melancholy Magic: Masochism, Stevenson, Anti-Imperialism." *Nineteenth-Century Literature* 56, no. 3 (2001): 364–400.

Lamos, Colleen. *Deviant Modernism: Sexual and Textual Errancy in T. S. Eliot, James Joyce, and Marcel Proust.* Cambridge: Cambridge University Press, 1998.

Lane, Christopher. *The Ruling Passion: British Colonial Allegory and the Paradox of Homosexual Desire.* Durham, NC: Duke University Press, 1995.

Letley, Emma. Introduction to Stevenson, *Travels with a Donkey.*

Linehan, Katherine. "Taking Up with Kanakas: Stevenson's Complex Social Criticism in 'The Beach of Falesá.'" *ELT* 33, no. 4 (1990): 407–22.

Maixner, Paul. *Robert Louis Stevenson: The Critical Heritage.* London: Routledge and Kegan Paul, 1981.

McGann, Jerome J. *The Textual Condition.* Princeton, NJ: Princeton University Press, 1991.

Melville, Herman. *Typee, Omoo, Mardi.* New York: Library of America, 1982.

Menikoff, Barry. Editor's preface to Stevenson, *Kidnapped.*

———. Introduction to *The Complete Stories of Robert Louis Stevenson.* Edited by David Menikoff. New York: Modern Library, 2002.

———. *Narrating Scotland: The Imagination of Robert Louis Stevenson.* Columbia: University of South Carolina Press, 2005.

———. "'These Problematic Shores': Robert Louis Stevenson in the South Seas." In *1876–1918: The Ends of the Earth,* edited by Simon Gatrell, 141–56. Vol. 4 of *English Literature and the Wider World.* London: Ashfield, 1992.

Miller, D. A. *Bringing Out Roland Barthes.* Berkeley: University of California Press, 1992.

———. *The Novel and the Police.* Berkeley: University of California Press, 1988.

Mitchell, Timothy. *Colonising Egypt.* Berkeley: University of California Press, 1991.

Porter, Bernard. *The Absent-Minded Imperialists: Empire, Society, and Culture in Britain.* New York: Oxford University Press, 2004.

Prebble, John. *The Lion in the North: One Thousand Years of Scotland's History.* Harmondsworth: Penguin, 1973.

Quigley, Christine. *The Corpse: A History.* Jefferson, NC: McFarland, 1996.

Rankin, Nicholas. *Dead Man's Chest: Travels after Robert Louis Stevenson.* London: Phoenix, 2001.

Redekop, Magdalene. "Beyond Closure: Buried Alive with Hogg's *Justified Sinner.*" *ELH* 52 (1985): 159–84.

Rennie, Neil. *Far-Fetched Facts: The Literature of Travel and the Idea of the South Seas.* Oxford: Clarendon Press, 1995.

———. Introduction to Stevenson, *In the South Seas.*

Robertson, Fiona. *Legitimate Histories: Scott, Gothic, and the Authorities of Fiction.* Oxford: Clarendon Press, 1994.

Rose, Jacqueline. *The Case of Peter Pan, or the Impossibility of Children's Fiction.* Philadelphia: University of Pennsylvania Press, 1993.

Rubiés, Joan Pau. "Travel Writing and Ethnography." In *The Cambridge Companion to Travel Writing,* edited by Peter Hulme and Tim Youngs, 242–60. New York: Cambridge University Press, 2002.

Ruskin, John. "The Nature of Gothic." From *The Stones of Venice.* In *The Longman Anthology of British Literature,* vol. 2, edited by David Damrosch, 1560–70. New York: Longman, 1999.

Sahlins, Marshall. *How "Natives" Think: About Captain Cook, for Example.* Chicago: University of Chicago Press, 1995.

Said, Edward W. *Culture and Imperialism.* New York: Vintage, 1994.

———. *Orientalism.* New York: Pantheon, 1978.

Sandison, Alan. *Robert Louis Stevenson and the Appearance of Modernism.* New York: St. Martin's, 1997.

Sedgwick, Eve Kosofsky. *Between Men: English Literature and Male Homosocial Desire.* New York: Columbia University Press, 1985.

———. *Epistemology of the Closet.* Berkeley: University of California Press, 1991.

Showalter, Elaine. *Sexual Anarchy: Gender and Culture at the Fin-de-Siècle.* New York: Viking, 1990.

Smith, Adam. *An Inquiry into the Nature and Causes of the Wealth of Nations.* Edited by Kathryn Sutherland. New York: Oxford University Press, 1993.

Smith, Vanessa. *Literary Culture and the Pacific: Nineteenth-Century Textual Encounters.* Cambridge: Cambridge University Press, 1998.

Spivak, Gayatri. *A Critique of Postcolonial Reason.* Cambridge, MA: Harvard University Press, 1999.

Sutherland, John. *The Stanford Companion to Victorian Fiction.* Stanford, CA: Stanford University Press, 1989.

Swearingen, Roger G. *The Prose Writings of Robert Louis Stevenson: A Guide.* Hamden, CT: Archon, 1980.

Symonds, John Addington. *The Letters of John Addington Symonds.* 3 vols. Edited by Herbert M. Schueller and Robert L. Peters. Vol. 3, 1885–1893. Detroit, MI: Wayne State University Press, 1969.

———. *The Memoirs of John Addington Symonds.* Edited Phyllis Grosskurth. Chicago: University of Chicago Press, 1986.

Veeder, William, and Gordon Hirsch, eds. *Dr. Jekyll and Mr. Hyde after One Hundred Years.* Chicago: University of Chicago Press, 1988.

Wallace, Lee. *Sexual Encounters: Pacific Texts, Modern Sexualities.* Ithaca, NY: Cornell University Press, 2003.

Weber, Max. *The Protestant Ethic and the Spirit of Capitalism.* Translated by Talcott Parsons. Los Angeles: Roxbury, 1998.

Weeks, Jeffrey. *Coming Out: Homosexual Politics in Britain from the Nineteenth Century to the Present.* Rev. ed. London: Quartet, 1990.

White, Hayden. *The Content of the Form: Narrative Discourse and Historical Representation.* Baltimore: Johns Hopkins University Press, 1987.

Wilde, Oscar. *The Artist as Critic: Critical Writings of Oscar Wilde.* Edited by Richard Ellmann. Chicago: University of Chicago Press, 1969.

———. *The Complete Letters of Oscar Wilde.* Edited by Merlin Holland and Rupert Hart-Davis. New York: Holt, 2000.

———. *The Picture of Dorian Gray.* Edited by Donald L. Lawler. New York: Norton, 1988.

Williams, Raymond. *Marxism and Literature.* New York: Oxford University Press, 1977.

# INDEX

*Robert Louis Stevenson is referred to throughout as RLS, except in the main entries devoted to him and to his works*

# Index

# Index